Measurement and Evaluation *for* Health Educators

Manoj Sharma, MBBS, MCHES, PhD, FAAHB
Professor, Health Promotion and Education
Professor, Environmental Health
University of Cincinnati

R. Lingyak Petosa, PhD, FAAHB
Professor, Health Promotion and Exercise Science
Professor, School of Allied Medical Professions, College of Medicine
The Ohio State University

JONES & BARTLETT
LEARNING

World Headquarters
Jones & Bartlett Learning
5 Wall Street
Burlington, MA 01803
978-443-5000
info@jblearning.com
www.jblearning.com

Jones & Bartlett Learning books and products are available through most bookstores and online booksellers. To contact Jones & Bartlett Learning directly, call 800-832-0034, fax 978-443-8000, or visit our website, www.jblearning.com.

Production Credits

Publisher: William Brottmiller
Executive Editor: Shoshanna Goldberg
Editorial Assistant: Sean Coombs
Production Manager: Julie Champagne Bolduc
Production Assistant: Stephanie Rineman
Senior Marketing Manager: Jennifer Stiles
VP, Manufacturing and Inventory Control: Therese Connell

Composition: Publishers' Design and
    Production Services, Inc.
Cover Design: Michael O'Donnell
Cover Image: © beaucroft/ShutterStock, Inc.
Printing and Binding: Edwards Brothers Malloy
Cover Printing: Edwards Brothers Malloy

Library of Congress Cataloging-in-Publication Data
Sharma, Manoj.
    Measurement and evaluation for health educators / by Manoj Sharma and Rick Lingyak Petosa.
       p. ; cm.
    Includes bibliographical references and index.
    ISBN 978-1-4496-2820-8 — ISBN 1-4496-2820-6
    I. Petosa, Rick Lingyak. II. Title.
    [DNLM: 1. Health Education—standards. 2. Educational Measurement—methods. 3. Evaluation
Studies as Topic. 4. Health Educators—standards. 5. Program Evaluation. WA 18]

    613—dc23
                                                                        2012027635

6048

Printed in the United States of America
16 15   10 9 8 7 6 5 4 3

To all my teachers and students.

M. S.

Students: To those who commit to promoting health and preventing disease, a noble effort.

My teachers: Gus Lingyak, Ken Briggs, Robert Baum, Robert Russell, David Duncan, Elena Sliepcevich, each a model of conscious commitment.

Marsha, Mazlow and Zane, your support enables my promise.

R. L. P.

Contents

Preface

Congratulations on choosing *Measurement and Evaluation for Health Educators* to complement your course! With this book you will study evaluation methods applied to health promotion and education programs. Health promotion and education remains a vital element of community efforts to promote positive health and prevent disease. This field has a truly noble mission: to empower individuals and communities to prevent health problems and to aspire to a higher quality of life. This mission is accomplished using systematic community organization efforts enabling people to promote informed decision-making, positive health practices, and development of health-enhancing environments. All of the major health challenges facing our society—medical care costs, chronic diseases, an aging population, and obesity—can be solved by addressing personal lifestyle choices.

In addition, there has been a steady growth in the knowledge base that is the foundation of health promotion. Considerable advances have been made in program planning models, health behavior theory, and evidence-based health promotion programs. Over the past 50 years there has been considerable growth in the number of scientific publications in the health promotion area. Most importantly, there is a marked growth in the quality and quantity of scientific publications verifying the effectiveness of health promotion activities. This growth has been fueled by the commitment of government agencies, private foundations, and health promotion professionals to an evidence-based approach to practice. This commitment is characterized by a consistent effort to evaluate the effects of different health promotion approaches among a variety of populations and settings. Over time, a data-driven decision-making process yields professional practices that are effective. The authors of this text are committed to the perspective that health promotion professionals should be experimenting practitioners who are responsible for creating new programs rooted in established knowledge about effective practices, in addition to proposing testable approaches to increase effectiveness. Such programs must be carefully evaluated to contribute to the existing literature on health promotion effectiveness.

One of the responsibilities for both entry-level and advanced-level health educators is to evaluate health education and health promotion programs. This book is designed to prepare all health educators for this responsibility and includes psychometric, statistical, political, managerial, and public health perspectives for measurement and evaluation. Geared toward undergraduate students, graduate students, and entry- or advanced-level practitioners in health education and health promotion, this text fills a market void. With years of hands-on experience in evaluating health education and health promotion programs at local, regional, national, and international levels, we have written this book based on our experiences in the health fields.

This book emphasizes the essentials of selecting or developing instruments for evaluating the effectiveness of health education and health promotion programs, as well as the design elements needed to carry out such evaluations. Topics covered include introduction to evaluation of health education and health promotion; planning for health education and health promotion evaluations; basics of measurement; steps in instrument development; reliability assessment; validity assessment; measurement errors; process evaluation; designs for quantitative evaluation; approaches to qualitative evaluation; sampling for evaluation; quantitative data analysis; and data interpretation and report writing. This book is especially valuable for those taking the CHES, MCHES, or CPH exams, as the competencies tested in these exams have been thoroughly considered while writing this book.

The straightforward language used in this book is designed to enhance the conceptual understanding of evaluation for both undergraduate and graduate students in health education, health promotion, and public health. Some advanced topics, such as factor analysis, can be skipped by undergraduate students. Pedagogical highlights of this book include:

- Key concepts and a set of learning objectives in each chapter help readers focus their attention and retain important information.
- Succinct chapter introductions and concise chapter summaries provide an opportunity for readers to prepare for exams and master key concepts by reinforcement.
- Practical Skill-Building Activities to help students gain mastery by applying concepts. These activities will enable students to hone their skills relating to various aspects of evaluation of health education and health promotion programs.
- Boxed items emphasizing important points and quotations to reinforce salient concepts.
- Focus Features that provide an account of interesting discoveries, anecdotes, examples, case studies, or future directions being pursued on a particular topic, which should help to consolidate interest on a topic and foster further reading.

- A Glossary at the end of the text provides the reader with a useful resource for looking up concepts in evaluation of health education and health promotion interventions.
- A detailed list of References in each chapter.
- Review Questions in each chapter help the reader prepare for exams.
- Web exercises with annotated guides provide interactive activities that directly relate to the chapter content and help students apply their new knowledge practically.

INSTRUCTOR RESOURCES

We have prepared a set of PowerPoint presentations for each chapter that instructors can use for classroom lectures. Instructors also have access to online Test Bank questions for each chapter. Contact your Jones & Bartlett Learning sales representative for access to these resources.

ACKNOWLEDGMENTS

We are indebted to the Health Science team at Jones & Bartlett Learning who aided in the publication process at all stages: Shoshanna Goldberg, Executive Editor; Sean Coombs, Editorial Assistant; and Julie Bolduc, Production Manager. We would also like to thank the reviewers of this book:

Paul Branscum, PhD, RD
Assistant Professor
Health and Exercise Science
The University of Oklahoma

Melinda J. Ickes, PhD
Assistant Professor
Department of Kinesiology and Health Promotion
University of Kentucky

Dr. Amar Shireesh Kanekar
Assistant Professor
Health Studies
East Stroudsburg University

About the Authors

Manoj Sharma, MBBS, MCHES, PhD, FAAHB, is a professor in the Health Promotion and Education program and the Department of Environmental Health at the University of Cincinnati. He is a physician by initial training and has also completed his doctorate in preventive medicine/public health from The Ohio State University. He has worked in community health for more than 25 years, designing and evaluating health education programs at all levels: local (Columbus Health Department, Omaha Healthy Start program, Lead Safe Omaha Coalition); state (Nebraska Health and Human Services, Ohio Commission on Minority Health, Ohio Department of Health); national (American School Health Association, Centers for Disease Control and Prevention, National Commission for Health Education Credentialing); and international, working on various programs in India, Italy, Mongolia, Nepal, United Arab Emirates, United Kingdom, and Vietnam. His research interests include childhood obesity, alternative and complementary systems of health, community-based participatory research, and designing and evaluating theory-based health education and health promotion programs. He enjoys yoga and meditation.

R. Lingyak Petosa, PhD, FAAHB, is a professor of health education at The Ohio State University. For the past 35 years he has engaged in the design and evaluation of health behavior change programs in schools, worksites, and healthcare and community settings. He is an advocate for the use of evaluation methods to support the continuous refinement of health behavior change programs. He has conducted evaluations sponsored by Centers for Disease Control and Prevention, the William T. Grant Foundation, Ohio Department of Education, Ohio Department of Health, and the Illinois Department of Public Health. His research interests include measurement methods, physical activity promotion, and validation of theory-based health behavior programs. He enjoys beer and winemaking, cooking, reading, boating, sports cars, cycling, tennis, and lacrosse.

CHAPTER 1

Introduction to Evaluation in Health Education and Health Promotion

THE FIELD OF HEALTH EDUCATION AND HEALTH PROMOTION

Health education professionals facilitate the modification of health behaviors in target populations. **Health education** has been defined in several ways. The 2000 Joint Committee on Health Education and Promotion Terminology (Gold & Miner, 2002, p. 3) defined health education as "any combination of planned learning experiences based on sound theories that provide individuals, groups, and communities the opportunity to acquire information and the skills needed to make quality health decisions." The World Health Organization (WHO, 1998, p. 4) defined health education as "compris[ing] consciously constructed opportunities for learning involving some form of communication designed to improve health literacy, including improving knowledge, and developing life skills which are conducive to individual and community health." Green and Kreuter (2005, p. G-4) defined health education as "any planned combination of learning experiences designed to predispose, enable, and reinforce voluntary behavior conducive to health in individuals, groups or communities."

From these definitions some things are clear. First, health education is a systematic and planned application. Second, the delivery of health education involves a set of techniques rather than just one, such as preparing health education informational brochures, pamphlets, and videos; delivering lectures; facilitating role plays or simulations; analyzing case studies; participating and reflecting in group discussions; reading; and interacting in computer-assisted training. In the past, health education encompassed a wider range of functions, including community mobilization, networking, and advocacy, which are now embodied in the term **health promotion**. Third, the primary purpose of health education is to influence antecedents of behavior so that healthy behaviors develop in a voluntary fashion (without any coercion). Examples of antecedents of behavior include awareness, information, knowledge, skills, beliefs, attitudes, and values. Finally, health education is performed at several levels. It can be done one-on-one, such as in a counseling session; it can be done with a group of people, such as through a group discussion; it can be done at an organizational level, such as through an employee wellness fair; or it can be done at the community level, such as through a multiple-channel, multiple-approach campaign.

Since the publication of *Healthy People: The Surgeon General's Report on Health Promotion and Disease Prevention* (U.S. Department of Health and Human Services [USDHHS], 1979), the term *health promotion* has gained popularity and continues to gain strength. This term has been used in the *Objectives for the Nation* (USDHHS, 1980), *Healthy People 2000* (USDHHS, 1990), *Healthy People 2010* (USDHHS, 2000), and *Healthy People 2020* (USDHHS, 2009) reports. **Table 1.1** summarizes the 42 focus areas in *Healthy People 2020*, which underscore the importance of health promotion.

> "*Healthy People 2020* reflects assessments of major risks to health and wellness, changing public health priorities, and emerging issues related to our nation's health preparedness and prevention."
>
> —USDHHS, 2012

Health education is a subset of health promotion. Green and Kreuter (2005, p. G-4) defined health promotion as "any planned combination of educational, political, regulatory and organizational supports for actions and conditions of living conducive to the health of individuals, groups or

TABLE 1.1 Focus Areas in *Healthy People 2020*	
Access to health services	HIV
Adolescent health	Immunization and infectious diseases
Arthritis, osteoporosis, and chronic back conditions	Injury and violence prevention
Blood disorders and blood safety	Lesbian, gay, bisexual, and transgender health
Cancer	Maternal, infant, and child health
Chronic kidney diseases	Medical product safety
Dementias including Alzheimer's disease	Mental health and mental disorders
Diabetes	Nutrition and weight status
Disability and health	Occupational safety and health
Early and middle childhood	Older adults
Educational and community-based programs	Oral health
Environmental health	Physical activity
Family planning	Preparedness
Food safety	Public health infrastructure
Genomics	Respiratory diseases
Global health	Sexually transmitted diseases
Health communication and health IT	Sleep health
Healthcare-associated infections	Social determinants of health
Health-related quality of life and well-being	Substance abuse
Hearing and other sensory or communication disorders	Tobacco use
Heart disease and stroke	Vision

communities." The 2000 Joint Committee on Health Education and Promotion Terminology (Gold & Miner, 2002, p. 4) defined health promotion as "any planned combination of educational, political, environmental, regulatory, or organizational mechanisms that support actions and conditions of living conducive to the health of individuals, groups, and communities." The Ottawa Charter for Health Promotion (WHO, 1986, p. 1) defined health promotion as "the process of enabling people to increase control over, and to improve their health." The Ottawa Charter identified five key action strategies for health promotion:

- Build healthy public policy.
- Create physical and social environments supportive of individual change.
- Strengthen community action.
- Develop personal skills such as increased self-efficacy and feelings of empowerment.
- Reorient health services to the population and partnership with patients.

These action areas were confirmed in 1997 in the Jakarta Declaration on Leading Health Promotion into the 21st Century (WHO, 1997). In addition, the Jakarta Declaration identified five priorities for health promotion:

- Promote social responsibility for health.
- Increase investments for health development.
- Expand partnerships for health promotion.
- Increase community capacity and empower the individual.
- Secure an infrastructure for health promotion.

> "*H*ealth for all: The attainment by all people of the world of a level of health that will permit them to lead a socially and economically productive life."
>
> —World Health Organization, 1986, p. 4

Once again, all these depictions of health promotion have some things in common. First, just like health education, health promotion is a systematic, planned application that qualifies as a science. Second, it entails methods beyond mere education such as community mobilization, community organization, community participation, community development, community empowerment, networking, coalition building, advocacy, lobbying, policy development, formulating legislation, and developing social norms. Third, unlike health education, health promotion does not endorse voluntary change in behavior, but utilizes measures that compel an individual's behavior change. These measures are uniform and mandatory. Often the behavior change in health promotion comes from measures that an individual may not like, such as an increase in insurance premiums for a smoker. Finally, health promotion is done at the group or community level.

DEFINING EVALUATION

Evaluation is essential for assessing the value of health education and health promotion interventions. The word *evaluate* is derived from *value*, which in turn is derived from the Latin word *valere* meaning "to be strong" or "to have worth." The American Evaluation Association defines *evaluation* as that which "involves assessing the strengths and weaknesses of programs, policies, personnel, products, and organizations to improve their effectiveness" (American Evaluation Association, n.d.).

There are several aspects of evaluation that need to be underscored. The first is that it is systematic and science-based. Evaluation in health education and health promotion usually employs techniques and methods rooted in social and behavioral sciences. Second, evaluation can be used to actively refine and improve health education and promotion programs. Evaluation provides concrete guidance with evidence to support program refinements. The third aspect of evaluation is that often it compares a set of observations with a known or ideal standard, so evaluation is always aiming for achieving standards of acceptability. The fourth aspect of evaluation is that it is intertwined with measurement. Measurement helps in collecting observations that are used during

> *E*valuation of health education and health promotion programs uses systematic, science-based methods to help improve a program, comparing it against ideal standards, and is related to behavior change.

evaluation to make inferences and deductions. Finally, evaluations in health education and health promotion are related to behavior change. These evaluations measure either processes used in behavior change, antecedents of behavior, behavior itself, or epidemiological indices related to behavior.

EVALUATION COMPETENCIES FOR HEALTH EDUCATORS

The history of health education dates to the late 19th century, when the first academic programs emerged for training school health educators (Allegrante et al., 2004). The 2003 *Directory of Institutions Offering Undergraduate and Graduate Degree Programs in Health Education* listed 258 institutions offering baccalaureate, masters, and doctoral degrees in health education (American Association for Health Education, 2003).

As the profession of health education has grown, greater interest has arisen in establishing standards and holding professionals accountable to those standards. In February 1978, a conference for health educators was convened in Bethesda, Maryland, to analyze the similarities and differences in preparing health educators from different practice settings and to discuss the possibility of developing uniform guidelines (National Commission for Health Education Credentialing [NCHEC], Society for Public Health Education [SOPHE], & American Association for Health Education [AAHE], 2006; U.S. Department of Health, Education and Welfare, 1978). Soon after, the Role Delineation Project was implemented, which looked at the role of the entry-level health education specialist and identified the desirable responsibilities, functions, skills, and knowledge for that level. These were verified by a survey of practicing health educators. The process led to publication of *A Framework for the Development of Competency-Based Curricula for Entry-Level Health Educators* (NCHEC, 1985).

In 1986, the second Bethesda Conference provided consensus for the certification process, and in 1988, the NCHEC was established. In 1989, a charter certification phase was introduced, during which time health educators could become certified by submitting letters of support and academic records. From 1990 to the present, the NCHEC has conducted competency-based national certification examinations. An individual who meets the required health education training qualifications, successfully passes the certification exam, and meets continuing education requirements is known as a **Certified Health Education Specialist (CHES)**. In June 2012, there were approximately 9,500 certified individuals (L. Lysoby, personal communication, June 27, 2012). There are seven basic responsibilities for entry-level health educators (NCHEC, 1985). These pertain to needs assessment; planning, implementing, and evaluating health education programs; coordinating health education; acting as a resource person in health education; and communicating the needs for health education.

In 1992, the AAHE and SOPHE began to determine graduate-level competencies, and a Joint Committee for the Development of Graduate-Level Preparation Standards was formed. *A Competency-Based Framework for Graduate Level Health Educators* was published in 1999 (AAHE, NCHEC, & SOPHE, 1999). The responsibilities for graduate-level health educators included needs assessment; planning, implementing, and evaluating health education programs; coordinating health education; acting as a resource person; communicating the need for health education; applying research principles; administering health education programs; and advancing the health education profession. Beginning in October 2011, the NCHEC started holding exams for the advanced-level credential, **Master Certified Health Education Specialist (MCHES)** (Rehrig, 2010).

In 1998 the profession launched the National Health Educator Competencies Update Project (CUP), a 6-year project to reverify the entry-level health education responsibilities, competencies, and subcompetencies and to verify the advanced-level competencies and subcompetencies (Airhihenbuwa et al., 2005; Gilmore, Olsen, Taub, & Connell, 2005). The CUP model identifies three levels of practice:

1. *Entry:* Competencies and subcompetencies performed by health educators with a baccalaureate or master's degree and less than 5 years of experience
2. *Advanced 1:* Competencies and subcompetencies performed by health educators with a baccalaureate or master's degree and more than 5 years of experience
3. *Advanced 2:* Competencies and subcompetencies performed by health educators with a doctoral degree and 5 years or more of experience

TABLE 1.2   Settings for Health Education Identified in the CUP Model
Community
School (K–12)
Health care
Business/industry
College/university
University health services

The CUP model contains 7 areas of responsibility, 35 competencies, and 163 subcompetencies, many of which are similar to previous models. These responsibilities pertain to assessing needs; planning, implementing, evaluating, researching, and administering health education strategies, interventions, and programs; serving as a resource person; and communicating and advocating for health and health education. Research and advocacy have been combined to form Area IV (evaluation and research), and communication and advocacy have been combined in Area VII (communication and advocacy for health and health education). The CUP model also identifies six settings for health education (see **Table 1.2**).

Health education also is an important and integral function of public health. The Institute of Medicine (1988) defined three core functions of public health in its *Future of Public Health* report:

1. *Assessment:* Every public health agency should regularly and systematically collect, assemble, analyze, and make available information on the health of the community.
2. *Policy development:* Every public health agency should assist in the development of comprehensive public health policies.
3. *Assurance:* Every public health agency should ensure that services necessary to achieve agreed-upon goals in communities are provided either directly or by regulations or other agencies.

Building on these identified functions, the Public Health Functions Steering Committee (1994) identified 6 public health goals and 10 essential public health services. The six goals are to do the following:

1. Prevent epidemics and the spread of disease
2. Protect against environmental hazards

3. Prevent injuries
4. Promote and encourage healthy behaviors
5. Respond to disasters and assist communities in recovery
6. 6. Assure the quality and accessibility of health services

The 10 essential public health services are to do the following:

1. Monitor health status to identify community health problems
2. Diagnose and investigate health problems and health hazards in the community
3. Inform, educate, and empower people about health issues
4. Mobilize community partnerships to identify and solve health problems
5. Develop policies and plans that support individual and community health efforts
6. Enforce laws and regulations that protect health and ensure safety
7. Link people to needed personal health services and ensure the provision of health care when it is otherwise unavailable
8. Ensure the availability of a competent public health and personal healthcare workforce
9. Evaluate the effectiveness, accessibility, and quality of personal and population-based health services
10. Research new insights and innovative solutions to health problems

It can be seen from both these lists that health education is a core and integral function of public health, and that health educators are key public health functionaries.

The Institute of Medicine published *The Future of the Public's Health in the 21st Century* in 2002, which echoed the vision articulated in *Healthy People 2010* (USDHHS, 2000): healthy people in healthy communities. It emphasized the following key areas of action:

- Adopt a focus on population health that includes multiple determinants of health
- Strengthen the public health infrastructure
- Build partnerships
- Develop systems of accountability
- Emphasize evidence
- Improve communication

Once again, all of these functions underscore the inextricable linkage between public health and health education. Health education is an important subset of public health. Just as there is a National Commission for Health Education Credentialing, since 2005 the National Board of Public Health Examiners (NBPHE, n.d.) has ensured that graduates from schools and programs of public health accredited by the Council on Education for Public Health (CEPH) have gained the required knowledge and skills related to public health. NBPHE is responsible for developing, preparing, administering, and evaluating a voluntary certification exam. People who pass this exam are called **Certified in Public Health (CPH)**. The first exam was conducted in 2008 and certified about 500 individuals. The exam consists of questions from five core areas—biostatistics, epidemiology, environmental health sciences, health policy and management, and social and behavioral sciences—along with seven cross-cutting areas: communication and informatics, diversity and culture, leadership, public health biology, professionalism, programs planning, and systems thinking.

In both the CUP model of health education and the field of public health, conducting evaluation and research related to health education is important. The first area where evaluation is important is for planning. Based on the NCHEC (2008b) framework, some of the functions that entry-level health educators perform in this regard are to cull out and fuse information from the literature, and consume and use evaluation-related literature. In addition, graduate-level health educators are responsible for locating existing valid and reliable instruments and assessing the advantages and disadvantages of various evaluation methods.

The second area of importance pertains to identifying evaluation procedures. In this category, the entry-level health educator is responsible for assessing data collection instruments and approaches and ascertaining changes in the health status of individuals. In addition, the graduate-level health educator sets benchmarks for effectiveness, describes methods to assess changes in health status, evaluates the efficacy and effectiveness of interventions, sets boundaries for evaluation, and chooses the methodology for evaluation.

The third area where evaluation is applied pertains to creating data-gathering tools. In this category, both the entry-level and graduate-level health educators are responsible for building psychometric tools that are valid and reliable to be used for data collection and evaluation.

The fourth area where evaluation is applied pertains to implementing evaluation plans. In this category, entry-level health educators choose appropriate methods, match methods with objectives, apply appropriate techniques, and evaluate changes in health status. Graduate-level health educators also evaluate the match between objectives and needs, use relevant technology in evaluation, and analyze data.

The fifth area is about interpretation of findings from evaluation. In this category, the entry-level health educator is responsible for data analysis from research and evaluation; comparison of findings across interventions, situations, and contexts; and preparing reports about the efficacy and effectiveness of programs. In addition, the graduate-level health educators contrast intervention activities against intervention objectives, identify suggestions based on findings, develop criteria for gauging attainment of program objectives, and convey the findings to all sections of the society.

The sixth area of evaluation is about coming up with inferences for future programs and interventions, and consists of responsibilities mainly for graduate-level health educators. These include ways to apply suggestions that emanate from the evaluation, use data from evaluation to further improve programs, and identify causal associations in evaluation. **Self-Assessment Worksheet 1.1** is an assessment of how much one perceives oneself as competent about evaluation. The score on this assessment can range from 0 to 60, with higher scores denoting higher competence. **Self-Assessment Worksheet 1.2** is a basic knowledge assessment of evaluation competency. It is not content valid (a concept which will be discussed later in the book), but merely taps into one item of basic knowledge related to evaluation competencies. It would require scoring by a competent expert, and the score could range from 0 to 15 based on correct or incorrect responses. Based on these two scales, a health educator can judge his or her perception of competence and actual competence. Often there is a poor correlation between the two, with a higher rating of perception of competence. This phenomenon has been called the **Dunning-Kruger effect**. In a series of studies, Kruger and Dunning (1999) found that humor, logic, and grammar test participants who scored low tended to overestimate their test performance and competence. It is very important for learning to have a true assessment of one's competence, so we recommend that you take these two tests.

SELF-ASSESSMENT WORKSHEET 1.1

Evaluation Competency Assessment of Health Educators

The following scale has been developed to gauge the evaluation competency of health educators based on NCHEC-developed standards. Please carefully self-reflect on each attribute and self-rate your present level of competence on the provided continuum. Please answer each question by checking the box that indicates your opinion about each item using the following rating continuum:

If asked *right now*, I am:

0   Not aware of this concept

1   Able to describe this concept

2   Able to demonstrate enough skill to complete a class project on this concept

3   Able to demonstrate enough skill to regularly apply in a real world setting

4   Able to demonstrate enough skill to flexibly apply and manipulate this concept to different challenging situations

	0	1	2	3	4
1. Identify existing sources of health-related databases					
2. Evaluate existing data-gathering instruments					
3. Evaluate existing data-gathering processes					
4. Select an appropriate qualitative evaluation design					
5. Select an appropriate quantitative evaluation design					
6. Develop a valid evaluation instrument					
7. Develop a reliable evaluation instrument					
8. Implement appropriate qualitative evaluation					
9. Implement appropriate quantitative evaluation techniques					
10. Apply evaluation technology as appropriate					
11. Implement strategies to analyze data from evaluation assessments					
12. Compare evaluation results to other findings					
13. Make recommendations from evaluation results					
14. Apply findings to refine/maintain programs					
15. Use evaluation findings in policy analysis and development					

SELF-ASSESSMENT WORKSHEET 1.2

Basic Knowledge Assessment of Evaluation Competency

Please mark an appropriate response. If you answer yes, please fill in the blank with the appropriate answer. (Maximum time 15 min.)

1. Name an existing health-related database.
    Don't know   Not sure   Yes, I know and it is:

    _____

2. Name any one criterion for evaluating an existing instrument.
    Don't know   Not sure   Yes, I know and it is:

    _____

3. Name any one data-gathering process used in evaluation.
    Don't know   Not sure   Yes, I know and it is:

    _____

4. Name any one qualitative evaluation technique.
    Don't know   Not sure   Yes, I know and it is:

    _____

5. Name any one quantitative evaluation design.
    Don't know   Not sure   Yes, I know and it is:

    _____

6. Name any one type of validity.
    Don't know   Not sure   Yes, I know and it is:

    _____

7. Name any one type of reliability.
    Don't know   Not sure   Yes, I know and it is:

    _____

8. Describe any one barrier in implementing a qualitative evaluation technique.
    Don't know   Not sure   Yes, I know and it is:

    _____

9. Describe any one barrier in implementing a quantitative evaluation technique.
    Don't know   Not sure   Yes, I know and it is:

    _____

SELF-ASSESSMENT WORKSHEET 1.2 (continued)

10. Name any one software used in evaluation.

    Don't know   Not sure   Yes, I know and it is:

    _____

11. Name any one statistical test used in evaluation to analyze data.

    Don't know   Not sure   Yes, I know and it is:

    _____

12. Name any one criterion for cause-effect linkage.

    Don't know   Not sure   Yes, I know and it is:

    _____

13. Name any one area for recommendations of evaluation results.

    Don't know   Not sure   Yes, I know and it is:

    _____

14. Name any one way to apply evaluation findings for refining programs.

    Don't know   Not sure   Yes, I know and it is:

    _____

15. Name any one way to apply evaluation findings for policy development.

    Don't know   Not sure   Yes, I know and it is:

    _____

HISTORICAL MILESTONES IN THE EVALUATION OF HEALTH EDUCATION AND HEALTH PROMOTION

The history of evaluation in health education and health promotion is related to the history of evaluation in the fields of education, medicine, public health, and the behavioral and social sciences. As we all know, the field of health education and health promotion is an applied field derived from these fields; as a result, the history of evaluation is also related to these disciplines.

The first influence on evaluation in health education and health promotion is from the field of education. In education, standardized tests are often used to evaluate students. The origin of these standardized tests can be traced back to China in the seventh century (Hall, 1999). These tests were used to recruit potential employees for working in the government and entailed testing of a person's knowledge and understanding of the philosophy of Confucius. In the United States, the educator Horace Mann initiated standardized testing in 1845 to test knowledge of spelling, math, and geography. At that time, *viva voce*

FOCUS FEATURE 1.1   HYPOTHETICAL ACCOUNT OF A HEALTH EDUCATOR'S EVALUATION RESPONSIBILITIES

John Doe completed his bachelor's and master's degrees in health education at the University of Cincinnati. He also passed an exam to become a Certified Health Education Specialist. He worked with the City of Cincinnati Health Department for 5 years. He has recently joined a health education consultation and evaluation firm as an evaluator. His job responsibilities are:

- To design and implement evaluation plans for assessment of the process, impact, and outcome of health education and health promotion programs

- To select or develop psychometrically robust tools for process, impact, and outcome evaluations

- To consult with client organizations to develop evaluation components in grant proposals

- To participate in local, regional, and national conferences to disseminate results of evaluation studies

- To write evaluation reports for clients

- To publish the results of evaluation studies in peer-reviewed journal articles, if clients want

He completed several courses related to health education in his master's program that helped him to get this job, such as:

- Principles of Health Promotion and Education

- Health Promotion Program Planning

- Community Mobilization or Organization

- Promoting Health Promotion Programs

- Health Promotion Program Management

- Analysis of Health Indices

- Resource Development and Fundraising

- Measurement and Evaluation in Health Education

- Research Methods

Based on these courses John was able to develop necessary skills that helped him get this job. The skills that he acquired pertained to planning, implementation, and evaluation of health education programs. He learned skills specifically pertaining to developing instruments, reviewing instruments, choosing evaluation designs, sampling, data analysis, and data interpretation. Such skills are vital for anyone aspiring to work in the field of evaluating health education programs.

or oral exams were common. These were replaced by written exams. In 1895, 36 secondary school, college, and university administrators from seven Midwestern states formed the North Central Association of Colleges and Secondary Schools. The current purpose of the association is "to require its Commission members to have accrediting processes that foster quality, encourage academic excellence, and improve teaching and learning" (North

Central Association of Colleges and Secondary Schools, n.d.). Currently, approximately 10,000 schools and colleges across the United States are members of this association.

In 1909, the Thorndike Handwriting Scale was introduced, which measured handwriting. In 1914, the multiple choice test was introduced by Frederick Kelly.

Another contribution to the field of evaluation from education was by Joseph Mayer Rice (1857–1934). He was a physician and educator, and is often credited as being the originator of evaluative research in education. He conducted a comparative experiment in which he compared learning outcomes between schools that spent 200 minutes a week learning spelling and those that spent 10 minutes a week. He found no significant differences (McDermott & Sarvela, 1999). This can be seen as an experimental study in education that paved the way for further evaluation studies.

Another contribution to the field of evaluation from education came from the work of Ralph Tyler (1902–1994), who published more than 700 articles and 16 books. Tyler introduced the term *evaluation* in the context of schooling. He used this concept as being separate from rote memorization examinations. He talked about an evidence collection process related to teaching and learning objectives (Kiester, 1978). He advocated that evaluation should focus on programmatic outcomes (Tyler, 1949). This paved the way for what in contemporary times is called a portfolio assessment.

In public health and medicine, mortality and morbidity data are used as a basis for evaluation. Records of vital events started being kept around 1532 by an unknown person in London (Declich & Carter, 1994). Surveillance of plague was first done in London during the 17th century, and surveillance of infectious diseases became established by the 18th century in Europe (Declich & Carter, 1994). In some colonies of America, such as Rhode Island, reporting of small pox, cholera, and yellow fever began in 1743. Surveillance data was used in an evaluation of public health in two hallmark reports in public health in the 19th century: Edwin Chadwick's report in England entitled "*The Sanitary Conditions of the Labouring Population*" and Lemuel Shattuck's "Report of Massachusetts Sanitary Commission" in the United States (Eylenbosch & Noah, 1988). In 1935, the first national health survey was done in the United States (Declich & Carter, 1994).

Another major influence on the evaluation of health education and health promotion came from work in medicine and public health. The randomized controlled trial (RCT) is considered to be the gold standard in evaluation. This approach first originated in a crude form around 600 BC, when Daniel of Judah compared the health effects of a vegetarian diet with a royal Babylonian diet for 10 days (Jadad, 1998). Modern application of RCTs began with the work of Austin Bradford Hill (1952). Today, RCTs are the basis of evaluation for all drugs and procedures in medicine, and they form the basis of the movement called evidence-based medicine (Stolberg, Norman, & Trop, 2004). RCTs are also used in the evaluation of health education efforts, and sometimes health promotion efforts.

The field of behavioral and social sciences has provided several contributions to evaluation in the form of psychometric instrumentation. The first contributor was Sir Francis Galton (1822–1911). He was an experimental psychologist who originated what is known as differential psychology, which deals with psychological differences between people, as opposed to classifying people by common traits. He also developed several psychometric tools. Another contributor was Louis Leon Thurstone (1887–1955) who developed an eponymous scale. He also contributed to the technique of factor analysis. A third contributor was Charles Edward Spearman (1863–1945), who is considered to be the father of classical test theory and a contributor to factor analysis (Jensen, 1994).

From these early influences, the field of health education and health promotion emerged. Although the history of health education dates to the late 19th century, when the first academic programs emerged for training school health educators (Allegrante et al., 2004), the field became established only after World War II. The 1960s saw the first major evaluations in health education. The first of these was the School Health Education Study (SHES) (Sliepcevich, 1964), which examined data pertaining to student health practices and school health education programs. The study was spread across 38 states involving 135 school systems (1,101 elementary schools and 359 secondary schools). The initial study found that the condition of health education was appalling, especially with regard to health practices, and that individual health education programs were not evaluated. The study recommended four major changes: (1) regular evaluations should be done; (2) both genders should be taught together; (3) wherever appropriate, locally developed curricula should be used; and (4) operational policies should be inspected. Based on this study, the School Health Curriculum Project (SHCP) was funded for 6 years to develop a model curriculum for schools.

In 1968, the *International Survey of Research and Studies in Health Education by Ministries of Health and Universities* (Roberts & Green, 1968) found that most evaluation efforts around the world were being done by health educators trained in the United States. Most of the evaluation was found to be descriptive, in the form of knowledge, attitudes, and practices (KAP) surveys, and almost no efforts were undertaken with regard to experimental evaluations (Green & Lewis, 1986).

In the 1970s there were several developments that influenced the evaluation of health promotion and education. In 1971, President Richard M. Nixon appointed the first presidential committee ever charged with addressing the state of health education in the United States (Guinta & Allegrante, 1992). The idea of forming such a committee originated from the issue of rising medical costs. The committee, which consisted of 19 members, found a paucity of evaluation literature related to health education programs, and emphasized the need to establish the efficiency and effectiveness of health education programs in all settings. It also sought to establish a National Center for Health Education to stimulate, coordinate, and evaluate health education programs.

The National Health Planning and Resources Act of 1974 (Public Law 93-641) was aimed at ensuring efficiency in healthcare delivery (Terenzio, 1976), and the National Consumer Health Information and Health Promotion Act of 1976 (Public Law 94-317) provided $31 million for basic research and demonstration projects in health information, health promotion, preventive health services, and education in the appropriate use of health care (Somers, 1976). Both of these public laws had a strong provision for evaluation of the programs. These measures strengthened the role of evaluation in health education and health promotion.

In 1976, the Office of Disease Prevention and Health Promotion was established within the U.S. Department of Health and Human Services (USDHHS). Some of the achievements of this office over the years have included participation in the formulation of Healthy People 2000, Healthy People 2010, and Healthy People 2020; maintenance of a National Health Information Center (NHIC), which is an Internet-accessible clearinghouse of health information for consumers and professionals that utilizes a database of over 1,700 organizations; development of physical activity guidelines; and development of dietary guidelines. Evaluation has been an important emphasis of this office.

In 1979, *Healthy People: Surgeon General's Report on Health Promotion and Disease Prevention* was published. The report had goals and evaluation targets. It identified five health promotion priority areas of smoking, alcohol and drug use, nutrition, exercise and fitness, and management of stress.

In the 1980s, Green and Lewis (1986) described the poverty cycle of health education wherein health education programs tend to set diffuse objectives. These diffuse objectives lead to implementation of diffuse methods and procedures, which in turn result in weak and sparse impact and outcome. As a result of low-quality or nonexistent evaluations of health promotion programs, the public did not have clear evidence that these programs were effective. As a result, there was inadequate support for health education. Green and Lewis (1986) advocated strong evaluation to break this cycle. Several years have elapsed since the introduction of the concept of this cycle in health education, yet we have not been able to completely emerge from this vicious circle.

In the late 1970s and early 1980s, several health education projects were funded to combat risk factors affecting cardiovascular disease. The first of these, which started in 1972, was the Stanford Three Community Study, which targeted three risk factors: smoking, high serum cholesterol, and high blood pressure (Farquhar, 1978; Farquhar et al., 1977). This was followed by the Stanford Five City Project in 1978 (Farquhar et al., 1985; Young, Haskell, Jatulis, & Fortmann, 1993), the Minnesota Heart Health Program in 1980 (Mittelmark et al., 1986), and the Pawtucket Heart Health Program in 1982 (Carleton, Lasater, Assaf, Lefebvre & McKinlay, 1987). Systematic evaluations were done in these studies. It was found that the outcome results were modest in changing physiological variables and influencing mortality and morbidity rates (Sharma & Galletly, 1997).

Another important development that occurred in the 1980s was the establishment of the Behavioral Risk Factor Surveillance System (BRFSS) by the Centers for Disease Control and Prevention (CDC). Between 1981 and 1983, a feasibility study of behavioral surveillance was conducted in 29 states, and in 1984 the BRFSS was established. The BRFSS is a state-level system composed of health surveys that collects data on health risk behaviors, healthcare access, and preventive health practices related to chronic diseases and injuries. Currently, the BRFSS interviews more than 350,000 adults each year, making it the largest telephone health survey in the world (Centers for Disease Control and Prevention, 2008). Based on the BRFSS, a youth counterpart, Youth Risk Behavior Surveillance System (YRBSS) has also been established. The YRBSS records selected health-risk behaviors and the prevalence of obesity and asthma among youth and young adults (National Center for Chronic Disease Prevention and Health Promotion, 2010). Both BRFSS and YRBSS have established the value of systematic data collection in evaluation.

In 1986, the American Evaluation Association was founded. The American Evaluation Association is "an international professional association of evaluators devoted to the application and exploration of program evaluation, personnel evaluation, technology, and many other forms of evaluation" (American Evaluation Association, n. d.). This association currently has 5,500 members and has a mission "to improve evaluation practices and methods, increase evaluation use, promote evaluation as a profession, and support the contribution of evaluation to the generation of theory and knowledge about effective human action" (American Evaluation Association, n. d.).

As mentioned earlier, in 1988, the National Commission for Health Education Credentialing (NCHEC) was established. This was an important step in the evaluation of health education personnel. The mission of NCHEC is "to enhance the professional practice of Health Education by promoting and sustaining a credentialed body of Health Education Specialists. To meet this mission, NCHEC certifies health education specialists, promotes professional development, and strengthens professional preparation and practice" (NCHEC, 2008a). The same year, the Institute of Medicine (1988) published the *Future of Public Health* report, which was mentioned earlier in this chapter. The report identified three core functions of public health functionaries, in which health educators were included: assessment, policy development, and assurance. All three functions entail the use of evaluation.

In 1990, the *Healthy People 2000* report was published. With the publication of this report, annual monitoring of 227 objectives in 15 priority areas began. This was a significant attempt at systematically using evaluation to gauge various health indicators spread across a variety of areas. There was greater focus on accountability, use of theory-based health education programs, and triangulation of qualitative and quantitative approaches in evaluating health education interventions.

The 1990s also saw evaluation of HIV/AIDS programs with several risk groups in a variety of settings. Many of these programs utilized behavioral theories and were found to be successful. For example, Kim and colleagues (1997) examined 40 adolescent AIDS risk reduction interventions and found that these interventions were effective in enhancing knowledge, attitudes, and behavioral intentions and reducing risky behaviors. These systematic evaluations strengthened the image of both health education and evaluation.

The 2000s started with the *Healthy People 2010* report, which had 467 objectives in 28 areas. Population-based health education and health promotion interventions that utilized multiple channels and multiple approaches became the norm in the 2000s. Use of behavioral theory in health education and health promotion interventions also became very popular.

In 2010, the *Healthy People 2020* report was published. This has 42 areas with several objectives that are currently being monitored; these were presented earlier in Table 1.1. The report has four overarching goals (USDHHS, 2010):

- Attain high-quality, longer lives free of preventable disease, disability, injury, and premature death.
- Achieve health equity, eliminate disparities, and improve the health of all groups.
- Create social and physical environments that promote good health for all.
- Promote quality of life, healthy development, and healthy behaviors across all life stages.

In 2011, the NCHEC started the Master Certified Health Education Specialist (MCHES) credential, thereby creating two cadres of health educators: one at the entry level and one at the master level.

The entire timeline of salient events shaping evaluation in health education and health promotion is summarized in **Table 1.3**.

TABLE 1.3   Timeline of Salient Events Shaping Evaluation in Health Education and Health Promotion

Year	Event
1532	Records of vital events started by an unknown person in London.
17th century	Surveillance of plague first done in London.
18th century	Surveillance of infectious diseases became established in Europe.
1743	Reporting of smallpox, cholera, and yellow fever began in American colonies.
1845	Educator Horace Mann initiated standardized testing.
1850	Lemuel Shattuck's *Report of Massachusetts Sanitary Commission* in the United States is based on surveillance data.
1895	North Central Association of Colleges and Secondary Schools formed.
1898	Joseph Mayer Rice conducted a comparative experiment in which he compared learning outcomes between schools.
1822–1911	Sir Francis Galton developed several psychometric tools.
1863–1945	Charles Edward Spearman was the father of classical test theory and a contributor to factor analysis.
1887–1955	Louis Leon Thurstone developed a scale he named after himself, and also contributed to the technique of factor analysis.
1909	The Thorndike Handwriting Scale was developed.
1914	The multiple choice test was introduced by Frederick Kelly.
1935	The first national health survey was done in the United States.
1949	Ralph Tyler advocated that evaluation should focus on programmatic outcomes.
1952	The application of randomized controlled trials began with the work of Austin Bradford Hill.
1961–63	The School Health Education Study (SHES) was completed.
1964	The School Health Curriculum Project (SHCP) began.
1968	The *International Survey of Research and Studies in Health Education by Ministries of Health and Universities* was published.
1971	President Richard M. Nixon appointed the first presidential committee ever charged with addressing the state of health education in the United States.
1974	The National Health Planning and Resources Act (Public Law 93-641) aimed at ensuring efficiency in healthcare delivery.
1976	The National Consumer Health Information and Health Promotion Act (Public Law 94-317) provided $31 million for basic research and demonstration projects in health information, health promotion, preventive health services, and education in the appropriate use of health care.
	The Office of Disease Prevention and Health Promotion was established.
Late 1970s and early 1980s	Several health education projects that had evaluation components were funded to combat risk factors affecting cardiovascular disease.
1980s	Green and Lewis (1986) described the poverty cycle of health education.
1984	The Behavioral Risk Factor Surveillance System (BRFSS) was established

(continues)

TABLE 1.3   Timeline of Salient Events Shaping Evaluation in Health Education and Health Promotion *(Continued)*

Year	Event
1986	The American Evaluation Association was founded.
1988	The National Commission for Health Education Credentialing (NCHEC) was established.
	The Institute of Medicine published the *Future of Public Health* report.
1990	The *Healthy People 2000* report was published.
1990s	Systematic evaluations of health education programs for HIV/AIDS were conducted.
2000	The *Healthy People 2010* report was published.
2000s	Population-based health education and health promotion interventions that utilized multiple channels and multiple approaches using behavioral theory became the norm.
2010	The *Healthy People 2020* report was published.
2011	The Master Certified Health Education Specialist (MCHES) certification started.

BASIC TERMS IN EVALUATION

Health education and health promotion have their roots in several disciplines: biological sciences, behavioral sciences, economics, political science, and other social sciences. As in any other field, certain terms and jargon are common to health education and health promotion professionals. In this section we present some of these terms that relate to evaluation.

Intervention

An **intervention** is another term for a health education or health promotion program. It is derived from the word *intervene*. An intervention signifies a systematic orientation and a planned approach, and entails an appropriate mix of behavioral-level (educational) and policy-level (promotion) approaches. It specifies target population, site(s), approach(es), and time(s).

Formative Evaluation

A **formative evaluation** is done during the development and/or implementation of a health education or health promotion intervention. This is usually done on a smaller scale as a pilot study or a field study and entails monitoring of activities. This evaluation can be used when developing a new health promotion intervention. The key purpose of a formative evaluation is to provide rapid (1 hour or 1 week) or short-term (1 week to 6 months) feedback to improve the program. Key questions would include: What aspects of the program are working? What aspects of the program should be refined? This type of evaluation usually uses qualitative or quasi-experimental designs. Experimental designs are almost never used. The feedback from a formative evaluation leads to program adjustments.

Summative Evaluation

A **summative evaluation** is done to understand the "end products" of a health education or health promotion program. It is generally presumed that the program has been refined and is working properly. It is now time to rigorously evaluate the program's outcomes to determine whether the program is effective. The summative evaluation is usually done on a larger scale than other evaluations and uses quantitative designs. The key queries that summative evaluation deals with are: What has happened? Who was affected? What was the most effective treatment? Was it cost effective? (Groteluseschen, 1982). In health education and health promotion programs it entails measurement of changes in antecedents of behavior, behavior, physiological outcomes, and epidemiological indicators.

Process Evaluation

A **process evaluation** is concerned with finding out to what extent the program adhered to the written plan. It is also interested in finding out the satisfaction of the recipients, implementers, sites, and other associated personnel with the program. Assurance of quality is another purpose of process evaluation. It usually uses nonexperimental designs and monitors procedures: How much (of the intervention), when (how much time), to whom, and by whom?

Impact Evaluation

An **impact evaluation** is concerned with assessing changes in health-related cognitive and behavioral domains. The usual time frame for this evaluation is 6 months to 2–3 years. This type of evaluation usually uses experimental or quasi-experimental designs. In this evaluation it is important to enhance internal validity or the degree to which the intervention produced (caused) changes in cognitive or behavioral domains within the target population. An example of an impact evaluation is a 6-month childhood obesity intervention that measures changes in physical activity behavior at the end of the program and compares it with a control group.

Outcome Evaluation

An **outcome evaluation** is concerned with assessing changes in health indicators such as mortality and morbidity in the target population. It is presumed that the impact evaluation has been completed and demonstrated that a significant portion of the target population has changed a health behavior. The outcome evaluation seeks to determine whether changes in health behavior have produced anticipated changes in health status. The time frame for this evaluation is usually long, often entailing 5–10 years. Controlling for secular trends (time related) is usually difficult in this type of evaluation.

Efficacy

Efficacy is the extent to which a new or untested approach produces an impact (cognitive or behavioral changes) and/or outcome (changes in health indicators such as mortality, morbidity, and the like) as tested under *optimal* conditions. In efficacy testing, controlled situations are created and internal validity is particularly important.

Effectiveness

Effectiveness is the extent to which an existing or tested approach produces an impact (cognitive or behavioral changes) and/or outcome (changes in health indicators such as mortality, morbidity, and the like) as tested under *real world* or *practice* conditions. In effectiveness testing, both internal and external validity (generalizability) are important.

Cost-Benefit Evaluation

A **cost-benefit evaluation** is an analysis carried out taking into account only financial costs and financial benefits. A financial (dollar) value is placed on every cost and every benefit, and then a comparison is made. Methodologically and politically it is very difficult to determine a universally acceptable way to estimate things such as a year of life in monetary terms. Therefore, the applicability of this evaluation is sometimes limited.

Cost-Effectiveness Evaluation

A **cost-effectiveness evaluation** analyzes the impact of a program as a ratio of program costs to some naturally occurring outcome, such as cost per case of breast cancer prevented. It is an excellent tool to compare different approaches being used for the same disease. However, it is not a useful method if one needs to compare across diseases.

Empowerment Evaluation

An **empowerment evaluation** entails the utilization of concepts, approaches, and results from evaluation to build improvement and self-determination (Fetterman, 2001). Fetterman (2007) defines empowerment evaluation as "an evaluation approach that aims to increase the probability of achieving program success by (1) providing program stakeholders with tools for assessing the planning, implementation, and self-evaluation of their program, and (2) mainstreaming evaluation as part of the planning and management of the program/organization." In this evaluation method, participants are responsible for evaluating their own programs instead of an evaluator doing so.

Goal-Free Evaluation

A **goal-free evaluation** aims at eliminating (or reducing) evaluator bias. When conducting this type of evaluation, the program's preset objectives are not revealed to the evaluator. As a result, a program's intended and unintended effects are both studied. One of the disadvantages of this type of evaluation is its lack of clear methodology.

Goal-Oriented Evaluation

A **goal-oriented evaluation** is based on predetermined objectives. This type of evaluation usually uses quantitative experimental designs that are typically grounded in theory. Efforts are made in this evaluation to enhance internal validity.

Hatchet Evaluation

The purpose of a **hatchet evaluation** is to demonstrate the weaknesses and failures of a program or an organization. This concept illustrates a potential political use of an evaluation, such as when a stakeholder in the community would like to see a health promotion program ended or downsized. The motive for such an evaluation is to discredit the program so that funding or political support is diminished or completely removed.

Ingratiating Evaluation

The primary purpose of an **ingratiating evaluation** is to show the success and strengths of the program. This approach to evaluation also is politically motivated. The goal of the stakeholders is to exaggerate the positive benefits of the program. Usually in such evaluations, considerations are not given to internal or external validity or whatever shortcomings the program may have had. This type of evaluation is typically done with the intent of ensuring continued funding and program survival, and gaining political support.

Illuminative Evaluation

An **illuminative evaluation** is a custom-built evaluation approach that does not necessarily have formal objectives, avoids (but does not exclude) statistical procedures, employs subjective methods, and is primarily interested in the "informing" function of an evaluation, rather than the more usual "inspectoral or grading" function of an evaluation (Richards, 1985). These evaluations are more holistic and responsive in their orientation.

Participatory Evaluation

A **participatory evaluation** entails partnership among all stakeholders—program developers, program implementers, target population, and funders—to develop a joint evaluation framework and implement it together. It entails joint identification of evaluation questions, planning the evaluation design, selecting the measures, analyzing the data, and interpreting the data together.

Transactional Evaluation

A **transactional evaluation** entails examination of the perspectives of all stakeholders. It is a very comprehensive evaluation and examines multiple outcomes. A main disadvantage of this type of evaluation is that it is often prone to dilution.

SKILL-BUILDING ACTIVITY

Certain fundamental questions can be posed before embarking upon any evaluation. We will apply those questions to some potential evaluation contexts. The questions are:

- WHAT will you evaluate?
- WHEN will you evaluate?
- WHY will you evaluate?
- WHO will evaluate?
- WHOM will you evaluate?
- WHERE will you evaluate?
- HOW will you evaluate?

Context 1: A 6-month childhood obesity prevention program is being implemented in upper elementary grades of a school district in Kentucky. The program is in its first year. You have been approached to evaluate this program.

Context 2: There is an on-the-job training program on use of the latest technology in health education for health educators in Ohio in which health educators from all counties in Ohio participate. The program is in its second year. You have been approached to evaluate this program.

Context 3: A diabetes education program for newly diagnosed diabetics at the Methodist Hospital in Atlanta has been running for the past 4 years. You have been approached to evaluate this program.

Context 4: Insurance of Omaha implements a wellness program for its employees. It is a large worksite with over 10,000 employees, and the program has been in existence for 5 years. You have been approached to evaluate this program.

Carefully evaluate each question for each of the four contexts. What similarities and differences did you find?

SUMMARY

Evaluation is the process of judging the strong points and weak points of programs/interventions, policies/procedures, personnel/staff, products/materials, and organizations/institutions to enhance their effectiveness. Evaluation is vital for health education and health promotion in six areas:

- Planning
- Identifying evaluation procedures
- Creating data-gathering tools
- Implementing evaluation plans
- Interpreting findings from evaluation
- Coming up with inferences for future programs and interventions (consists of responsibilities mainly for graduate-level health educators)

The history of evaluation in health education and health promotion is related to the history of evaluation in the fields of education, medicine, public health, and behavioral and social sciences. Some of the salient events that have influenced the evaluation of health education and health promotion programs include educator Horace Mann's initiation of standardized testing in 1845, the first national health survey in the United States in 1935, application of the randomized controlled trial by Austin Bradford Hill in 1952, the School Health Education Study (SHES) in 1961–63, the first presidential committee ever charged with addressing the state of health education in the United States in 1971, establishment of the Office of Disease Prevention and Health Promotion in 1976, formation of the American Evaluation Association in 1986, formation of the National Commission for Health Education Credentialing (NCHEC) in 1988, and systematic evaluations of health education programs for HIV/AIDS in the 1990s.

REVIEW QUESTIONS

1. Define health education, health promotion, and evaluation.
2. Describe the evaluation competencies for health educators.
3. Discuss the historical contributions of the field of education to the development of evaluation in health education and health promotion.
4. Discuss the key events from the 1970s, 1980s, and 1990s that shaped evaluation in health education and health promotion.
5. Differentiate between formative evaluation and summative evaluation.
6. Differentiate among process, impact, and outcome evaluation.
7. Differentiate between cost-benefit evaluation and cost-effectiveness evaluation.
8. Define empowerment evaluation and participatory evaluation.
9. What is transactional evaluation?

WEBSITES TO EXPLORE

American Evaluation Association

http://www.eval.org
The American Evaluation Association website contains links to information about the organization, readings that include links to journals and newsletters, links to various events, community links to listservs and Facebook, career links for posting and searching resumes, ways to find an evaluator, and a members-only area. Review these links and learn about the organization. *Click on the Find an Evaluator link and choose Search Evaluator Listings. For your state, locate evaluators who have experience in health education. What did you find? Do you know any of these people?*

Empowerment Evaluation Blog

http://eevaluation.blogspot.com
This is a blog created by the originator of empowerment evaluation, David Fetterman. It is a forum for exchange and discussion about empowerment evaluation. The website provides a complete profile of David Fetterman and links to various discussions. *Read one of the discussions and reflect on what you think about empowerment evaluation.*

Eta Sigma Gamma

http://www.etasigmagamma.org

This is the website of Eta Sigma Gamma, which is the national health education honorary. Links on this website have been provided for information about the organization, awards and grants, career opportunities, chapter information, membership information, publications, upcoming events, and a few others. *Review the chapter information. Does your program have a chapter? If yes, then visit its website. If no, find out more about starting a chapter.*

Participatory Evaluation

http://www.evaluativethinking.org/docs/EvaluationEssentials2010.pdf

This is a guide to participatory evaluation called *Participatory Evaluation Essentials. A Guide for Nonprofit Organizations and Their Evaluation Partners*, which was updated by the Bruner Foundation in 2010. *Browse through this guide and read some sections. What are some skills and tools needed for participatory evaluation?*

REFERENCES

Airhihenbuwa, C. O., Cottrell, R. R., Adeyanju, M., Auld, M. E., Lysoby, L., & Smith, B. J. (2005). The National Health Educator Competencies Update Project: Celebrating a milestone and recommending next steps to the profession. *American Journal of Health Education, 36*, 361–370.

Allegrante, J. P., Airhihenbuwa, C. O., Auld, M. E., Birch, D. A., Roe, K. M., & Smith, B. J. (2004). Toward a unified system of accreditation for professional preparation in health education: Final report of the National Task Force on Accreditation in Health Education. *Health Education and Behavior, 31*, 668–683.

American Association for Health Education. (2003). Directory of institutions offering undergraduate and graduate degree programs in health education. 2003 edition. *American Journal of Health Education, 34*(4), 219–235.

American Association for Health Education, National Commission for Health Education Credentialing, & Society for Public Health Education. (1999). *A competency-based framework for graduate-level health educators.* Allentown, PA: National Commission for Health Education Credentialing.

American Evaluation Association. (n. d.). About us. Retrieved from http://www.eval.org/aboutus/organization/aboutus.asp

Carleton, R. A., Lasater, T. M., Assaf, A., Lefebvre, R. C., & McKinlay, S. M. (1987). The Pawtucket Heart Health Program: I. An experiment in population-based disease prevention. *Rhode Island Medical Journal, 70*(12), 533–538.

Centers for Disease Control and Prevention. (2008). About the BRFSS. Retrieved from http://www.cdc.gov/brfss/about.htm

Declich, S., & Carter, A. O. (1994). Public health surveillance: Historical origins, methods and evaluation. *Bulletin of the World Health Organization, 72*(2), 285–304.

Eylenbosch, W. J., & Noah, N. D. (1988). *Surveillance in health and disease.* Oxford: Oxford University Press.

Farquhar, J. W. (1978). The community-based model of life style intervention trials. *American Journal of Epidemiology, 108*(2), 103–111.

Farquhar, J. W., Fortmann, S. P., Maccoby, N., Haskell, W. L., Williams, P. T., Flora, J. A., . . . Hulley, S. B. (1985). The Stanford Five-City Project: Design and methods. *American Journal of Epidemiology, 122*(2), 323–334.

Farquhar, J. W., Maccoby, N., Wood, P. D., Alexander, J. K., Breitrose, H., Brown, B. W. Jr., . . . Stern, M. P. (1977). Community education for cardiovascular health. *Lancet, 1*(8023), 1192–1195.

Fetterman, D. (2001). Empowerment evaluation and self determination: A practical approach toward program improvement and capacity building. In N. Schneiderman, M. A. Speers, J. M. Silva, H. Tomes, & J. H. Gentry (Eds.), *Integrating behavioral and social sciences with public health* (pp. 321–350). Washington, DC: American Psychological Association.

Fetterman, D. (2007). Empowerment evaluation: Principles in practice. Retrieved from http://wwwstatic.kern.org/gems/region4/DavidFettermanPresentation.pdf

Gilmore, G. D., Olsen, L. K., Taub, A., & Connell, D. (2005). Overview of the National Health Educator Competencies Update Project, 1998–2004. *Health Education and Behavior, 32,* 725–737.

Gold, R. S., & Miner, K. R., for the 2000 Joint Committee on Health Education and Promotion Terminology. (2002). Report of the 2000 Joint Committee on Health Education and Promotion Terminology. *Journal of School Health, 72,* 3–7.

Green, L. W., & Kreuter, M. W. (2005). *Health program planning: An educational and ecological approach* (4th ed.). Boston: McGraw-Hill.

Green, L. W., & Lewis, F. M. (1986). *Measurement and evaluation in health education and health promotion.* Palo Alto, CA: Mayfield.

Groteluseschen, A. D. (1982). Program evaluation. In A. B. Knox and Associates (Eds.), *Developing, administering, and evaluating adult education* (pp. 75–87). San Francisco: Jossey Bass.

Guinta, M. A., & Allegrante, J. P. (1992). The President's Committee on Health Education: A 20-year retrospective on its politics and policy impact. *American Journal of Public Health, 82*(7), 1033–1041.

Hall, E. (1999). The history of standardized test. Retrieved from http://www.ehow.com/about_5392902_history-standardized-test.html

Hill, A. B. (1952). The clinical trial. *New England Journal of Medicine, 247,* 113–119.

Institute of Medicine. (1988). *Future of public health.* Washington, DC: National Academies Press.

Institute of Medicine. (2002). *The future of the public's health in the 21st century.* Washington, DC: National Academies Press.

Jadad, A. R. (1998). *Randomised controlled trials: A user's guide.* London, England: BMJ Books.

Jensen, A. R. (1994). Spearman, Charles Edward. In R. J. Sternberg (Ed.), *Encyclopedia of intelligence* (Vol. 1, pp. 1007–1014). New York: Macmillan.

Kiester, E. (1978). Ralph Tyler: The educator's educator. *Change, 10*(2), 28–35.

Kim, N., Stanton, B., Li, X., Dickersin, K., & Galbraith, J. (1997). Effectiveness of the 40 adolescent AIDS-risk reduction interventions: A quantitative review. *Journal of Adolescent Health, 20*(3), 204–215.

Kruger, J., & Dunning, D. (1999). Unskilled and unaware of it: How difficulties in recognizing one's own incompetence lead to inflated self-assessments. *Journal of Personality and Social Psychology, 77*(6), 1121–1134.

McDermott, R. J., & Sarvela, P. D. (1999). *Health education evaluation and measurement. A practitioner's perspective* (2nd ed.). New York: McGraw-Hill.

Mittelmark, M. B., Luepker, R. V., Jacobs, D. R., Bracht, N. F., Carlaw, R. W., Crow, R. S., . . . Blackburn, H. B. (1986). Community-wide prevention of cardiovascular disease: Education strategies of the Minnesota Heart Health Program. *Preventive Medicine, 15*(1), 1–17.

National Board of Public Health Examiners. (n.d.). National Board of Public Health Examiners. Retrieved from http://www.nbphe.org/aboutnbphe.cfm

National Center for Chronic Disease Prevention and Health Promotion, Division of Adolescent and School Health. (2010). YRBSS in brief. Retrieved from http://www.cdc.gov/HealthyYouth/yrbs/brief.htm

National Commission for Health Education Credentialing. (1985). *A framework for the development of competency-based curricula for entry-level health educators.* New York: Author.

National Commission for Health Education Credentialing. (2008a). Mission and purpose. Retrieved from http://www.nchec.org/aboutnchec/mission/

National Commission for Health Education Credentialing. (2008b). Responsibilities and competencies for health education specialists. Retrieved from http://www.nchec.org/credentialing /responsibilities/

National Commission for Health Education Credentialing, Society for Public Health Education, & American Association for Health Education. (2006). *Competency-based framework for health educators—2006.* Whitehall, PA: Author.

North Central Association of Colleges and Secondary Schools. (n. d.). Mission and purposes. Retrieved from http://www.northcentralassociation.org/PURPOSE%20OF%20THE%20 NORTH%20CENTRAL%20ASSOCIATION.htm

Public Health Functions Steering Committee. (1994). Public health in America. Retrieved from http://www.health.gov/phfunctions/public.htm

Rehrig, M. (2010, Winter). The long awaited advanced credential, MCHES, don't miss out. *CHES Bulletin, 21*(1), 1.

Richards, H. (1985). *The evaluation of cultural action.* Basingstoke, England: Macmillan.

Roberts, B. J., & Green, L. W. (1968). *International survey of research and studies in health education by Ministries of Health and Universities.* Berkeley, CA: University of California School of Public Health.

Sharma, M., & Galletly, C. (1997, Spring). Lessons for health promotion from selected community-based heart disease prevention programs. *Health Educator, 28,* 21–26.

Sliepcevich, E. M. (1964). *School health education study: A summary report of a nationwide study of health instruction in the public schools, 1961–1963.* Washington, DC: School Health Education Study.

Somers, A. R. (1976). *Promoting health: Consumer education and national policy.* Germantown, MD: Aspen Systems.

Stolberg, H. O., Norman, G., & Trop, I. (2004). Randomized controlled trial. *American Journal of Roentgenology, 183,* 1539–1544.

Terenzio, J. V. (1976). The National Health Planning and Resources Act of 1974 (Public law 93-641). *Bulletin of New York Academic Medicine, 52*(10), 1236–1243.

Tyler, R. (1949). *Basic principles of curriculum and instruction.* Chicago: University of Chicago Press.

U.S. Department of Health and Human Services. (1979). *Healthy people: The surgeon general's report on health promotion and disease prevention.* Washington, DC: Author.

U.S. Department of Health and Human Services. (1980). *Promoting health—preventing disease. Objectives for the nation.* Washington, DC: Author.

U.S. Department of Health and Human Services. (1990). *Healthy people 2000. National health promotion and disease prevention objectives.* Washington, DC: Author.

U.S. Department of Health and Human Services. (2000). *Healthy people 2010* (Vols. 1–2). Washington, DC: Author.

U.S. Department of Health and Human Services. (2012). Healthypeople.gov. Retrieved from http:// www.healthypeople.gov/HP2020/default.asp

U.S. Department of Health and Human Services. (2010). About Healthy People. Retrieved from http://www.healthypeople.gov/2020/about/default.aspx

U.S. Department of Health, Education and Welfare. (1978). *Preparation and practice of community, patient, and school health educators: Proceedings of the workshop on commonalities and differences.* Washington, DC: Division of Allied Health Professions.

World Health Organization. (1986). *Ottawa charter for health promotion, 1986*. Geneva, Switzerland: Author.

World Health Organization. (1997). *The Jakarta Declaration on leading health promotion into the 21st century*. Geneva, Switzerland: Author.

World Health Organization. (1998). Health promotion glossary. Retrieved from http://www.who.int/hpr/NPH/docs/hp_glossary_en.pdf

Young, D. R., Haskell, W. L., Jatulis, D. E., & Fortmann, S. P. (1993). Associations between changes in physical activity and risk factors for coronary heart disease in a community-based sample of men and women: The Stanford Five-City Project. *American Journal of Epidemiology, 138*(4), 205–216.

CHAPTER 2

Planning Evaluations for Health Education and Health Promotion Programs

KEY CONCEPTS _____

- activities
- comprehensive evaluation
- continuous health program improvement
- evaluation rigor
- impact
- impact evaluation
- implementation fidelity
- inputs
- logic model
- outcome evaluation
- outcomes
- outputs
- political climate
- process evaluation
- program stakeholder
- team approach to program planning and evaluation
- utilization-focused evaluation

CHAPTER OBJECTIVES _____

- Describe the relationship between evaluation and continuous health program improvement
- Explicate the role of logic models in program evaluation
- Explain the advantages of a team approach to program planning and evaluation
- Identify differences in expectations of different stakeholders
- Explain the components of a comprehensive evaluation
- Identify key concepts to promote utilization-focused evaluation

EVALUATION AND CONTINUOUS HEALTH PROGRAM IMPROVEMENT _____

Evaluation is an essential part of the continuous health program improvement model, which is illustrated in **Figure 2.1**. **Continuous health program improvement** is a cyclical model that starts with the skilled application of the health education knowledge base that informs needs assessment leading to high-quality program planning and implementation.

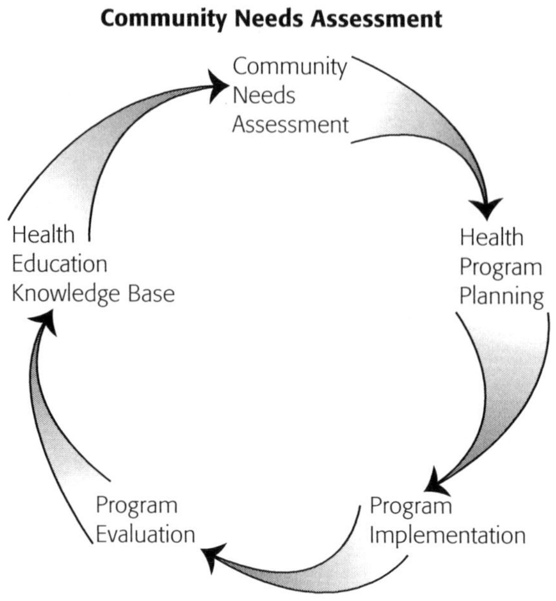

Community Needs Assessment

Figure 2.1 Continuous health education and health promotion model.

This is followed by program evaluation, which contributes back to the health education knowledge base.

In this model, the process begins with professionals who are well versed in the health education knowledge base. The knowledge base includes skills in the application of systematic models of needs assessment, health behavior theory, health education program planning, and program evaluation. The knowledge base also includes a detailed understanding of the linkages between determinants of health and the health status of communities. Needs assessment is conducted to systematically identify the health needs and interests of the target community. Needs assessment also is a time to engage the target population in the process. Consumer participation supports the development of relevant health program and program ownership. This phase is essential for designing health programs that are "on target" with participants' interests. Based on information gathered in the needs assessment phase, program planning establishes health status goals, health behavior objectives, and strategies to achieve these goals. Evaluation planning begins by reviewing the goals and objectives. Are the goals and objectives measurable? Can they be refined to increase the precision and rigor of the evaluation? Evaluators, program planners, and stakeholders should collaborate on setting goals and objectives that are attainable and measurable.

During health program implementation, evaluation procedures begin. Pretesting is typically done before the health program begins. Assessments are carefully administered to gather information essential to the evaluation, but not disruptive of the program. Posttesting and follow-up assessments are used to determine the impact of the health program on program participants: knowledge, skills, beliefs, attitudes, health behaviors, and health status. The results of the program evaluation are uti- lized by program planners, program managers, and stake- holders to refine and improve the health program. Evaluation results also feed back into the health education knowledge base. This knowledge base enables practitioners to continu- ously refine their decision making based on evidence of effec- tive and ineffective practices. On the local level it empowers decision makers to improve their health education programs. On a broader professional level, the health education knowl- edge base improves. Conceptualized in this way, evaluation is an essential process for improving the effectiveness of health education programs.

> *Continuous health program im- provement is a cyclical model that starts with the skilled application of the health education knowledge base that informs needs assessment, leading to high-quality program planning and implementation. This is followed by program evaluation, which contributes back to the health education knowl- edge base.*

LOGIC MODEL FOR HEALTH EDUCATION AND HEALTH PROMOTION PROGRAMS

Evaluators must be skilled in working with program planning models used in the field of health education and promotion. Health professionals draw on a variety of planning models to systematically assess the health needs of the community and plan programs in response to those needs. Examples of health education and promotion planning models include:

- The *Planning Approach to Community Health (PATCH)* was developed by the Cen- ters for Disease Control and Prevention (n.d.) to enable people in communities to take greater control of their health by systematically assessing health needs and targeting health programs.
- The *PRECEDE/PROCEED model* (Green & Kreuter, 2005) outlines a systematic process of gathering data to make informed decisions about community health needs. The acronym *PRECEDE* stands for predisposing, reinforcing, and enabling constructs in educational/environmental diagnosis and evaluation. The acronym *PROCEED* stands for policy, regulatory, and organizational constructs in educa- tional and environmental development. After identification of needs, the PRE- CEDE/PROCEED model encourages practitioners to consider policy, regulatory, educational, and environmental solutions.
- The *Community Health Improvement Process (CHIP) model*, developed by Durch, Bai- ley, and Stoto (1997), involves health problem prioritization and health program implementation. This model was linked to the assessment and performance mea- sures of Healthy People 2000 model standards.
- MATCH stands for the *Multilevel Approach to Community Health* (Simons-Morton, Simons-Morton, Parcel, & Bunker, 1988). MATCH employs an ecological planning perspective that targets a variety of objectives and target populations.
- The health education model RE-AIM stands for *Reach, Effectiveness, Adoption, Imple- mentation.* The RE-AIM framework is used for individual behavior change pro- grams and has been useful in organizing a health program flowchart for evaluations (Glasgow, Nelson, Strycker, & King, 2006).

Although there are many different program planning models for health education and health promotion, there are some important, common themes across all models. One important principle of contemporary health education and health promotion planning models is community participation. Consumers and professionals are viewed as community resources who can contribute to shared decision making about the health needs of the community. Active participation can yield many insights into both the goals and methods to achieve goals in a particular community. Active participation should increase program relevance, ownership, and participation. A second important principle is data-based decision making. Data can include perceptions of consumers, community mortality and morbidity statistics, medical care costs, and behavior risk factor data. The data can be used to inform decision making, set priorities, and target specific health concerns, behaviors, and resources. Ultimately the process results in defining a target population in the community that will receive the health program. Goals and objectives are set to enable health professionals to target resources and programs in an attempt to improve the public's health. The final step is to develop the health education and health promotion activities that the target population will receive. The careful delineation of health program goals and objectives provides a foundation for the evaluation of the program. The design of health education and promotion activities is also critical to the evaluation process. In an ideal situation, the planning of the health program and the planning of the evaluation are occurring simultaneously. The common themes across health education and health promotion planning models are summarized in **Table 2.1**.

It has become increasingly common to use logic models to design health programs and evaluations. A **logic model** is a systematic graphic representation of how an intervention is designed to produce its results by showing its relationship to resources and activities. The Centers for Disease Control and Prevention (CDC) and the Kellogg Foundation use logic models to design and evaluate programs. The advantage of logic models is that they can be applied to the wide range of program planning models in health education and health promotion. The logic model approach provides a means of communication and understanding across professionals from a range of disciplines.

A logic model is a systematic way to map out the relationships among resources for the program, health education/promotion program activities, and the intended results. The model is used to describe how objectives will be achieved. Each step in the logic model (**Figure 2.2**) is described in the following list:

- *Inputs:* These include the human, financial, and community resources that are available to support the health education/promotion program. From an administrative perspective, inputs are all of the resources needed to deliver health programs to target populations.

TABLE 2.1   Common Themes Across Health Education and Health Promotion Planning Models

Community participation

Data-based decision making

Defining a target population

Objectives that identify specific targets

Activities to promote health actions

A logic model is a systematic way to map the relationships among program resources, health education/promotion activities, and targeted objectives. A logic model serves as a graphic representation of how an intervention is designed to achieve goals by illustrating a program's relationship to resources and activities.

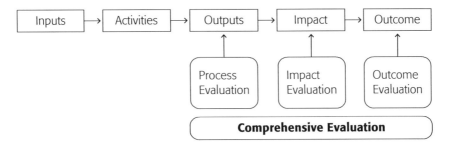

Figure 2.2   Logic model of health education and health promotion planning.

- *Activities:* These are all of the educational processes, tools, events, and environmental supports planned to make up the health education/promotion program. Specifically, this is the health program planning component designed to achieve program objectives.
- *Outputs:* These are the direct services that participants receive as delivered by the health program. These program activities are designed to promote participant behavioral capability and provide environmental supports to encourage health practices and enhance health status. This includes health education programs as well as environmental supports, including health policy, incentives, and access to facilities.
- *Impact:* This is the change in participants' knowledge, skills, motivation, and health behavior. Impact also includes environmental supports that participants may receive. Examples include incentives, policies, or access to facilities that support health behaviors. Short-term impact should be measureable from the final session of the health program to 6 months after program exposure. Long-term impacts are attainable from 6 months to 5 years after program exposure.
- *Outcome:* This is the change in participants' or communities' health status or quality of life produced by the health education/promotion program activities. The time frame for outcome-level changes depends on the temporal relationship between health behavior change and detectable changes in health status. Generally, outcomes are assessed 6 months to several years after health program implementation.

Fundamental to evaluation planning is an understanding of the logic used to design a health program. The logic model should identify the goals and objectives of the program. The evaluator may need to help revise program goals and objectives to ensure they are clear and measurable. The activities of the program should be mapped out to explain how they are expected to achieve goals and objectives. A logic model is a tool that can assist the evaluation team with this process.

LOGIC MODEL AND COMPREHENSIVE EVALUATION

Close examination of the logic model (Figure 2.2) suggests different potential points for evaluation. Starting with the Outputs section of the logic model, **process evaluation** methods can be used to assess the degree to which the program was implemented as designed.

Process evaluation methods can be used to assess the degree to which a program was implemented as designed.

Evaluators develop procedures for measuring the extent to which the program participants received matched the program that was planned. Basch and colleagues (1985) clearly indicate that it is not wise to assume a program is implemented as designed. Failing to document program implementation can affect stakeholders' interpretation of the impact and outcome evaluations. **Implementation fidelity** is the extent to which the program was implemented as planned. It is important for several reasons. First, it is a management tool. For accountability purposes, program administrators need to know how well program staffs are delivering programs. Implementation fidelity is also an important foundation of an evaluation plan. If the purpose of an evaluation is to determine the impact of a health program on a target population's health behavior or health status, we must first establish that the program was actually delivered.

Beyond implementation, a process evaluation can also gather information about program quality, and the satisfaction levels of participants, implementers, sites, and other personnel associated with the program. Often key insights can be identified to improve the program. Overall, quality assurance of a health program is an important element of process evaluation.

The impact evaluation focuses on changes in participants' health knowledge, health skills, health motivations, social support, perceived risk, and health behaviors.

The impact section of the logic model targets specific changes in participants produced by the health program. The **impact evaluation** can focus on participant changes in determinants of health behavior, including health knowledge, health skills, health motivations, social support, and perceived risk. Determinants can also include forces outside the individual. These factors are the product of health promotion strategies, and can include health incentives, health policy, and supportive environments. Another important target of the impact evaluation is health behaviors. Impact evaluation methods are used to determine the degree to which health education and health promotion interventions produced (caused) changes in health behaviors or the determinants of health behaviors in the target population.

First, let us focus on the determinants of health behaviors. Most health programs work to empower participants with knowledge, motivation, and skills to adopt health practices. To evaluate these changes requires attention to measurement. Have the objectives addressing health behavior determinants been stated in measurable terms? Does a measurement tool exist to validly assess the determinant? Are the resources available to develop a valid measurement tool for the determinant? Many determinants are conceptual in nature and not directly observable, such as health motivation, self-efficacy, perceived risk, and personal susceptibility. The second element of impact evaluation addresses health behavior changes in the target population. The logic model suggests the following chain of events. First, the health program was delivered as designed. Second, the program produced the intended enhancements in determinants of health behavior. Third, the determinants are sufficient to produce sustainable changes in health practices among the target population.

A key issue is how enduring the changes in health practices are. Most health practices will impact health status only if practiced consistently and correctly over a sustained period of time. As a consequence, the impact evaluation should sample the health behavior changes over a period of time. For example, were initial changes in the health behavior (exercise, reduction of fat in diet, etc.) maintained 3, 6, or 12 months after the health program ended?

Attainment of health status goals (Figure 2.2) are addressed in the **outcome evaluation**. This level of evaluation is concerned with assessing changes in the health status of the target population that are produced by changes in health practices. Careful attention needs to be directed towards the amount of time a health practice needs to be adopted before changes in health status are likely to be detectable. For example, if adults at a worksite adopt regular aerobic exercise designed to produce gains in fitness, measurable changes in fitness level (VO_2) can be detected in 6 to 8 weeks. If, on the other hand, these same adults adopt the exercise to produce changes in body fat or blood pressure, considerably more time will need to pass. As an extreme example, if the same adults adopt the exercise to produce changes in mortality, decades may need to pass to detect changes. This example underscores the importance of the evaluation team carefully thinking through the best evidence on the time window for each link between a health behavior and a health status outcome. Combining this analysis with time and resources for the evaluation project can promote sound decision making about the objectives that can be measured in a reasonable time frame.

> *Outcome evaluation is concerned with assessing changes in health status of the target population that are produced by changes in health practices.*

A **comprehensive evaluation** is one that includes process, impact, and outcome evaluation methods. It can yield important insights into how a health program produces results or fails to produce results. Unfortunately, comprehensive evaluations often are not conducted. There are significant barriers to conducting comprehensive evaluations. They can be expensive and take several years to conduct. Consider the amount of time that would be needed for a program to be fully implemented, and for health behavior changes to accumulate in the target population. Then consider how much time it would take for the health behavior changes to produce changes in health status. To illustrate, a school-based program to reduce smoking will take several decades to produce changes in heart disease or cancer among the target population. On the other hand, a patient education program on diabetes that covers behaviors related to diet, exercise, medication, and blood glucose monitoring could produce dramatic improvements in health status in a matter of weeks. These two examples illustrate the importance of thinking through the logic of the program to determine what the focus of the evaluation should be and how much time and resources will be needed. In most health promotion settings the evaluation questions address a specific set of goals or objectives, which narrows the range of the evaluation to one or two stages of the logic model. Ultimately, organization administrators must decide on the scope and type of evaluation needed at a given time. The evaluator should help clarify evaluation options and cost estimates. However,

> *A comprehensive evaluation is one that includes process, impact, and outcome evaluation methods.*

the evaluator and administration need to be on the same page regarding the scope and purpose of the evaluation project.

HEALTH PROGRAM PLANNING AND EVALUATION: INTEGRATION

Planning a health education or health promotion program and planning the evaluation for that program should be part of the same process. Ideally, planning for the health education or health promotion program and evaluation should begin at the same time and be directly linked to one another during the planning and implementation phases. When program planning and evaluation planning are conducted simultaneously, they can be carefully and precisely integrated with each other. Evaluation procedures can be planned to minimize disruption to program implementation, and in some cases, evaluation procedures can be part of the educational process. As one example, program instructors can use pretesting on key concepts or knowledge to tailor educational experiences to the program participants. Conceptually, the evaluation should seamlessly fit to the precise goals and objectives of the health education program. This is best done when health program planners and evaluators are at the same table, on the same page, working together to build the best program and best evaluation.

The team approach to program planning and evaluation is a joint collaboration between those responsible for planning the health education or health promotion program and those responsible for evaluating it.

The health professionals responsible for program planning should be in regular communication with the professionals responsible for evaluation. Ideally there would be one team of professionals working together to design the program and actively participating in the design, implementation, and evaluation of the program. The **team approach to program planning and evaluation** is defined as a joint collaboration between those responsible for planning the health education or health promotion program and those responsible for evaluating it.

There are several advantages to the team approach to program planning and evaluation:

- Builds staff trust and support
- Increases opportunities for evaluation to be integrated into everyday practice
- Contributes to staff development
- Enhances communication among project staff
- Sets realistic expectations for the program and the evaluation
- Builds utilization-based evaluation

There are many advantages to a team-based approach. There are also many advantages to program planning and evaluation planning occurring at the same time. However, these are ideal situations that may not occur in many actual settings. Often evaluation planning begins after health programs are designed. It is not unusual for evaluations to begin several months or even years after a health program has been up and running. Often an evaluator is hired as an outside consultant to conduct an evaluation. In these cases, it is important that the evaluator fully understand the circumstances under which the evaluation will take place. There are three critical areas of information an evaluator needs to know before assuming responsibility for evaluating a health program.

First, the evaluator should learn the history of the program being evaluated. Is the program currently in the design phase, the implementation phase, or has it been implemented several times in the recent past? Have evaluations been conducted on the health program in the past? If so, what types of evaluations were conducted and what were the results?

Second, who will be actively involved in making decisions about the evaluation? These decision makers can inform the evaluator of the potential budget, time line, and purpose of the evaluation. Evaluations can be designed at different levels of evaluation rigor, which will involve different amounts of time and resources. For example, a comprehensive evaluation following a large cohort of subjects ($n = 200$) over multiple years to track health behavior and health status changes produced by the health program would result in a considerable investment of time and money. In contrast, an evaluation could focus on one set of participants ($n = 30$) and examine changes in their health practices 1 week after exposure to the health program. It is important to determine the time frame and resource base upon which an evaluation will be planned.

Third, what is the purpose of the evaluation? Most directly, what decisions will be made based on the results of the evaluation? Is the purpose of the evaluation to provide feedback for program refinement or is the evaluation being conducted to determine whether the health program should continue in the future? The answers to these questions can have an impact on the design, rigor, and cost of the evaluation, and they can also help the evaluator decide if his or her participation is feasible (time commitment) or personally acceptable (professional consequences).

POLITICAL CLIMATE AND EVALUATION

Program evaluation is different from research; evaluation takes place in an action setting. Professionals are delivering programs to consumers in real community settings. Consumers are participating in these programs, making efforts to improve their health. Evaluators are endeavoring to insert evaluation procedures into the health promotion process to determine whether the health program works. It would be naïve for an evaluator to assume that an evaluation does not exist in a political climate. The **political climate** can be defined as the conditions surrounding the political powers in an evaluation. For example, if the evaluation is being done in a situation where the administrator has an authoritarian management style, that style might have adverse effects on the outcomes of the evaluation. Programs and professionals are being judged and worth is being estimated. Suppose that a rigorous evaluation of a teen pregnancy prevention program has been conducted. Regardless of the results of the evaluation, interpretations of the data may vary widely. Supporters and opponents of the program are likely to have sharply different perspectives. An evaluator should expect decision makers (program funders, program managers, program professionals) to carefully scrutinize the evaluation results in the context of a whole range of political concerns. Evaluators should attempt to identify the stakeholders for a health program. By identifying the motives of stakeholders, the evaluator can attempt to respond to the wide range of concerns that will ultimately determine the usefulness of an evaluation.

POLITICAL CLIMATE AND PROGRAM STAKEHOLDERS

A **program stakeholder** is a person or organization having a keen interest in the development, implementation, or evaluation of a health education/promotion program. **Table 2.2** lists potential stakeholders and some of their underlying interests in the program.

Examples of stakeholders include funders, health organization administrators, professional personnel, target populations, the general public, and evaluators. The results of program evaluation will likely affect the person in either a positive or a negative way. As a consequence, the evaluation team needs to consider the perspectives of stakeholders when designing the evaluation. Each of these stakeholders may look at the purpose of the evaluation from a different perspective. First is the funder of the program. Almost all health education and health promotion programs require some sort of funding to start and sustain themselves. Often this funding comes from the federal government (e.g., National Institutes of Health, Centers for Disease Control and Prevention, etc.), state government (e.g., state department of health, state commission on minority health, etc.), local government (e.g., county health department, city health department, etc.), or a foundation or organization (e.g., Robert Wood Johnson Foundation, American Heart Association, American Cancer Society, etc.). The funding organization is usually interested in: (1) the documented benefits of the health program, (2) whether the funds have been judiciously and appropriately used, (3) what is the most efficient use of resources to accomplish the program's goals, (4) whether the program can be replicated at other sites, (5) how to present the results to their donors, or taxpayers in the case of government, and (6) whether the program can be self-supporting (sustenance).

The second stakeholder in the program is the organization implementing the health education or health promotion program. Examples include a not-for-profit organization (e.g., American Heart Association), a governmental organization (e.g., county health department), or an academic institution (e.g., a university). The administrators of the organization are interested in finding out: (1) level of program impact, (2) level of staff performance, (3) whether the materials developed by the program were useful, (4) whether funds were used efficiently, (5) how much it would cost to offer the program again and where those resources would come from, and (6) whether the program can run on its own (sustenance).

The third stakeholder in the program consists of the members of the target population for whom the health education or health promotion program was implemented. Examples of target populations include employees at a worksite, patients at a healthcare facility, schoolchildren and their parents at a school setting, members of a church, college students in a university setting, or members of a target audience in a defined community. Usually the target population is interested in finding out: (1) whether the health program is perceived as worth the time and effort to participate, (2) whether the program will continue, (3) the pros and cons of the program, (4) who will be running the program, and (5) whether the funds have been judiciously and appropriately used.

The fourth stakeholder is the professional personnel responsible for delivery of the health program These health professionals are interested in finding out: (1) whether the program was successful in reaching its goals, (2) whether he or she individually performed well, (3) whether the materials developed in the program were useful, (4) how to gain

TABLE 2.2   Potential Stakeholders' Interests in a Health Education or Promotion Program Evaluation

Health Education/Promotion Program Funders

What was the overall impact of the health education/promotion program?

Were resources (funds) used judiciously and appropriately?

What is the most efficient way to accomplish goals?

Can the health education/promotion program be replicated at other sites?

How can the program be promoted for political purposes?

How can the program support itself in the future (sustenance)?

Health Education/Promotion Program Organization

Demonstrate program effectiveness.

Describe professional staff performance in the program.

Meet funding agencies' requirements for accountability.

Determine health education/promotion program costs.

Build support for program needs (funds, facilities, staff, activities, etc.).

Estimate costs of health education/promotion program dissemination.

Make decisions about future health education/promotion program plans.

Health Education/Promotion Program Administrator

How can resources be managed more effectively?

Was the health education/promotion program implemented as designed?

Do evaluation results justify administrative decisions?

Demonstrate program effectiveness to justify more support.

Increase administrator status in organization.

Were program staff members qualified to develop and implement the program?

Target Population of Health Education/Promotion Program

Is the health program perceived as worth the time and effort to participants?

Should the health education/promotion program continue?

What are the pros and cons of the program?

Have program funds been used judiciously and appropriately?

General Public

Is the health education/promotion program consistent with community values?

Are tax dollars being used efficiently and appropriately?

Professional Staff

Were goals and objectives achieved?

Did the target audience benefit from program participation?

Will the evaluation results make the health education/promotion program look effective?

Evaluator

Advance career through professional contributions (presentations, publications).

Determine the overall impact of the health education/promotion program.

Serve as an advocate for the usefulness of health promotion and education.

Compare the program outcomes with expert knowledge.

support for program continuation, and (5) whether the program was implemented in the way it was designed. The professional staff has a vested interest in doing a quality job and ensuring the effectiveness of the health program.

The fifth stakeholder group is the general public. In an age of accountability, members of the general public want to know if resources are being used efficiently. In some cases, the members of the general public will also want to know if resources are used in a manner consistent with community values. Some health education or health promotion programs are controversial, such as family planning agencies that include abortion services or school-based sex education programs that explain contraceptive use. Controversial programs may provoke members of the community who do not support these programs. It may be important to engage these members of the community to understand their concerns. There may be ways for the evaluation to address their concerns. Ignoring their interests is likely to provoke political action that may undermine the health program.

The final stakeholder is the program evaluator. This person can be an internal evaluator of the program who was involved with development of the program or an external evaluator who was not involved with the development of the program. The evaluator is interested in finding out: (1) whether the program goals and objectives were met, (2) whether the program had an impact, (3) whether the program contributed to broader health outcomes, (4) whether the program was implemented in the way it was designed, (5) what the qualifications were of those developing and implementing the program, (6) whether the target population was satisfied with the program, and (7) how the program outcomes compare with expert knowledge. He or she is also interested in presenting the findings at conferences, publishing the results in peer-reviewed journals, and making recommendations for continuation (or not) of the program.

Stakeholders for the evaluation of health education and health promotion programs include funders, health organizations, program administrators, professional staff, members of the target population, the general public, and program evaluators.

Stakeholders for a particular health program share many common and/or complementary interests, but it is also clear that some of the interests among the stakeholders are at odds with one another. Taken together, stakeholders' interests create a political climate that the evaluator has to work in. Occasionally the different interests of stakeholders can create a questioning of motives or conflict. Other times, some stakeholders can be disappointed that the evaluation did not address their specific concerns. The evaluator should make an effort to become familiar with stakeholders and their specific concerns. One method is to have personal meetings with the different stakeholders to ensure that their interests are understood. Another method is to form a formal coalition or an advisory group of representative stakeholders. Meetings can then be held so that stakeholders can develop an understanding of and sensitivity to a wide variety of concerns that may need to be addressed in the evaluation. Another method is to form an evaluation team that includes representatives from key stakeholders for a health program. As part of the evaluation team, the stakeholders participate in shared decision making regarding the evaluation design. Regardless of the method used, understanding and responding to different stakeholders' interests can increase the relevance of the evaluation and ultimately increase the acceptance and utilization of evaluation results. The evaluator should make special efforts to be sensitive to different stakeholder perspectives when designing the evaluation. In addition, the evaluation final report should attempt to place the results and conclusions in the context of stakeholder concerns.

BALANCE BETWEEN EVALUATION RIGOR AND UTILIZATION

As the evaluator prepares to meet with stakeholders to design the evaluation, he or she should consider two important perspectives on evaluation. These views can be seen as falling on ends of a continuum, with evaluation rigor on one end and utilization on the other (**Figure 2.3**). Establishing high **evaluation rigor** involves utilization of design methods including measurement, sampling, random assignment, and random selection to ensure high levels of internal and external validity in the conduct of the evaluation. Following these procedures will help control for alternative explanations for the observed results. On the other end of the continuum is a concern for utilization of evaluation findings. The key focus here is on the relevance of the evaluation to program decision makers. Often decision makers need to be pragmatic; they are primarily concerned with "real world" constraints. As a consequence, decisions regarding evaluation rigor and utilization can be a series of tradeoffs. In some instances these perspectives are reconcilable. In other cases compromises are inevitable. Evaluators should be sensitive to the need to balance these perspectives.

CONDUCTING A UTILIZATION-FOCUSED EVALUATION

The results of an evaluation need to focus specifically on the needs of consumers and practitioners. This view is essential to designing an evaluation that is relevant to stakeholders. Cronbach (1982) suggests that evaluation should focus on the needs of program decision makers and stakeholders. The goal is to provide useful information that is sensitive to political realities and program constraints. Patton (1997) argues that the primary concern is utilization of evaluation results. As a consequence, the evaluation should be designed around the information needs of program managers, program staff, and consumers (Mercier, 1997).

To conduct a **utilization-focused evaluation** requires that the evaluator actively engage decision makers (e.g., funders, program managers, professional staff) in the evaluation planning process. The planning is oriented towards an evaluation that provides a utility in the real world (Dibella, 1990). The evaluator works with each group of decision makers to discuss the principles of utilization-focused evaluation, which are listed in **Table 2.3**. The evaluator will discuss the

> *A utilization-focused evaluation requires that the evaluator actively engage decision makers (e.g., funders, program managers, professional staff) in evaluation and that the evaluation provides a utility in the real world.*

Focus on	Balance	Focus on
evaluation rigor		utilization

Figure 2.3 Evaluation rigor versus utilization continuum.

TABLE 2.3   Principles of Utilization-Focused Evaluation
1. Actively engage program decision makers.
2. Identify the decisions to be made based on the evaluation.
3. Specify the evidence needed to make a decision.
4. Develop a plan for implementing decisions.

potentials and limitations of the evaluation data in the hope of setting realistic expectations. A critical step is carefully defining the evidence needed to make program decisions. Generally speaking, the rigor of the evaluation (measurement, design, etc.) should match the importance and consequences of the decision to be made. For example, if an evaluation is being conducted to determine whether a health program should be eliminated or expanded, considerable rigor should focus on program effectiveness. Finally, a method for implementation of decisions should be outlined (Florio, Behrmann, & Goltz, 1995). This step clarifies the specifics of how the evaluation data will be interpreted and how the evaluation conclusions will be used by the organization to improve or refine the health program.

CONDUCTING A RIGOROUS EVALUATION

There is an old saying about evaluation, "Garbage in, garbage out." When evaluation methods are not well-defined, rigorous, and reproducible you have a "garbage-in" situation likely to produce a low-quality (garbage) evaluation. The following are some examples of specific factors contributing to garbage-in evaluations:

- Health program goals and objectives are not stated in measurable terms.
- Data-gathering instruments do not have established validity and reliability.
- Data-gathering instruments do not match the goals and objectives.
- Sampling methods do not produce representative samples, reach the target population, or allow for meaningful comparisons between treatment and control conditions.
- Alternative explanations of the evaluation results are not addressed by the evaluation design.

If the evaluation methods are not rigorous, the resulting evaluation results may not be useful in making decisions. Further, stakeholders may debate the accuracy and interpretation of the results. In such situations, the evaluation is likely to produce more heat than light, more debate than data-based decisions. An evaluator cannot dismiss scientific concerns. They are the one stakeholder who must do their best to ensure the scientific credibility of the evaluation. An important role of the evaluator is to make sure that the garbage-in situation is prevented, or at least reduced to reasonable limits. To do so requires the following steps:

1. Clearly define the purpose(s) of the evaluation.
2. Create measurable program goals and objectives.

3. Use rigorous scientific methods to produce high-quality data.
4. Ensure that conclusions are grounded in the high-quality data.

Attending to these steps will go a long way towards ensuring a utilization-focused evaluation. Utilization-focused evaluation was developed by Patton (1997). His approach emphasizes close collaboration with stakeholders who will actually use the evaluation findings.

Active collaboration on the issues listed will enable the evaluation to produce information that can be used.

Clearly Define the Purpose(s) of the Evaluation

Whether the evaluator is negotiating with a single administrator or a team of stakeholders, it is critical to come to a precise agreement on the purpose of the evaluation. Often the evaluator can detail a set of options ranging from an evaluation that is limited to one stage of the logic model (**Focus Feature 2.1**) to a comprehensive evaluation focused on all stages of the health program. Some key issues to discuss are:

- Who will be using the evaluation results?
- What decision(s) will be made based on the evaluation results?

The answers to these questions will enable the evaluator to propose an evaluation that is best suited to the needs of the organization. It also provides an opportunity for the evaluator to clarify expectations about the limitations of evaluation designs and the impact of these limits on the quality of data and results.

Create Measurable Program Goals and Objectives

Existing health programs generally have a set of goals and objectives. A key task of the evaluator is to carefully examine all of the goals and objectives. There are several criteria that need to be considered. First, is each goal and objective measurable? Is there a valid and reliable available method of measuring each objective? Do the goals and objectives fall within the time frame of the evaluation? Often the evaluator can work with project staff to revise objectives, ensuring that they do meet these criteria.

Use Rigorous Scientific Methods to Produce High-Quality Data

The evaluator has to perform a balancing act in implementing an evaluation plan. On the one hand, the evaluator is committed to using rigorous scientific methods including sampling, measurement, design, and analysis. But rigor needs to be balanced with real world concerns such as feasibility, cost, time, and health program disruption (Card, Greeno, & Peterson, 1992). Experience, creativity, and cooperation with program staff are needed to develop a plan to employ the maximum feasible evaluation rigor with reasonable cost and program disruption.

FOCUS FEATURE 2.1   PLANNING A HEALTH EDUCATION/PROMOTION PROGRAM EVALUATION

1. What is/are the purpose(s) of the evaluation?
   What decisions will be made based on the evaluation?
   Who will have access to the evaluation report and results?

2. Will formative evaluation be needed?
   Is health education/promotion program refinement needed before process evaluation?

3. What is the history of the program to be evaluated?
   How long has the program been operating?
   Has the program been evaluated before? What were the results?

4. Who will be members of the evaluation design team?
   Program managers, program staff, stakeholders, evaluation consultants?

5. Is process evaluation to be conducted?
   Program delivery: Will health program implementation be assessed?
   Efficiency: Will resource utilization be assessed?
   Fiscal: Did program activities stay within budget?
   Legal: Are legal and ethical practices to be assessed?
   Recruitment: Will the reach into the target audience be assessed?
   How many program cycles will be evaluated?

6. Is impact evaluation to be conducted?
   Are educational objectives to be assessed?
   Are health behaviors to be assessed?
   When should the follow-up assessment of health behavior take place (6 months, 1 year, 2 years)?

7. Is outcome evaluation to be conducted?
   Are health status goals to be assessed?
   When should the follow-up assessment of health status goals take place (1–5 years)?

8. What type of evaluation sample should be used?
   Should it be a probability or nonprobability sample?
   What should be the sample size?

9. Which evaluation design should be used?
   Experimental design with randomization
   Quasi-experimental design
   Nonexperimental design

10. How should the evaluation budget be determined?
    How many resources are available for the evaluation project?

Ensure That Conclusions Are Grounded in the High-Quality Data

Report writing is a critical phase in the evaluation project. The report should explain how evaluation methods were employed, the quality of the data collected, data analysis methods, and results. Conclusions should be directly linked to data. The limitations of the evaluation methods should be described so that readers of the report have a context for understanding the conclusions.

CRITICAL ISSUES FOR AN EVALUATION PROJECT

Focus Feature 2.1 outlines a set of issues to be addressed in the planning of an evaluation. The list is offered as a guide to facilitate discussion of critical decisions. Following these steps can get funding agencies, program administration, health program staff, stakeholders, and evaluators on the same page. The list is somewhat like a menu of options; not all settings or situations will require a comprehensive evaluation. Thus, not all issues need to be addressed in every situation. For example, a new program may only need a formative evaluation in the first year of operation. Some program managers are only interested in process evaluations. Each of these evaluators can use this list as a planning tool to review the evaluation options with program managers to help clarify agency needs. Many of the issues listed come with significant cost considerations; for example, choosing an experimental design with randomization can significantly increase the cost of the project. A realistic conversation needs to balance the tradeoffs between design rigor and cost to come to the right decision for a particular setting.

SKILL-BUILDING ACTIVITY

Consider any health education program that changes any health behavior in a target population—for example, a physical activity promotion program in upper elementary school children. Using the SMART way of writing objectives shown in **Table 2.4**, write at least two process evaluation objectives, two impact evaluation objectives, and two outcome evaluation objectives for this program.

TABLE 2.4	The SMART Way to Write Evaluation Objectives	
Acronym	**Description**	**Example**
S	Specific	What is being evaluated and in whom
M	Measurable	Percentage of participants who will change
A	Action verb	List, describe, identify, explain, etc.
R	Realistic	Must be attainable
T	Time frame	End of the session, end of 1 year, etc.

SUMMARY

Evaluation is an essential part of continuous health program improvement. Continuous health program improvement starts with the skilled application of the health education knowledge base that informs needs assessment, leading to high-quality program planning and implementation. Evaluation is used to determine the effects of the health program, which contributes back to the health education knowledge base. Over time, the effectiveness of the health program increases. There are many different program planning models for health education and health promotion. The logic model includes the common themes across these different models, including: community participation, data-based decision making, definition of a target population, setting objectives, and defining program activities that promote health actions. Addressing the themes of the logic model creates a foundation for program evaluation. It also serves as an important communication tool helping different stakeholders understand the various elements of the health program.

A comprehensive evaluation is one that includes process, impact, and outcome evaluation methods. Process evaluation methods can be used to gather information about program quality, satisfaction levels of participants, implementers, sites, and the degree to which the program was implemented as designed. Quality assurance of a health program is an important element of process evaluation. Impact evaluation methods are used to determine the degree to which health interventions produced changes in health behaviors or the determinants of health behaviors in the target population. Outcome evaluation is concerned with assessing changes in health status of the target population that are produced by changes in health practices. Comprehensive evaluation can yield many important insights into how a health education or health promotion program works and does not work; however, comprehensive evaluations can be expensive and take several years to conduct. In most health promotion settings the evaluation questions address a specific set of goals or objectives, which narrows the range of the evaluation to one or two stages of the logic model. Ultimately, organization administrators must decide on the scope and type of evaluation needed at a given time.

A program stakeholder is a person or organization having a keen interest in the development, implementation, or evaluation of a health education/promotion program. Examples of stakeholders include: funders, health organizations, administrators, professional personnel, members of the target population, the general public, and evaluators. Stakeholders for a particular health program may share many complementary interests, but there will also be areas of interest unique to different stakeholders. Taken together, stakeholders' interests create a political climate that the evaluator has to take into consideration. The evaluator should make an effort to become familiar with stakeholders and their specific concerns.

The results of an evaluation need to focus specifically on the needs of consumers and practitioners. This view is essential to designing an evaluation that is relevant to stakeholders. The goal is to provide useful information that is sensitive to political realities and program constraints. To conduct a utilization-focused evaluation requires that the evaluator actively engage decision makers (e.g., funders, program managers, professional staff) in the evaluation planning process. The evaluator works with each group of decision makers to discuss the principles of utilization-focused evaluation. The evaluator will discuss the potentials and limitations of the evaluation data in hopes of setting realistic expectations. A critical step is carefully defining the evidence needed to make program decisions. The rigor of the evaluation should match the importance and consequences of the decision to be made.

Measurement is fundamental to quality program evaluation. Answering evaluation questions requires the measurement of key variables. The usefulness of the data is grounded in the quality of the measurement tools used. Evaluators need skills to judge the appropriateness and quality of existing instruments with established validity and reliability. Evaluators also need to be skilled in developing valid and reliable instruments for specific programs. Health programs are regularly innovating and evolving. It is often necessary to develop new instruments to precisely match program goals and objectives. It is also important that instruments be validated for particular target populations.

The creative and skilled use of applied scientific methods is essential for evaluation. There are many research designs and sampling methods appropriate for use in health program evaluations. The evaluator should familiarize him- or herself with a wide range of design options. This will increase the likelihood of sound decision making in balancing concerns of evaluation rigor with practical concerns and real world constraints.

REVIEW QUESTIONS

1. Define continuous health program improvement. What is its relationship with evaluation?
2. Discuss some common health education and health promotion planning models. What are some common themes for evaluation in these models?
3. Discuss a logic model for evaluation of health education and health promotion programs.
4. Identify the key features of comprehensive evaluation.
5. What is the team approach to program planning and evaluation? Discuss its advantages.
6. Define *political climate*. How does it affect evaluation?
7. Identify the key stakeholders in a program evaluation. Discuss each one's key interests in evaluation.
8. Discuss the principles of utilization-focused evaluation.
9. What are the steps in conducting a rigorous evaluation?

WEBSITES TO EXPLORE

Evaluation Logic Model

http://www.uwex.edu/ces/pdande/evaluation/evallogicmodel.html
This website was developed by the University of Wisconsin—Extension office. It shows a logic diagram. Several links have been provided, including links to templates for drawing

logic diagrams. *Review this website. Using the provided template, draw a logic diagram for a teen pregnancy prevention program.*

Framework for Program Evaluation in Public Health

http://www.cdc.gov/mmwr/preview/mmwrhtml/rr4811a1.htm
This is a report from the Centers for Disease Control and Prevention (CDC) that was published in *Morbidity and Mortality Weekly Report (MMWR)*. The framework in this report guides public health professionals in their use of program evaluation. *Read this report. The report identifies four standards for evaluation: utility, feasibility, propriety, and accuracy. Describe in your own words what these mean to you. How can these be achieved?*

The Power of Proof: An Evaluation Primer by the Tobacco Technical Assistance Consortium

http://www.ttac.org/services/power-of-proof/index.html
This website presents a primer on evaluation. It has seven parts and associated links: setting the stage, evaluation planning, writing objectives, data collection, types of evaluation, interpreting the data, and reporting results. *Review this website. Pay special attention to the writing evaluation objectives. Can you articulate process, impact, and outcome evaluation objectives for a fictitious health education program?*

Utilization-Focused Evaluation Checklist

http://web.idrc.ca/uploads/user-S/10905198311Utilization_Focused_Evaluation.pdf
This checklist on utilization-focused evaluation was developed by the originator of the concept of utilization-focused evaluation, Michael Quinn Patton. This is a 12-part checklist. *Review this checklist. Prepare a critique of the approach and checklist.*

REFERENCES

Basch, C. E., Sliepcevich, E. M., Gold, R. S., Duncan, D. F., & Kolbe, L. J. (1985). Avoiding type III errors in health education program evaluations: A case study. *Health Education Quarterly, 12*, 315–331.

Card, J. J., Greeno, C., & Peterson, J. (1992). Planning an evaluation and estimating its costs. *Evaluation and the Health Professions, 12*(4), 75–89.

Centers for Disease Control and Prevention. (n.d.). Planned approach to community health: Guides for local coordinators. Retrieved from http://www.cdc.gov/nccdphp/publications/PATCH/index.htm

Cronbach, L. (1982). *Designing evaluations of educational and social programs.* San Francisco: Jossey-Bass.

Dibella, A. (1990). The research manager's role in encouraging evaluation use. *Evaluation Practice, 11*(2), 115–119.

Durch, J. S., Baily, L. A., & Stoto, M. A. (Eds.). (1997). *Improving health in the community: A role for performance monitoring.* Washington, DC: National Academies Press. Retrieved from http://www.nap.edu/readingroom/books/improving

Florio, D. H., Behrmann, M., & Goltz, D. L. (1995). What do policy makers think of evaluational research and evaluation? Or do they? *Educational Evaluation and Policy Analysis, 1*, 61–87.

Glasgow, R., Nelson, C., Strycker, L., & King, D. (2006). Using RE-AIM metrics to evaluate diabetes self-management support interventions. *American Journal of Preventive Medicine, 30*(1), 67–73.

Green, L., & Kreuter, M. (2005). *Health promotion planning: An educational and ecological approach* (4th ed.). Palo Alto, CA: Mayfield.

Mercier, C. (1997). Participation in stakeholder-based evaluation: A case study. *Evaluation and Program Planning, 20*(4), 467–475.

Patton, M. (1997). *Utilization-focused evaluation: The new century text* (3rd ed.). Thousand Oaks, CA: Sage.

Simons-Morton, D., Simons-Morton B., Parcel, G., & Bunker, J. (1988). Influencing personal and environmental conditions for community health: A multilevel intervention model. *Family and Community Health, 1*(2), 25–35.

CHAPTER 3

Basics of Measurement

CHAPTER OBJECTIVES

- Define measurement, validity, and reliability
- Describe four scales of measurement
- Identify statistical tests that can be used with each of the four types of scales
- Explain the conceptual paradigm of measurement
- List the benefits of using theory in health education and health promotion
- Identify different types of variables that are used in health education and health promotion, and give examples for each type

DEFINITION OF MEASUREMENT

Measurement is foundational to evaluation activities. The quality of the evaluation rests upon the reliability and validity of the measurement methods used. Consider evaluating a childhood obesity prevention program in a school setting. First, you would need some way to decipher whether the program is being implemented in the way it was planned. For this you would need measurement tools. Second, you would want to see whether the program had any effect on antecedents of behaviors as well as behaviors such as physical activity, dietary behaviors, or screen time behaviors. For each of these variables you would need a measurement method. Finally, you may be interested in seeing whether your program had any effect on obesity rates in your region. For this, once again you would need measurement tools. Clearly, the quality of each of the measurement methods would be directly linked to the quality of the entire evaluation effort. If you use valid measures, the evaluation will, in turn, be accurate and useful.

Measurement is the systematic application of a set of procedures and processes so that concepts can be objectively reduced to numbers for the purpose of comparison.

What is measurement? Stevens (1959, p. 24) defined measurement as, "the assignment of numerals to aspects of objects or events according to rule." Green and Lewis (1986, p. 58) defined measurement as, ". . . the assignment of numbers to objects, events, or people according to specified rules." Nunnally and Bernstein (1994, p. 1) stated, "[m]easurement consists of rules for assigning symbols to objects so as to (1) represent quantities of attributes numerically (scaling) or (2) define whether the objects fall in same or different categories with respect to a given attribute (classification)." Our definition of measurement is the systematic application of a set of procedures and processes so that concepts can be accurately assigned numbers for the purpose of comparison. In health education and health promotion, the concepts we are interested in assigning numbers to are: (1) the health *needs* of a community, such as which things need to be changed; (2) *processes*, including intervention quality, intervention implementation fidelity, and the like; (3) *impacts*, such as changes in health behaviors and changes in the antecedents of health behaviors (knowledge, attitudes, skills, values, etc.); and (4) health *outcomes*, such as changes in mortality and morbidity indicators. The tools that are developed for evaluating these concepts must be relevant, reliable, and valid. **Validity** is the ability to say that an instrument is actually measuring what it is purporting to measure, and **reliability** is the ability of an instrument to measure repeatedly the same results and be internally consistent. By **relevance**, we mean that the instrument is appropriate and important to the measure being examined.

Once the concepts have been reduced to numbers, you can perform mathematical operations on them. For example, a childhood obesity prevention program may be able to measure height and weight for students. It can then compute body mass index (BMI) as a function of weight (in kg) divided by height (in m^2). It can also calculate the mean (average) BMI of the school students. It can then compare this average BMI with that of another school. It could also compare the average BMI calculated before the childhood obesity prevention program to the average calculated after the program took place. Statistical tests (such as paired t-test) can be done on this and deductions made about significant changes.

SCALES OR LEVELS OF MEASUREMENT

Statistics ascribes different meanings to different numbers. One common conceptualization of different numbers is by scales or levels of measurement. There are four commonly used scales: nominal, ordinal, interval, and ratio (Kuzma & Bohnenblust, 2005). DiIorio

(2005) has assigned a property to each of these scales—nominal/kind, ordinal/order, interval/equal intervals, and ratio/ratios.

The **nominal scale** is used to categorize or classify individuals, objects, issues, or events into different groups (e.g., sex, race, marital status, etc.). As mentioned earlier, this scale is characterized by "kind" or "type." Variables that yield nominal-level data are also called **qualitative variables** because they merely classify into qualitative categories and not quantitative categories. In some computer statistical packages, nominal variables are called **grouping variables**. Another name for nominal-level variables is **categorical variables**. For example, the variable *sex* is categorized into two categories or kinds: male and female. Variables such as sex are also called **dichotomous variables** because they have only two categories.

> *The nominal scale (or categorical scale, grouping scale, or qualitative scale) is used to categorize or classify individuals, objects, issues, or events into different groups such as sex, race, marital status, and the like.*

It is important to note that the categories defined in the nominal scale must be mutually exclusive, so that an individual, object, issue, or event can be categorized under only one category and should have no chance of being classified into another category or categories of the scale. When coding a nominal scale you can choose any number. For example, to code sex you can assign 0 to males and 1 to females, or 1 to males and 2 to females, or vice versa. You can choose any other numbers as well, but by convention 0 and 1 or 1 and 2 are usually used. Nominal scales are not quite restrictive with regard to numbers because the categorization of the levels remains unchanged. If you choose a higher number, it does not mean that the category is higher. It is simply done to differentiate the two categories. Only frequencies and percentages can be calculated for different categories. Mathematical operations such as multiplication and division cannot be performed on nominal scales. Therefore, some measurement experts have questioned whether nominal scales are true forms of measurement (Lord & Novick, 1968). Commonly used nominal-level variables in health education and health promotion include identification number (ID), Social Security number, zip code, gender (sex), hair color, marital status, name of college or university, and disease status (presence or absence).

The second scale that is used is the **ordinal scale**, which is used to classify individuals, objects, issues, or events into categories that have a meaningful order. This is a hierarchical order where one category is higher than the other category but we do not know exactly how much higher. For example, one may classify the top five causes of death as heart disease (#1), cancer (#2), stroke (#3), chronic respiratory disease (#4), and unintentional injury (#5). Another example is year in college as freshmen, sophomore, junior, and senior, where an increasing number of credit hours denotes the different categories. Another commonly used scale in health education and health promotion is the **Likert scale**, which is an ordinal scale. A classical Likert scale uses the following responses:

> *An ordinal scale is used to classify individuals, objects, issues, or events into categories that have a meaningful hierarchical order.*

- Strongly agree
- Agree
- Neither agree nor disagree

- Disagree
- Strongly disagree

A person who marks "strongly agree" has a more favorable attitude toward something than a person who has marked "strongly disagree," thus showing a hierarchy. Addition or multiplication by a constant does not alter the order of an ordinal scale.

The third scale is the **interval scale**, which is used to classify individuals, objects, issues, or events into categories that have a meaningful order, implying higher levels have more of the attribute; at the same time, this scale has equal intervals so it is possible to tell how much difference there is between one category and another. One unit on the interval scale represents the same magnitude of the characteristic or criterion being measured across the entire range of the scale. An interval scale does not have a true zero point or a point at which there is no value of the attribute. Therefore, it is not possible to make statements about how many times higher a given score is compared to another. A difference between the interval scale and ordinal scale is that an interval scale is a continuous measure, whereas an ordinal scale is separated into distinct groups.

> *An interval scale is used to classify individuals, objects, issues, or events into categories that have a meaningful order, implying higher levels have more of the attribute; at the same time this scale has equal intervals, so it is possible to tell how much difference there is between one category and another.*

An example of an interval scale is a knowledge score on a 100-item scale. One can say that a person scoring 50 points on the scale had 5 points less than a person scoring 55 points, and that this difference is the same as that between a person scoring 65 points and another one scoring 70 points. However, because this scale does not have a true zero it is not possible to say that a person with a score of 30 was twice as knowledgeable as a person with a score of 15. Further, a score of 0 on this knowledge scale is arbitrary—a person scoring a 0 does not imply that his or her knowledge is 0 on the subject being tested. In health education and health promotion, summated rating scales (in which items are summed to derive a score) are also assumed to be interval scales. An interval scale can be transformed by addition or multiplication by a constant.

> *A ratio scale has all the characteristics of an interval scale, but in addition has a true zero point.*

The fourth scale is the **ratio scale**, which has all the characteristics of an interval scale, but in addition has a true zero point. The ability to have a true zero gives this scale an ability to express meaningful ratios. An example of a ratio scale is body weight, which can be measured in pounds or kilograms. A person weighing 50 kilograms is 5 kilograms heavier than one weighing 45 kilograms and is twice as heavy as one weighing 25 kilograms. Further, the ratio of differences can also be expressed: we can say that the difference between 25 kilograms and 50 kilograms is the same as the difference between 50 kilograms and 75 kilograms. Both interval and ratio scales are often referred to as **metric scales** or **quantitative variables**.

Table 3.1 shows the statistical tests that can be done with each of the four types of scales. Fewer tests can be done with nominal scales whereas the most tests can be done with ratio scales.

TABLE 3.1	Permissible Statistical Tests with the Four Types of Scales
Scale	**Statistical Tests**
Nominal	Frequencies, percentages, mode, chi-square
Ordinal	Frequencies, percentages, mode, chi-square, median, percentile, rank order correlation coefficient
Interval	Arithmetic mean, standard deviation, Pearson product moment correlation, t-test,* analysis of variance (ANOVA),* regression
Ratio	Arithmetic mean, standard deviation, Pearson product moment correlation, t-test,* analysis of variance (ANOVA),* regression, geometric mean, harmonic mean, percentage of variation, structure equation modeling

* These tests require the independent variable to be nominal and the dependent variable to be metric.

Often, any given variable can be operationalized in more than one scale, especially if it is a metric variable. For example, let's look at the variable of age. As an ordinal-level variable, one could classify age into the following categories: 0–5 years, 6–18 years, 19–45 years, 46–64 years, and 65 years and older. The same variable of age also could be operationalized as an interval/ratio scale where one could be asked to write one's age in years. When operationalizing variables, it is desirable to have the highest level of measurement—that is, ratio level—if possible.

CONCEPTUAL PARADIGM OF MEASUREMENT

In health education and health promotion, just like in behavioral and social sciences, we cannot measure concepts directly. So we have to convert these concepts into numbers called *variables.* Green and Lewis (1986, p. 68) described a **concept** as, ". . . merely an abstraction created by generalization drawn from particulars. It is induced from particular situations, statements, gestures, responses, or observations. As an abstraction, a concept is not directly observable or measurable." So a concept is a broad entity that cannot be directly measured or observed. An example of a concept could be health beliefs about physical activity. These may be statements of perceived facts or impressions about physical activity.

> A concept is a broad entity that cannot be directly measured or observed.

The core concepts in behavioral and social sciences are organized in the form of theories. Theories are developed as a result of research. Kerlinger and Lee (2000) defined theory as "a set of interrelated concepts, definitions, and predispositions that present a systematic view of events or situations by specifying relations among variables in order to explain and predict the events or situations." Health education and health promotion professionals are primarily interested in predicting or explaining changes in behaviors or environments. Use of theory is becoming almost mandatory for practitioners of health education and health promotion. The theoretical paradigm is often used in measurement and evaluation of health education and health promotion programs. These days, even for entry-level health educators, competency for developing a logical scope and sequence plan for health education is a requirement (National Commission for Health Education Credentialing, Society for Public Health Education, & American Association for Health Education, 2006). For graduate-level health educators, use of theory is a must. Theories help articulate assumptions and hypotheses regarding the strategies and targets of interventions and their evaluation (National Cancer Institute, 2005).

Polit and Hungler (1999) have classified theories into three types. First are the macro theories or grand theories that purport to explain and describe large segments of the environment or human experience—for example, Talcott Parsons's (1951) theory on social functioning. Second are middle-range theories that describe or explain phenomena such as specific behaviors—for example, Albert Bandura's (1986, 2004) social cognitive theory. Finally there are descriptive theories that describe or explain a single discrete phenomenon—for example, Hans Selye's (1974) general adaptation syndrome.

Glanz, Rimer, and Viswanath (2008) have classified theories as either explanatory theories (or theories of the problem) or change theories (or theories of action). Explanatory theories help describe and identify why a problem exists and search for modifiable constructs. Change theories guide the development of interventions and form the basis of evaluation.

Theories start from discussing concepts or ideas that are abstract entities. As mentioned earlier, these concepts are not measurable or observable. They are adopted into theories and become known as **constructs** (Kerlinger & Lee, 2000). For example, in social cognitive theory (Bandura, 1986, 2004), self-efficacy for a given behavior is a construct. The constructs of a theory are constantly refined from empirical testing. Ideally, a theory must be able to demonstrate predictive power. Behavioral theories must be able to make significant changes on affect (feelings or conation), thought (cognition), and action (volition). Ideally a theory must be able to provide practical guidance on what, why, and how. An ideal theory must be testable and must be generalizable. The constructs of the theory must be able to explain phenomena, which for health education and health promotion are behaviors or environmental conditions. **Figure 3.1** shows a generic depiction of a behavioral theory.

A construct is a concept adopted for use in a theory.

Using theory derived from behavioral or social science helps the practice of health education and health promotion in several ways. First, it helps in developing program objectives that are measurable. For example, if the health education program uses social cognitive theory (Bandura, 1986, 2004) to change physical activity behavior in elementary school students, then the objectives can be based on three constructs derived from the theory. The objectives could be as follows:

1. At the end of the program, 80% of the participants are able to demonstrate positive change in their physical activity expectations score from before to after the intervention.
2. At the end of the program, 80% of the participants are able to demonstrate positive change in their physical activity self-efficacy score from before to after the intervention.

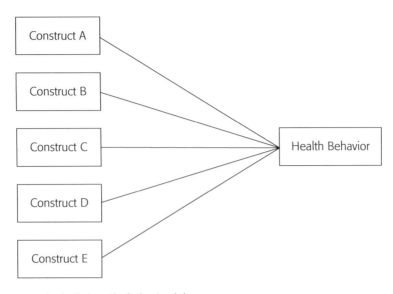

Figure 3.1   A generic depiction of a behavioral theory.

3. At the end of the program, 80% of the participants are able to demonstrate positive change in their physical activity self-control score from before to after the intervention.

Second, the theory helps in identifying the method to use in health education or health promotion. For example, continuing with the previous example, the theory prescribes that in order to change self-efficacy the behavior must be taught in small steps, so demonstration could be used as a method. Third, the theory helps in deciding the timing of the intervention. For example, theoretically it would make sense to design more interventions that prevent use of tobacco at the middle school level because the behavior is beginning to get started at that point. Fourth, the theory helps in choosing the right mix of strategies and methods. In the earlier example, three constructs were chosen for the social cognitive theory because the theory suggests that those three are important for early-stage adolescents. Fifth, theory aids communication between professionals. The constructs of each theory remain the same in different applications, and thus readers can understand across the studies what was done. Sixth, the use of theory helps in replication of the program because the same constructs can be used from one intervention to the other. Finally, behavioral and social science theories help in making programs more effective (greater impact) and efficient (less time). These benefits are summarized in **Table 3.2**.

TABLE 3.2   Benefits of Theory in Health Education and Health Promotion

Helps in discerning measurable program outcomes

Specifies methods for behavior change

Identifies the timing for interventions

Helps in choosing the right mix of strategies

Enhances communication between professionals

Improves replication

Improves program efficiency and effectiveness

When specific properties are assigned to the construct, it becomes an indicator.

The variable or quantitative score, which varies from one individual to another, is derived from the indicator. A variable can be measured and observed, and it takes on different values in the form of numbers.

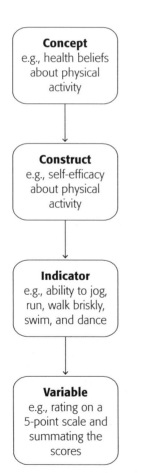

Figure 3.2 Conceptual paradigm of measurement.

Constructs are further refined into indicators. When specific properties are assigned to the construct, it becomes an **indicator**. Indicators are also known as indices, operators, or indicants (Green & Lewis, 1986). For example, five items may be written in the form of a questionnaire for the construct of self-efficacy for physical activity, constituting what the construct means. These items may be the ability to jog, ability to run, ability to swim, ability to walk briskly, and ability to dance. These are the properties that have been ascribed to the construct. It is the task of the person developing the instrument or conducting the evaluation to select the best properties that are possible for the target population. These properties should also be representative of all the possible choices. However, one has to make a decision as to whether one wants an exhaustive list of properties to be listed or, more practically, the ones that are salient.

From the indicator is derived the **variable** or quantitative score, which varies from one individual to another. A variable can be measured and observed, and it takes on different values in the form of numbers. For example, in the five-item physical activity questionnaire, each item can be ranked on a five-point rating scale of not at all sure (1), slightly sure (2), moderately sure (3), very sure (4), and completely sure (5); the summation of all five items yields a score ranging from 5 to 25. This conceptual paradigm of measurement is depicted in **Figure 3.2**.

TYPES OF VARIABLES IN HEALTH EDUCATION AND HEALTH PROMOTION

Health education and health promotion professionals are interested in a variety of variables. The following sections discuss variables that are commonly used in the evaluation of health education and health promotion programs.

Demographic Variables

Demographic variables are characteristics of a human population. These variables are used to classify target population and conduct subgroup-specific analyses. Some of the demographic variables commonly used in health education and health promotion are:

- *Gender:* Nominal level (male and female, or men and women, or boys and girls)
- *Age:* Usually metric, but sometimes ordinal (usually in years, sometimes for newborns in days or weeks)
- *Race:* Nominal level; usually used in the United States because of diversity issues (Caucasian American, African American, Hispanic American, Asian American, Native American, Pacific Islanders, and Other)
- *Ethnicity:* Nominal level; again, usually used in the United States because of diversity issues (the census uses Hispanic origin and non-Hispanic origin)
- *Occupation:* Nominal level (can include different options depending on the study's focus)
- *Education:* Ordinal level (less than high school, high school or GED, some college, bachelor's degree, master's degree, professional degree, doctorate)
- *Zip code of residence:* Nominal level
- *National origin:* Nominal level
- *Religion:* Nominal level
- *Income:* Can be metric, but people usually like to answer in categories as a nominal level
- *Family size:* Usually metric
- *Disability status:* Usually dichotomous (disabled, not disabled)
- *Home ownership:* Nominal level

Knowledge Scores

Health education and health promotion programs are often interested in gauging whether the target population acquired knowledge on a given subject. The learning of facts and gaining of insights is called **knowledge**. Bloom (1956) identified knowledge as part of the cognitive domain and identified six categories of cognitive learning. The first of these categories is knowledge, which entails recalling data or information—for example, reciting the symptoms of a disease or knowing safety procedures. The second level is comprehension, or understanding the meaning, translation, interpolation, and interpretation of instructions and problems. An example is the ability to state a problem in one's own words. The third level is application, which entails using a concept in a new situation. It also means applying what was learned in the classroom setting to novel situations in the workplace. The fourth level is analysis, in which the person is able to separate concepts into component parts so their organizational structure may be understood—for example, a health educator collects information about a community and then prioritizes the needs to decide what program to offer in the community. The fifth level is synthesis, in which the parts are put together to form a whole, with emphasis on creating a new meaning or structure. The sixth and final level is evaluation, where one makes judgments about the value of ideas or materials.

Knowledge can be tested as being correct or incorrect. The usual methods by which knowledge is tested are true/false questions or multiple choice questions. An example of a knowledge scale is presented in **Focus Feature 3.1**.

Skills/Performance

In performing any action, a set of psychomotor **skills** is required. Performance of these skills entails physical movement, coordination, and use of the motor skill. Development of these skills requires practice and is measured in terms of speed, precision, distance, procedures, or techniques in execution (Simpson, 1972). Seven categories, ranging from the simplest skill to the most complex skill, have been identified:

1. *Perception:* The ability to use sensory cues to guide motor activity.
2. *Set:* The readiness to act. It includes mind-set, which predetermines a person's response to different situations.
3. *Guided response:* Early stages in learning a complex skill, which include imitation and trial and error.
4. *Mechanism:* Learned responses have become habitual and the movements can be performed with some confidence and proficiency.

FOCUS FEATURE 3.1   EXAMPLE OF A SCALE MEASURING KNOWLEDGE

Assessing the Basics of Stress Management

For the following questions, circle the correct response. *Each question is worth 5 points (50 points total).*

1. The Social Readjustment Rating Scale (SRRS) measures the chronic stressors faced by an individual in the past year. **True / False**
2. People who are not competitive and have no time urgency are not successful in life and have stress. **True / False**
3. It is not the stressor but our perception of stress that is important. **True / False**
4. Stressors have the potential to produce beneficial effects. **True / False**
5. The contraction of skeletal muscles that results from stress can lead to tension headaches. **True / False**
6. Generally speaking, the sympathetic nervous system is responsible for conserving energy (e.g., decreasing respiratory rate). **True / False**
7. One major stressful event like the death of someone close to us is much more important in causing ill effects of stress than everyday small hassles. **True / False**
8. Thomas Holmes described the General Adaptation Syndrome. **True / False**
9. Progressive muscle relaxation was first described by Edmund Jacobson. **True / False**
10. Stress increases the amount of saliva in the mouth. **True / False**

SCORING:

1, 2, 6, 7, 8, and 10 are false.

3, 4, 5, and 9 are true.

5. *Complex overt response:* Performance without hesitation; automatic performance.
6. *Adaptation:* Skills are well developed, and the individual can modify movement patterns to fit special requirements.
7. *Origination:* The person creates new movement patterns to fit a particular situation or specific problem.

Psychomotor skills are required in almost all health education programs. These are tested by demonstration and redemonstration. For example, in a cardiopulmonary resuscitation (CPR) program, the instructor first shows the correct technique and then watches the participants perform CPR to see whether they have learned the technique correctly.

Beliefs

Beliefs are convictions that a phenomenon is true or real (Rokeach, 1970). In other words, beliefs are statements of perceived fact or impressions about the world. These are neither correct nor incorrect. For example, a student may enter a classroom and say that the classroom is big. She may be used to smaller classrooms, and thus from her perspective the current classroom seems big. Another student may enter the same classroom and say that it is small. He may be used to bigger classrooms and thus his perspective finds the classroom smaller. Health education and health promotion programs are often interested in gauging the beliefs they are trying to change, for example, beliefs about physical activity.

Attitudes

Attitudes are relatively constant feelings, predispositions, or sets of beliefs directed toward an idea, object, person, or situation (Mucchielli, 1970). Put another way, attitudes can be considered as beliefs with an evaluative component. Attitudes have an affective component and demonstrate what one likes and what one does not like. For example, building on the example presented earlier about beliefs, a student might find a room small and may qualify that belief by saying that it is an ugly, small room. Because an evaluation has been done that the student dislikes the room, it becomes an attitude. Likewise, another student might find the same room to be a small, cozy room, and thus demonstrate an attitude of liking the object.

Most of the constructs in behavioral theories tap into attitudes such as subjective norm (from the theory of reasoned action and theory of planned behavior), perceived behavioral control (from the theory of planned behavior), self-efficacy for a given behavior (from social cognitive theory), situational perception (from social cognitive theory), consciousness raising (from the transtheoretical model), perceived susceptibility (from the health belief model), and the like. Attitudes are typically measured by self-reporting scales, such as Likert scales. Likert scales list several sentences about an object and then ask respondents whether they strongly agree, agree, disagree, or strongly disagree with each statement. The scores are then summed to measure the respondent's attitude toward that object. **Focus Feature 3.2** shows a scale measuring attitudes.

FOCUS FEATURE 3.2   EXAMPLE OF A SCALE MEASURING ATTITUDES

This scale is based on social cognitive theory and measures selected constructs of the theory for four childhood obesity prevention behaviors: physical activity for 60 minutes, watching TV for less than 2 hours per day, drinking water instead of sweetened beverages, and eating five or more servings of fruits and vegetables each day.

IRB#: _____

Promoting Healthy Lifestyles: Survey   **Name:** _____

Assent and Directions: This survey is voluntary, which means you may choose not to complete it or not to answer individual questions. There is no direct benefit of this survey to you. All data from this survey will be kept secret. It will not be used for grading. Some of you may be asked to complete this two times. If you do not take the survey you will do another task assigned by the teacher. There will be no penalty if you do not participate. Please put an X mark by the response that correctly describes your view. Thank you for your help!

1. How old are you today?
   - ☐ Younger than 9 years old
   - ☐ 9 years old
   - ☐ 10 years old
   - ☐ 11 years old
   - ☐ 12 years old
   - ☐ 13 years old
   - ☐ older than 13 years
2. Are you a . . . ?
   - ☐ Boy
   - ☐ Girl
3. What is your race?
   - ☐ White
   - ☐ Black or African American
   - ☐ Asian
   - ☐ American Indian
   - ☐ Hispanic
   - ☐ Other _____
4. How many times have you been taught in school about healthy eating?
   - ☐ Never
   - ☐ Once
   - ☐ Twice
   - ☐ Three or more class lessons
5. How many times have you been taught in school to do physical activity or exercise at home?
   - ☐ Never
   - ☐ Once
   - ☐ Twice
   - ☐ Three or more class lessons
6. Since yesterday at this time, how many minutes did you exercise at home? (please write)
   _____ minutes
7. Since yesterday at this time, how many hours of TV did you watch? (please write)
   _____ hour(s)

FOCUS FEATURE 3.2   EXAMPLE OF A SCALE MEASURING ATTITUDES *(Continued)*

8. Since yesterday at this time, how many glasses of water did you drink? (please write)
   _____ glass(es)
9. Since yesterday at this time, how many servings of fruit did you eat? (please write)
   _____ serving(s)
10. Since yesterday at this time, how many servings of vegetables did you eat? (please write)
    _____ serving(s)

		Never	Hardly Ever	Sometimes	Almost Always	Always

If I exercise 60 minutes daily at home I will . . .

11.	. . . not get sick as often.					
12.	. . . have more confidence.					
13.	. . . have more fun.					
14.	. . . look better.					

If I watch TV less than 2 hours/day I will . . .

15.	. . . have more friends.					
16.	. . . have more free time.					
17.	. . . have more fun.					
18.	. . . be more relaxed.					

If I drink water instead of sweetened beverages I will . . .

19.	. . . be more relaxed.					
20.	. . . feel better.					
21.	. . . have more energy.					
22.	. . . have a better weight.					

If I eat 5 or more servings of fruits and vegetables each day I will . . .

23.	. . . have more energy.					
24.	. . . feel better.					
25.	. . . not get sick as often.					
26.	. . . have a better weight.					

(continues)

FOCUS FEATURE 3.2 EXAMPLE OF A SCALE MEASURING ATTITUDES (Continued)

How important is it to you that you . . .

		Not at All Important	Slightly Important	Moderately Important	Very Important	Extremely Important
27.	. . . not get sick as often?					
28.	. . . have more confidence?					
29.	. . . have more fun?					
30.	. . . look better?					
31.	. . . have more friends?					
32.	. . . have more free time?					
33.	. . . be more relaxed?					
34.	. . . feel better?					
35.	. . . have more energy?					
36.	. . . have a better weight?					

How sure are you that you can . . .

		Not at All Sure	Slightly Sure	Moderately Sure	Very Sure	Completely Sure
37.	. . . exercise every day for 30 minutes at home?					
38.	. . . exercise for 30 minutes at home even if you are tired?					
39.	. . . exercise for 30 minutes at home even if you are busy?					
40.	. . . set goals to exercise every day for 30 minutes at home?					
41.	. . . reward yourself with something you like for exercising?					
42.	. . . watch TV no more than 2 hours per day?					
43.	. . . reduce watching TV even if your favorite shows are coming?					

FOCUS FEATURE 3.2   EXAMPLE OF A SCALE MEASURING ATTITUDES (Continued)

		Not at All Sure	Slightly Sure	Moderately Sure	Very Sure	Completely Sure
44.	. . . reduce watching TV even if everyone else in the family is watching?					
45.	. . . set goals to watch TV no more than 2 hours per day?					
46.	. . . reward yourself with something you like for reducing watching TV?					
47.	. . . drink more water?					
48.	. . . drink water every day instead of sweet drinks?					
49.	. . . drink more water every day even if you do not feel thirsty?					
50.	. . . set goals to replace sweet drinks with water every day?					
51.	. . . reward yourself with something you like for drinking water instead of sweet drinks?					
52.	. . . eat 5 or more servings of fruits and vegetables every day?					
53.	. . . eat 5 or more servings of fruits and vegetables every day even if you do not like them?					
54.	. . . eat 5 or more servings of fruits and vegetables every day even if others in your family do not like them?					
55.	. . . set goals to eat 5 or more servings of fruits and vegetables?					
56.	. . . reward yourself with something you like for eating 5 or more servings of fruits and vegetables every day?					

Thank you for your time!

(continues)

FOCUS FEATURE 3.2   EXAMPLE OF A SCALE MEASURING ATTITUDES
(Continued)

Scoring on the Scale:
Number each rating scale from 1–5.

Expectations for physical activity:
Multiply Item 11 × Item 27; Item 12 × Item 28; Item 13 × Item 29; Item 14 × Item 30. Then sum all the products to get the score for expectations for physical activity.

Expectations for watching < 2 hours of TV:
Multiply Item 15 × Item 31; Item 16 × Item 32; Item 17 × Item 29; Item 18 × Item 33. Then sum all the products to get the score for expectations for watching < 2 hours of TV.

Expectations for drinking water instead of sweetened beverages:
Multiply Item 19 × Item 33; Item 20 × Item 34; Item 21 × Item 35; Item 22 × Item 36. Then sum all the products to get the score for expectations for drinking water instead of sweetened beverages.

Expectations for eating 5 or more servings of fruits and vegetables each day:
Multiply Item 23 × Item 35; Item 24 × Item 34; Item 25 × Item 27; Item 26 × Item 36. Then sum all the products to get the score for expectations for eating 5 or more servings of fruits and vegetables each day.

Self-efficacy for physical activity:
Sum Item 37 + Item 38 + Item 39

Self-control for physical activity:
Sum Item 40 + Item 41

Self-efficacy for watching < 2 hours of TV:
Sum Item 42 + Item 43 + Item 44

Self-control for watching < 2 hours of TV:
Sum Item 45 + Item 46

Self-efficacy for drinking water instead of sweetened beverages:
Sum Item 47 + Item 48 + Item 49

Self-control for drinking water instead of sweetened beverages:
Sum Item 50 + Item 51

Self-efficacy for eating 5 or more servings of fruits and vegetables each day:
Sum Item 52 + Item 53 + Item 54

Self-control for eating 5 or more servings of fruits and vegetables each day:
Sum Item 55 + Item 56

Psychometric properties of the scale discussed in: Sharma, M., Wagner, D. I., & Wilkerson, J. (2005–2006). Predicting childhood obesity prevention behaviors using social cognitive theory. *International Quarterly of Community Health Education, 24*(3), 191–203.

Values

A collection of beliefs and attitudes comprises a value system. **Values** are enduring beliefs or systems of beliefs regarding whether a specific mode of conduct or end state of behavior is personally or socially preferable (Rokeach, 1970). Let us take the example of the student who likes small, cozy classrooms. He also likes the students and the instructor in the classroom, and likes the textbook that has been assigned by his instructor. He likes to read and to complete his assignments on time. Such a student can be said to have a value system that values education.

Personality

A set of attributes that categorize individuals is known as personality. It consists of the sum total of the physical, mental, emotional, and social characteristics of an individual. Sometimes the evaluation of health education and health promotion programs is interested in gauging some personality styles or traits such as Type A and Type B personality (Friedman & Rosenman, 1974) or health locus of control (internal or external) (Rotter, 1954).

Behaviors

Health education and health promotion are primarily interested in changing unhealthy behaviors and replacing those with healthy behaviors, so measurement of behaviors becomes essential in the evaluation of health education and health promotion programs. Some of the behaviors that are commonly measured include physical activity behaviors, healthy dietary behaviors (such as eating five or more servings of fruits and vegetables each day, controlling portion size, drinking water instead of sweetened beverages, avoiding fast food, etc.), safer sex behavior (such as monogamy, using condoms, etc.), sleep behaviors, anger management behaviors, anxiety reduction behaviors, avoiding smoking behaviors, avoiding drinking behaviors, and avoiding drug use behaviors.

Physiological Profiles

Many health education and health promotion programs are interested in altering physiological profiles. Examples of these include:

- *Body mass index (BMI), which is a function of weight (kg)/height (m²); waist circumference; skinfold thickness; and the like:* For interventions aiming to alter body weight and body composition such as overweight/obesity prevention/control programs
- *Blood pressure:* For hypertension prevention/control interventions
- *Total cholesterol, HDL (high density lipoproteins), LDL (low density lipoproteins), very low density lipoproteins (VLDL), triglycerides:* For interventions aiming to change lipid profile
- *Blood glucose, hemoglobin a1c:* For diabetes education/prevention/control programs
- *Serum cotinine:* For smoking cessation interventions
- *Salivary cortisol:* For stress management programs

Program Process

An important area in evaluation of health education and health promotion programs is to decipher actual aspects of program implementation. Was the program implemented in the way it was planned? What was the response of the site where the program was implemented? What was the quality of the educational materials provided? What was the competency of the implementers?

Health Service Utilization

Often health education and health promotion programs are interested in enhancing utilization of health services, so this variable is also of interest to evaluators in health education and health promotion.

Environmental Variables

These variables are particularly of interest to health promotion interventions. Examples include changes in policies, changes in laws, changes in vending machine choices, and the like.

Epidemiological Indices

When conducted for a long period of time and intensively, health education and health promotion programs can bring about changes in epidemiological indices such as mortality rates (e.g., death rates due to HIV/AIDS) and morbidity rates (e.g., incidence of HIV/AIDS, prevalence of HIV/AIDS). This type of evaluation is known as outcome evaluation, and is done after several years of intensive programming.

Table 3.3 summarizes all the potential variables that evaluators of health education and health promotion programs are interested in.

TABLE 3.3   List of Potential Variables That Interest Evaluators of Health Education and Health Promotion Programs

Demographic variables	Behaviors
Knowledge scores	Physiological profiles
Skills/performance	Program process
Beliefs	Health service utilization
Attitudes	Environmental variables
Values	Epidemiological indices
Personality	

SKILL-BUILDING ACTIVITY

Imagine you have been hired to evaluate a safer sex intervention among college students that is based on social cognitive theory. Identify the variables you would study for process and impact evaluation of this intervention. Also, if this intervention was part of several other interventions in the area, what variables would you choose for outcome evaluation? After identifying the variables, choose which scale of measurement you would apply for each of those variables.

SUMMARY

Measurement is the systematic application of a set of procedures and processes so that concepts can be objectively reduced to numbers for the purpose of comparison. The instruments that are developed for measurement must be valid and reliable. Validity is the ability to say that the instrument is actually measuring what it is purporting to measure, and reliability is the ability of the instrument to measure repeatedly the same results and be internally consistent.

There are four commonly used scales: nominal, ordinal, interval, and ratio. With a nominal scale the property "kind" is assigned; for an ordinal scale the property "order" is assigned; for an interval scale the property "equal intervals" is assigned; and with a ratio scale, "ratios" is assigned. The nominal scale is used to categorize or classify individuals, objects, issues, or events into different groups (e.g., sex, race, marital status, etc.). The ordinal scale is used to classify individuals, objects, issues, or events into categories that have a meaningful order. The interval scale is used to classify individuals, objects, issues, or events into categories that have a meaningful order, implying higher levels have more of the attribute. At the same time, this scale has equal intervals so it is possible to tell how much difference there is between one category and another. The ratio scale has all the characteristics of an interval scale, but in addition has a true zero point.

Health education and health promotion professionals cannot measure concepts directly, so concepts are converted into constructs, then constructs into indicators, and then indicators into variables or numbers. A concept is a broad entity that cannot be directly measured or observed. An example of a concept could be health beliefs about physical activity. A construct is a concept adopted for use in theory. An example would be self-efficacy for physical activity. When specific properties are assigned to the construct, then it becomes an indicator.

A variety of variables are important in health education and health promotion, including demographic variables, knowledge scores, skills/performance, beliefs, attitudes, values, personality, behaviors, physiological profiles, program processes, health service utilization, environmental variables, and epidemiological indices.

REVIEW QUESTIONS

1. Define *measurement*, *validity*, and *reliability*.
2. Differentiate among the nominal, ordinal, interval, and ratio scales.

3. Identify statistical tests that can be used for nominal, ordinal, interval, and ratio scales.
4. Describe the conceptual paradigm of measurement.
5. Differentiate between concept and variable.
6. Describe the benefits of using theory in health education and health promotion.
7. List any five types of variables that are used in the evaluation of health education and health promotion programs.
8. Differentiate between beliefs and attitudes.

WEBSITES TO EXPLORE

Evaluation and Measurement: Some Dilemmas for Health Education

http://www.ncbi.nlm.nih.gov/pmc/articles/PMC1653552/

This is an article by Larry Green published in 1977 in *American Journal of Public Health* [67(2): 155–161]. The article identifies six dilemmas: (1) rigor of experimental design versus significance or program adaptability, (2) internal validity or "true" effectiveness versus external validity or feasibility, (3) experimental versus placebo effects, (4) effectiveness versus economy of scale, (5) risk versus payoff, and (6) measurement of long-term versus short-term effects. *Read the abstract and the article. Do you think these dilemmas are still true after so many years?*

Measurement Issues in Health Education Evaluation

http://www.aahperd.org/aahe/publications/iejhe/loader.cfm?csModule=security
/getfile&pageid=39319

This website contains an article by Mohammad Torabi and Kele Ding published in 1998 in the *International Electronic Journal of Health Education* [1:26–38]. This article presents a review of literature related to some statistical and measurement issues and problems related to research in education, particularly health education. *Read this article and prepare a one-page summary and critique.*

OECD Health Data—2010—List of Variables

http://www.oecd.org/document/9/0,3746,en_2649_34631_2085193_1_1_1_1,00.html

This is the website of the Directorate for Employment, Labour, Social Affairs at the Organisation for Economic Co-operation and Development (OECD), which has its headquarters in Paris, France. On this website you can download the complete list of variables used by the OECD. *Download the list in PDF format. Go through this exhaustive list and identify which variables would be of value in evaluating health education programs.*

Statistics Glossary

http://www.stats.gla.ac.uk/steps/glossary/presenting_data.html

This website was developed by Valerie Easton and John McColl and presents several statistical concepts related to presenting data. *Read about nominal, ordinal, interval, and ratio scales. How does discrete data differ from continuous data?*

REFERENCES

Bandura, A. (1986). *Social foundations of thought and action.* Englewood Cliffs, NJ: Prentice Hall.

Bandura, A. (2004). Health promotion by social cognitive means. *Health Education and Behavior, 31,* 143–164.

Bloom, B. S. (1956). *Taxonomy of educational objectives. Handbook I: The cognitive domain.* New York: David McKay.

DiIorio, C. K. (2005). *Measurement in health behavior. Methods for research and education.* San Francisco, CA: Jossey-Bass.

Friedman, M., & Rosenman, R. H. (1974). *Type A behavior and your heart.* New York: Fawcett Crest.

Glanz, K., Rimer, B. K., & Viswanath, K. (2008). *Health behavior and health education. Theory, research, and practice* (4th ed.). San Francisco: Jossey-Bass.

Green, L. W., & Lewis, F. M. (1986). *Measurement and evaluation in health education and health promotion.* Palo Alto, CA: Mayfield.

Kerlinger, F. N., & Lee, H. B. (2000). *Foundations of behavioral research* (4th ed.). Fort Worth, TX: Harcourt College.

Kuzma, J. W., & Bohnenblust, S. E. (2005). *Basic statistics for the health sciences* (5th ed.). Boston: McGraw-Hill.

Lord, F. M., & Novick, M. R. (1968). *Statistical theories of mental test scores.* Reading, MA: Addison-Wesley.

Mucchielli, R. (1970). *Introduction to structural psychology.* New York: Funk and Wagnalls.

National Cancer Institute. (2005). *Theory at a glance: A guide for health promotion practice* (2nd ed.). Washington, DC: U.S. Department of Health and Human Services. Retrieved from http://www.nci.nih.gov/theory/pdf

National Commission for Health Education Credentialing, Society for Public Health Education, & American Association for Health Education. (2006). *Competency-based framework for health educators—2006.* Whitehall, PA: Author.

Nunnally, J. C., & Bernstein, I. H. (1994). *Psychometric theory.* New York: McGraw-Hill.

Parsons, T. (1951). *The social system.* New York: Free Press.

Polit, D. F., & Hungler, B. P. (1999). *Nursing research: Principles and methods* (6th ed.). Philadelphia: Lippincott.

Rokeach, M. (1970). *Beliefs, attitudes and values.* San Francisco: Jossey Bass.

Rotter, J. B. (1954). *Social learning and clinical psychology.* New York: Prentice Hall.

Selye, H. (1974). *The stress of life.* New York: McGraw-Hill.

Sharma, M., Wagner, D. I., & Wilkerson, J. (2005–2006). Predicting childhood obesity prevention behaviors using social cognitive theory. *International Quarterly of Community Health Education, 24*(3), 191–203.

Simpson, E. J. (1972). *The classification of educational objectives in the psychomotor domain.* Washington, DC: Gryphon House.

Stevens, S. S. (1959). Measurement, psychophysics, and utility. In C. W. Churchman & P. Ratoosh (Eds.), *Measurement definitions and theories* (pp. 18–63). New York: Wiley.

CHAPTER 4

Steps in Instrument Development

BASIC PRINCIPLES OF INSTRUMENT DEVELOPMENT _____

An **instrument** or a scale is a tool used to measure concepts and constructs by reducing them into variables. An instrument typically has items that participants rate on a scale. A critical oversight by many health educators planning an evaluation is to use existing instruments that do not precisely meet the measurement needs of a particular health program. This text promotes the idea that evaluators should very carefully review existing published instruments to determine whether they precisely match the needs of the evaluation. If they do not, evaluators should consider the importance of developing instruments to precisely and completely measure the constructs as they are addressed in a particular health intervention. The steps in instrument development are summarized in **Table 4.1**. Each of the items in the table will be discussed in the following sections.

Define the Purpose of Instrument Development

The first step in developing an instrument is to *define the purpose of instrument development*. The usual purposes in health education are to measure knowledge on a subject, gauge attitudes about a topic, or measure health behaviors. The usual purposes in health promotion are to measure changes in environment, policies, laws, and regulations. If the purpose is not clarified, there is a chance the instrument may not be relevant for the study. The purpose is also dependent on whether one is doing process, impact, or outcome evaluation. For process evaluation, a researcher is usually interested in developing checklists of tasks planned and done. For impact evaluation, the researcher is interested in antecedents of health behavior; health behavior; and environmental, organizational, or policy changes. For outcome evaluation a researcher is interested in instruments that measure epidemiological indices of health status, such as rates of illness, death, obesity, fitness levels, and so on.

TABLE 4.1   Steps in Instrument Development

1. Define the purpose of instrument development.
2. Review existing instruments related to the purpose.
3. Identify objects of interest.
4. Constitutively define each object of interest (concept–construct).
5. Prioritize how many objects of interest are to be measured.
6. Operationally define selected objects of interest (indicator–variable).
7. Choose the scale of measurement.
8. Develop items.
9. Prepare a draft with directions, scoring, and layout.
10. Test for readability and adjust according to the target population.
11. Send to a panel of experts (typically six) for face and content validation.
12. Conduct a minimum of two rounds with the panel of experts, and revise the instrument based on their feedback.
13. Conduct a pilot test with a small sample of the target population for readability, comprehension, time of completion, and other important issues.
14. Establish reliability: internal consistency and stability.
15. Establish construct validity: confirmatory factor analysis.
16. Establish criterion validity, if applicable: comparison with other scales of the same measure.

Review Existing Instruments Related to the Purpose

The second step in instrument development is to *review existing instruments related to the purpose*. Articles about instrument development can be found in several databases. Some of the common ones in health education and health promotion are MEDLINE (PubMed), ERIC, CINAHL, Sport Discus, Google Scholar, and Academic Search Premier. **Health and Psychosocial Instruments (HaPI)** is a specialized database that lists only instruments in the health-related disciplines, the behavioral and social sciences, and the organizational behavior field. It offers quick access to measurement instruments and tools (such as checklists, coding schemes/manuals, index measures, interview schedules, projective techniques, questionnaires, rating scales, vignettes/scenarios, and tests). The instruments are helpful for administrators, educators, evaluators, practitioners, students, and researchers and can be used for evaluation and research. A drawback to HaPI is that not all institutions subscribe to it. If your institution does not subscribe to it, you cannot access it.

Carefully study the purpose and actual items of an existing instrument. It is quite possible that an instrument that sounds like it might suit your needs may not. A common mistake is for health educators to mistakenly apply an existing instrument that does not precisely match the measurement needs of their program. For example, let us assume you have located an instrument that assesses knowledge of "Self-Care for People with Diabetes." You think this might be a good instrument to evaluate your diabetes education program. It is advisable to carefully review the items of this instrument to determine whether they match the content of the educational program you wish to evaluate. The knowledge items that this instrument is measuring may not be the knowledge areas that your program has covered. It is very important to have a direct match between the lesson plan of your program and the instrument so you can correctly evaluate what is indeed being covered by the program.

Upon review of existing instruments, if you find an instrument that matches your purpose and has adequate psychometric properties, then you can use that instrument and stop further instrument development. However, often professionals are not able to find an instrument that meets their purpose or that has adequate psychometric properties. In that case, you need to proceed to the next step.

Identify Objects of Interest

The third step is to *identify objects of interest*. Suppose you have a social cognitive theory–based problem-solving skills intervention for sixth-grade schoolchildren that you want to evaluate for impact. In this case, the objects of interest would be problem-solving skills and antecedents of these skills based on social cognitive theory (SCT). We will use the example of developing this scale in illustrating all the steps of instrument development. The final scale is depicted in **Focus Feature 4.1** (p. 82).

Constitutively Define Each Object of Interest (Concept–Construct)

The fourth step is to *constitutively define each object of interest*. In the previous example, this would mean defining *problem-solving skills* as an ability by the sixth-grade schoolchildren to identify and define stressors, generate sufficient solutions in dealing with the stressors, analyze the advantages and disadvantages of various solutions, and choose a solution. This also means defining the nine constructs of social cognitive theory (Bandura, 1986, 2004). The first construct of SCT is *knowledge*, which entails learning facts and gaining insights related to an action, idea, object, person, or situation. The second construct of SCT is *outcome expectations*, which is the anticipation of the probable outcomes that would ensue as a result of engaging in the behavior under discussion. The third construct, which goes hand-in-hand with outcome expectations, is *outcome expectancies*, which refers to the value

Constitutive definition is how a given concept is operationalized into a construct.

a person places on the probable outcomes that result from performing a behavior. The fourth SCT construct is *situational perception*, which refers to how one perceives and interprets the environment around oneself. The fifth construct of SCT, *environment*, refers to the physical or social circumstances or conditions that surround a person. The sixth construct is *self-efficacy*, which is the confidence a person has in his or her ability to pursue a behavior. Self-efficacy is behavior-specific and is in the present. The seventh construct is *self-efficacy in overcoming impediments*, which refers to the confidence a person has in overcoming barriers while performing a given behavior. The eighth construct is *goal setting or self-control*, which refers to setting goals and developing plans to accomplish chosen behaviors. The final construct in SCT is *emotional coping*, which refers to the techniques employed by the person to control the emotional and physiological states associated with acquisition of a new behavior. These constructs are depicted in **Figure 4.1**.

Prioritize How Many Objects of Interest Are to Be Measured

The fifth step is to *prioritize how many objects of interest are to be measured*. It is quite clear that if a researcher measures all constructs of social cognitive theory then the measurement will be very long, detailed, impractical, and not feasible. So we need to prioritize which constructs to focus on. Let us choose *situational perception for stressors, outcome expectations for problem-solving skills, outcome expectancies about problem-solving skills, self-efficacy about problem-solving skills, self-efficacy in overcoming barriers while applying problem-solving skills*, and *self-control for problem solving* along with *problem-solving skills*.

Operationally Define Selected Objects of Interest (Indicator–Variable)

The sixth step is to *operationally define selected objects of interest*. The *situational perception for stressors* would be operationally defined as the occurrence and emotional perception of the sixth-grade children to explicate: (1) chronic stressors at school, including being late with homework; (2) chronic stressors about performance at school, including taking tests; (3) chronic stressors about peer relationships, including being teased by classmates; and (4) chronic stressors at home, including parents arguing at home. These will be measured by summing the multiplicative score on a four-item Likert-type self-reporting rating scale measuring occurrence and feeling of stressors.

The construct of *outcome expectations about problem-solving skills* would be operationally defined as the anticipated outcome benefits perceived by the sixth-grade students from

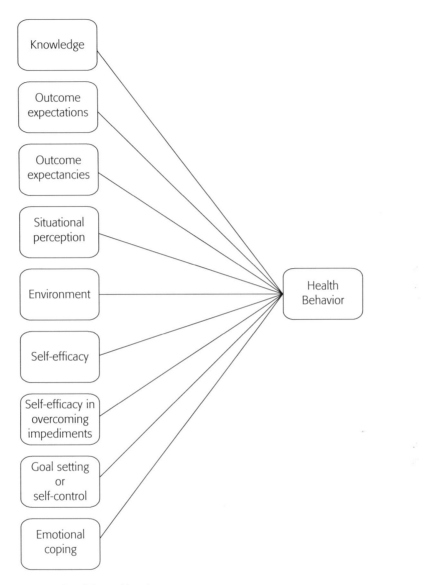

Figure 4.1 Constructs of social cognitive theory.

learning problem-solving skills consisting of having more friends, using class time productively, ability to learn other subjects better, ability to get better grades, and having more fun. The construct of *outcome expectancies about problem-solving skills* would be operationally defined as the personal value placed on the listed benefits by a sixth-grade student. These would be measured through summing a multiplicative score between expectations (five items) and expectancies (five items) on a 10-item Likert-type self-reporting rating scale.

The construct of *self-efficacy about problem-solving skills* would be operationally defined as the confidence of the sixth-grade student to (1) generate sufficient solutions in dealing with the chronic stressors at school, in school performance, in peer relationships, and at home; (2) discuss the advantages and disadvantages of various solutions; and (3) choose a solution as measured through a summative score on a four-item Likert-type self-reporting rating scale.

The construct of *self-efficacy in overcoming barriers while applying problem-solving skills* would be operationally defined as the ability to practice these steps when angry, tired, or busy. This would be measured through a summative score on a four-item Likert-type self-reporting rating scale.

The construct of *self-control for problem-solving skills* would be operationally defined as the ability of the sixth-grade student to self-reward on successful accomplishment of problem-solving steps as measured through a summative score on a four-item Likert-type self-reporting rating scale. *Problem-solving skills* would be operationally defined as the ability to identify and define chronic stressors at school, about performance at school, about peer relationships, and at home; generate sufficient solutions in dealing with these stressors; analyze the advantages and disadvantages of various solutions; and choose a solution. Overall frequency counts of number of students who faced and identified problems in the past week at school and at home, number of students who thought of many ways to deal with that problem, number of students who thought of good and bad points of each way, and number of students who chose one solution will be obtained through scoring by two raters.

> *Operational definition is how a given construct is transformed for measurement into a variable with a score range.*

Choose the Scale of Measurement

The seventh step is to *choose the scale of measurement*. In our example of situational perception of stressors, the following scales will be used:

How often does it happen to you?: Never (1), Hardly Ever (2), Sometimes (3), A Lot (4), Almost Always (5)

How bad does it make you feel?: Not Bad (1), A Little Bad (2), Pretty Bad (3), Really Bad (4), Terrible (5)

The ratings will be multiplied and then summed. The summated score will range from 4 to 64 and will be a metric score. For *outcome expectations about problem-solving skills*, the following scale will be used: Never (1), Hardly Ever (2), Sometimes (3), A Lot (4), Almost Always (5). For *outcome expectancies about problem-solving skills* the scale will be Not Important at All (1), Not Important (2), Somewhat Important (3), Important (4), Very Important (5), and the ratings will be multiplied and summed. The score of expectations (outcome expectations × outcome expectancies) will range from 5 to 125 and will be a metric score.

For *self-efficacy about problem-solving skills*, the scale Really Unsure (1), Sort of Unsure (2), Somewhat Sure (3), Sort of Sure (4), Really Sure (5) will be used. The scores will be summed across four situations, and the resulting metric score will range from 16 to 64. For *self-efficacy in overcoming barriers about problem-solving skills*, the scale Really Unsure (1), Sort of Unsure (2), Somewhat Sure (3), Sort of Sure (4), Really Sure (5) will be used. The scores will be summed across four situations, and the resulting metric score will range from 12 to 48. For *self-control about problem-solving skills*, the scale Really Unsure (1), Sort of Unsure (2), Somewhat Sure (3), Sort of Sure (4), Really Sure (5) will be used. The scores will be summed across four situations, and the resulting metric score will range from 4 to 16.

Develop Items

The eighth step is to *develop items*. One item should be developed corresponding to each property. It should be clear and tap into only one attribute. In our example, the items for each construct can be seen in Focus Feature 4.1.

When the concept has been reduced to a variable, the scale of measurement chosen, and the items developed, then the instrument is also called a **questionnaire**. Questionnaire is a generic term that refers to instruments in which respondents answer questions directly. In a questionnaire one can identify specific items and corresponding variables that are being measured. The conventional format for questionnaires is paper-and-pencil with closed-ended questions; however, electronic questionnaires are becoming quite popular.

Prepare a Draft with Directions, Scoring, and Layout

The ninth step is to *prepare a draft with directions, scoring, and layout*. The directions are very important in any instrument. They should be optimized as much as possible. They should be neither too vague nor too detailed, and should not be confusing to the reader. The directions should describe what is expected of the respondent in very clear terms. If the instrument has to be administered to children, then the directions can also include the assent statement or the agreement about the willingness of the child to participate. Sometimes directions can include a sample response or an example of how to mark the responses.

The instrument should have clear guidance about scoring—how each item will be scored, how different subscales will be scored, whether there will be one scorer or more, what the range of scores will be, and what high and low scores mean.

Finally, the instrument should have a good layout. For instruments that are to be administered as paper and pencil tests, there should be enough white space so that the instrument does not appear cluttered. The font size should be large enough for respondents to see clearly. Generally speaking, the demographic information should be placed at the end and not in the beginning. For instruments to be administered electronically by Survey Monkey or Qualtrics, the layout is equally important. Ideally no more than five questions should be forced on a single screen. It is a good practice to provide an indicator as to how much questionnaire remains after each screen. Also, a person should be able to revisit his or her answers in electronic questionnaires.

Test for Readability and Adjust According to the Target Population

The tenth step is to *test for readability and adjust according to the target population*. Microsoft Word has the capability of assessing the readability of any document. When Microsoft Word finishes checking spelling and grammar, it can display information about the reading level of the document, including two readability scores: the Flesch Reading Ease score and the Flesch-Kincaid Grade Level score. The readability score is based on the average number of syllables per word and words per sentence. The **Flesch Reading Ease score** rates text on a 100-point scale; the higher the score, the easier it is to understand the document. The formula for the Flesch Reading Ease score is:

$$206.835 - (1.015 \times ASL) - (84.6 \times ASW)$$

where:

> ASL = average sentence length (the number of words divided by the number of sentences)
> ASW = average number of syllables per word (the number of syllables divided by the number of words)

A score of 60 to 70 is considered a good score on this index. Achieving a perfect 100 is often difficult.

The **Flesch-Kincaid Grade Level score** rates text on a U.S. school grade level. For example, a score of 5.0 means that a fifth grader can understand the document. The formula for the Flesch-Kincaid Grade Level score is:

$$(0.39 \times ASL) + (11.8 \times ASW) - 15.59$$

where:

> ASL = average sentence length (the number of words divided by the number of sentences)
> ASW = average number of syllables per word (the number of syllables divided by the number of words)

Many instruments in health education and health promotion must be prepared at grade 7.0 to 8.0. If the reading level is found to be higher, then words with more syllables should be replaced with simpler words.

Send to a Panel of Experts (Typically Six) for Face and Content Validation

After establishing satisfactory readability of the instrument, it needs to be *sent to a panel of experts for face and content validation.* **Face validity** measures whether each item measures the intended construct as operationally defined and whether the instrument looks like an instrument. Green and Lewis (1986) describe face validity as the judgment of an instrument by an expert who logically determines whether the instrument "looks like" what it is supposed to measure. **Content validity** measures whether the items adequately assess each construct within the universe of content as operationally defined. DiIorio (2005, p. 213) defines content validity as, "the assessment of the correspondence between the items composing the instrument and the content domain from which the items are selected." Both face and content validity are determined by a panel of experts. An expert is a professional with experience in content or process. Typically the panel of experts is composed of six people: two subject experts (including theory, if theory has been used), two experts in measurement and instrument development, and two experts in the target population.

The panel is sent the operational definitions and the draft instrument prepared through the tenth step, with instructions to determine the face validity of each item and the content validity of each subscale.

Conduct a Minimum of Two Rounds with the Panel of Experts, and Revise the Instrument Based on Their Feedback

The twelfth step is to *conduct a minimum of two rounds with the panel of experts, and revise the instrument based on their feedback.* The panel may suggest deleting certain items, adding others, or rewording items for conceptual clarity to increase face and content validity. Changes are made after receiving the input from the first round with the panel of experts. In the second round, once again the panelists are approached to check whether their suggestions have been sufficiently incorporated. The goal is to try to achieve consensus among the panel of experts that the revised items represent face and content validity. Usually two rounds are sufficient, but sometimes a third round may be needed.

Conduct a Pilot Test with a Small Sample of the Target Population for Readability, Comprehension, Time of Completion, and Other Important Issues

The thirteenth step is to *conduct a pilot test with a small sample of the target population for readability, comprehension, time of completion, and other important issues.* After the panelists have approved the instrument, a pilot test of the instrument should be conducted with members of the target population. Some professionals like to conduct this pilot test before the expert panel review. This is a matter of professional judgment. In this pilot test, the target population members are instructed to circle any words they do not understand or any statements that are not clear. They are also timed to determine approximately how much time it would take to complete the instrument in a real-world setting. They are also asked to provide any suggestions with regard to improving the instrument's readability.

Establish Reliability: Internal Consistency and Stability

The fourteenth step is to *establish reliability: internal consistency and stability.* **Internal consistency** is the indication of how much each item in the scale relates to other items in the scale, or how much the items gel together (Green & Lewis, 1986). An essential requirement for calculating an internal consistency coefficient is that the scale must have more than one item that measures the variable (DiIorio, 2005). There are different methods for determining internal consistency, but one that is commonly used is Cronbach's alpha. **Stability** is the degree of association between a measurement that is repeat-measured in a retest situation. The method used to assess stability is the test-retest method. Usually a small sample of at least 30 members from the target population is taken and the instrument is administered to them. After 2 weeks the instrument is once again administered to the same group. Steps are taken so that each person's retest can be matched against their original test. A correlation coefficient is then calculated.

Establish Construct Validity: Confirmatory Factor Analysis

The penultimate step in instrument development is to *establish construct validity: confirmatory factor analysis*. **Construct validity** is the degree to which an instrument measures the same theme under study (Polit & Hungler, 1999). This requires administering the scale to an adequate sample of the target population and then conducting a statistical procedure called *confirmatory factor analysis* on all the subscales. This is a desirable step for field evaluations, but often is not done; it is primarily done in research studies.

Establish Criterion Validity, if Applicable: Comparison with Other Scales of the Same Measure

The final step in instrument development is to *establish criterion validity, if applicable: comparison with other scales of the same measure*. This step is only applicable if similar instruments are available on the same object of interest.

FOCUS FEATURE 4.1   EXAMPLE OF A THEORY-BASED SCALE

Problem Solving Questionnaire

You are requested to fill in your name; however, all information will be kept secret and will *not* be used for grading.

Your name: _____

Your school: _____

Your class teacher: _____

The following sentences will be read to you. Please put an **"X" mark** by the response that correctly describes your view. Your answers will help us in developing a good health education program for students like you. Remember, there are no right or wrong answers.

    1. How old are you?   __ younger than 10 years old
                                            __ 10 years old
                                            __ 11 years old
                                            __ 12 years old
                                            __ 13 years old
                                            __ 14 years old
                                            __ older than 14 years

    2. What is your sex?   __ Male (Boy)
                                            __ Female (Girl)

    3. What is your race?   __ White
                                            __ Black or African American
                                            __ Asian
                                            __ American Indian
                                            __ Hispanic
                                            __ Other, _____

FOCUS FEATURE 4.1   EXAMPLE OF A THEORY-BASED SCALE (Continued)

4. Have you ever been taught in school about problem solving as a way to deal with stress?
   __ Yes, I have had three or more class lessons on problem solving.
   __ Yes, I have had one or two class lessons on problem solving.
   __ Yes, but I have not had a complete class lesson on problem solving.
   __ No, I have had no class lesson on problem solving.

5. In the past week, name something that happened to you at school or home that you would call a problem.

   _____

   _____

   What steps did you follow in solving this problem?

   _____

   _____

   _____

   _____

   _____

   _____

   _____

Table 1

	How often does it happen to you?				How bad does it make you feel?			
	Never	Hardly Ever	A Lot	Almost Always	Not Bad	A Little Bad	Really Bad	Terrible
6. Not have home-work done on time.								
7. Worry about taking tests.								
8. Get teased by classmates.								
9. Hear your parents argue.								

(continues)

FOCUS FEATURE 4.1   EXAMPLE OF A THEORY-BASED SCALE
(Continued)

Table 2

If I can solve daily problems better:	Never	Hardly Ever	A Lot	Almost Always
10. I will be more popular with kids my age.				
11. I will learn more quickly at school.				
12. I will get better grades.				
13. I will have more fun with my family.				
14. I will have more fun at school.				

Table 3

How important is it that you:	Not Important at All	Somewhat Important	Important	Very Important
15. Be popular with kids your age.				
16. Learn more quickly at school.				
17. Get good grades.				
18. Have fun with your family.				
19. Have fun at school.				

Table 4

	Very Unsure	Sort of Unsure	Sort of Sure	Very Sure
20. Imagine yourself worrying about handing in homework late. How sure are you that you can follow each of these steps:				
a. Think of many ways to deal with this problem?				
b. Think of good points about each way?				
c. Think of bad points about each way?				
d. Choose one way to deal with this problem?				
e. Follow these steps even when you are angry?				
f. Follow these steps even when you are tired?				
g. Follow these steps even when you are busy?				
h. Reward yourself with something you like for following these steps?				

FOCUS FEATURE 4.1   EXAMPLE OF A THEORY-BASED SCALE (Continued)

Table 5

	Very Unsure	Sort of Unsure	Sort of Sure	Very Sure
21. Imagine yourself worrying about taking tests. How sure are you that you can follow each of these steps:				
a. Think of many ways to deal with this problem?				
b. Think of good points about each way?				
c. Think of bad points about each way?				
d. Choose one way to deal with this problem?				
e. Follow these steps even when you are angry?				
f. Follow these steps even when you are tired?				
g. Follow these steps even when you are busy?				
h. Reward yourself with something you like for following these steps?				

Table 6

	Very Unsure	Sort of Unsure	Sort of Sure	Very Sure
22. Imagine yourself worrying about getting teased by classmates. How sure are you that you can follow each of these steps:				
a. Think of many ways to deal with this problem?				
b. Think of good points about each way?				
c. Think of bad points about each way?				
d. Choose one way to deal with this problem?				
e. Follow these steps even when you are angry?				
f. Follow these steps even when you are tired?				
g. Follow these steps even when you are busy?				
h. Reward yourself with something you like for following these steps?				

(continues)

FOCUS FEATURE 4.1   EXAMPLE OF A THEORY-BASED SCALE (Continued)

Table 7

	Very Unsure	Sort of Unsure	Sort of Sure	Very Sure
23. Imagine yourself worrying about your parents arguing. How sure are you that you can follow each of these steps:				
a. Think of many ways to deal with this problem?				
b. Think of good points about each way?				
c. Think of bad points about each way?				
d. Choose one way to deal with this problem?				
e. Follow these steps even when you are angry?				
f. Follow these steps even when you are tired?				
g. Follow these steps even when you are busy?				
h. Reward yourself with something you like for following these steps?				

Skills Exercise

Directions: In this exercise we are interested in finding out how you solve problems. Two situations are presented below which will be read to you. You may have had some of these problems yourself, while some others may be new to you. Be sure to listen carefully and work as best as you can. You have 10 minutes to write answers to each situation. That is a total of 20 minutes.

Please work on your own and do not discuss with anyone. Please remember spelling will not count. Your answers will *not* be graded by your teachers and will be kept secret. No parents, teachers, or other kids will see your answers.

24. John is a sixth-grade student at Lakeview Elementary School. He has been studying at this school since second grade. For the past few weeks he has handed in his homework late many times. He is worried.

   a. What do you think John's problem is?

   _____

   _____

FOCUS FEATURE 4.1   EXAMPLE OF A THEORY-BASED SCALE
(Continued)

Table 8

b. Please list different **ways** in which he can solve this problem:	c. Discuss the **good** points of each way:	d. Discuss the **bad** points of each way:

e. From the above list, choose the best solution to deal with this problem:

_____

_____

_____

(continues)

FOCUS FEATURE 4.1   EXAMPLE OF A THEORY-BASED SCALE (Continued)

25. Candi is a sixth-grade student at Forest Wood Elementary School. She has an older brother who is in the ninth grade and a younger sister who is in the third grade. For the past few months her parents have been arguing a lot. Often these arguments are in a loud voice. She is worried.

a. What do you think Candi's problem is?

_____

_____

Table 9

b. Please list different **ways** in which she can solve this problem:	c. Discuss the **good** points of each way:	d. Discuss the **bad** points of each way:

FOCUS FEATURE 4.1   EXAMPLE OF A THEORY-BASED SCALE (*Continued*)

e. From the above list choose the best solution to deal with this problem:

_____

_____

THANK YOU VERY MUCH FOR YOUR TIME AND EFFORT!

SCORING INSTRUCTIONS

For Item #5:

If the student marks "yes" in the problem and writes out the problem [Criteria: (1) legibly written (spelling doesn't count) and (2) makes sense to the reader in terms of being a coherent thought, (3) for item 1 pertains to school and item 2 pertains to home], count it in the tally sheet in the column of "problem identified" and progress further.

If the student marks "no" or marks "yes" but does not describe the problem [Criteria: (1) leaves the space blank, (2) writes out something that does not make any sense to the reader as a coherent thought (spelling doesn't count), (3) for item 1 does not pertain to school and for item 2 does not pertain to home] count it in the tally sheet in "no problem identified" and stop from scoring any further.

In the steps, for both items separately, if the student writes:

(1) "Thought of many ways" or something similar to that effect then count it in the column of "yes many ways." If nothing to this effect is mentioned, mark in the tally sheet in the column "not many ways."

(2) "Think of good and bad points about each way" or something similar to that effect then count it in the column of, "yes good and bad points." If nothing to that effect is mentioned, mark in the tally sheet in the column, "no good and bad points."

(3) "Chose one solution" or something to that effect then count it in, "yes chose solution." If nothing to that effect is mentioned, mark in the tally sheet in the column, "did not choose solution."

Table 10

Tally Sheet

	Problem Identified	No Problem Identified	Yes Many Ways	Not Many Ways	Yes Good and Bad Points	No Good and Bad Points	Yes Chose Solution	Did Not Choose Solution
a. School								
b. Home								

(continues)

FOCUS FEATURE 4.1   EXAMPLE OF A THEORY-BASED SCALE *(Continued)*

Scoring Situational Perception About Stressors

Use Items 6–9:

Scoring is:

How often does it happen to you?: Never (1), Hardly Ever (2), A Lot (3), Almost Always (4)
How bad does it make you feel?: Not Bad (1), A Little Bad (2), Real Bad (3), Terrible (4)

Multiply "How often does it happen to you score" with "How bad does it make you feel score" for each item from 6 to 9, and then sum the totals for items 6–9 (Range: 4–64).

Scoring Outcome Expectations and Outcome Expectancies About Problem-Solving Skills (Expectations About PSS)

Use Items 10–19:

Scoring is:

Expectations (Items 10–14): Never (1), Hardly Ever (2), A Lot (3), Almost Always (4)

Expectancies (Items 15–19): Not Important At All (1), Somewhat Important (2), Important (3), Very Important (4)

Multiply the score from Item 10 with Item 15, Item 11 with Item 16, Item 12 with Item 17, Item 13 with Item 18, and Item 14 with Item 19. Then sum to obtain the score of expectations of problem-solving skills (Range: 5–80).

Scoring Self-Efficacy About Problem-Solving Skills

Use Items 20–23, sections a through d:

Scoring: Very Unsure (1), Sort of Unsure (2), Sort of Sure (3), Very Sure (4)

Sum the scores for Items 20–23 on sections a through d (Range: 16–64).

Scoring Self-Efficacy in Overcoming Barriers While Implementing Problem-Solving Skills

Use Items 20–23, sections e through g:

Scoring: Very Unsure (1), Sort of Unsure (2), Sort of Sure (3), Very Sure (4)

Sum the scores for Items 20–23 on sections e through g (Range: 12–48).

Scoring Self-Control About Problem-Solving Skills

Use Items 20–23, section h:

Scoring: Very Unsure (1), Sort of Unsure (2), Sort of Sure (3), Very Sure (4)

Sum the scores for Items 20–23 on section h (Range: 4–16).

FOCUS FEATURE 4.1   EXAMPLE OF A THEORY-BASED SCALE *(Continued)*

Scoring Problem-Solving Skills (Items 24 and 25)

Situation 1 (Item 24):

1. Did the student identify the stressor?
   (For accurate identification—handing in homework late or similar meaning words—give 1; for inaccurate, give 0.)

2. How many alternative solutions [Criteria: (1) legibly written (spelling doesn't count), (2) makes sense to the reader as a coherent thought] did the student come up with?
   (For no solution, give 0;
   for 1 solution, give 1;
   for 2 solutions, give 2;
   for 3 solutions, give 3;
   for 4 or more, give 4.)

3. How many good and bad points did the student come up with [Criteria: (1) legibly written (spelling doesn't count), (2) makes sense to the reader as a coherent thought]?
   (For no points, give 0;
   for 1 way for 1 good and 1 bad point, give 1;
   for 1 way with more than 1 good or bad point for each, give 2;
   for 2 ways with 1 good and 1 bad point each, give 2;
   for 2 ways with more than 1 good or bad point for each, give 3;
   for 3 ways with 1 good and 1 bad point each, give 3;
   for 3 ways with more than 1 good and bad point each, give 4;
   for 4 or more ways with 1 good and 1 bad point each or more, give 4.)

4. Did the student pick one solution from the alternatives [Criteria: (1) legibly written (spelling doesn't count), (2) makes sense to the reader as a coherent thought]?
   (For picking a solution, give 1; for not picking, give 0.)

Situation 2 (Item 25):

5. Did the student identify the stressor?
   (For accurate identification—taking tests or similar-meaning words—give 1; for inaccurate, give 0.)

6. How many alternative solutions did the student come up with [Criteria: (1) legibly written (spelling doesn't count), (2) makes sense to the reader as a coherent thought]?
   (For no solution, give 0;
   for 1 solution, give 1;
   for 2 solutions, give 2;
   for 3 solutions, give 3;
   for 4 or more, give 4.)

7. How many good and bad points did the student come up with [Criteria: (1) legibly written (spelling doesn't count), (2) makes sense to the reader as a coherent thought]?
   (For no points, give 0;
   for 1 way for 1 good and 1 bad point, give 1;
   for 1 way with more than 1 good or bad point for each, give 2;
   for 2 ways with 1 good and 1 bad point each, give 2;

> ## FOCUS FEATURE 4.1   EXAMPLE OF A THEORY-BASED SCALE (Continued)
>
> for 2 ways with more than 1 good or bad point for each, give 3;
> for 3 ways with 1 good and 1 bad point each, give 3;
> for 3 ways with more than 1 good and bad point each, give 4;
> for 4 or more ways with 1 good and 1 bad point each or more, give 4.)
>
> 8. Did the student pick one solution from the alternatives [Criteria: (1) legibly written (spelling doesn't count), (2) makes sense to the reader as a coherent thought]? (For picking a solution, give 1; for not picking, give 0.)
>
> Total both situations to come up with a total score of PSS.
>
> *Source:* Instrument taken from: Sharma, M. (1997). Evaluation of a coping intervention developing problem solving skills among upper elementary school children based on social cognitive theory. Retrieved from ProQuest Dissertations and Theses (UMI No. AAT 9801785).

GENERAL PRINCIPLES OF WRITING ITEMS

Some general principles need to be kept in mind when writing items for a new instrument. Keeping these principles in mind will improve the quality of the instrument. It also will increase the likelihood that your subjects will understand and answer the items accurately. This goes a long way to enhancing the validity and reliability of the instrument. The principles are summarized in **Table 4.2**.

TYPES OF INSTRUMENTS MEASURING KNOWLEDGE

One of the common measures that health education and health promotion professionals are interested in evaluating is knowledge. Knowledge is among the most evaluated domains by health education and health promotion programs. Health educators commonly use two types of knowledge tests: (1) constructed response items instruments, and (2) selected response items instruments (McDermott & Sarvela, 1999). In **constructed response items instruments**, the test taker develops his or her own answer in response to the questions. Examples of constructed response items instruments are (1) item completion questions or fill in the blanks, (2) short essays, and (3) extended item essays. These tests are helpful when the program objectives are to explain, describe, define, state, or write about topics (Roid & Haladyna, 1982). In **selected response items instruments**, the test takers choose the answers from a set of possible answers. Examples of selected response items instruments are (1) true–false questions, (2) multiple choice questions, and (3) matching the response questions. These tests are helpful when the program objectives are to identify, differentiate, distinguish, and match (Roid & Haladyna, 1982).

A good item is concise, clear, relevant, nonbiased, non-negative, and not double-barreled.

TABLE 4.2 Principles to Keep in Mind While Developing Items for New Instruments

Principle

1. *Compose clear items.*

   Clear item: "The item is short." Here the item is tapping in only one dimension and is clear.

   Unclear item: "The item is short, precise, and brief." Here the item is tapping several things.

2. *Do not use jargons, abbreviations, or multisyllable words.*

   Good item: "The American College of Sports Medicine recommends moderately intense cardio exercise for 30 minutes a day for at least 5 days a week."

   Bad item: "The ACSM recommends moderately intense cardio for 30 min/day for at least 5 days/wk."

3. *Avoid double-barrel items.*

   Good item: "The item is short."

   Double-barrel item: "The item is short and clear." Here the item could be short but not clear, thus posing a problem to the respondent.

4. *Keep items short. Long items tend to be confusing and convoluted.*

   Short item: "The item is short."

   Long item: "The item is decidedly short and precise but is not optimal in length."

5. *Try to avoid negative items.*

   Positive item: "The item is good."

   Negative item: "The item is not good." Here the respondent may have a difficult time interpreting negativity.

6. *Try to avoid biased items.*

   Neutral item: "Evaluate the items in this scale."

   Biased item: "Good items constitute this scale." Here the respondent may be swayed to mark positively.

7. *Include only relevant items. Remove irrelevant items. Focus only on items that match with operational definitions.*

   For example, for self-efficacy to jog:

   Relevant item: "How sure are you that you can jog for 30 minutes?"

   Irrelevant item: "How sure are you that you can run for 30 minutes?"

8. *Frame an item such that the respondent is able to answer it completely.*

   For example, for self-efficacy to jog:

   Complete item: "How sure are you that you can jog for 30 minutes?"

   Incomplete item: "How sure are you that you can jog?"

To test knowledge about the previous paragraph, we can use all six types of questions. Here are examples of such questions:

1. *Item completion question:* Instruments that require the test takers choose the answers from a set of possible answers are known as _____ items instruments.
2. *Short essay:* Describe the two types of knowledge tests.
3. *Extended essay:* Describe the two types of knowledge tests. Provide examples for each of the two types and explain which objectives would be appropriate for which test.
4. *True–false question:* Indicate whether the following statement is true or false: In constructed response items instruments, the test takers choose the answers from a set of possible answers. (Answer: false)
5. *Multiple choice question:* Circle the most appropriate choice:
   All of the following are examples of selected response items instruments, except:
   a. true–false questions
   b. multiple choice questions
   c. item completion questions
   d. matching the response questions
   (Answer: c)
6. *Matching the response question:* The phrases below describe the various terms about knowledge tests used in health education. Match the description with the term.
   _____ Test takers choose the answers from a set of possible answers.
   _____ Fill in the blanks.
   _____ The test taker develops his or her own answer in response to the questions.
   _____ Pick one choice from several choices.

   a. constructed response items instruments
   b. selected response items instruments
   c. item completion questions
   d. multiple choice questions
   (Answer: b, c, a, d)

With regard to formulating item completion and short essay questions, Ebel and Frisbie (1991) have some suggestions:

- Before writing the item, think of the answer. Then write the question so that the desired answer is the only appropriate choice.
- There should be a single, unique answer.
- Use a direct question as much as possible.
- Ensure there are no unintended clues toward the answer in the question.
- Be concise in composing the question.

Ebel and Frisbie (1991) also have some suggestions regarding formulating essay questions:

- Ask questions that are determinate, meaning that it should be generally agreed that one answer is better than any other.

- Ask questions so that the respondent can demonstrate essential knowledge.
- Have specific questions that can be answered briefly.
- Compose a model answer to each question.
- Avoid giving options. Have respondents answer all questions.

Ebel and Frisbie (1991) also have the following suggestions regarding formulating true–false questions:

- Both memory and understanding must be tested.
- Questions should test knowledge of important ideas.
- There should be one correct answer.
- Avoid using negatives or double negatives.
- Keep sentences short.
- Use only a single idea in the question.

Ebel and Frisbie (1991) offer the following tips for formulating matching questions:

- Questions and answers should constitute a homogenous set of content.
- Directions should be clear.
- The premise in the matching question should be longer than the response.

With regard to multiple choice questions there also are some suggestions:

- There should be four or five choices per question.
- There should be one correct answer with no ambiguity.
- The incorrect answers, also known as distracters, should be closely related to the answer.
- These types of questions can be used to test knowledge, understanding, problem solving, and decision making.

When developing items for knowledge tests, identify the precise answer first before developing the question.

TYPES OF INSTRUMENTS MEASURING ATTITUDES

Attitudes are relatively constant feelings, predispositions, or sets of beliefs directed toward an idea, object, person, or situation (Mucchielli, 1970). Attitudes are enduring beliefs with a strong evaluative component. They also have an affective component and demonstrate what one likes and what one does not like. Health educators are often required to measure health-related attitudes. Most of the constructs in behavioral theories are essentially attitudes, such as subjective norm (from the theory of reasoned action and theory of planned behavior), perceived behavioral control (from the theory of planned behavior), self-efficacy for a given behavior (from social cognitive theory), situational perception (from social cognitive theory), consciousness raising (from the transtheoretical model), and perceived susceptibility (from the health belief model). Attitudes are typically measured by self-reporting scales. In health education there are six common types of self-report instruments measuring attitudes:

1. Summated rating Likert scales
2. Equal appearing interval scales (e.g., Thurstone)

3. Cumulative scales (e.g., Guttman)
4. Semantic differential rating scales
5. Forced choice (paired comparisons) scales
6. Visual analog scales (VAS)

Summated Rating Likert Scales

Summated rating Likert scales are the most often used scales in health education and health promotion. These are composed of items that are approximately equal in their attitudinal value, and the respondents respond to these items in terms of the extent of agreement or disagreement (Kerlinger & Lee, 2000). This type of scale was first developed by Rensis Likert for his dissertation (Likert, 1932). The scale uses several items to measure any given attribute, and the responses are summed to obtain a total score. These scales are also sometimes called agreement scales (Henderson, Morris, & Fitz-Gibbon, 1978). An example of the summated rating Likert scale is the Rosenberg self-esteem scale (Rosenberg, 1965, 1989). This scale is shown in **Focus Feature 4.2**. The scale also shows the role of reverse coding, where a score of 0 is assigned to what would be marked as 3 and vice versa. This reversing is helpful to keep someone from marking everything positive or everything negative.

> *Summated rating Likert scales are often used in health education and health promotion.*

Construction of these scales is very well suited within the theoretical framework discussed in this chapter, including reducing concepts into constructs, into indicators, and then into variables. The traditional Likert scale has the response rating strongly agree (5), agree (4), neutral (3), disagree (2), and strongly disagree (1). In this response rating the neutral point posed problems because it was neither positive nor negative and was given a scoring of 3. Contemporary researchers have eliminated the neutral point. They also use other variations of the response scale such as not at all important (1), not important (2), somewhat important (3), important (4), and very important (5) or never (1), hardly ever (2), sometimes (3), a lot (4), and almost always (5).

Another thing to keep in mind while making these scales is that all the items in the scale should be one-dimensional or measuring the same thing. If more dimensions are required, then different subscales should be constructed. If a theoretical framework is not being used, then discrimination indices should be used. One can use discrimination indices to decipher which items differentiate most clearly between those people who have favorable and unfavorable responses toward the attitude. Then one can select at least six items that have the best discrimination indices to form the scale (Miller & Salkind, 2002).

Equal Appearing Interval Scales

Equal appearing interval scales consist of items measuring attitude; each item has a scale value indicative of the strength of attitude toward the item. An example of this type of scale is the **Thurstone scale** (Thurstone & Chave, 1929). These days, these scales are rarely used in health education and health promotion.

FOCUS FEATURE 4.2   ROSENBERG SELF-ESTEEM SCALE

Instructions: Below is a list of statements dealing with your general feelings about yourself. If you strongly agree, circle **SA**. If you agree with the statement, circle **A**. If you disagree, circle **D**. If you strongly disagree, circle **SD**.

1.	On the whole, I am satisfied with myself.	SA	A	D	SD
2.*	At times, I think I am no good at all.	SA	A	D	SD
3.	I feel that I have a number of good qualities.	SA	A	D	SD
4.	I am able to do things as well as most other people.	SA	A	D	SD
5.*	I feel I do not have much to be proud of.	SA	A	D	SD
6.*	I certainly feel useless at times.	SA	A	D	SD
7.	I feel that I'm a person of worth, at least on an equal plane with others.	SA	A	D	SD
8.*	I wish I could have more respect for myself.	SA	A	D	SD
9.*	All in all, I am inclined to feel that I am a failure.	SA	A	D	SD
10.	I take a positive attitude toward myself.	SA	A	D	SD

Scoring: SA = 3, A = 2, D = 1, SD = 0. Items with an asterisk are reverse scored, that is, SA = 0, A = 1, D = 2, SD = 3. Sum the scores for the 10 items. The higher the score, the higher the self-esteem.

Source: Rosenberg, Morris. 1989. *Society and the Adolescent Self-Image*. Revised edition. Middletown, CT: Wesleyan University Press. Available at http://www.bsos.umd.edu/socy/research/rosenberg.htm

In order to construct a Thurstone scale, a large number of items (approximately 100) related to the attitude are gathered. Then expert judges sort these items into 11 groups ranging from highest to lowest or most favorable to least favorable. The median rank value is selected as the item's weight. Statements that are judged differently by different judges are eliminated as being irrelevant or ambiguous. The final step is to choose a representative set of items from the total set that includes favorable, neutral, and unfavorable attitudes.

A hypothetical example of a Thurstone scale examining attitudes toward heart disease is as follows:

- I believe heart disease hinders one's normal living. (Scale value 0.5)
- I believe heart disease requires some adjustment in one's life. (Scale value 5.5)
- I believe heart disease requires no change in one's life. (Scale value 9.5)

Cumulative Scales

Cumulative scales are scales composed of a set of items arranged by their degree of positivity or favorableness toward the variable under study. An example of this scale is the

Guttman scale, developed by Louis Guttman (1944). Here is an example of this scale created by Mueller (1986):

Abortion should be given on demand.	Yes	No
Abortion is acceptable for family planning.	Yes	No
Abortion is acceptable in rape cases.	Yes	No
Abortion is acceptable if the fetus is malformed.	Yes	No
Abortion is acceptable when a mother's life is in danger.	Yes	No

In this example, a person who agrees with the first statement is likely to agree with all the other statements and is most liberal. He or she would receive a score of 5. A person who agrees with the second statement is likely to agree with the remaining statements and would receive a score of 4. A person who agrees with the third statement is likely to agree with the remaining two and would receive a score of 3. A person who agrees with the fourth statement is likely to agree with the remaining one and would receive a score of 2. A person who agrees with the last statement is not likely to agree with the preceding statements and would receive a score of 1. It is a difficult scale to construct, and therefore is not commonly used in health education and health promotion work.

Semantic Differential Rating Scales

Semantic differential rating scales are scales that use bipolar adjectives. Osgood (1952) first developed the semantic differential scale. An example of a semantic differential scale is the operationalization of the construct of behavioral beliefs from the theory of planned behavior (Ajzen, 1991) about physical activity in schoolchildren:

If I am physically active at least 60 minutes a day, I will:

1. . . . be healthier.	Unlikely	1	2	3	4	5	6	7	Likely
2. . . . have more energy.	Unlikely	1	2	3	4	5	6	7	Likely
3. . . . have more confidence.	Unlikely	1	2	3	4	5	6	7	Likely
4. . . . lose/maintain my weight.	Unlikely	1	2	3	4	5	6	7	Likely
5. . . . be less stressed.	Unlikely	1	2	3	4	5	6	7	Likely

Semantic differential scales are commonly used by health education researchers and evaluators who use the theory of reasoned action or the theory of planned behavior in their work. DiIorio (2005) notes that semantic differential scales generally measure three dimensions: (1) *evaluation*, as measured by bad/good, nice awful, fair/unfair; (2) *potency*, as measured by small/large, weak/strong, hard/soft; and (3) *activity*, as measured by active/passive, slow/fast, and sharp/dull. Some of the bipolar adjectives commonly used in semantic differential scales in health education and health promotion are:

Healthy	____	____	____	____	____	____	____	Unhealthy
Effective	____	____	____	____	____	____	____	Ineffective
Efficient	____	____	____	____	____	____	____	Inefficient
Easy	____	____	____	____	____	____	____	Difficult
Safe	____	____	____	____	____	____	____	Unsafe

Stress-free	____	____	____	____	____	____	____	Stressful
Moral	____	____	____	____	____	____	____	Immoral
Happy	____	____	____	____	____	____	____	Sad
Harmless	____	____	____	____	____	____	____	Harmful
Sufficient	____	____	____	____	____	____	____	Insufficient

Forced Choice (Paired Comparisons) Scales

Forced choice (paired comparisons) scales involve having a respondent select one item from two choices. With a series of such items, a score is then derived. An example of a paired comparison with regard to physical activity attitudes is:

Pair 1: Choose one of the two choices:
  • A physically active life is good.
  • A sedentary life is good.
Pair 2: Choose one of the two choices:
  • Playing basketball is good.
  • Playing chess is good.
Pair 3: Choose one of the two choices:
  • Playing football is good.
  • Reading is good.

A person who chooses the first choice in all three pairs values a physically active life more than someone who chooses all the second choices. These scales have limited utility in health education and health promotion.

Visual Analog Scales (VAS)

Visual analog scales are a type of graphic rating scales. The first visual analog scale was described by Freyd in 1923 for assessing personality traits. These scales are popular in medicine and nursing, where they are used to measure attributes such as pain, nausea, dyspnea, and fatigue. A straight horizontal or vertical line of 100 mm in length is drawn; on one side of the line is written "no pain" and on the other side is "worst pain." The patient would then be asked to mark their rating at the appropriate point on the line. (See **Figure 4.2**.) Each respondent's numeric score is determined by measuring the distance from one end to the point marked. The 100 mm line has a special meaning because it helps the evaluator to measure on a continuous scale from 0 (none) to 100 (maximum). Sometimes gradations (10, 20, 30, etc.) are also provided on this scale to help the respondent make a more accurate response.

No pain |————————————————————————————————| Worst pain

Figure 4.2 Example of a visual analog scale (VAS).

TYPES OF INSTRUMENTS MEASURING HEALTH BEHAVIOR

A very important indicator of change in health education and health promotion programs is health behavior. Both health education and health promotion programs are interested in changing unhealthy behaviors and developing healthy behaviors, so measurement of behavior assumes importance and is a critical impact variable. Three things are required when measuring behavior: frequency, intensity, and duration. Health behavior is often measured in two ways: self-report and direct observation. More recently, behavior is being measured in a third way—by technology such as accelerometers and pedometers.

Self-Report of Behavior

Self-report of behavior is a common approach in the measurement of health-related behaviors. For some behaviors, such as safer sex behaviors, this is the only way one can measure behavior. Examples of methods of self-reporting behaviors include nutrition diaries, stressor diaries, physical activity logs, and the like. Romas and Sharma (2010) have developed a stress awareness log that records various stressors in the following format:

- Time of day
- Signals
- Stressors
- How am I dealing with the stressors?
- How effective have I been?
- What else can I do?

There are both advantages and disadvantages to keeping logs and diaries. Some of the advantages are that issues with recall are minimized, there is a fairly accurate record of the behavior being observed, and it provides a written record. Some of the disadvantages are that they are time consuming, data varies from one participant to another, they require frequent reminders from the evaluators, not all participants complete their records, and they tend to have social desirability bias (people like to write things they think evaluators may like to see).

There are also self-report behavioral questionnaires that elicit response about behaviors from participants. Examples of such questionnaires are the Behavioral Risk Factor Surveillance System (BRFSS) questionnaire and the Youth Risk Behavior Surveillance System (YRBSS) questionnaire. The following are some of the questions from the BRFSS questionnaire pertaining to tobacco behavior (Centers for Disease Control and Prevention, 2010):

11.1 Have you smoked at least 100 cigarettes in your entire life?
Note: 5 packs = 100 cigarettes.
    1 Yes
    2 No [Go to Q11.5]
    7 Don't know/Not sure [Go to Q11.5]
    9 Refused [Go to Q11.5]

11.2 Do you now smoke cigarettes every day, some days, or not at all?
  1 Every day
  2 Some days
  3 Not at all [Go to Q11.4]
  7 Don't know/Not sure [Go to Q11.5]
  9 Refused [Go to Q11.5]

11.3 During the past 12 months, have you stopped smoking for one day or longer because you were trying to quit smoking?
  1 Yes [Go to Q11.5]
  2 No [Go to Q11.5]
  7 Don't know/Not sure [Go to Q11.5]
  9 Refused [Go to Q11.5]

11.4 How long has it been since you last smoked cigarettes regularly?
  0 1 Within the past month (less than 1 month ago)
  0 2 Within the past 3 months (1 month but less than 3 months ago)
  0 3 Within the past 6 months (3 months but less than 6 months ago)
  0 4 Within the past year (6 months but less than 1 year ago)
  0 5 Within the past 5 years (1 year but less than 5 years ago)
  0 6 Within the past 10 years (5 years but less than 10 years ago)
  0 7 10 years or more
  0 8 Never smoked regularly
  7 7 Don't know/Not sure
  9 9 Refused

11.5 Do you currently use chewing tobacco, snuff, or snus every day, some days, or not at all?
  Note: Snus (rhymes with "goose") is Swedish for snuff. It is a moist smokeless tobacco, usually sold in small pouches that are placed under the lip against the gum.
  1 Every day
  2 Some days
  3 Not at all
  7 Don't know/Not sure
  9 Refused

Observation of Behavior

This method entails direct **observation of behavior** and is sometimes called an obtrusive measure. Although observations are generally more accurate than self-reports. they are utilized less often in evaluations because they are expensive and time consuming. When using observations, evaluators must establish reliability every time they observe the behavior, thus adding to the cost of the procedure. Observations are particularly valuable in assessing fidelity to intervention in process evaluations.

In making observation checklists for behaviors, the following questions should be kept in mind:

- How many observers will there be?
- What is the unit of observation?
- What are the details of what is to be observed?
- How many observations should be made?
- How much time should be devoted for observation?
- What is the method of recording?

There must be a minimum of two observers so that rater/interrater reliability can be established. In selecting behaviors to be observed, the evaluator must decide what constitutes a unit. Polit and Hungler (1999) have described two approaches. The first is the *molar approach*, which entails observing large units of behavior and treating them as a whole. For example, in observing physical activity in children, all movements involving large muscle groups would be counted as being physically active. The second approach is the *molecular approach*, which entails measuring small and highly specific behaviors as the unit of observation. For example, in observing physical activity, the observer may be interested in documenting the kicking movement. The choice of which approach to use depends on the type of evaluation problem and the preference of the evaluator.

The question of how many observations should be made and how much time is needed for observations depends on the type of behavior and the resources available for observations. With regard to recording of behavior, the observer can do so with his or her sensory perception or use audio or video recordings to aid in the process. **Table 4.3** summarizes the advantages and disadvantages of observation of behavior as a method.

PHYSIOLOGICAL AND BIOMEDICAL INSTRUMENTS: OUTCOMES OF BEHAVIOR

Sometimes health education and health promotion programs require instruments that measure physiological and biomedical variables. Although the health educator would most likely not be developing instruments or measuring these variables on their own, some

TABLE 4.3 Advantages and Disadvantages of Observation of Behavior
Advantages
1. Observers are able to capture behaviors an individual may not be aware of.
2. Observers are human beings, which are sensitive and intelligent tools.
3. Dishonesty in self-report is not an issue.
Disadvantages
1. Often it is not ethical to observe all behaviors.
2. There may be a lack of consent to being observed.
3. Observation is a demanding task and subject to errors and subjectivity.
4. Observation is subject to observational biases.

understanding of these variables would be helpful for the health educator. **Table 4.4** summarizes some of these physiological and biomedical variables.

SKILL-BUILDING ACTIVITY

In this activity, you will consider social cognitive theory using the constructs of expectations, expectancies, and self-efficacy. Consider the behavior of physical activity in college students. You are to develop an instrument for these three constructs for physical activity behavior in college students. Operationally define each of the three constructs and generate potential items. Then choose a rating scale and prepare a draft instrument.

SUMMARY

An instrument or a scale is a tool that measures concepts and constructs by reducing them into variables. There are 16 steps in instrument development:

1. Defining the purpose of instrument development
2. Reviewing existing instruments related to the purpose
3. Identifying objects of interest
4. Constitutively defining each object of interest (concept–construct)

TABLE 4.4 Common Physiological and Biomedical Variables in Health Education and Health Promotion Programs

Domain	Examples
Cardio-respiratory fitness	Submaximal exercise capacity
	Maximal oxygen uptake
	Maximal aerobic power
	Blood pressure
	Electrocardiograph (ECG)
Muscular strength	Arm curls
	Bench presses
Flexibility	Sit and reach tests
	Trunk extension
Body composition	Body mass index (BMI)
	Waist circumference
	Skinfold test
	Underwater weighing
Blood chemistry	Cholesterol (HDL, LDL, VLDL)
	Blood glucose (fasting/postprandial)
	Hemoglobin a1c
	HIV/AIDS screening
	Serum cotinine
Stress	Salivary cortisol
	Electroencephalograph (EEG)
	Electromyograph (EMG)
	Galvanic skin response (GSR)

5. Prioritizing how many objects of interest are to be measured
6. Operationally defining selected objects of interest (indicator–variable)
7. Choosing the scale of measurement
8. Developing items
9. Preparing a draft with directions, scoring, and layout
10. Testing for readability and adjusting according to the target population
11. Sending it to a panel of experts (usually six) for face and content validation
12. Conducting a minimum of two rounds with the panel of experts and revising the instrument based on feedback
13. Conducting a pilot test with a small sample of the target population for readability, comprehension, time of completion, and the like
14. Establishing reliability: internal consistency and stability
15. Establishing construct validity: confirmatory factor analysis
16. Establishing criterion validity, if applicable: comparison with other scales of the same measure

When developing items for new instruments, one must compose clear items; not use jargon, abbreviations, or multisyllable words; avoid double-barrel items; keep items short; try to avoid negative items; avoid biased items; include only relevant items; and frame an item such that the respondent is able to answer it completely. Health educators commonly use two types of knowledge tests: constructed response items instruments and selected response items instruments.

In health education there are six common types of self-report instruments measuring attitudes: (1) summated rating Likert scales, (2) equal appearing interval scales (e.g., Thurstone), (3) cumulative scales (e.g., Guttman), (4) semantic differential rating scales, (5) forced choice (paired comparisons) scales, and (6) visual analog scales (VAS). Health behavior is often measured in two ways: self-report and direct observation. More recently, behavior is being measured in a third way—by technology such as accelerometers and pedometers.

REVIEW QUESTIONS

1. Define an instrument in the context of health education and health promotion programs. Describe the steps in instrument development.
2. Differentiate between constitutive definition and operational definition with the help of an example.
3. Differentiate between the Flesch Reading Ease score and the Flesch-Kincaid Grade Level score.
4. Differentiate between face validity and content validity.
5. Differentiate between internal consistency and stability.
6. Describe the types of instruments used in health education and health promotion for measuring knowledge.
7. Describe the types of instruments used in health education and health promotion for measuring attitudes.

8. Differentiate between the Guttman scale and the Thurstone scale.
9. Describe the types of instruments used in health education and health promotion for measuring behavior.
10. Give examples of commonly used physiological and biomedical instruments in health education and health promotion.

WEBSITES TO EXPLORE

Guttman Scaling

http://www.socialresearchmethods.net/kb/scalgutt.php
This website describes the process of Guttman scaling. Read the account and the example provided. Relate it to the reading in this chapter. *Develop a draft of a Guttman scale on a health topic of your choice.*

Likert Scaling

http://www.socialresearchmethods.net/kb/scallik.php
This website describes the process of Likert scaling. Read the account and the example provided. Relate it to the reading in this chapter. *Develop a draft of a Likert scale on a health topic of your choice.*

Pain Scale

http://www.ttuhsc.edu/som/clinic/forms/ACForm3.02.A.pdf
This website shows several different scales used to measure pain: Faces Pain Scale, Visual Analog Scale (VAS), Pain Assessment of Infants Scale, and Nonverbal Pain Assessment Scale. *Review these four scales and discuss the advantages and disadvantages of each.*

Thurstone Scaling

http://www.socialresearchmethods.net/kb/scalthur.php
This website describes the process of Thurstone scaling. Read the account and go through the example provided. Relate it to the reading in this chapter. *Develop some items for Thurstone scaling on a health topic of your choice.*

What Are Assessment Instruments?

http://www.jmu.edu/assessment/pass/assmntresources/instruments.htm
This is the website of the Program Assessment Support Service of James Madison University. The website defines assessment instruments and discusses criteria for developing or selecting an instrument. Read the webpage and pay attention to the "How Do I Create Instruments?" section. *Compare the steps discussed in this chapter with the steps described on the website. What are the similarities and differences?*

REFERENCES

Ajzen, I. (1991). The theory of planned behavior. *Organizational Behavior and Human Decision Process, 50,* 179–211.

Bandura, A. (1986). *Social foundations of thought and action.* Englewood Cliffs, NJ: Prentice Hall.

Bandura, A. (2004). Health promotion by social cognitive means. *Health Education and Behavior, 31,* 143–164.

Centers for Disease Control and Prevention (CDC). (2010). *Behavioral risk factor surveillance system survey questionnaire.* Atlanta, GA: U.S. Department of Health and Human Services, Centers for Disease Control and Prevention.

DiIorio, C. K. (2005). *Measurement in health behavior. Methods for research and education.* San Francisco, CA: Jossey-Bass.

Ebel, R. L., & Frisbie, D. A. (1991). *Essentials of educational measurement* (5th ed.). Englewood Cliffs, NJ: Prentice Hall.

Freyd, M. (1922). The measurement of interests in vocational selection. *Journal of Personnel Research, 1,* 319–328.

Green, L. W., & Lewis, F. M. (1986). *Measurement and evaluation in health education and health promotion.* Palo Alto, CA: Mayfield.

Guttman, L. (1944). A basis for scaling qualitative data. *American Sociological Review, 9*(2), 139–150.

Henderson, M. E., Morris, L. L., & Fitz-Gibbon, C. T. (1978). *How to measure attitudes.* Beverly Hills, CA: Sage.

Kerlinger, F. N., & Lee, H. B. (2000). *Foundations of behavioral research* (4th ed.). Fort Worth, TX: Harcourt College.

Likert, R. (1932). A technique for the measurement of attitudes. *Archives of Psychology, 22*(140), 5–55.

McDermott, R. J., & Sarvela, P. D. (1999). *Health education evaluation and measurement. A practitioner's perspective* (2nd ed.). New York: McGraw-Hill.

Miller, D. C., & Salkind, N. J. (2002). *Handbook of research design and social measurement* (6th ed.). Thousand Oaks, CA: Sage.

Mucchielli, R. (1970). *Introduction to structural psychology.* New York: Funk and Wagnalls.

Mueller, D. J. (1986). *Measuring social attitudes.* New York: Teachers College Press.

Osgood, C. E. (1952). The nature and measurement of meaning. *Psychological Bulletin, 49*(3), 197–237.

Polit, D. F., & Hungler, B. P. (1999). *Nursing research: Principles and methods* (6th ed.). Philadelphia: Lippincott.

Roid, G. H., & Haladyna, T. M. (1982). *A technology for test-item writing.* New York: Academic Press.

Romas, J. A., & Sharma, M. (2010). *Practical stress management. A comprehensive workbook for managing change and promoting health* (5th ed.). San Francisco: Benjamin Cummings.

Rosenberg, M. (1965). *Society and the adolescent self-image.* Princeton, NJ: Princeton University Press.

Rosenberg, M. (1989). *Society and the adolescent self-image* (Rev. ed.). Middletown, CT: Wesleyan University Press.

Sharma, M. (1997). Evaluation of a coping intervention developing problem solving skills among upper elementary school children based on social cognitive theory. Retrieved from ProQuest Dissertations and Theses (UMI No. AAT 9801785).

Thurstone, L. L., & Chave, E. J. (1929). *The measurement of attitude: A psychophysical method and some experiments with a scale for measuring attitude toward the church.* Chicago: University of Chicago Press.

CHAPTER 5

Reliability Assessment

KEY CONCEPTS

- alternative-forms reliability
- classical test theory
- Cohen's kappa
- Cronbach's alpha
- equivalence
- internal consistency reliability
- interobserver reliability
- intraobserver reproducibility
- intrarater reliability
- Kuder-Richardson Formula-20 (KR-20)
- Kuder-Richardson Formula-21 (KR-21)
- parallel tests
- rater-interrater reliability
- Spearman-Brown split-half reliability method
- split-half method
- stability
- test-retest reliability
- variance

CHAPTER OBJECTIVES

- Define reliability
- List types of reliability
- Describe internal consistency reliability and how it is measured
- Explain test-retest reliability (stability) and how it is measured
- Describe interobserver (rater-interrater) reliability and how it is measured
- Explain intraobserver reproducibility
- Describe equivalence
- Use PASW to calculate reliability statistics

DEFINITION OF RELIABILITY

Reliability is an essential attribute for assessing the adequacy and quality of any instrument to be used in an evaluation. The term *reliability* has several synonyms such as consistency, repeatability, reproducibility, precision, dependability, and stability. We define reliability as the ability of an instrument to measure repeatedly the same results and be internally

> *Reliability is the ability of an instrument to measure repeatedly the same results and be internally consistent.*

consistent. Polit and Hungler (1999, p. 397) define reliability as "the degree of consistency with which it measures the attribute it is supposed to be measuring." It is important to note that the reliability of an instrument is not a property of the instrument per se but is a function of the target population to which it is administered and the conditions under which it is administered. That is why reliability needs to be determined every time an instrument is used. The concepts of reliability and validity are shown in **Figures 5.1 to 5.3**. Hitting the bull's eye equates to being valid, and hitting the same spot again and again is reliability.

Based on classical test theory, DiIorio (2005, p. 176) defines reliability as "the proportion of observed score variance that is explained by the true-score variance." **Classical test theory** is a set of propositions that was developed to explain the concept of reliability. According to this theory, there is always a true score associated with an individual's responses on any given instrument. This true score is the individual's real level of knowledge, strength of attitude, or measure of behavior measured under ideal conditions. In reality, however, such ideal conditions cannot be replicated so all measurements will have some error. This concept can be depicted in the following mathematical equation:

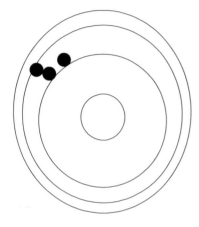

Figure 5.1 Example of something being reliable but not valid.

$$\text{Observed score (X)} = \text{True score (T)} + \text{Error score (E)}$$

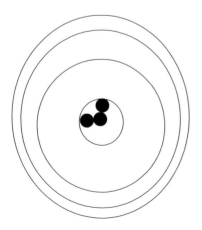

Figure 5.2 Example of something being reliable and valid.

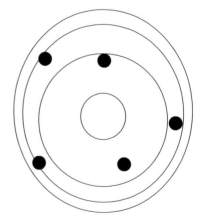

Figure 5.3 Example of something being neither reliable nor valid.

Both the true score (T) and error (E) are unobservable (latent), but the greater the error is the more unreliable the instrument will be. A reliable instrument is one that maximizes the true score component and minimizes the error component. There are three assumptions in this equation: (1) If multiple tests are done, the sum and mean of the error scores are zero—sometimes the error increases the score, but sometimes the error decreases the score, thereby cancelling out and resulting in zero; (2) the true score and error score are uncorrelated; and (3) error scores across **parallel tests** are uncorrelated (parallel tests are tests that have the same mean, variance, and correlations with other tests, such as Form A or Form B on the GRE).

In order to understand the concept of reliability you need to first understand variance. **Variance** is the variation or dispersion in a set of scores or a measure of how far a set of numbers are spread out from each other. Variance in observed scores is a function of true differences among respondents and error. This is depicted in the following mathematical equation:

Observed variance (OV) = True variance (TV) + Error variance (EV)

Both the true variance (TV) and error variance (EV) are unobservable (latent). Reliability, as you saw earlier, is the proportion of variance in the observed score that is explained by the true score. This is shown mathematically as:

Reliability coefficient (r^2) = TV/OV

OV = TV + EV, so we can substitute and get the following equation:

Reliability coefficient (r^2) = TV / (TV + EV)

From this equation it is evident that when the EV is low, the reliability coefficient will move toward 1; however, when the EV is large, the reliability coefficient will move toward 0. Hence the reliability coefficient ranges from 0 to 1, with higher values indicating a higher proportion of variance. However, it is important to note that a perfect instrument that has a perfect reliability has not, does not, and is not likely to exist.

TYPES OF RELIABILITY

There are four types of reliability. The classification of reliability is dependent on two factors, namely, type of instrument and time of application. In terms of the type of instrument, consideration is given as to whether the instrument is self-report or observation. Time of application refers to whether the instrument is administered once or more than once at different times. Based on these two factors, the different types of reliability are depicted in **Table 5.1**.

TABLE 5.1 Types of Reliability		
Type of Instrument/Time	**Same Time**	**Different Time**
Self-report	Internal consistency reliability	Test-retest reliability (stability)
Observer	Interobserver (rater-interrater) reliability	Intraobserver reproducibility

In addition, there is one more type of reliability called equivalence or correlation between parallel tests.

Internal Consistency Reliability

Internal consistency reliability measures the extent to which each item in an instrument is related to other items. Nunnally and Bernstein (1994) define internal consistency reliability as the degree to which items hang together. Green and Lewis (1986, p. 86) explain internal consistency reliability as that which "examines the intercorrelations or covariance of all the individual items making up the instrument." Internal consistency reliability is the extent of association, correlation, or covariance of a set of measurements that are developed to measure the same unidimensional concept.

> *Internal consistency reliability measures the extent to which each item in an instrument is related to other items.*

When evaluating internal consistency, an assumption is made that the instrument must be self-report, linear, and summative (Nunnally & Bernstein, 1994). It can be inferred from this assumption that the instrument must be unidimensional or measuring only one dimension. Hence, if you have a scale based on social cognitive theory that has reified the constructs of situational perception, outcome expectations, outcome expectancies, self-efficacy, and self-control, then you will have to determine the internal consistency of five subscales separately, each representing one dimension. Also important to note is that internal consistency can only be calculated if the scale has multiple items. The concept of internal consistency reliability does not apply to single-item scales.

There are three primary approaches to calculating internal consistency reliability: Cronbach's alpha, Kuder-Richardson Formula-20, and the split-half method.

Cronbach's Alpha

This is the most popular approach, and is commonly used in health education and health promotion. **Cronbach's alpha** is a summary measure of internal consistency reliability that is based on calculating the amount of intercorrelation or relationship between all items at the same time (Cronbach, 1951). Cronbach's alpha is computed by taking the mean of the individual item-to-item correlations and adjusting for the total items. Cronbach's alpha can be calculated using correlation or a variance-covariance matrix (DiIorio, 2005). The mathematical equation for calculating Cronbach's alpha using correlation is as follows (DiIorio, 2005):

$$\alpha = N\rho \ / \ [1 + \rho(N - 1)]$$

where,

α = Cronbach's alpha
N = Number of items
ρ = Mean inter-item correlation

The mathematical equation for calculating Cronbach's alpha using a variance-covariance matrix is as follows (DiIorio, 2005):

$$\alpha = N/(N-1) \; [1 - \Sigma\sigma^2_i \,/\, \Sigma\sigma^2_i + 2(\Sigma\sigma^2_{ii})]$$

where,

α = Cronbach's alpha
N = Number of items
$\Sigma\sigma^2_i$ = Sum of item variances
$2(\Sigma\sigma^2_{ii})$ = Twice the sum of the covariances below (or above) the diagonal

The value of Cronbach's alpha ranges from 0 to 1, with values closer to 1 indicative of higher internal consistency. An acceptable level for scales is generally considered to be equal to or over 0.70 (Carmines & Zeller, 1979; Nunnally & Bernstein, 1994). For newer scales, lower values may be considered acceptable. DeVellis (2003) suggests that a Cronbach's alpha below 0.60 is unacceptable, between 0.60 and 0.65 is undesirable, between 0.65 and 0.70 is minimally acceptable, between 0.70 and 0.80 is respectable, and between 0.80 and 0.90 is very good; for scores above 0.90 DeVellis recommends shortening the scale.

Cronbach's alpha is a summary measure of internal consistency reliability that is based on calculating the amount of intercorrelation or relationship between all items at the same time. Calculating Cronbach's alpha is the most popular and commonly used approach in health education and health promotion.

Some of the scales that have used Cronbach's alpha are the Adolescent Physical Activity Perceived Benefits and Barriers scales (Robbins, Wu, Sikorskii, & Morley, 2008), a child nutrition questionnaire (Wilson, Magarey, & Mastersson, 2008), the Family Eating and Activity Habits Questionnaire (Golan & Weizman, 1998), an instrument designed to assess the HIV/AIDS knowledge of university students (Balogun et al., 2010), a mood disorder questionnaire (Chung, Tso, & Chung, 2009), and a violence screening tool for primary care (Sigel, Hart, Hoffenberg, & Dodge, 2011).

Table 5.2 shows the Cronbach's alphas of a number of problem-solving subscales. All of the values are acceptable.

Kuder-Richardson Formula-20

Kuder-Richardson Formula-20 (KR-20) is a method of internal consistency reliability testing employed when the scale consists of dichotomous items (Richardson & Kuder,

TABLE 5.2 Cronbach's Alphas of the Problem-Solving Subscales ($n = 254$)	
Subscale	**Cronbach's Alpha**
Expectations for problem-solving skills	0.75
Self-efficacy for problem-solving skills	0.87
Self-efficacy in overcoming barriers while applying problem-solving skills	0.92
Self-control for problem-solving skills	0.90

1937). Dichotomous items are those with a yes/no or true/false response. The following mathematical equation is used (DiIorio, 2005):

$$KR20 = N/(N-1)\ [1 - \Sigma pq/\sigma^2_i]$$

where,

$KR20$ = Kuder-Richardson-20 coefficient
N = number of dichotomous items
p = proportion of correct (or positive) responses
q = proportion of incorrect (or negative) responses
σ^2_i = variance of the total test

Just like Cronbach's alpha, the values of KR-20 vary from 0 to 1, and values closer to 1 are indicative of higher internal consistency reliability. Some examples of where KR-20 has been used are as follows: Cancer Knowledge Scale for Elders (Su, Chen, & Kuo, 2009), Diabetes Numeracy Test (Huizinga et al., 2008), General Symptom Distress Scale (Badger, Segrin, & Meek, 2011), HIV/AIDS knowledge scale (Yancey, Wang, Goodin, & Cockrell, 2003), and the Preschool Developmental Assessment Scale for assessment of developmental disabilities (Leung, Mak, Lau, Cheung, & Lam, 2010).

> *Kuder-Richardson Formula-20 is a method of internal consistency reliability testing employed when a scale consists of dichotomous items.*

A related statistic to KR-20 is **Kuder-Richardson Formula-21 (KR-21)**, which represents a lower limit for the computed value of KR-20 and is also used for determining internal consistency reliability of dichotomous scales (Charter, 2007).

Split-Half Method

The **split-half method** is a technique by which an instrument is divided into two equal parts and the correlation between these two halves is considered as an estimate of the instrument's internal consistency reliability. It is also called the **Spearman-Brown split-half reliability method** (Brown, 1910; Spearman, 1910). In coming up with the two halves, one of the following approaches is used:

1. Odd-numbered and even-numbered items are considered as two halves.
2. The first half and second half are considered as two halves.
3. Random selection is done to determine the two halves.

The mathematical equation for split-half reliability is known as the Spearman-Brown prophecy formula, and is as follows (Polit & Hungler, 1999):

$$r^1 = 2r\ /\ (1 + r)$$

where,

r = the correlation coefficient computed on split halves
r^1 = the estimated reliability of the entire test

A drawback of this method is that the reliability estimates will vary depending on the method of splitting chosen. Some will underestimate and some will overestimate. As a result, it is not very popular in health education and health promotion. But it is commonly used for knowledge tests.

Just like Cronbach's alpha and KR-20, the split-half coefficient values vary from 0 to 1, and values closer to 1 are indicative of higher internal consistency reliability. This method has been used by several studies. Some examples include the development of a measure of emotional regulation following acquired brain injury (Cattran, Oddy, & Wood, 2011), a physician's spiritual well-being scale (Fang et al., 2011), and the Purdue Pharmacist Directive Guidance Scale (Marr-Lyon, Anderson, & Gupchup, 2010).

Test-Retest Reliability (Stability)

Test-retest reliability, also known as **stability**, is the extent of association between two or more measurements taken over time. This stability over time is a critical attribute to look for in an instrument when your evaluation design requires pre- and post-testing. In testing for stability, the instrument is administered once to a sample from the target population, and then after an interval the *same* instrument is once again administered to the *same* sample from the target population. Then the correlation coefficient is calculated between the first time and the second time. The interval between first measurement and second measurement should not be so small that participants remember their responses, and it should not be so large that external events cause a change in the responses. Generally speaking, stability coefficients are higher if the interval is short and lower if the interval is long term. Nunnally and Bernstein (1994) suggest an interval of 2 weeks. The need to readminister the instrument on two occasions and match the participants makes it somewhat challenging at times. Therefore, often this procedure is carried out with a small sample of 30 participants. Attempts must be made to keep the method of administration and the site for the second time as close to the first time as possible. Test-retest reliability coefficients are generally not recommended for measures that change over short periods of time. Test-retest reliability coefficients can be calculated for self-reports (attitudes, knowledge, behaviors), observations (behaviors), and physiological measures. Stability indices are most useful for relatively enduring attributes such as one's ability on a task or certain physical attributes such as height.

The correlation coefficient in stability determinations can be expressed as Pearson product-moment correlation coefficients or Spearman rank correlation coefficients. The choice between the two is based on the fulfillment of underlying assumptions. Coefficient values can vary from −1 to +1; values closer to +1 are indicative of higher stability. Negative or inverse correlations are theoretically possible where a person marks the highest on the first instance of an attribute and lowest on the second instance, but usually in practice one does not find such variations. Nunnally and Bernstein (1994) recommend a value of 0.70 as acceptable, 0.80 as better, and 0.90 as excellent. Carmines and Zeller (1979) note that the lower value of the test-retest reliability coefficient may be due either to change in the underlying concept or reactivity that refers to change due to the very process of measuring a phenomenon.

Test-retest reliability, also known as stability, is the extent of association between two or more measurements of the same instrument taken over time.

Some of the scales that have used test-retest reliability or stability are the Activity Questionnaire for Adults and Adolescents and the Physical Activity Scale for the Elderly (Liu et al., 2011), the Edinburgh Depression Scale (Bergink et al., 2011), a trail walking test (Yamada & Ichihashi, 2010), and the Traumatic Brain Injury Screening Instrument (TBISI; Van Dyke, Axelrod, & Schutte, 2010).

The test-retest reliability coefficients of the problem-solving subscales are presented in **Table 5.3**. Except for self-control, all of the items in the table are acceptable.

Interobserver (Rater-Interrater) Reliability

Interobserver or **rater-interrater reliability** is calculated when different observers are using the same instrument to measure the same phenomena at the same time. It is very important for observation of behaviors. It is sometimes also referred to as equivalence, which is discussed later in this chapter. Interobserver or rater-interrater reliability is typically measured as a correlation coefficient or as a percentage agreement score, which is determined by the following formula:

% agreement = # of agreements / (# of agreements + # of disagreements) × 100

When there are two observers and interrater reliability is needed between qualitative (categorical) items, then **Cohen's kappa** can be used (Cohen, 1960). The formula for Cohen's kappa is:

$$\kappa = \Pr(a) - \Pr(e) / 1 - \Pr(e)$$

where,

$\Pr(a)$ = Observed percentage of agreement
$\Pr(e)$ = Expected percentage of agreement

Analysis of variance also can be used to determine interobserver or rater-interrater reliability where different means obtained by different observers can be compared (Goodwin & Prescott, 1981). If correlation coefficients are used, the acceptable standard is usually

TABLE 5.3 Test-Retest Reliability Coefficients of the Problem-Solving Subscales ($n = 254$)	
Subscale	**Test-Retest Reliability Coefficients**
Situation perception of stressors	0.84
Expectations for problem-solving skills	0.79
Self-efficacy for problem-solving skills	0.82
Self-efficacy in overcoming barriers while applying problem-solving skills	0.75
Self-control for problem-solving skills	0.62

0.80; with percentage agreement it also is desirable to have over 80% agreement. Cohen's kappa can range from –1 to +1. A value of Cohen's kappa equal to +1 implies perfect agreement between the two raters, whereas that of –1 means perfect disagreement. If Cohen's kappa has a value of 0, this implies that there is no relationship between the ratings of the two raters. A Cohen's kappa of 0.70 is generally considered to be satisfactory. A standard checklist with explicit criteria, adequate training of observers, and adequate experience in observing are some ways in which this agreement score can be enhanced and disagreement minimized. Use of a third rater to break the discrepancy between two raters who disagree is also helpful (Green & Lewis, 1986).

Several instruments and scales have used interobserver reliability; however, they are used more in the medicine and nursing fields than in health education and health promotion. In health education and health promotion they are particularly useful for testing the reliability of process evaluation checklists. Some examples include the Active-Learning Inventory Tool (Van Amburgh, Devlin, Kirwin, & Qualters, 2007), an instrument to assess the quality of health information on the World Wide Web (Bernstam, Shelton, Walji, & Meric-Bernstam, 2005), and the Time and Change (T&C) Test for dementia screening (Inouye, Robison, Froehlich, & Richardson, 1998).

Intraobserver Reproducibility

Intraobserver reproducibility, also known as **intrarater reliability**, is the extent to which a single rater agrees upon the characteristics of an observation repeatedly over time (McDermott & Sarvela, 1999). It assumes there is no change over time in the phenomenon being observed; therefore, it is seldom used in health education and health promotion work. It is helpful to use this method for tasks such as rating of CPR for a large group of individuals by the same instructor. In order to measure intrarater reliability, it is important to have explicit checklists that detail the observation task. Then percentage agreements can be calculated. The percentage agreement score is determined using the following formula:

% agreement = # of agreements / (# of agreements + # of disagreements) × 100

Equivalence

Equivalence is the estimation of correlation between parallel tests. Another name for this is **alternative-forms reliability**. Alternative or parallel forms of the same instrument are taken, and they are assessed to determine whether they are equivalent. To gauge equivalence the evaluator administers both the forms to the same group of people. The respondents complete the forms one after the other in the same sitting. The scoring on the two forms is compared with the help of a correlation coefficient. The value of the correlation coefficient will range from –1 to +1. The closer the value is to +1, the better is the equivalence.

We use computer software to calculate reliability statistics. One popular software is IBM-SPSS. **Focus Feature 5.1** presents various commands for IBM-SPSS that can be used to calculate reliability statistics.

FOCUS FEATURE 5.1   USING IBM-SPSS TO CALCULATE RELIABILITY STATISTICS

To calculate Cronbach's alpha:

1. From the data editor screen, click *Analyze*, and then click *Scale*.
2. Click *Reliability analysis*.
3. Highlight and transfer the scale items to be analyzed in the column. *Alpha* is the default, and is used for Cronbach's alpha.
4. Click OK.

To calculate KR-20:

1. From the data editor screen, click *Analyze*, and then click *Scale*.
2. Click *Reliability analysis*.
3. Highlight and transfer the scale items (dichotomous) to be analyzed in the column. *Alpha* is the default and is used for KR-20.
4. Click OK. In the output it will say Cronbach's alpha, but because the scale is dichotomous it is KR-20.

To calculate split-half coefficient:

1. From the data editor screen, click *Analyze*, and then click *Scale*.
2. Click *Reliability analysis*.
3. Highlight and transfer the scale items to be analyzed in the column.
4. Select *Split-half* from the pull-down menu.
5. Click OK.

To calculate test-retest reliability coefficient and equivalence:

1. From the data editor screen, click *Analyze*, and then click *Correlate*.
2. Click *Bivariate*.
3. Move the variables in the column. *Pearson* and *two-tailed* are defaults.
4. Click OK.

To calculate Cohen's kappa:

1. From the data editor screen, click *Analyze*, and then click *Descriptive statistics*.
2. Click *Crosstabs*.
3. In the dialog box, click on the *Statistics* button.
4. Select the *Kappa* option box.
5. Move variables in rows and columns.
6. Click OK.

TIPS TO INCREASE THE RELIABILITY OF AN INSTRUMENT

It is always desirable to make your instruments as reliable as possible. If you get low scores on reliability, what do you do? In order to enhance the reliability of any instrument, one can take some measures to improve the instrument, improve the administration of the instrument, and improve the response on the part of the respondents (Green & Lewis, 1986). Efforts to be undertaken in each of these three categories of factors are summarized in **Table 5.4.**

TABLE 5.4	Tips to Increase the Reliability of an Instrument
Category	**Effort to Be Undertaken**
Instrument	Improve the clarity of items.
	Replace complicated words with simple words.
	Remove ambiguous items.
	Improve layout in both paper/pencil and electronically administered instruments.
	Improve directions.
Administration	Have same controlled conditions for each administration.
	Make the environment for taking the instrument as comfortable as possible.
Respondents	Must be from the target population being studied.
	Emotional arousal should be minimized.

SKILL-BUILDING ACTIVITY

Take an existing instrument you have created or that you have access to. Enter the instrument in PASW and create a mock data set for 30 respondents. Also add retest data for these 30 subjects. Calculate the Cronbach's alpha, test-retest reliability coefficient, and split-half coefficient on this data set. Interpret the results.

SUMMARY

Reliability is the ability of an instrument to measure repeatedly the same results and be internally consistent. The term *reliability* has several synonyms such as consistency, repeatability, reproducibility, precision, dependability, and stability. Based on classical test theory, reliability is defined as the proportion of observed score variance that is explained by the true-score variance. There are four types of reliability: (1) internal consistency reliability, (2) test-retest reliability (stability), (3) interobserver (rater-interrater) reliability, and (4) intraobserver reproducibility (or intrarater reliability). In addition there is one more type of reliability called equivalence or correlation between parallel tests.

Internal consistency reliability measures the extent to which each item in an instrument is related to other items. There are three primary approaches to calculating internal consistency reliability: (1) Cronbach's alpha, (2) Kuder-Richardson Formula-20, and (3) Spearman-Brown split-half reliability method. Test-retest reliability, also known as stability, is the extent of association between two or more measurements taken over time. Interobserver or rater-interrater reliability is calculated when different observers are using the same instrument to measure the same phenomena at the same time. Intraobserver reproducibility, also known as intrarater reliability, is the extent to which a single rater agrees upon the characteristics of an observation repeatedly over time. Equivalence is the estimation of correlation between parallel tests. Another name for this is alternative-forms reliability.

To enhance the reliability of any instrument one can take some measures to improve the instrument, improve the administration of the instrument, and improve the response on the part of the respondents.

REVIEW QUESTIONS

1. Define reliability. List the types of reliability.
2. Describe internal consistency reliability and the methods for assessing it.
3. Explain test-retest reliability (stability) and how it is measured.
4. Describe interobserver (rater-interrater) reliability and how it is measured.
5. Explain intraobserver reproducibility.
6. Describe equivalence.
7. Suppose you have tested the reliability of an instrument and it has come out to be low. What measures will you employ to increase reliability on the second round?

WEBSITES TO EXPLORE

Essentials of a Good Psychological Test

http://wilderdom.com/personality/L3-2EssentialsGoodPsychologicalTest.html
This website briefly discusses properties that are required for a good psychological test. *Review this information. What are the similarities and differences between the information provided on this website and what you read in the text?*

How to Improve Test Reliability and Validity

http://oct.sfsu.edu/assessment/evaluating/htmls/improve_rel_val.html
This webpage was developed by San Francisco State University and discusses how to improve test reliability. *Review this website and prepare a list of ideas to keep in mind for improving the reliability of an instrument. Dovetail those ideas with the ones presented in this chapter.*

Test Reliability

http://www.indiana.edu/~best/test_reliability.shtml
This webpage was developed by Lucy C. Jacobs at Indiana University and discusses several important issues related to reliability. It identifies sources of error as: (1) item sampling, (2) construction of items, (3) test administration, (4) scoring, (5) difficulty of the test, and (6) student factors. It also discusses ways to improve reliability of tests. *Review this list and compare it with the list provided in this chapter. What were the similarities and what were the differences?*

Types of Reliability

http://www.socialresearchmethods.net/kb/reltypes.php
This is on the website of the Web Center for Social Research Methods. This webpage discusses different types of reliability and has some graphics. *Review the information on this webpage. How is the information similar to and different than what you learned in this chapter?*

REFERENCES

Badger, T. A., Segrin, C., & Meek, P. (2011). Development and validation of an instrument for rapidly assessing symptoms: The general symptom distress scale. *Journal of Pain and Symptom Management, 41*(3), 535–548.

Balogun, J. A., Abiona, T. C., Lukobo-Durrell, M., Adefuye, A., Amosun, S., Frantz, J., & Yakut, Y. (2010). Evaluation of the content validity, internal consistency and stability of an instrument designed to assess the HIV/AIDS knowledge of university students. *Education for Health, 23*(3), 400.

Berginck, V., Kooistra, L., Lambregtse-van den Berg, M. P., Wijnen, H., Bunevicius, R., van Baar, A., & Pop, V. (2011). Validation of the Edinburgh Depression Scale during pregnancy. *Journal of Psychosomatic Research, 70*(4), 385–389.

Bernstam, E. V., Shelton, D. M., Walji, M., & Meric-Bernstam, F. (2005). Instruments to assess the quality of health information on the World Wide Web: What can our patients actually use? *International Journal of Medical Informatics, 74*(1), 13–19.

Brown, W. (1910). Some experimental results in the correlation of mental abilities. *British Journal of Psychology, 3*(3), 296–322.

Carmines, E. G., & Zeller, R. A. (1979). *Reliability and validity assessment.* Newbury Park, CA: Sage.

Cattran, C., Oddy, M., & Wood, R. (2011). The development of a measure of emotional regulation following acquired brain injury. *Journal of Clinical and Experimental Neuropsychology.* [Epub ahead of print]. PMID: 21416425.

Charter, R. A. (2007). A practical use for the KR-21 reliability coefficient. *Psychological Reports, 101*(2), 673–674.

Chung, K. F., Tso, K. C., & Chung, R. T. (2009). Validation of the Mood Disorder Questionnaire in the general population in Hong Kong. *Comprehensive Psychiatry, 50*(5), 471–476.

Cohen, J. (1960). A coefficient of agreement for nominal scales. *Educational and Psychological Measurement, 20*(1), 37–46.

Cronbach, I. J. (1951). Coefficient alpha and the internal structure of tests. *Pyschometrika, 16*, 297–334.

DeVellis, R. F. (2003). *Scale development. Theory and applications* (2nd ed.). Newbury Park, CA: Sage.

DiIorio, C. K. (2005). *Measurement in health behavior. Methods for research and education.* San Francisco, CA: Jossey-Bass.

Fang, C. K., Li, P. Y., Lai, M. L., Lin, M. H., Bridge, D. T., & Chen, H. W. (2011). Establishing a "Physician's Spiritual Well-Being Scale" and testing its reliability and validity. *Journal of Medical Ethics, 37*(1), 6–12.

Golan, M., & Weizman, A. (1998). Reliability and validity of the Family Eating and Activity Habits Questionnaire. *European Journal of Clinical Nutrition, 52*(10), 771–777.

Goodwin, I. D., & Prescott, P. A. (1981). Issues and approaches to estimating interrater reliability in nursing research. *Research in Nursing and Health, 4*, 323–337.

Green, L. W., & Lewis, F. M. (1986). *Measurement and evaluation in health education and health promotion.* Palo Alto, CA: Mayfield.

Huizinga, M. M., Elasy, T. A., Wallston, K. A., Cavanaugh, K., Davis, D., Gregory, R. P. . . . Rothman, R. L. (2008). Dev elopment and validation of the Diabetes Numeracy Test (DNT). *BMC Health Services Research, 8*, 96.

Inouye, S. K., Robison, J. T., Froehlich, T. E., & Richardson, E. D. (1998). The time and change test: A simple screening test for dementia. *Journal of Gerontology Series A Biological Sciences and Medical Sciences, 53*(4), M281–M286.

Leung, C., Mak, R., Lau, V., Cheung, J. & Lam, C. (2010). Development of a preschool developmental assessment scale for assessment of developmental disabilities. *Research in Developmental Disabilities, 31*(6), 1358–1365.

Liu, R. D., Buffart, L. M., Spiering, M., Kersten, M. J., Brug, J., van Mechelen, W., & Chinapaw, M. J. (2011). Psychometric properties of two physical activity questionnaires, the AQuAA and the PASE, in cancer patients. *BMC Medical Research Methodology, 11*(1), 30.

Marr-Lyon, L. R., Anderson, J. R., & Gupchup, G. V. (2010). Split-half and parallel reliabilities of the Purdue Pharmacist Directive Guidance Scale. *Psychological Reports, 107*(3), 726.

McDermott, R. J., & Sarvela, P. D. (1999). *Health education evaluation and measurement. A practitioner's perspective* (2nd ed.). New York: McGraw-Hill.

Nunnally, J. C., & Bernstein, I. H. (1994). *Psychometric theory* (3rd ed.). New York: McGraw-Hill.

Polit, D. F., & Hungler, B. P. (1999). *Nursing research: Principles and methods* (6th ed.). Philadelphia: Lippincott.

Richardson, G. F., & Kuder, M. (1937). The theory of estimation of test reliability. *Psychometrika, 2*, 135–138.

Robbins, L. B., Wu, T. Y., Sikorskii, A., & Morley, B. (2008). Psychometric assessment of the Adolescent Physical Activity Perceived Benefits and Barriers scales. *Journal of Nursing Measurement, 16*(2), 98–112.

Sigel, E., Hart, J., Hoffenberg, A., & Dodge, M. (2011). Development and psychometric properties of a violence screening tool for primary care. *Journal of Adolescent Health, 48*(4), 358–365.

Spearman, C. (1910). Correlation calculated from faulty data. *British Journal of Psychology, 3*, 271–295.

Su, C. C., Chen, Y. M., & Kuo, B. J. (2009). Development and psychometric testing of the Cancer Knowledge Scale for Elders. *Journal of Clinical Nursing, 18*(5), 700–707.

Van Amburgh, J. A., Devlin, J. W., Kirwin, J. L., & Qualters, D. M. (2007). A tool for measuring active learning in the classroom. *American Journal of Pharmaceutical Education, 71*(5), 85.

Van Dyke, S. A., Axelrod, B. N., & Schutte, C. (2010). Test-retest reliability of the Traumatic Brain Injury Screening Instrument. *Military Medicine, 175*(12), 947–949.

Wilson, A. M., Magarey, A. M., & Masterssson, N. (2008). Reliability and relative validity of a child nutrition questionnaire to simultaneously assess dietary patterns associated with positive energy balance and food behaviours, attitudes, knowledge and environments associated with healthy eating. *International Journal of Behavioral Nutrition and Physical Activity, 5*, 5.

Yamada, M., & Ichihashi, N. (2010). Predicting the probability of falls in community-dwelling elderly individuals using the trail-walking test. *Environmental Health and Preventive Medicine, 15*(6), 386–391.

Yancey, E. M., Wang, M. Q., Goodin, L., & Cockrell, T. (2003). HIV/AIDS knowledge scale in relation to HIV risks among African-American women. *Psychological Reports, 92*(3 Pt 1), 991–996.

CHAPTER 6

Validity Assessment

DEFINITION OF VALIDITY _____

Validity is the ability to say that an instrument is actually measuring what it is purporting to measure. Green and Lewis (1986, p. 101) define validity as "the extent to which the instrument adequately measures the concepts under study." Validity addresses the question: Does my instrument accurately tap the underlying concepts? Validity is not considered as an attribute of the instrument, but is the extent of support obtained for the interpretations of scores on an instrument when the instrument is being used for its intended purpose (American Educational Research Association, American Psychological Association,

Validity is the ability of an instrument to actually measure what it is purporting to measure.

& National Council on Measurement in Education, 1999). So validity can be seen as the ability of an instrument to accurately represent the ideas one is trying to study. For example, let's say there is a problem-solving skills scale that is valid for sixth-grade children. It implies that it is able to measure the ability to solve problems by a group of sixth-grade children. If the scale were administered to first-grade children, it would not be valid any longer because it will not be able to measure problem-solving skills. So, in essence, it is not the instrument that is validated, but the scores and their interpretations for any given target population (Messick, 1989). It can also be said that an instrument measuring one characteristic is valid for only one group of people. It may or may not be valid for another group of people. This phenomenon is what is called as **situational validity** (McDermott & Sarvela, 1999).

It is also important to note that validity is dependent on the purpose and context for which the instrument is being used (Smith & Glass, 1987). If the purpose is to test problem-solving skills, then the instrument will only be valid for testing problem-solving skills. If the instrument is based on social cognitive theory, then the validity will only pertain to the constructs of social cognitive theory.

Like reliability, validity also has several aspects, and associated with those aspects are different approaches to assess it. Compared to reliability, validity is more difficult to assess. There are no clear-cut mathematical techniques for establishing validity that can be employed; the determination often depends on the expertise of experts in the field. Reliability is believed to lower random error in an instrument, whereas validity is supposed to lower systematic error and ensure adequate representation of the concept. It is also important to appreciate that an unreliable instrument cannot be valid, but a reliable instrument can be invalid. In other words, high reliability of an instrument is not indicative of its validity for a given purpose; however, low reliability of an instrument is indicative of low validity. A comparison of validity and reliability is depicted in **Table 6.1**.

TYPES OF VALIDITY

There are four basic types of validity: (1) face validity, (2) content validity, (3) construct validity, and (4) criterion validity. Face validity is the determination as to whether the instrument "looks like" what it is supposed to measure. Content validity is the extent to

TABLE 6.1	**Comparison of Validity and Reliability**	
Attribute	**Validity**	**Reliability**
Definition	The ability to say that the instrument is actually measuring what it is purporting to measure	The ability of the instrument to measure repeatedly the same results and be internally consistent
Assessment	Difficult	Relatively easy
Focus	Lower systematic error and ensure adequate representation of the concept	Lower random error in an instrument
Relationship	An unreliable instrument cannot be valid.	A reliable instrument can be invalid.

which an instrument has adequately sampled the total meanings or substrata of a concept. Construct validity is a determination of how well the items in a given instrument measure the same construct and are related to each other. **Criterion validity** is the extent of correlation of the instrument with another instrument of the same phenomenon. In some cases there is a gold standard criterion measure of a construct. In such cases, one can test criteria against that gold standard.

ASSESSING FACE AND CONTENT VALIDITY

Face validity is the most basic type of validity that an instrument can hold, and is a prerequisite for having any other type of validity. McDermott and Sarvela (1999, p. 141) wrote that, "if on the 'face' of things, the instrument appears to measure the construct under consideration, and appears to be appropriate for the audience for which it is intended," then the instrument is face valid. So how can face validity be assessed? The only way to tell is to have a panel of experts make that determination.

Content validity also can be determined by the same panel of experts. Content validity is the extent to which an instrument has adequately sampled the total meanings or substrata of a concept; in other words, it determines whether the items selected in the instrument are adequately representative of the universe of concept as defined. When creating a potentially content-valid scale it is important to first do a thorough literature search to find previous instruments and studies on the topic such that all properties of the construct can be identified. Then one must do a personal reflection to define the boundaries of the construct being operationalized and separate it into a single dimension without any overlap with any other construct. Then the items can be generated and the scale is ready for validation by the panel of experts. **Table 6.2** depicts a rating form by a panel of experts.

Content validity is the extent to which an instrument has adequately sampled the total meanings or substrata of a concept.

Typically, the panel of experts is composed of six people: two subject experts (including theory, if theory has been used), two experts in measurement and instrument development, and two experts on the target population. Usually the panel can be identified by searching on databases such as MEDLINE (PubMed), CINAHL, or ERIC using keywords related to the instrument. After locating the email addresses of researchers who have worked on similar projects, one would write to those researchers and check their availability to serve as panelists. (See **Focus Feature 6.1** for a sample letter.) One could also locate panelists by talking to an adviser or faculty mentor who is working in that area to see whether they can recommend some well-known researchers. The panel is sent the operational definitions of the variables and the draft instrument with instructions to determine the face validity of each item and the content validity of each subscale. A qualitative agreement in two rounds between all panelists usually is considered sufficient. Sometimes three rounds may be needed if panelists are divided on certain issues. Sometimes the evaluator may employ an agreement scoring for each item and panelists may have to express their agreement or disagreement with each item. **Table 6.3** summarizes the steps of expert panel review.

TABLE 6.2   Rating Form by a Panel of Experts for an Outcome Expectations of a Problem-Solving Skill Subscale

Constitutive Definition: Outcome Expectations

Bandura (1986) proposed the construct of *outcome expectations* as anticipatory determinants of behavior. A person develops expectations about a behavior before they encounter the situation through previous experiences (performance attainments), observing others (vicarious learning), advice from other people (social persuasion), and emotional or physical responses (physiological arousal).

Operational Definition: Outcome Expectations

For this study, the construct of outcome expectations about problem-solving skills has been defined as the anticipated outcome benefits perceived by the sixth-grade students from learning problem-solving skills, consisting of having more friends, using class time productively, ability to learn other subjects better, ability to get better grades, and having more fun.

Scoring: Outcome Expectations

Never (1), Hardly Ever (2), Sometimes (3), A Lot (4), Almost Always (5)

If I can solve daily problems better:	Never	Hardly Ever	Some-times	A Lot	Almost Always

1. I will be more popular with my friends.

Is the item readable?

Yes   No   *If no, suggestion*

_____

Is the item face valid?

Yes   No   *If no, suggestion*

_____

2. I will learn quicker at school.

Is the item readable?

Yes   No   *If no, suggestion*

_____

Is the item face valid?

Yes   No   *If no, suggestion*

_____

3. I will get better grades.

Is the item readable?

Yes   No   *If no, suggestion*

_____

Is the item face valid?

Yes   No   *If no, suggestion*

_____

TABLE 6.2 Rating Form by a Panel of Experts for an Outcome Expectations of a Problem-Solving Skill Subscale *(Continued)*

4. I will have more fun with my family.

Is the item readable?

Yes   No   *If no, suggestion*
_____

Is the item face valid?

Yes   No   *If no, suggestion*
_____

5. I will have more fun at school.

Is the item readable?

Yes   No   *If no, suggestion*
_____

Is the item face valid?

Yes   No   *If no, suggestion*
_____

Is the subscale content valid (the items of the subscale adequately assess each social cognitive theory construct within the universe of content as operationally defined)?

Yes   No   *If no, suggestions* _____

_____

TABLE 6.3 Steps of an Expert Panel Review

Step	What to Do
1.	Develop operational definitions of constructs.
2.	Choose scale of measurement.
3.	Develop items.
4.	Prepare a draft with directions, scoring, and layout.
5.	Email or mail request to panel of experts.
6.	Collect feedback from panel of experts.
7.	Incorporate feedback from panel of experts. Identify any dissension among panelists.
8.	Resubmit revised instrument back to panelists and point out any dissension.
9.	Aim for consensus among panelists.
10.	Your instrument is finalized when consensus is achieved.

FOCUS FEATURE 6.1   FORM LETTER TO PANEL OF EXPERTS FOR FACE AND CONTENT VALIDATION

(ADDRESS)

Dear _____,

I am _____ at _____ and am conducting a study entitled, "_____
_____."

Based on your expertise in the area of _____, you have been identified as an expert to help me establish the face and content validity of my instrument. Attached please find the operational definitions of my variables and the draft instrument with all the subscales. Please read the operational definitions and look at the corresponding items on the subscales, and then determine the following:

>   Face validity: Does each item appear to measure the intended construct as operationally defined?

>   Content validity: Do the items in each subscale adequately assess the construct within the universe of content as operationally defined?

>   Readability: Is the meaning of each item clear and language appropriate for the _____ grade level?

Kindly respond to all aspects and return the instrument with your valuable comments to me by _____ [usually 2-week time period]. After receiving your inputs and inputs from other experts I will revise the instrument and send it to you again on _____ [usually 2 weeks later] for a second review. The comments on second review would be expected by _____ [usually 2 weeks later]. If you have any questions I can be reached at ( ) _____ (phone), ( ) _____ (fax), or _____ (email).

I am extremely thankful for your time, and would like to convey my anticipatory gratitude for your valuable comments on the instrument.

With warm regards.

Sincerely,

_____

enc. as above

CONSTRUCT VALIDITY AND FACTOR ANALYSIS

Construct validity is a determination of how well the items in a given instrument measure the same construct and are related to each other. When an instrument is measuring a construct from a theory, construct validity becomes very important. Theory tells us which constructs to use, and the identity of those constructs is ascertained by construct validation. The idea of construct validation was first suggested by Cronbach and Meehl (1955).

> *Construct validity is a determination of how well the items in a given instrument measure the same construct and are related to each other.*

There are two common forms of construct validity:

- *Convergent validity:* The degree to which constructs (composed of items measuring alternative but related substrata or dimensions) relate to each other
- *Discriminant validity:* The degree to which constructs (dimensions) are not correlated with the constructs (dimensions) with which they are not expected to correlate

A statistical approach for assessing construct validity is factor analysis. **Factor analysis** is a statistical method in which correlations between items are measured, and as a result, factor scores are developed. Thurstone (1931) first introduced the concept of factor analysis. There are several applications of factor analysis, including the following:

- To reduce a large number of variables to a smaller number of factors for purposes of modeling. This is also called data reduction.
- To detect structure in the relationships between variables. This is also called classifying variables.
- To handle multicollinearity in multiple regression by creating a set of factors that are uncorrelated.
- To validate an instrument by demonstrating that its constituent items load on the same factor. The items that cross-load on more than one factor can be dropped.

Two different types of factor analyses exist (Kim & Mueller, 1978; Stevens, 1996): exploratory and confirmatory. Typically, **exploratory factor analysis** is used for data reduction to a smaller number of factors, to ascertain the minimum number of unobservable common factors that can account for observed correlations among variables, or to explore the underlying dimensions in a data set. If there is a hypothesis about the dimensionality of underlying factors, then **confirmatory factor analysis** is used. Confirmatory factor analysis seeks to determine whether the number of factors and the loadings of measured variables or indicator variables on them conform to what is expected on the basis of theory. Indicator variables are selected on the basis of pre-established theory, and factor analysis is used to see whether they load as predicted on the expected number of factors. The researcher's *a priori* assumption is that each factor is associated with a specified subset of indicator variables. Confirmatory factor analysis is used for construct validation. For confirmatory factor analysis, some statisticians recommend building a model, specifying the presumed effect of latent variables, and then testing the model using structural equation modeling (SEM) (Schumacker & Lomax, 1996; Thompson, 2004).

Sample Size

The first question in conducting factor analysis is how many participants should one sample for factor analysis. There are different opinions on this subject. The first one depends on the subjects-to-variables ratio (STV ratio), and suggests that it should be no lower than 5 (Bryant & Yarnold, 1995). Hatcher (1994) recommends the number of subjects should be the larger of 5 times the number of variables, or 100. Even more subjects are needed when communalities are low and/or few variables load on each factor (Hatcher, 1994). Hutcheson and Sofroniou (1999) recommend at least 150–300 cases—more toward the 150 end when there are a few highly correlated variables, as would be the case when collapsing highly multicollinear (related or correlated) variables. Gorsuch (1983) recommends there should be at least 200 cases, regardless of STV. Lawley and Maxwell (1971) recommend that there should be 51 more cases than the number of variables, to support chi-square testing. Comrey and Lee (1992) provide a guide to sample size: a sample size of 50 is very poor; 100 is poor; 200 is fair; 300 is good; 500 is very good; and 1,000 is excellent. Tabachnick and Fidell (2007, p. 613) write, "As a general rule of thumb, it is comforting to have at least 300 cases for factor analysis." We agree with this recommendation, and suggest one has at least 300 participants to do factor analysis.

Assumptions in Factor Analysis

Certain assumptions need to be considered in performing factor analysis. **Table 6.4** summarizes these assumptions (Tabachnick & Fidell, 2007).

The maximum likelihood method of factor extraction is the most important method used for confirmatory factor analysis.

Factor Extraction Techniques

Several factor extraction techniques are employed in factor analysis. Most of these are available in SPSS. These are summarized in **Table 6.5** (Tabachnick & Fidell, 2007).

How Many Factors to Retain

One of the decisions in factor analysis is how many factors to retain. In confirmatory factor analysis it is important to establish which criteria to use in order to say that this is a single factor. There are three criteria that help in this decision making. The first is the **Kaiser criterion** (Kaiser, 1960). According to this criterion, one can retain those components that have an Eigenvalue greater than 1. An **Eigenvalue** is the amount of variance in the original variable set that is explained by each component. It is sometimes also called latent root. In principal component analysis, the sum of the Eigenvalues for all of the principal components equals the total variance for the original set of variables. This criterion is the default in PASW. It is more accurate when the number of variables is small (usually 10 to 15) and the communalities are high (> 0.70) (Stevens, 1996). **Communality** is the proportion of variance on a variable accounted for by the set of factors.

TABLE 6.4   Assumptions in Factor Analysis
Assumption
1.   Interval data.
2.   Multivariate normality: All variables are normally distributed (assessed by skewness and kurtosis).
3.   Linearity: Relationships among pairs of variables are linear (assessed by scatterplots).
4.   Absence of outliers.
5.   Absence of multicollinearity and singularity (look at squared multiple correlations (SMC): If one, then singularity is present. If very large, then multicollinearity is present. (Delete variable, if present.)
6.   Factor interpretations and labels must have face validity and/or be rooted in theory.

TABLE 6.5   Summary of Factor Extraction Techniques

Technique	Purpose	Comments
Principal component analysis (PCA)	To maximize extracted variance. The principal components are ordered, with the first component extracting the most variance. It transforms a set of correlated variables into uncorrelated components. It deals with total variance.	The default in IBM-SPSS, but often not the best choice because the first component extracts maximum variance. More information from Harman (1976).
Maximum likelihood method	To estimate factor loadings for population that maximize the likelihood of sampling the observed correlation matrix. It deals with common variance.	Most appropriate for confirmatory factor analysis (CFA). More information from Joreskog and Lawley (1968).
Unweighted least squares	To minimize squared residual correlations.	Generally not used for CFA. More information from Joreskog (1977).
Generalized least squares	Weights are applied to variables.	Generally not used for CFA.
Principal axis factoring	To maximize variance extracted. However, the method is not as good as others in reproducing the correlation matrix.	Sometimes used for CFA, but not the preferred method.
Alpha factoring	To maximize the generalizability of the factors.	More information from Kaiser and Caffry (1965).
Image factoring	To distribute among factors the variance of an observed variable that is reflected by other variables.	More information from Kaiser (1963).

The second criterion is a graphical method called the **scree test** (Cattell, 1966). In this method, the Eigenvalues are plotted on the vertical axis and their ordinal rank on the horizontal axis. The magnitude of the successive Eigenvalues drops off sharply and then levels off. The criterion recommends retention of all factors in the sharp descent of the curve before the first Eigenvalue on the line where the Eigenvalues begin to level off or where the "elbow" is forming.

The third criterion is to retain as many factors as will account for a specified amount of total variance. Stevens (1996) recommends accounting for at least 70% of the total variance.

Enhancing Interpretation by Rotation

In order to enhance interpretation, sometimes a rotation of factor matrix may be needed. Rotation aids in simplified interpretation of the rotated factors. Two broad categories of rotation are available:

1. *Orthogonal:* The factors remain uncorrelated.
2. *Oblique:* The factors are correlated.

Table 6.6 summarizes commonly used rotational techniques in IBM-SPSS. This is not an exhaustive list; only the common techniques are presented. Other rotations that are not discussed are equamax, orthogonal with gamma, parsimax, orthooblique, promax, and procrustes (Tabachnick & Fidell, 2007).

TABLE 6.6 Commonly Used Rotational Techniques in IBM-SPSS			
Type of Technique	**Name of Technique**	**Purpose**	**Comments**
Orthogonal	Varimax rotation	Each factor tends to load high on a lesser number of variables and load low on other variables.	Most frequently used.
Orthogonal	Quartimax rotation	Maximizes variance of loadings on each variable.	The problem with this approach is that most of the variables tend to load on a single factor.
Oblique	Direct oblimin	This technique simplifies factors by reducing cross-products of loadings.	Allows different factor intercorrelations.
Oblique	Direct quartimin	This technique simplifies factors by reducing the sum of cross-products of squared loadings.	Allows fairly high correlations among factors.

With regard to rotations, one can try different rotations and see whether the interpretation is somewhat improved. Stevens (1996) is in favor of rotating both orthogonally and obliquely to improve interpretation. Pedhazur and Schmelkin (1991, p. 615) recommend, "The preferred course of action is, in our opinion, to rotate both orthogonally and obliquely." Further, *SAS STAT User's Guide* (SAS Institute, 1990, p. 776) notes that:

> Rotating a set of factors does not change the statistical explanatory power of the factors. You cannot say that any rotation is better than any other rotation from a statistical point of view; all rotations are equally good statistically. Therefore, the choice among different rotations must be based on nonstatistical grounds. For most applications, the preferred rotation is that which is most easily interpretable.

Interpretation of Factors

Before describing the interpretation of factors, one term needs clarification: factor loadings. **Factor loadings** are simply Pearson product moment correlation coefficients between items and factors (Gorsuch, 1983; Kim & Mueller, 1978; Stevens, 1996). Tabachnik and Fidell (2007, p. 649) propose a rule of thumb that factor loadings of 0.32 (absolute value) or higher be used to identify variables that load on each factor. Comrey and Lee (1992) recommend that loadings in excess of 0.71 are considered excellent, 0.63 are very good, 0.55 are good, 0.45 are fair, and 0.32 are poor. Stevens (1996, p. 371) recommends that sample size and a stringent alpha should also be considered in this interpretation. According to his recommendation, the minimum acceptable factor loading for a sample size of 250 and an alpha of 0.01 would be 2(0.16) or 0.32. For a sample size of 200 and an alpha of 0.01, acceptable factor loading would be 2(0.18) or 0.36. For a sample size of 300 and an alpha of 0.01, acceptable factor loading would be 2(0.149) or 0.30. So the higher the sample size, the lower the factor loading that would be acceptable. Besides factor loadings, the factor must also have an Eigenvalue greater than 1.

Judging Goodness of Fit

Often, after confirmatory factor analysis one needs to determine whether the model is a good model. This can be done by looking at several model fit indices. IBM-SPSS provides an index called goodness of fit chi-square. A p-value of greater than 0.05 is considered acceptable (Hair, Andersen, Tatham, & Black, 1992). Another measure is goodness of fit index, which ranges from 0 (poor fit) to 1 (perfect fit). Adjusted goodness of fit index is a measure that adjusts for degrees of freedom (df); a value greater than 0.90 is considered acceptable (Byrne, 1998). Another measure is root mean square residual (RMR), which should be less than 0.05 (Byrne, 1998). Good fitting models have a small RMR. A final measure is root mean square error of approximation (RMSEA). Values of RMSEA < 0.05 indicate good fit; 0.05–0.08 are indicative of a fair fit; 0.08–0.10 signify poor fit; and > 0.10 is a very poor fit (Browne & Cudeck, 1993; Byrne, 1998). Most of these indices can be calculated on SAS. **Focus Feature 6.2** provides commands for conducting confirmatory factor analysis using IBM-SPSS. **Focus Feature 6.3** presents a case study of confirmatory factor analysis.

CRITERION VALIDITY

Criterion validity is the degree of correlative association of an instrument with another instrument or another criterion of the same observable fact. McDermott and Sarvela (1999) define criterion validity as the systematic relationship of test scores to one or more outcome criteria—for example, the ability of SAT scores to predict final college grade point average (GPA). Green

> *Criterion validity is the degree of correlative association of an instrument with another instrument or another criterion of the same observable fact.*

and Lewis (1986) identify two types of criterion validity: (1) **concurrent validity**, which measures the degree of correlation between two instruments at the same point in time, and (2) **predictive validity**, which measures the degree of correlation between one instrument and a future measure of the same observable fact. An example of concurrent validity would be the correlation between one instrument that measures physical activity by self-report and another instrument, administered at the same time, that measures physical activity by pedometer. An example of predictive validity would be the correlation between SAT scores and GPA in the first year of college. Measurement of criterion validity yields Pearson product moment correlation coefficients that can potentially range from 0 to 1; the higher the coefficient, the better the criterion validity.

FOCUS FEATURE 6.2   USING IBM-SPSS FOR CONFIRMATORY FACTOR ANALYSIS

1. From the data editor screen, click *Analyze*, then click *Dimension reduction*, and then click *Factor*.
2. In *Factor*, open *Descriptives* and click on *Initial solution* (usually the default). (If you want univariate descriptives, click on that as well; if you want any attributes of correlation matrix, click on those.)
3. In *Factor*, open *Extraction*. Choose *Maximum likelihood* method. The default is an Eigenvalue greater than 1 and maximum iterations of 25. (Leave them as is.)
4. In *Factor*, use *Rotation* only if needed.
5. In *Factor*, use *Scores* and *Options* only if needed.
6. Move items you want to test for confirmatory factor analysis in variables and click OK.

FOCUS FEATURE 6.3   CASE STUDY OF CONFIRMATORY FACTOR ANALYSIS

A convenience sample of 257 sixth-grade students drawn from 10 different classrooms of the same school from a suburban school district in the Midwest participated in this validation. Summary of the distribution of demographic variables of this sample is presented in Table 1.

Table 1

Summary of Distribution of Demographic Variables of the Data Set Collected for Developing Instruments ($n = 257$)

Variable	Subgroups	Frequency	Percent
Gender	Males	123	47.9
	Females	134	52.1
	Total	257	100.0
Age	11 years	92	35.8
	12 years	156	60.7
	13 years	8	3.1
	14 years	1	0.4
	Total	257	100.0
Race	White	224	87.5
	Black or African American	10	3.9
	Asian	7	2.7
	American Indian	1	0.4
	Hispanic	3	1.2
	Others	11	4.3
	Total	256	100.0
Previous exposure to problem-solving training	None	18	7.2
	Not a complete session	22	8.8
	One to two sessions	110	43.8
	Three or more sessions	101	40.2
	Total	251	100.0

FOCUS FEATURE 6.3   CASE STUDY OF CONFIRMATORY FACTOR ANALYSIS *(Continued)*

It is evident from this table that although both genders were almost equally represented, a majority of the children were 12-year-olds (60.7%) and were predominantly white (87.5%). It is also worthwhile to note that in this sample, a majority of the kids had been exposed to some form of problem-solving training prior to this data collection (Eighty-four percent self-reported to participating in one or more sessions on problem solving.)

The mean scores with standard deviations on various construct subscales and total problem-solving skill scores are reported in Table 2. It is interesting to note that mean scores for situational perception about stressors (summation of multiplicative scores of frequency and magnitude dimensions) and expectations about problem-solving skills (summation of multiplicative scores of outcome expectations and outcome expectancies dimensions) were generally on the lower side, whereas self-efficacy about problem-solving skills, self-efficacy in overcoming barriers, and self-control about problem-solving skills were toward the higher side of the possible range.

Table 2

Summary of Means and Standard Deviations of Subscale Scores (*n* = 257)

	Variable	No. of Responses	Possible Range	Observed Range	Means	Standard Deviations
1.	Situational perception of stressors	243	4–64	4–52	18.35	9.08
2.	Expectations of problem-solving skills (PSS)	250	5–125	11–80	44.75	15.09
3.	Self-efficacy of PSS	249	16–64	16–64	47.57	9.04
4.	Self-efficacy in overcoming barriers while applying PSS	249	12–48	12–48	31.32	'9.45
5.	Self-control for applying PSS	254	4–16	4–16	12.04	3.93
6.	Problem-solving skills (Rater 1)	257	0–40	0–36	15.57	7.01

Because no previous scale for problem-solving skills based on SCT has been developed, the nature of the relationship was not established *a priori*. For confirmatory factor analyses, the maximum likelihood extraction method was performed on each of the seven hypothesized dimensions. The criteria of Eigenvalues greater than 1.0 and factor loadings greater than 0.32 had been established *a priori*.

The results from the confirmatory factor analysis on the magnitude dimension of the situational perception of stressors are presented in Table 3. The analysis confirmed the presence of one factor, and both the criteria of Eigenvalue > 1.0 and factor loadings > 0.32 were satisfied.

(continues)

FOCUS FEATURE 6.3   CASE STUDY OF CONFIRMATORY FACTOR ANALYSIS *(Continued)*

Table 3

Summary of the Confirmatory Factor Analysis on the Dimension of Stressor Magnitude of the Subscale Measuring Situational Perception of Stressors ($n = 243$)

Item	Factor 1 (factor loadings)	Variance Explained by the Factor (Eigenvalue)
How bad does it make you feel?		
1. Not have homework done on time	0.5323	1.0883
2. Worry about taking tests	0.4872	
3. Get teased by classmates	0.5431	
4. Hear your parents argue	0.5221	

The results from the confirmatory factor analysis on the outcome expectations dimension of problem-solving skills are presented in Table 4. The analysis confirmed the presence of one factor, and both criteria of Eigenvalue > 1.0 and factor loadings > 0.32 were satisfied.

Table 4

Summary of the Confirmatory Factor Analysis on the Dimension of Outcome Expectations About Problem-Solving Skills of the Subscale Measuring Expectations of Stressors ($n = 251$)

Item	Factor 1 (factor loadings)	Variance Explained by the Factor (Eigenvalue)
If I can solve daily problems better:		
1. I will be more popular with my friends	0.4193	2.0244
2. I will learn more quickly at school	0.7093	
3. I will get better grades	0.7384	
4. I will have more fun with my family	0.6402	
5. I will have more fun at school	0.6248	

The results from the confirmatory factor analysis on the outcome expectancies dimension of problem-solving skills are presented in Table 5. The analysis confirmed the presence of one factor. Both the criteria of Eigenvalue greater than 1.0 and factor loadings greater than 0.32 were satisfied, except for the first expectancy, that is, how important is it that you be popular with friends. It was speculated that perhaps this was because of the way this item was worded, and hence, in consultation with subject experts, its wording was revised to: How important is it that you are popular with *kids your age.*

FOCUS FEATURE 6.3   CASE STUDY OF CONFIRMATORY FACTOR ANALYSIS *(Continued)*

Table 5

Summary of the Confirmatory Factor Analysis on the Dimension of Outcome Expectancies About Problem-Solving Skills of the Subscale Measuring Expectations of Stressors ($n = 255$)

Item	Factor 1 (factor loadings)	Variance Explained by the Factor (Eigenvalue)
How important is it that you:		
1. Be popular with friends	0.2101	1.1131
2. Learn more quickly at school	0.4402	
3. Get good grades	0.3478	
4. Have fun with your family	0.5563	
5. Have fun at school	0.6670	

The results from the confirmatory factor analysis on the self-efficacy for problem-solving skills are presented in Table 6. The Eigenvalue was greater than 1.0 and factor loadings were greater than 0.32 for all items except two, which pertained to thinking about bad points of dealing with being late for homework and taking tests. Further, it was identified in the subscale that more components had Eigenvalues greater than 1.0. Hence, a two-factor solution and three-factor solution were also run with varimax and promax rotations. From these solutions it became clear that Factor 1 contained a representation of all items, as revealed by factor loadings over 0.32 for this factor in all the cases. Hence, it was concluded that the dimension identified by the experts is construct valid. Further, it was found that a second component of this overall dimension seems to be relevant, as is clear in the two-factor solution (Table 7) and the three-factor solution (Table 8). This factor can be called the self-efficacy for thinking about bad points for different solutions that have been thought about in solving any problem. It was decided that, for the primary purpose of the evaluation, besides comparing self-efficacy of problem-solving skills in experimental and comparison classrooms (before and after the interventions), it may also be worthwhile to compare changes specifically in this component represented by four items.

(continues)

FOCUS FEATURE 6.3   CASE STUDY OF CONFIRMATORY FACTOR ANALYSIS *(Continued)*

Table 6

Summary of the Confirmatory Factor Analysis on the Dimension of Self-Efficacy About Problem-Solving Skills ($n = 249$)

Item (abbreviated)	Factor 1 (factor loadings)	Variance Explained by the Factor (Eigenvalue)
1. Many ways to deal with late homework	0.6183	4.9035
2. Good points about each way	0.6483	
3. Bad points about each way	0.2878	
4. Choose one way	0.5067	
5. Many ways to deal with taking tests	0.6005	
6. Good points about each way	0.6756	
7. Bad points about each way	0.3028	
8. Choose one way	0.6473	
9. Many ways to deal with teasing	0.5889	
10. Good points about each way	0.5620	
11. Bad points about each way	0.3307	
12. Choose one way	0.5672	
13. Many ways to deal with parents arguing	0.6613	
14. Good points about each way	0.6184	
15. Bad points about each way	0.4060	
16. Choose one way	0.5960	

FOCUS FEATURE 6.3   CASE STUDY OF CONFIRMATORY FACTOR ANALYSIS *(Continued)*

Table 7

Summary of the Factor Analysis Specifying a Two-Factor Solution on the Dimension of Self-Efficacy About Problem-Solving Skills ($n = 249$)

Item (abbreviated)	Factor 1 (factor loadings)	Factor 2 (factor loadings)
1. Many ways to deal with late homework	0.5961	−0.0902
2. Good points about each way	0.6296	−0.1201
3. Bad points about each way	0.3574	0.5055
4. Choose one way	0.4928	−0.0691
5. Many ways to deal with taking tests	0.5851	−0.0734
6. Good points about each way	0.6578	−0.0982
7. Bad points about each way	0.3912	0.6656
8. Choose one way	0.6280	−0.0816
9. Many ways to deal with teasing	0.5883	0.0100
10. Good points about each way	0.5561	−0.1073
11. Bad points about each way	0.4099	0.5570
12. Choose one way	0.5548	−0.0409
13. Many ways to deal with parents arguing	0.6555	−0.3263
14. Good points about each way	0.6178	−0.2350
15. Bad points about each way	0.4748	0.3914
16. Choose one way	0.5914	−0.3012
Variance explained by each factor (Eigenvalues)		
	4.9623	1.4768

(continues)

FOCUS FEATURE 6.3   CASE STUDY OF CONFIRMATORY FACTOR ANALYSIS *(Continued)*

Table 8

Summary of the Factor Analysis Specifying a Three-Factor Solution on the Dimension of Self-Efficacy About Problem-Solving Skills ($n = 249$)

Item (abbreviated)	Factor 1 (factor loadings)	Factor 2 (factor loadings)	Factor 3 (factor loadings)
1. Many ways to deal with late homework	0.5963	−0.0546	−0.3855
2. Good points about each way	0.6230	−0.0746	−0.1713
3. Bad points about each way	0.3274	0.4832	0.0208
4. Choose one way	0.4860	−0.0424	−0.1367
5. Many ways to deal with taking tests	0.5886	−0.0534	−0.3776
6. Good points about each way	0.6600	−0.0433	−0.2584
7. Bad points about each way	0.3454	0.6400	−0.0863
8. Choose one way	0.6265	−0.0294	−0.2301
9. Many ways to deal with teasing	0.5712	0.0621	−0.0435
10. Good points about each way	0.5503	−0.0674	0.0735
11. Bad points about each way	0.3913	0.6319	0.1842
12. Choose one way	0.5444	−0.0035	−0.1101
13. Many ways to deal with parents arguing	0.6955	−0.3134	0.2050
14. Good points about each way	0.6465	−0.2202	0.2256
15. Bad points about each way	0.4795	0.4565	0.3102
16. Choose one way	0.6460	−0.3063	0.3839
Variance explained by each factor (Eigenvalues)			
	5.0087	1.5156	0.8567

The results from the confirmatory factor analysis on the self-efficacy for overcoming barriers in solving problems are presented in Table 9. Both the criteria of Eigenvalue greater than 1.0 and factor loadings greater than 0.32 were satisfied. The results from confirmatory factor analysis on the dimension of self-control for applying problem-solving skills are presented in Table 10. Both the criteria of Eigenvalue greater than 1.0 and factor loadings greater than 0.32 were satisfied.

FOCUS FEATURE 6.3   CASE STUDY OF CONFIRMATORY FACTOR ANALYSIS *(Continued)*

Table 9

Summary of the Confirmatory Factor Analysis on the Dimension of Self-Efficacy for Overcoming Barriers ($n = 249$)

Item (abbreviated)	Factor 1 (factor loadings)	Variance Explained by the Factor (Eigenvalue)
1. Apply PSS steps to deal with late homework when angry.	0.5593	6.1105
2. Apply PSS steps to deal with late homework when tired.	0.5874	
3. Apply PSS steps to deal with late homework when busy.	0.6200	
4. Apply PSS steps to deal with tests when angry.	0.6433	
5. Apply PSS steps to deal with tests when tired.	0.6720	
6. Apply PSS steps to deal with tests when busy.	0.6794	
7. Apply PSS steps to deal with teasing when angry.	0.7288	
8. Apply PSS steps to deal with teasing when tired.	0.8252	
9. Apply PSS steps to deal with teasing when busy.	0.8627	
10. Apply PSS steps to deal with parents arguing, when angry.	0.7518	
11. Apply PSS steps to deal with parents arguing, when tired.	0.7879	
12. Apply PSS steps to deal with parents arguing, when busy.	0.7740	

Table 10

Summary of the Confirmatory Factor Analysis on the Dimension of Self-Control for Applying Problem-Solving Skills ($n = 254$)

Item (abbreviated)	Factor 1 (factor loadings)	Variance Explained by the Factor (Eigenvalue)
1. Self-reward for applying PSS for dealing with late homework	0.9003	2.7844
2. Self-reward for applying PSS for dealing with taking tests	0.8685	
3. Self-reward for applying PSS for dealing with teasing	0.8086	
4. Self-reward for applying PSS for dealing with parents arguing	0.7522	

Source: Sharma, M. (1997). Evaluation of a coping intervention developing problem solving skills among upper elementary school children based on social cognitive theory. Retrieved from ProQuest Dissertations and Theses (UMI No. AAT 9801785).

Related concepts that are used in epidemiological and physiological instruments are sensitivity and specificity. **Sensitivity** is the conditional probability that a test is positive given that there is disease. It is the true positives divided by the sum of the true positives and false negatives:

$$Sensitivity = P\ (Test + |\ Disease) = TP\ /\ TP + FN$$

where P is the probability, TP is the true positives, and FN is the false negatives.

Specificity is the conditional probability that the test is negative given that there is no disease. It is the true negatives divided by the sum of the true negatives and false positives:

$$Specificity = P\ (Test - |\ No\ Disease) = TN\ /\ TN + FP$$

where P is the probability, TN is the true negatives, and FP is the false positives.

Based on these two terms, **predictive value** can be defined as the conditional probability of the disease being present given that the test is positive. It is the true positives divided by the sum of the true positives and false positives:

$$Predictive\ value = P\ (Disease\ |\ Test +) = TP\ /\ TP + FP$$

where P is the probability, TP is the true positives, and FP is the false positives.

Likewise, **negative predictive value** can be defined as the conditional probability of absence of disease given that the test is negative. It is the true negatives divided by the sum of true negatives and false negatives:

$$Negative\ predictive\ value = P\ (No\ Disease\ |\ Test -) = TN\ /\ TN + FN$$

where P is the probability, TN is the true negatives, and FN is the false negatives.

SKILL-BUILDING ACTIVITY

If you have a scale for expert panel validation, then describe and apply the steps for doing that. If not, then choose a behavior commonly used in health education, such as physical activity behavior or safer sex behavior. Conduct a database search of MEDLINE (PubMed), CINAHL, and ERIC using the keywords related to that behavior and adding confirmatory factor analysis or construct validity. Locate an article that has performed confirmatory factor analysis for construct validation on an instrument related to that behavior. Answer the following questions:

- What is the sample size? Is it adequate for factor analysis?
- Does the article describe whether the assumptions for factor analysis have been met?
- What method of factor extraction has been used?
- What are the criteria for factors to be retained?
- Has rotation been done?
- What factor loading has been used for interpretation of factors? Is it adequate?
- What are the criteria for judging goodness of fit? Are these adequate?

SUMMARY

Validity is the ability to say that an instrument is actually measuring what it is purporting to measure. There are four basic types of validity: (1) face validity, (2) content validity, (3) construct validity, and (4) criterion validity. Face validity is the determination as to whether the instrument "looks like" what it is supposed to measure. Content validity is the extent to which an instrument has adequately sampled the total meanings or substrata of a concept. Construct validity is a determination of how well the items in a given instrument measure the same construct and are related to each other. Criterion validity is the extent of correlation of the instrument with another instrument of the same phenomenon. Face and content validity are determined by a panel of experts. Typically, the panel of experts consists of six people: two subject experts (including theory, if theory has been used), two experts in measurement and instrument development, and two experts of target population.

Confirmatory factor analysis is used for construct validation. There are different recommendations for sample size for factor analysis. Generally speaking, one should have at least 300 participants to do factor analysis. The maximum likelihood method of factor extraction is the most important method used for confirmatory factor analysis. There are three criteria for retaining factors: (1) Kaiser criterion—retain those components that have an Eigenvalue greater than 1; (2) scree test—retain all factors in the sharp descent of the curve before the first Eigenvalue on the line where the Eigenvalues begin to level off or where the "elbow" is forming; and (3) retain as many factors as will account for a specified amount of total variance, typically at least 70% of the total variance.

To enhance interpretation, sometimes a rotation of factor matrix may be needed. Two broad categories of rotation are available: orthogonal (the factors remain uncorrelated) and oblique (the factors are correlated). In interpretation of factor analysis, one should also consider factor loadings, which are Pearson product moment correlation coefficients between items; factors should generally be over 0.32. Often after confirmatory factor analysis one needs to determine whether the model is a good model. This can be done by looking at several model fit indices such as goodness of fit chi-square, goodness of fit index, adjusted goodness of fit index, root mean square residual (RMR), and root mean square error of approximation (RMSEA).

REVIEW QUESTIONS

1. Define validity. Differentiate between reliability and validity.
2. Describe how the face and content validity of an instrument are established.
3. Differentiate between convergent and discriminant validity.
4. Define factor analysis. Differentiate between exploratory and confirmatory factor analysis.
5. Differentiate between principal components analysis and maximum likelihood analysis methods of extraction of factors.
6. Why is rotation done in factor analysis? Describe some common types of rotation.
7. Define criterion validity. Differentiate between predictive and concurrent validity.
8. Differentiate between sensitivity and specificity.

WEBSITES TO EXPLORE

Content Validity

http://www.experiment-resources.com/content-validity.html
This website explains the concept of content validity very well. Read the information provided about content validity. Click on the links to highlighted words. *Describe a plan for establishing the content validity of an instrument you are developing.*

Face Validity

http://www.experiment-resources.com/face-validity.html
This website explains the concept of face validity very well. Read the information provided about face validity. Click on the links to highlighted words. Explore related links on the website for validity and reliability, types of validity, external validity, and internal validity. *Describe a plan for establishing the face validity of an instrument you are developing.*

Factor Analysis

http://www.psych.cornell.edu/darlington/factor.htm
This website, written by Richard Darlington at Cornell University, presents an interesting account about factor analysis. Read this account and compare it with what is written in this chapter. *Based on these two accounts, describe how you would go about applying confirmatory factor analysis for construct validation.*

Reliability and Validity of a Pain Scale

http://www.painphysicianjournal.com/linkout_vw.php?issn=1533-3159&vol=14&page=61
This is an article by Gentile and colleagues (2011) published in *Pain Physician* [*14*(1):61–70]. The article describes the validation of a pain scale. Download the article in PDF format and read it. *Summarize in approximately 250 words how the researchers established the different types of validity and reliability.*

Validity and Reliability of a Physical Activity Social Support Assessment Scale

http://www.scielosp.org/scielo.php?script=sci_arttext&pid=S0034-89102011000200008&lng=en&nrm=iso&tlng=en
This is an article by Reis and colleagues (2011) published in *Revista de Saúde Pública* [*45*(2)] that describes the assessment of validity and reliability of a physical activity social support scale in adults. Read this article. *Summarize in approximately 250 words how the researchers established the different types of validity and reliability.*

REFERENCES

American Educational Research Association, American Psychological Association, & National Council on Measurement in Education. (1999). *Standards for educational and psychological testing.* Washington, DC: American Educational Research Association.

Bandura, A. (1986). *Social foundations of thought and action.* Englewood Cliffs, NJ: Prentice Hall.

Browne, M. W., & Cudeck, R. (1993). Alternative ways of assessing model fit. In K. A. Bollen & J. S. Long (Eds.), *Testing structural equation models* (pp. 136–162). Newbury Park, CA: Sage.

Bryant, F. B. & Yarnold, P. R. (1995). Principal components analysis and exploratory and confirmatory factor analysis. In L. G. Grimm and P. R. Yarnold (Eds.), *Reading and understanding multivariate statistics* (pp. 99–136). Washington, DC: American Psychological Association Books.

Byrne, B. M. (1998). *Structure equation modeling with LISREL, PRELIS, and SIMPLIS. Basic concepts, applications and programming.* Mahwah, NJ: Lawrence Erlbaum.

Cattell, R. B. (1966). The meaning and strategic use of factor analysis. In R. B. Cattell (Ed.), *Handbook of multivariate experimental psychology* (pp. 174–243). Chicago: Rand McNally.

Comrey, A. L., & Lee, H. B. (1992). *A first course in factor analysis* (2nd ed.). Hillsdale, NJ: Lawrence Erlbaum.

Cronbach, L. J., & Meehl, P. E. (1955). Construct validity in psychological tests. *Psychological Bulletin, 52*(4), 281–302.

Gorsuch, R. L. (1983). *Factor analysis.* Hillsdale, NJ: Lawrence Erlbaum.

Green, L. W., & Lewis, F. M. (1986). *Measurement and evaluation in health education and health promotion.* Palo Alto, CA: Mayfield.

Hair, J. F. Jr., Andersen, R. E., Tatham, R. M., & Black, W. C. (1992). *Multivariate data analysis with readings* (3rd ed.) New York: Macmillan.

Harman, H. H. (1976). *Modern factor analysis* (3rd ed.). Chicago: University of Chicago Press.

Hatcher, L. (1994). *A step-by-step approach to using the SAS system for factor analysis and structural equation modeling.* Cary, NC: SAS Institute.

Hutcheson, G., & Sofroniou, N. (1999). *The multivariate social scientist: Introductory statistics using generalized linear models.* Thousand Oaks, CA: Sage.

Joreskog, K. G. (1977). Factor analysis by least-square and maximum likelihood method. In K. Enslein, A. Ralston, & S. Wilf (Eds.), *Statistical methods for digital computers* (Vol. 3, pp. 125–153). New York: John Wiley & Sons.

Joreskog, K. G., & Lawley, D. N. (1968). New methods in maximum likelihood factor analysis. *British Journal of Mathematical and Statistical Psychology, 21,* 85–86.

Kaiser, H. F. (1960). The application of electronic computers to factor analysis. *Educational and Psychological Measurement, 20,* 141–151.

Kaiser, H. F. (1963). Image analysis. In C. W. Harris (Ed.), *Problems in measuring change* (pp. 156–166). Madison: University of Wisconsin Press.

Kaiser, H. F., & Caffry, J. (1965). Alpha factor analysis. *Psychometrika, 30,* 1–4.

Kim, J., & Mueller, C. W. (1978). *Factor analysis. Statistical methods and practical issues.* Newbury Park, CA: Sage.

Lawley, D. N., & Maxwell, A. E. (1971). *Factor analysis as a statistical method.* London: Butterworth.

McDermott, R. J., & Sarvela, P. D. (1999). *Health education evaluation and measurement. A practitioner's perspective* (2nd ed.). New York: McGraw-Hill.

Messick, S. (1989). Validity. In R. Linn (Ed.), *Educational measurement* (3rd ed., pp. 13–103). New York: Macmillan.

Pedhazur, E., & Schmelkin, L. (1991). *Measurement, design, and analysis.* Hillsdale, NJ: Lawrence Erlbaum.

SAS Institute. (1990). *SAS/STAT user's guide, version 6.* (Vol. 1, 4th ed.). Cary, NC: Author.

Schumacker, R. E., & Lomax, R. G. (1996). *A beginner's guide to structural equation modeling.* Mahwah, NJ: Lawrence Erlbaum.

Sharma, M. (1997). Evaluation of a coping intervention developing problem solving skills among upper elementary school children based on social cognitive theory. Retrieved from ProQuest Dissertations and Theses (UMI No. AAT 9801785).

Smith, M., & Glass, G. (1987). *Research and evaluation in education and the social sciences.* Englewood Cliffs, NJ: Prentice Hall.

Stevens, J. (1996). *Applied multivariate statistics for the social sciences* (3rd ed.). Mahwah, NJ: Lawrence Erlbaum.

Tabachnick, B. G., & Fidell, L. S. (2007). *Using multivariate statistics* (5th ed.). Boston, MA: Pearson Education.

Thompson, B. (2004). *Exploratory and confirmatory factor analysis: Understanding concepts and applications*. Washington, DC: American Psychological Association.

Thurstone, L. L. (1931). Multiple factor analysis. *Psychological Review, 38*(5), 406–427.

CHAPTER 7

Measurement Errors

KEY CONCEPTS

- acquiescence bias
- bias
- central tendency bias
- deviation bias
- end-aversion bias
- expectation bias
- extreme responses bias
- faking bad bias
- halo effect
- insensitive measure bias
- measurement error
- middle range bias
- nay sayers bias
- observer reactivity
- optimizing approach
- random error
- recall or memory bias
- response sampling error
- response set biases
- satisficing approach
- social desirability bias
- systematic error
- yeasayers bias

CHAPTER OBJECTIVES

- Define measurement error
- Identify types of measurement error
- Differentiate between random error and systematic error
- Describe common measurement errors due to situational and environmental factors
- Identify measurement errors due to administrative differences
- Describe instrument-related measurement errors
- Explain response set biases
- Categorize intrapersonal errors
- Identify errors due to sampling of response

DEFINITION OF MEASUREMENT ERROR

Validity is the ability of an instrument to actually measure what it is purporting to measure, and reliability is the ability of an instrument to measure repeatedly the same results

M *easurement error is defined as the degree of deviation from high levels of validity and reliability.*

and be internally consistent. Reliability is believed to lower random error in an instrument, whereas validity is supposed to lower systematic error and ensure adequate representation of the concept. Despite our efforts to achieve high levels of validity and reliability, it is never really possible to have that perfection. No instrument ever yields perfectly valid and reliable scores. The instrument, the procedures involved in applying the instrument, the respondent, and the object being measured are vulnerable to several influences that could result in deviation from yielding perfectly valid and reliable scores. It is in this context that **measurement error** is defined as the degree of deviation from high levels of validity and reliability. Efforts must be made to identify and control for measurement errors. The goal is to reduce measurement error to a minimum, which will increase the validity and reliability of measurement and improve the quality of the evaluation. Some of these errors can be controlled whereas others cannot. Likewise, some of these errors can be identified whereas some others cannot. One must realize that it is not always possible to identify and control for all errors; there will always be some amount of measurement error.

There are two types of measurement error: random error and systematic error. This can be written mathematically as:

Obtained score = True score ± Random error ± Systematic error

R *andom error lowers reliability and does not affect the mean, but only the variability around the mean; systematic error lowers validity and affects the mean.*

The true score is a hypothetical entity; it is never known. The obtained score could be, for example, the score one gets on completing a knowledge scale. **Random error** is the type of error in measurement that occurs due to chance (DiIorio, 2005). When taking a test, a person may not have known the correct answers and may have guessed and gotten them right, thus inflating the obtained score. Likewise, while completing a test a person might have a headache and thus be unable to concentrate, therefore marking some incorrect answers and thus lowering the obtained score. Both of these situations represent random errors—one inflating the true score and the other one deflating the true score. Viswanathan (2005) has described two types of random errors: generic and idiosyncratic. Generic random errors affect a substantial number of people; an example would be unclear instructions. Idiosyncratic random errors affect a small number of participants; an example is a distraction while completing an instrument. Random error lowers reliability. Random error does not affect the mean, but only the variability around the mean, as shown in **Figure 7.1**.

The other type of error that can also inflate or deflate the obtained score is systematic error. **Systematic error** occurs due to a systematic mechanism of either increasing or decreasing the true score. Another name for systematic error is **bias** (Camilli & Shepard, 1994; Hartman, Forsen, Wallace, & Neely, 2002). For example, a multiple choice question on a knowledge test may be designed in such a way that the answer is quite obvious; this will inflate the obtained score. Likewise, a similar question may be designed in such a way that it makes the person mark the wrong choice; that will deflate the obtained score. Systematic error lowers validity. Systematic error also affects the mean, as shown in **Figure 7.2**.

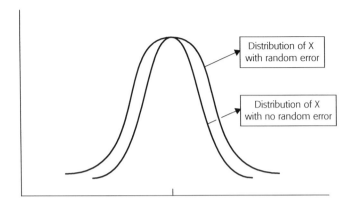

Figure 7.1   Effects of random error.

CLASSIFICATION OF MEASUREMENT ERRORS

Besides random and systematic classification of measurement errors, they also can be classified in several other ways. One such classification is presented in **Table 7.1**. We will discuss each of these categories in detail. The purpose of identifying these categories of measurement errors is to become cognizant of them and, wherever possible, avoid having them occur so that the instrument can be as valid and reliable as possible.

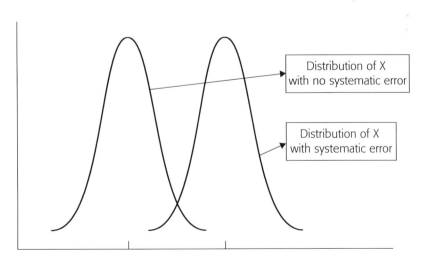

Figure 7.2   Effects of systematic error.

TABLE 7.1 Classification of Measurement Errors	
Type of Error	**Example**
Situational or environmental factors	Lighting in the room where the instrument is being completed
Administrative differences	Different instructions by different administrators of the instrument at different locations
Instrument-related factors	Unclear directions on the instrument
Response set biases	Social desirability bias, such as marking a choice because it is socially acceptable
Intrapersonal errors	Tiredness on the part of the participant
Errors due to sampling of response	Selection of items from a pool of items

Situational or Environmental Factors

Several factors are present in the environment or the situation where the instrument is being administered that can alter the participants' responses. Some of these factors may inflate the score whereas others may deflate it. Some examples of such factors are as follows:

- *Temperature of the room where the instrument is being administered (either too hot or too cold):* This can be overcome by maintaining a soothing temperature for the room where the instrument will be administered.
- *Outside or inside noise in the room where the instrument is being administered:* Sources of noise can be minimized by measures such as shutting the door or asking the participants to be quiet.
- *Environmental factors such as rain or snow that may distract the participants:* Not much can be done about environmental disturbances, but efforts can be taken so that their impact is minimized, such as not conducting the evaluation on a snow day, if possible.
- *Lighting in the room where the instrument is being administered (either too bright or too dim):* This can be rectified by having proper lighting in the room where the instrument will be administered.
- *Humidity in the room where the instrument is being administered (either too high or too low):* If possible, the humidity levels should be controlled in the room where the instrument is to be administered.
- *Time of day when the instrument is being administered:* Some people may have difficulty concentrating early in the morning or late in the day. If possible, a time should be chosen that most people find to be conducive—10:00 am and 11:00 am are usually good times.
- *Location of the data collection:* Efforts should be made to locate a site that is convenient to most of the participants and to ensure arrangements are also conducive to them, such as means of getting there, adequate seating, etc.
- *Current events that may affect the responses:* Not much can be done in this regard. If an event occurs that adversely affects the scoring on the instrument, then it should be noted as a measurement error.

- *Past events that may affect the responses:* Once again, not much can be done about this. If it is known that a past event such as 9/11 is going to affect the responses of some groups on a violence prevention questionnaire, then the instrument questions can be altered or instructions made such that its effect is minimized.

> "*Situational or environmental contaminants can be avoided by having instructions and procedures that are (1) standardized, (2) unambiguous, (3) clear, and (4) evaluated thoroughly.*"
>
> —Nunnally & Bernstein, 1994

- *Observer reactivity:* In situations where an observer is observing a phenomenon (usually behavior), the behavior of participants is altered (Merrell, 2003). This is called **observer reactivity**. Such reactivity can be reduced by making the observation inconspicuous or by having some informal observation prior to formal observation.
- *Friendliness of the researchers or instrument administrators:* This also can affect the responses provided by participants. This can be minimized by having the instrument administrators maintain an objective disposition.

Besides the methods described with each of the possible situational or environmental contaminants, it is also worth noting that these errors can be avoided by having instructions and procedures that are (1) standardized, (2) unambiguous, (3) clear, and (4) evaluated thoroughly (Nunnally & Bernstein, 1994). *Standardized* means that the instructions and procedures are detailed and are applied the same way each time the process is repeated. *Unambiguous* means that the instructions and procedures are unequivocal and are not subject to different interpretations. *Clear* means that the instructions and procedures are explicit such that anyone applying them does it the same way as others would. *Thorough evaluation* means that the instructions and procedures are revisited constantly, and any deficiencies are identified and plugged.

Administrative Differences

The second set of measurement errors can arise out of variations in administration. Some examples of such administration differences are as follows:

- A physiological test such as a lipid profile (cholesterol, HDL, LDL) will have different values depending on whether the person is fasting (which is recommended) or not fasting. To reduce such errors, the directions need to be standardized and unambiguous.
- Different instructions given by different administrators of the same instrument at different locations can result in measurement error. To reduce such errors, once again the directions and instructions need to be standardized and unambiguous.
- In a structured interview, if the interviewer changes one or more words for any reason it can also result in variations of responses. To reduce this error, the script for the interview should not be changed at any cost once it is finalized.
- When observing behavior or other phenomena, if the observer changes his or her coding category or definition of what is being observed then there could be a potential measurement error. To reduce such errors it is very important to develop a coding plan and adhere to it religiously.

- If different versions of the instrument are administered to different respondents, there is potential for measurement error. To reduce the chances of this happening as much as possible, the same version of the instrument should be used for all respondents.

Once again, to reduce administrative variations it is very important to have standardized and explicit protocols that are adhered to rigidly. Deviations from established plans should be avoided at all costs. It needs to be appreciated that despite all measures there will be some administrative variations that cannot be avoided and will add to measurement error.

Instrument-Related Factors

There are some inherent factors in the instrument itself that make it prone to measurement errors. This is often a major component of the measurement error. Some examples of instrument-related errors are as follows:

- *Paucity of instructions:* The instructions that have been provided may be deficient, and as a result subject to varying interpretations. To reduce this error, optimal instructions should be provided for each instrument. The instructions should allow the respondent to complete the tasks without having to worry about different interpretations.
- *Too many instructions:* Sometimes the instructions may be too detailed, which can cause confusion among respondents, thereby causing errors. To reduce this error, once again optimal instructions should be provided for each instrument.
- *Improper formatting and layout:* If there is a problem with the formatting and layout, then the respondents could incorrectly mark their responses, thereby causing measurement error. It is very important that the instrument be formatted properly. It should have a proper arrangement of items, proper placement of scale(s), enough white space (empty space) so that the instrument does not appear cluttered, and correct numbering of items. In addition, if it is a Web-based instrument, then an indicator also is needed that tells how much remains to be completed.
- *Improper sequencing of items:* If the items are not logically sequenced then that can also lead to measurement error. To reduce this error the items must be arranged logically.
- *Open-ended versus closed-ended questions:* These two types of questions yield different kinds of information and are susceptible to different kinds of measurement errors. For example, open-ended questions are difficult to code, while closed-ended questions are too restrictive. In order to reduce errors, the questions must be clearly worded.

Instrument-related errors can be minimized by careful planning, validation by a panel of experts, pilot testing, paying attention to detail, providing clear instructions, and providing staff training.

- *Use of acronyms and difficult terms:* Acronyms and difficult terms in the instrument are subject to varying interpretations, and thus can cause measurement error. In order to reduce such errors, acronyms should be avoided; if they are necessary they should be spelled out. As much as possible the instrument should use simple terms and language that is appropriate for the target audience's grade level.

- *Variation in scales:* Sometimes instruments use some five-point scales and some seven-point ones, or similar combinations. Respondents on these scales can very easily make mistakes when transitioning from one level of scale to another level, thereby causing measurement errors. To avoid such errors the scales must use only one type of scale for all subscales. Such uniformity of scale ensures less chance of measurement errors.

- *Mismatch between items and chosen scale:* Often there is a mismatch between the items and the chosen scale; for example, the item may be an agreement item and the response scale may be a frequency scale (such as never, hardly ever, sometimes, almost always, always). Marking the response on such a scale is likely to produce measurement error. This type of error can be reduced by judicious choice of an appropriate scale for each item being scored.

- *Oral form versus written form:* Responses will vary depending on whether the question is asked orally versus in a written form. This can lead to measurement error. To reduce such errors the questions should be asked using only one of the two methods.

- *Possibility of marking in a certain way by a certain group of respondents:* Sometimes some items on an instrument are written in such a fashion that they are marked in a certain way by a certain group of people and in another way by other groups of people. Such differential marking will result in measurement error. To reduce this error the items should be designed so that they are interpreted in the same way by all respondents.

- *Poor calibration of physiological tools:* Physiological tools, such as instruments for measuring blood pressure, serum cholesterol, or weight, are prone to calibration defects. This can cause variation in results and deviation from accuracy. To reduce this error the instruments must be checked and calibrated according to set standards.

- *Insensitive measure bias:* **Insensitive measure bias** occurs when an instrument is not sensitive enough to detect what might be important differences in the variable of interest (Hartman, Forsen, Wallace, & Neely, 2002). To reduce this error better instruments need to be designed; therefore, researchers constantly strive to make better and better instruments.

- *Recall or memory bias:* In instruments requiring recall of a behavior or another attribute there is a potential measurement bias called **recall or memory bias**. Often a person recalls positive events more than negative events, which can lead to selective error (Hartman, Forsen, Wallace, & Neely, 2002). In an interview situation some people may be questioned more vigorously than others, thereby improving their recall; others may not be questioned in the same way, thus causing additional measurement error. To reduce this error the recall period should be reasonable for a given behavior.

- *Inadequate directions for observation:* For instruments that require observation, sometimes directions may be inadequate, confusing, or poorly understood. In such situations the likelihood of making measurement errors increases. To reduce such errors observers must be adequately trained and provided with detailed directions.

Response Set Biases

Sometimes systematic measurement errors occur when people provide responses that are not related to the content of the item but are based on some other criteria. These are called **response set biases** (Pedhazur & Schmelkin, 1991). They can take different forms, including the following:

- *Social desirability bias:* When respondents mark responses that portray a favorable image of themselves, the error is called **social desirability bias** (Edwards, 1957; Polit & Hungler, 1999). In such situations respondents tend to feign their attitudes by providing responses that are more in line with the existing social norms. For example, a respondent may strongly agree with an item such as "I exercise for 30 minutes daily," despite the fact that he may not be a daily exerciser. Social desirability is influenced by several factors such as the person, the person's gender and cultural background, the specific item, and the context (i.e., face to face or anonymous) in which the question is asked (Streiner & Norman, 2003). The Differential Reliability Index (DRI) can be used to assess social desirability (Jackson, 1970). It is very difficult to reduce this error, but attempts can be made to provide indirect questioning, which is sometimes helpful.

- *Faking bad bias:* Sometimes the opposite of social desirability bias may occur, in which the respondent portrays him- or herself as bad; this is called **faking bad bias**. This usually happens when teenagers responding to behavior surveys mark that they smoke marijuana or take other illicit drugs when they may not be using any of those. Once again, it is difficult to reduce this bias, but better articulation of items can help somewhat.

- *Deviation bias:* **Deviation bias** is the tendency of respondents to respond to test items with deviant responses (Berg, 1967). This is related to the faking bad bias, but can occur in any direction. For example, on an attitude test a respondent may mark that it is acceptable to kill someone, whereas he or she may not actually believe that. There are two ways in which this can be reduced (Streiner & Norman, 2003). The first approach is to disguise the purpose of the test so that the respondent does not know what is being looked for. The second approach is to use subtle items so that the respondent is not aware of the behavior being measured.

- *Acquiescence bias:* Some people tend to agree with all statements in an instrument, regardless of their content; this is known as **acquiescence bias** or **yeasayers bias** (Couch & Keniston, 1960). This was first identified by Cronbach (1946) in true–false questions, for which some people have a tendency to choose true over false. In an empirical study, Krosnick (1999) estimated that there is an average of about 10% acquiescence effect in favor of answering yes. To reduce this type of bias to some extent, one can choose a scale that is not Likert (strongly agree, agree, disagree, strongly disagree). Also, by counterbalancing positively and negatively worded statements this bias can be reduced (Polit & Hungler, 1999).

- *Nay sayers bias:* The opposite of acquiescence bias is when the respondent disagrees with each item irrespective of the content; this is called **nay sayers bias**. It is less common than acquiescence bias. The strategies described with acquiescence bias, namely choosing a nonagreement scale and counter-balancing positively and negatively worded statements, also work to reduce this bias.

- *Extreme responses bias:* Some individuals have a tendency to express their attitudes in extreme terms (such as strongly agree or strongly disagree); this is called **extreme responses bias**. Such choices distort reality. There is not much that can be done to reduce this type of error, but it can be detected. Polit and Hungler (1999) note that the distortion produced by extreme response bias is not very powerful.

- *Middle range bias:* Just as there is an extreme response bias, there are some individuals who only endorse middle-range choices, thereby causing **middle range bias**. This is also called **end-aversion bias** and **central tendency bias**. This also distorts reality. There are two ways of dealing with this bias (Streiner & Norman, 2003). The first approach is to avoid extreme terms (such as *never* and *always*) in the scale and only use terms such as *almost always*. The second approach is to use a wider scale; for example, if you want to use a five-point scale then use a seven-point scale.
- *Halo effect:* **Halo effect** is when the ratings made on individual aspects of a person's performance or behavior are influenced by the respondent's overall impression of the person (Thorndike, 1920; Wells, 1907). It can lead to both high and low ratings, and is especially important in instruments involving observation. It can be reduced by thorough training of the observers, using more than one observer, and observing larger samples of behavior.

Intrapersonal Factors

There are several factors related to the respondent that affect the score on any instrument, causing measurement errors. Both self-report instruments and interviews are susceptible to these errors on the part of the respondents. Some of these errors are:

- *Fatigue or tiredness:* Sometimes the respondent(s) may be tired or fatigued and therefore unable to concentrate. This can lead to measurement errors. To avoid this, choosing an appropriate time of day is very important. Also, the respondents should not be given other tasks on the day the measurement is going to take place.
- *Hunger:* Sometimes the respondents may be hungry and thus unable to concentrate on completion of the instrument, thereby causing measurement errors. In order to avoid this error the instrument administration should not be planned around breakfast, lunch, or dinner times.
- *Anxiety:* Undue anxiety about completing the instrument or for any other reason may cause measurement errors. If it is anticipated that anxiety is likely to play a role, then relaxation exercises can be used before administering the instrument.
- *Mood:* Sometimes the mood of the respondent may not be good, which could affect completion of the instrument. Not much can be done in this regard, except being cognizant that this is a potential source of measurement error.

- *Boredom:* Often the respondent does not want to take the instrument and is simply bored with the idea of having to complete a questionnaire for evaluation or research. Such boredom can also result in measurement errors. Measures to make the task of instrument completion interesting can keep the interest of the respondents and reduce error in this regard.
- *Failure to follow instructions:* Sometimes the respondent may not read or follow the instructions that have been provided to complete the instrument, and in the process may make errors. To reduce these errors it sometimes helps to read the instructions to the target population.
- *Guessing:* Especially on knowledge tests, sometimes the respondent may guess and get the answers correct, thereby inflating his or her score. Negative marking can be used in some cases to discourage respondents from guessing answers on multiple choice questions.
- *Providing partial answers:* Sometimes the respondent may answer some of the items on the instrument or answer the questions partially. This is particularly an issue with open-ended questions. Such partial responses can lead to errors. To reduce this error, clear instructions to answer all questions and their subparts must be given to the respondents.
- *Providing inconsistent answers:* Sometimes the respondent may not be paying attention or may purposely provide inconsistent answers, which leads to measurement error. For example, a child may be asked to report minutes of physical activity and minutes spent on computers and television, and may mark more than 12 hours in each of those activities. Not only does that sound unrealistic, but if you add them together the total is more than 24 hours, which is not possible. It is difficult to stop respondents from doing this, but once again clear instructions and carefully worded items can reduce this type of error.
- *Incorrect marking:* Sometimes the respondent may incorrectly mark the response, such as by putting a cross mark on a Scantron sheet instead of filling in the bubble; may inadvertently mark in the wrong column; or may make other such mistakes. It is difficult to predict all such errors and prevent them, but once again clear instructions and clear layout can reduce such errors.
- *Lying:* Sometimes the respondent may purposely lie while completing the instrument. He or she may be influenced by some of the response set biases discussed earlier. As a result, the respondent may overreport or underreport agreement with items, frequency of events, and positive or negative attitudes. This is especially a problem in doing evaluation studies with children and adolescents, who tend to exaggerate their responses. Nothing can be done to prevent this from happening; it can just be mentioned as one of the assumptions for research and evaluation that people will respond honestly.
- *Copying:* Sometimes the respondents may copy from each other, thus inflating scores on knowledge tests. To avoid or reduce this type of error careful proctoring of the instrument is necessary.
- *Optimizing approach versus satisficing approach:* Krosnick (1991) described two kinds of approaches in completing instruments. One is the **optimizing approach**, in which

the respondent tries to do his or her best with the most optimal mental attitude, such as when taking a test for an exam on which he or she will be graded. The other one is the **satisficing approach**, in which the respondent applies just enough effort to complete the task, such as when completing a questionnaire for a researcher in which there is no tangible benefit to the respondent. There are more measurement errors in the satisficing approach due to the respondent not reading directions, improperly marking the instrument, or committing other such errors. Streiner and Norman (2003) note the following types of errors that may occur in the satisficing approach:

- The person may select the first response option that seems reasonable without paying attention to other responses.
- The person may simply agree with every statement.
- The person may endorse the status quo.
- The person may choose one answer for the first item and then use this response for all the remaining items.
- The person may simply mark "I do not know" or place a mark in the neutral point.
- The person may choose a random response.

To reduce error in this regard, efforts must be made so that respondents are in optimizing approach mode rather than satisficing approach. If that is not possible, then the task should be kept simple (i.e., questions should be short). Another approach is to keep the motivation of the respondents high by recruiting people who are interested or by giving some sort of incentive to the respondents. Another approach is to emphasize that the instrument is being used to evaluate the health program, and that their responses are very important and they should do their best. Finally, respondents can be made more accountable for their responses (i.e., they may be asked to explain why they chose a particular answer).

Sampling of Response

The final category of measurement errors is due to sampling of responses and errors on the part of observers. Following are some examples of such errors:

- *Response sampling error:* Sometimes errors may result from the items that have been chosen from the pool of potential items; this is called **response sampling error**. This selection may not be capturing the entire possible universe of items, and thus the instrument may not be content valid. As an example, for a knowledge test of 50 items, depending on which 50 questions are chosen from the pool of 500 questions, a respondent may get 40 correct answers on one test but on the other he or she may score only 30 correct answers. This type of error can be reduced by developing the instrument carefully with a panel of experts who establish the content validity systematically.
- *Expectation bias:* This type of bias occurs in instruments requiring observation when the observer may tend to observe things in favor of the treatment group. To reduce this type of error, a careful protocol for observation needs to be developed and adhered to. Another approach is to not inform the observers as to which group they are assessing, treatment or control.

FOCUS FEATURE 7.1   STRATEGIES TO MINIMIZE ERRORS IN SELF-REPORT INSTRUMENTS

You have seen in the discussion in this chapter that a number of measurement errors can affect self-report instruments. How do we reduce these errors? Here are some strategies that help in reducing measurement errors in self-report instruments:

- Use an appealing invitation to participate that highlights benefits to the person so that he or she is in an optimizing approach rather than a satisficing approach (Krosnick, 1991).

- Provide an optimal level of instructions that are neither too sparse nor too overwhelming.

- Create an attractive layout of the instrument with enough white space, clear titles, explicit response scales, enough space between questions, and judicious use of color if it is not black and white. Most of these suggestions also apply to Web-based instruments.

- Put the demographic items at the end and place items relevant to the instrument at the beginning (Dillman, 2000).

- Place sensitive items about halfway through the instrument (Dilorio, 2005).

- Keep items simple, short, and carefully worded.

- The items should be designed so that they are interpreted in the same way by all respondents.

- Acronyms and difficult terms should not be used in the instrument.

- The instrument should ask the respondent to mark it in a way that is easy and not prone to error.

- The instrument should have logically sequenced items.

- The instrument should use enough points on the response scale (at least five or seven points) so that it is not unduly affected by middle range bias or extreme response bias.

- As far as possible one should avoid using the agreement scale to avoid acquiescence bias.

- The same type of scale (such as five points) should be used for all subscales in the instrument. The wording may change, but the points must remain uniform.

- There must be counterbalancing of positively and negatively worded statements to reduce bias.

- If the instrument requires recalling a behavior, then the recall period should be kept as reasonable as possible.

FOCUS FEATURE 7.2   STRATEGIES TO MINIMIZE ERRORS IN INTERVIEWS

This chapter has discussed a number of measurement errors that can affect interviews. Here are some strategies that help in reducing measurement errors in interviews:

- Develop a detailed protocol for the interview.

- Use carefully worded questions that have been pilot tested. Instruction must be given to interviewers not to alter any words.

- All the interviewers must be trained on the prepared protocol and what to do (such as follow the instructions, stick to the protocol, read the items as written) and what not to do (such as provide interpretation for responses, skip items, use inappropriate probes, record responses inappropriately, and lead participants in a certain direction).

- Have interviewers practice delivery of the questions.

- Tape the interview, if possible, and then later have it transcribed.

- Emphasize to interviewers that they need to collect accurate and complete data.

FOCUS FEATURE 7.3   STRATEGIES TO MINIMIZE ERRORS IN OBSERVATIONS

A variety of measurement errors can affect observations. The following are some strategies to help reduce measurement errors in observations:

- Use more than one observer to avoid a halo effect (Thorndike, 1920; Wells, 1907).

- A careful protocol for observation needs to be developed and adhered to.

- Provide detailed directions to observers.

- Observe large samples of behavior.

- Provide thorough and identical training for all observers. Some of the aspects of training include learning careful observation of small units of the behavior, careful recording of the observation, giving attention to time, and how to shed preconceived notions.

- Have a plan for recording or coding the behavior being observed.

- To reduce observer reactivity (Merrell, 2003), the observation process can be made inconspicuous or there can be some informal observation prior to formal observation.

SKILL-BUILDING ACTIVITY

You are to observe the physical activity behavior of upper elementary school students while they are in physical education class. Develop an observation protocol to observe this behavior. Also develop a training protocol for training observers to record this behavior. Make a list of all potential errors in both protocols. How would you reduce these?

SUMMARY

Measurement error is defined as the degree of deviation from perfect validity and reliability. There are two types of measurement error: random error and systematic error. Random error is an error in measurement that occurs due to chance. Systematic error or bias is an error in measurement that occurs due to a systematic mechanism of either increasing or decreasing the true score. Another way of classifying measurement errors is as: (1) situational or environmental factors, (2) administrative differences, (3) instrument-related factors, (4) response set biases, (5) intrapersonal errors, and (6) errors due to sampling of response. Situational or environmental factors include temperature, noise, rain, snow, lighting, humidity, time of day, location of the data collection, current events, past events, observer reactivity (when an observer is observing a phenomenon the behavior of the participants is altered), and friendliness of the researchers. Administrative differences include varying instructions, changing of words in a set protocol, changes in coding category, and using different versions of the instrument. Instrument-related factors include paucity of instructions, too many instructions, improper formatting and layout, improper sequencing of the items, use of open-ended questions, use of acronyms and difficult terms, variation in scales, mismatch between items and chosen scale, possibility of marking in a certain way by a certain group of respondents, poor calibration of physiological tools, insensitive measure bias (when the instrument used is not sensitive enough to detect what might be important differences in the variable of interest), recall or memory bias, and inadequate directions for observation. Response set biases include social desirability bias, faking bad bias, deviation bias, acquiescence bias (yeasayers bias), nay sayers bias, extreme responses bias, middle range bias (end-aversion bias or central tendency bias), and halo effect. Intrapersonal errors include factors such as fatigue or tiredness, hunger, anxiety, mood, boredom, failure to follow instructions, guessing, providing partial answers, providing inconsistent answers, incorrect marking, lying, copying, and using a satisficing approach (in which the respondent just puts in a good enough effort such as when completing a questionnaire for a researcher in which there is no tangible benefit to him or her) as opposed to an optimizing approach. Finally, there are errors due to sampling of response, which include response sampling error and expectation bias (when the observer may tend to observe things in favor of the treatment group).

REVIEW QUESTIONS

1. Define measurement error. Identify the types of measurement error.
2. Differentiate between random error and systematic error.

3. Describe common measurement errors due to situational and environmental factors.
4. Identify measurement errors due to administrative differences.
5. Describe instrument-related measurement errors.
6. Explain response set biases.
7. Describe intrapersonal errors.
8. Identify errors due to sampling of response.

WEBSITES TO EXPLORE

Major Sources of Bias in Research Studies

http://www.umdnj.edu/idsweb/shared/biases.htm

This website from the University of Medicine and Dentistry of New Jersey (UMDNJ) discusses selection biases, measurement biases, and intervention biases in research studies. Read this description. There is a link to an article on this website that works for only that university's subscribers. *Using your library, locate and retrieve that article. Prepare a review of all biases based on your reading of that article.*

Measurement Error

http://www.socialresearchmethods.net/kb/measerr.php

This website of the Web Center for Social Science Research Methods presents a discussion on measurement error. Both random error and systematic error are discussed, along with ways to reduce them. *Read the description and prepare a list of ways to reduce measurement error.*

Measurement Error and Correlation Coefficients

http://www.bmj.com/content/313/7048/41.extract

This is an article by Bland and Altman (1996) published in the *British Medical Journal* (Volume 313, Number 7048, page 41). You can get the full article by registering on the website; if you do not want to register you may be able to get it from your library. *Read this article and summarize it in 250 words.*

Measurement Error in Education

http://www.wcpss.net/evaluation-research/reports/2000/mment_error.pdf

This website of Wake County Public Schools discusses the concept of measurement error. It was written by Johnson, Dulaney, and Banks in 2000. *Read this article and define standard error of measurement and standard error of mean.*

REFERENCES

Berg, I. A. (1967). The deviation hypothesis: A broad statement of its assumptions and postulates. In I. A. Berg (Ed.), *Response set in personality assessment* (pp. 146–190). Chicago: Aldine.

Camilli, G., & Shepard, L. A. (1994). *Methods for identifying biased test items.* Thousand Oaks, CA: Sage.

Couch, A., & Keniston, K. (1960). Yeasayers and naysayers: Agreeing response set as a personality variable. *Journal of Abnormal and Social Psychology, 60*, 151–174.

Cronbach, L. J. (1946). Response sets and test validity. *Educational and Psychological Measurement, 6,* 475–494.

DiIorio, C. K. (2005). *Measurement in health behavior. Methods for research and education.* San Francisco, CA: Jossey-Bass.

Dillman, D. A. (2000). *Mail and Internet surveys. The tailored design method.* New York: Wiley.

Edwards, A. L. (1957). *The social desirability variable in personality assessment research.* Orlando, FL: Dryden Press.

Hartman, J. M., Forsen, J. W., Wallace, M. S., & Neely, J. G. (2002). Tutorials in clinical research: Part IV: Recognizing and controlling bias. *Laryngoscope, 112,* 23–31.

Jackson, D. N. (1970). A sequential system for personality scale development. In C. D. Spielberger (Ed.), *Current topics in clinical and community psychology* (Vol. 2, pp. 61–96). New York: Academic Press.

Krosnick, J. A. (1991). Response strategies for coping with the cognitive demands of attitude measures in surveys. *Applied Cognitive Psychology, 5,* 213–236.

Krosnick, J. A. (1999). Survey research. *Annual Review of Psychology, 50,* 537–567.

Merrell, K. W. (2003). *Behavioral, social, and emotional assessment of children* (2nd ed.). Mahwah, NJ: Lawrence Erlbaum.

Nunnally, J. C., & Bernstein, I. H. (1994). *Psychometric theory.* New York: McGraw-Hill.

Pedhazur, E. J., & Schmelkin, L. P. (1991). *Measurement, design, and analysis: An integrated approach.* Mahwah, NJ: Erlbaum.

Polit, D. F., & Hungler, B. P. (1999). *Nursing research: Principles and methods* (6th ed.). Philadelphia: Lippincott.

Streiner, D. L., & Norman, G. R. (2003). *Health measurement scales. A practical guide to their development and use* (3rd ed.). Oxford: Oxford University Press.

Thorndike, E. L. (1920). A constant error in psychological ratings. *Journal of Applied Psychology, 4,* 25–29.

Viswanathan, M. (2005). *Measurement error and research design.* Thousand Oaks, CA: Sage.

Wells, F. L. (1907). A statistical study of literary merit. *Archives of Psychology, 1*(7).

CHAPTER 8

Process Evaluation

CHAPTER OBJECTIVES

- Identify the targets of a process evaluation
- Describe the importance of implementation fidelity
- Utilize methods to assess implementation fidelity
- Describe how process evaluation can be used as a quality control tool
- Identify the conditions that indicate a formative evaluation is needed
- Identify the use of formative evaluation for program refinement
- Differentiate between the purposes of formative and summative evaluation

Health programs should be carefully designed based on the needs of the target audience, as well as the health promotion and education knowledge base. **Process evaluation** methods describe what happens when the health program is implemented in "real world" conditions. Process evaluation methods can be used for several purposes. First, they can be used as a quality control method. **Quality control** is a set of procedures designed to ensure that a program or intervention

Quality control is a set of procedures designed to ensure that a program or intervention adheres to a defined set of characteristic criteria or meets the requirements of the participants or consumers.

adheres to a defined set of professional standards or meets the requirements of the participants or consumers. It can ensure that standards are being met. This information is useful for program managers, funding agencies, and the general public. Process evaluation methods also can be used to document the actual level of implementation of the program in community settings. In practice, many different factors can prevent full implementation of a program. Determining the actual level of program implementation is foundational to the interpretation of impact and outcome evaluation results.

Formative evaluations use methods similar to process evaluations, but serve a different purpose. Formative evaluations are used to generate rapid feedback to refine health programs before widespread implementation. Using formative evaluation methods is one step evaluators can take to increase the likelihood that the health program is tailored to the specific community for which it is intended. It is generally recommended that formative evaluations be conducted when a new program has been developed or an established program is being used in a new setting.

DEFINING PROCESS EVALUATION

Health education and health promotion interventions systematically organize programs designed to change health behaviors in target populations. As a part of the program planning process, considerable effort is devoted to conducting community needs assessment, gathering program resources, and designing the intervention. After much work, the intervention is implemented in the community. Stakeholders and funding agencies want to know that the intervention is being delivered as planned. Process evaluation verifies what the intervention looks like in the field and assesses the degree to which the program was delivered as designed to the target population (Scheirer, 1994). The goal of process evaluation is to carefully document how much of the intervention was provided and how well the intervention was delivered to its intended audience. Process evaluation does not attempt to assess the effects of the intervention on the consumer or participant; that is the focus of impact and outcome evaluations.

Figure 8.1 illustrates the role of process evaluation in the context of the logic model. As shown in Figure 8.1, process evaluations can focus on five potential targets. The overall purpose of the process evaluation is to document the health program's strengths and deficiencies in the field (Mark & Pines, 1995). It is a form of quality control that program administrators can use to manage resources effectively. Process evaluation methods describe what happens when the intervention is implemented in "real world" conditions. Results from a process evaluation provide data about the interactions between an intervention's components and consumers. This enables stakeholders to make data-based decisions regarding how well the intervention is delivered and how the program is received by the intended audience.

TARGETS OF PROCESS EVALUATION

Process evaluations are designed to address important questions about the delivery of health promotion and education interventions. **Table 8.1** lists a set of potential questions that may be addressed in a process evaluation. At first glance this list of potential questions may

Figure 8.1   Process evaluation in the logic model.

appear overwhelming. Indeed, many process evaluations identify a subset of these questions to focus on in a particular setting. The evaluation team should discuss these questions with
key stakeholders to decide which of these questions should be
addressed in the process evaluation.

> *Targets of process evaluation in
> health education and health
> promotion programs pertain to quality
> control, program reach, implementa-
> tion fidelity, consumer satisfaction, and
> program management.*

Quality Control

In Table 8.1, quality control is listed first. **Quality** is defined as the appropriateness of a set
of professional activities employed to meet a set of objectives. To assess quality, an established set of standards is applied to the observed performance of professional activities in
the field (Pearson et al., 2005). **Quality standards** are the minimum acceptable levels of

TABLE 8.1 Target Questions for Process Evaluation	
Quality control:	Are resources, including staff, facilities, money, and time, adequate to support high qual-ity delivery of the intervention? Do intervention staff work effectively with each other?
Program reach:	How many consumers received the intervention? Who was the intended target popula-tion, and how far did the intervention "reach" into this group? Did the intervention attract members of the community who were not targeted? Do members of the target population know that the program is available?
Implementation fidelity:	Did participants receive the intended amount, type, and quality of intervention services? Was the intervention delivered as it was designed? Are the essential intervention com-ponents being delivered well? Is program delivery consistent across different interven-tion sites? Does program quality vary across program staff?
Consumer satisfaction:	Are intervention participants satisfied with the program they receive? Do they participate in the entire intervention? Was attendance adequate for program delivery?
Program management:	Is the program in compliance with the requirements of professional standards, legal standards, funding agencies, and agency administration? Is the utilization of resources well organized so that resources are used efficiently?

performance used to judge the quality of professional practice. One responsibility of the evaluator is to identify a set of professional standards for health promotion and education practice. These standards are used to review the professional staff. Considerable progress has been made in the identification of standards for the Certified Health Education Specialist (CHES). Through expert panel review, competencies for CHESs have been identified and verified. **Table 8.2** lists a sampling of paraphrased competencies that could be used to review professional health education staff.

Using a set of *a priori* standards, the evaluator would review needs assessment and program planning documents to determine the degree to which standards were met. In addition, the evaluator would observe implementation of the health education or health promotion intervention to also determine the degree to which standards were reflected in practice. This external review by the evaluator is a form of quality assurance that seeks to verify that professional standards were met in designing and implementing the health education or health promotion program.

Targets of Process Evaluation: Program Reach

Program reach is the subject of the second set of questions listed in Table 8.1. Essentially the key issue is whether the program is being delivered to the intended audience (Sobo, Seid, & Gelhard, 2006). To address this question requires careful definition of the intended target audience of the program. For example, a worksite physical activity program is designed specifically for 300 employees who have been identified as sedentary and are overweight or obese. Over the course of the year, how many of the 300 employees who were targeted for the intervention actually participated in the health program? Did the program "reach" 50 highly motivated volunteers, 150 of the target population, or all 300

TABLE 8.2 Selected Paraphrased Certified Health Education Competencies Relevant to Health Education/Promotion Program Delivery	
Category	**Competency Practice Standard**
Needs assessment	1. Select valid sources of information about health needs.
	2. Prioritize health needs and target populations.
Planning health programs	1. Use research results when planning programs.
	2. Design developmentally appropriate interventions.
	3. Match health education services to program activities.
	4. Plan a sequence of learning activities that meet objectives.
Implement health interventions	1. Use community organization to facilitate health behaviors.
	2. Use instructional technology effectively.
	3. Use a code of ethics in professional practice.
	4. Apply theoretical models to improve program delivery.
	5. Implement intervention strategies to facilitate health behavior.
	6. Incorporate culturally sensitive techniques in health programs.

of the sedentary employees? Each of these three options will have a considerable effect on the interpretation of the subsequent evaluation results.

Occasionally evaluators may find that the program is reaching a different audience than intended. For example, in the previous example, it is possible the physical activity program is attracting participants who are already physically active. The targeted audience of sedentary employees was not reached. Careful review of recruitment methods and gathering descriptive data on program participants are essential for evaluating program reach.

Targets of Process Evaluation: Implementation Fidelity

Table 8.1 lists a set of questions related to program **implementation fidelity**. It is often assumed that health programs are delivered in the field as they are designed on paper. Imagine the frustration an evaluator might experience if the results of a multi-year evaluation to assess changes in health behavior and health status show that it is compromised because the program was not delivered as it was designed due to extensive modifications. It is critical that evaluators pay sufficient attention to carefully assessing the degree of program implementation. In most cases, monitoring the degree of program implementation can increase fidelity of implementation. This is accomplished by evaluators and program delivery professionals precisely identifying critical components of the program and then monitoring implementation. This process can enhance on-task behavior in the field. Using these procedures increases the confidence with which one can assert that the program was delivered according to plan (Spilane et al., 2007). Methods to measure implementation fidelity will be described in more detail later in this chapter.

Targets of Process Evaluation: Consumer Satisfaction

Table 8.1 identifies **consumer satisfaction** as another target for process evaluation. Consumer satisfaction is the extent to which a health program meets or exceeds the expectations of participants. Health programs cannot be delivered if participants do not consistently attend the planned sessions. Further, it is important that consumers of health programs be interested in and satisfied with the program they receive. Participants' learning and motivation to change their health practices will be influenced by the degree to which they are favorably impressed by the health program. The health program will be more effective in recruiting new participants if consumers are generally pleased with the health program. Interviews, focus groups, and surveys can be used to assess customer satisfaction with a health program.

Targets of Process Evaluation: Program Management

Process evaluations also can be utilized as a program management tool to monitor accountability and responsibility. **Program management** refers to the program's compliance with the requirements of professional standards, legal standards, funding agencies, and agency administration. **Program accountability** means being able to document to stakeholders and sponsors that health programs were delivered. **Responsibility** refers to health professionals ensuring that programs and services are delivered according to quality standards.

Documentation that health education or health promotion programs were delivered is known as program accountability.

Program managers are generally required to keep records documenting health program delivery. Each domain of program accountability requires planning and oversight. Rossi, Lipsey, and Freeman (1999) have identified core areas of accountability (**Table 8.3**).

Process evaluation procedures can be designed to carefully document these accountability domains. First, the process evaluation needs to keep track of all service delivery, not only how many programs were delivered, but also indicators of program quality. Utilization of program resources should be recorded, including staff, materials, and facilities needed to deliver health programs. This will enable the program manager to establish costs for program delivery. Keeping track of program participants is vital: who they are, attendance records, and services received. These process evaluation activities can be invaluable to program managers in meeting requirements for accountability. This information can also enable program managers to monitor staff efforts and resource utilization.

Careful documentation of how the intervention was actually implemented in the field can be essential context for the interpretation of the results produced from the impact and outcome evaluations. Listed in **Table 8.4** are some examples in which the process evaluation provided insights essential to the interpretation of program effectiveness.

TABLE 8.3   Types of Program Accountability

Efficiency:	Resources are used without waste or redundancy.
Fiscal accountability:	Resources are used following a budget.
Legal accountability:	Legal and ethical standards are maintained.
Coverage accountability:	The intended target audience receives the health program.
Service delivery accountability:	The intervention is provided as planned.
Impact accountability:	Program participants benefit from the health program.

TABLE 8.4   Examples of Process Evaluation Leading to Insights into How a Health Education or Health Promotion Program Works

1. Attendance records reveal that participants who attended 80% of the program sessions did change their health behavior. Those with attendance below 80% did not change their health behavior.

2. A new program employs innovative content and methods; test to see whether consumers accept the new program approach.

3. A well-established, effective program is ready for dissemination to a wider audience. However, staff were not comfortable with the program, resulting in low implementation fidelity. The new program requires significant training for new methods to increase staff skill and comfort.

4. Program implementation varied widely based on site and/or instructor. Sites with implementation fidelity were effective in changing health practices. Sites with low implementation fidelity were not effective in changing health practices.

5. In terms of program reach, the program reached only those who were already physically active and did not reach the intended target audience (sedentary adults). As a consequence, the program did not increase physical activity levels or improve fitness levels in the target population.

IMPLEMENTATION FIDELITY

Imagine a situation in which considerable effort has been expended in the development of a quality health behavior intervention. Everyone assumes that the program was delivered as designed. The impact evaluation reveals that the intervention did not produce positive changes in consumers' health behavior. Yet we do not know *why* the intervention failed to produce the intended results. Basch, Sliepcevich, Gold, Duncan, and Kolbe (1985) have described failure to implement a health intervention as designed as a potential explanation for program failure. Failure to implement a health intervention as designed is labeled a **Type III error**. There are many reasons why an intervention may not be implemented as planned. Consider the following:

> *Type III error occurs when one assumes a health education/promotion program has been implemented fully and correctly when it has not been.*

- Health promotion staff members were not adequately trained, so they did not know how to deliver the program correctly. They may not understand an underlying theory, concept, or technology. Lack of understanding may produce "blind spots" in which they unintentionally wander away from the intervention design.
- Health promotion staff did not fully buy into or accept the program. Staff may have preferred different intervention methods and, as a consequence, deviated from the program design. Experienced health staff may be more likely to have preferred methods, and thus may "reinvent" interventions by selectively implementing parts of the new intervention combined with favorite activities from past programs. Occasionally staff may decide they know what consumers need and simply ignore the program plan.
- Inadequate resources (time, money, facilities) did not allow for adequate implementation. For example, only 4 hours of instructional time did not allow staff to fully implement the 10-hour program. Practitioners experience many real-world constraints in the field. Inadequate facilities, educational technology, and the like may also prevent full implementation.
- Consumers did not like the new program and did not fully participate or adequately attend the intervention sessions. Consumer acceptance is foundational to program success. Consumers must see the value of the program and willingly attend and participate in sessions. Without consumers, the program does not get disseminated.

Experience suggests that a program evaluator should *not* assume an intervention has been implemented (Mihalic, Fagan, & Argamaso, 2008). Using process evaluation methods, evaluators should document the degree of implementation for the intervention. Implementation fidelity refers to the degree to which the program was delivered as planned. In theory, implementation fidelity can vary from 0% to 100%. In practice, implementation fidelity varies by site, situation, and health promotion practitioners (Hill, Maucicone, & Hood, 2007). In most cases, adequately trained health promotion professionals make a good faith effort to implement the program, but rarely does implementation fidelity reach 100%. Thus, it is important for evaluators to measure implementation fidelity. The degree of implementation fidelity provides a critical context for understanding the results of the impact and outcome evaluations.

Measuring Implementation Fidelity

The following methods will help professionals to measure implementation fidelity:

- *Identify critical intervention components:* Program developers and evaluation staff decide which intervention components are critical for adequate implementation.
- *Develop methods to measure each critical intervention component:* Evaluation staff develop observational assessments to assess the degree of implementation of each critical program component.
- *Assess intervention fidelity in the field:* Typically an evaluator attends intervention sessions and completes the observational assessment as each critical component is implemented.
- *Perform data analysis to determine quality and degree of implementation:* Evaluation staff members review observation forms to determine the degree of implementation fidelity.
- *Discuss how to increase program implementation fidelity in the future:* Evaluation, program development, and program delivery staff discuss barriers and solutions to increasing implementation fidelity in the field. This problem-solving discussion may focus on additional training of staff, overcoming barriers to implementation, or actually modifying the program to increase implementation fidelity.
- *Discuss relationships between program implementation and program impact:* After impact evaluations are completed, it may be instructive to look for patterns between program implementation and participant learning. It is assumed that higher implementation fidelity will lead to superior participant learning. This assumption should be tested when the data becomes available.

FOCUS FEATURE 8.1   EXAMPLE OF IMPLEMENTATION FIDELITY ASSESSMENT

The following is a very concise intervention plan designed as one part of a program to prevent back injuries at the Acme Company. A careful review of the plan reveals that the program uses a variety of methods to inform, motivate, and enhance the skills of employees. Instructional methods include lecture, guest lecture, demonstrations, practice, and videotape feedback. Policy requires employees to wear back braces, and incentives are provided for employees to remain back injury free. The intervention plan begins with a health status goal to reduce healthcare costs associated with back injuries at the worksite. The two behavioral objectives are for employees to use proper lifting techniques and to regularly wear back braces. The lesson then details the educational content to be delivered, the educational process to deliver the content, and the amount of time allocated for each educational process. A detailed intervention plan enables an evaluator to develop a method to observe and assess the degree of implementation.

Intervention Plan: Preventing Back Injury at Acme Company

Health Status Goal: Reduce healthcare costs associated with back injuries by 35% at the Acme Company by June 1, 2018.

FOCUS FEATURE 8.1   EXAMPLE OF IMPLEMENTATION FIDELITY ASSESSMENT *(Continued)*

Behavioral Objectives:

- Every day, Acme employees will consistently use proper lifting techniques during work to prevent back injuries.

- Every day, Acme employees will wear their back brace during work to prevent back injuries.

Educational Objectives:

- Participants will demonstrate lifting techniques to prevent injury.

- Participants will list three reasons why back injuries are serious.

- Participants will describe how a back injury could affect work, family, and recreational lifestyle.

- Participants will be able to describe the incentives provided by Acme for preventing back injury.

Educational Content	Educational Process	Time Required (in minutes)
Back injuries cost Acme Co.: $450,000 for treatment $250,000 in sick days $500,000 in lost productivity	Lecture on costs to Acme	10
Back injuries affect quality of life, causing changes in work, family, and recreation. Injury-causing incident: symptoms, surgery, rehab, costs. Inability to: exercise, golf, motorcycle, play with kids, tie shoes.	Guest lecture: Employee with back injury discusses personal experience with back injury.	25
Proper lifting requires keeping back erect, bending knees to lower body, and using leg muscles to lift object.	Lecture describing lifting method	10
	Show video of proper lifting sequence	10
	Demo lifting by instructor	10
	In pairs, students practice lifting 5-, 10-, and 20-pound objects. Partner videotapes lift technique. Self-evaluate lift method with videotape.	10
Policy: Employees must wear back braces	Lecture on policy	10
	Instructor distributes braces	5
Incentives: employee gets $50 incentive each year he or she does not experience back injury	Lecture: Inform employees about incentive policy	10
	Personnel office monitors back injuries and insurance claims and provides incentive to injury-free employees	10

(continues)

FOCUS FEATURE 8.1   EXAMPLE OF IMPLEMENTATION FIDELITY ASSESSMENT *(Continued)*

Program Implementation Observation

The following table is an implementation observation form used to assess the degree of implementation of the intervention plan. Careful review of the form reveals that time and educational process are used to segment the different elements of the intervention plan into observational units. Using this form, an evaluator can either videotape or directly observe practitioners in the field. By timing the delivery of each planned educational process the evaluator can quantify the degree of implementation of the intervention. The far right column provides a scale to record estimates of implementation quality.

IMPLEMENTATION OBSERVATION FORM: PREVENTING BACK INJURY AT ACME COMPANY

Observation Point	Planned Time (min)	Actual Time (min)	Low	Quality Rating Medium	High
1. Lecture on back injury costs to Acme	10	___	L	M	H
2. Guest lecture described:					
Workplace injury incident	15	___	L	M	H
Surgery, rehabilitation costs	5	___	L	M	H
Impact on family and recreation	5	___	L	M	H
3. Proper lifting technique					
Lecture to describe proper method	10	___	L	M	H
Video demonstration	10	___	L	M	H
Instructor demonstration	10	___	L	M	H
Student practice in pairs, videotape	10	___	L	M	H
Student evaluation of videotape	10	___	L	M	H
4. Policy on back braces					
Lecture on policy to wear back brace	10	___	L	M	H
Distribution of back braces	5	___	L	M	H
5. Incentives					
Lecture on employee incentives	10	___	L	M	H

List other classroom observations:

_____

_____

_____

_____

_____

PROCESS EVALUATION: FOUNDATIONAL TO IMPACT AND OUTCOME EVALUATION

The results of a carefully designed process evaluation can enhance stakeholders' ability to interpret impact and outcome evaluations of the same program. For example, process evaluation may reveal that a health program was not implemented with fidelity. It is likely that the subsequent outcome evaluation will reveal that participants did not learn as much as was intended, and their health behavior change was not adequate. If a process evaluation had not been conducted, it would be easy to conclude that the program design was not effective. However, in this example, the primary interpretation would be implementation failure. The program was not implemented adequately and thus we cannot claim to have adequately tested the health program. It is also likely that this case would be followed up to determine why the program was not implemented well. Perhaps the professional staff was not trained adequately. Another possibility is that the health professionals responsible for delivery have judged the program to be inappropriate for the target audience. In either case, understanding why the program was not implemented well can lead to problem-solving strategies to enhance program implementation.

A process evaluation can provide insights about *why* a program is effective or not effective. In another example, a health program is implemented with a high degree of fidelity, but posttests reveal the participants' knowledge, motivation, and skill levels did not increase as much as intended. In this case, the evaluator is likely to conclude that the health program was adequately tested and in its current form is not sufficient to produce the targeted changes in participants. The evaluator is likely to conclude that the program requires significant revisions.

PRAGMATIC PLANNING FOR A PROCESS EVALUATION

This chapter has identified five conceptual issues that a process evaluation can focus on: quality control, program reach, implementation fidelity, consumer satisfaction, and program management. Often it is not practical, feasible, or desirable for all five issues to be addressed in a particular process evaluation. It is often helpful for the evaluator to meet with program sponsors, program management, and program professionals to determine the direction the process evaluation will take. Once the set of conceptual foci of the process evaluation have been identified, it is time for pragmatic planning. **Table 8.5** lists questions that should be reviewed when deciding how the process evaluation will be conducted. Open discussion of these questions can ensure that the program staff members are well informed. Program staff need to know why the process evaluation is being conducted and the specific procedures of the process evaluation. The goal is for a quality process evaluation to be conducted efficiently and with a minimum of health program disruption.

TABLE 8.5 Pragmatic Issues to Discuss in Planning a Process Evaluation

What decisions need to be made based on the process evaluation?
What data needs to be collected to make these decisions?
What methods will be used to gather this data?
Who will be gathering, coding, and interpreting the data?
How much will it cost to conduct the proposed process evaluation?

Careful consideration of these questions is designed to lead the evaluation team towards a process evaluation that is affordable, practical, and directly relevant to the needs of a particular site. These questions can also provide a basis for examining options and assigning responsibilities for different aspects of the process evaluation. Discussions around these questions provide a forum for educating the professional staff and creating a climate of trust.

FORMATIVE EVALUATION

A special use of process evaluation methods is to conduct formative evaluations. Formative evaluation refers to the rapid, diagnostic feedback about the quality of implementation of health program methods, activities, and resources (**Figure 8.2**).

The purpose of formative evaluation methods is to provide rapid, meaningful feedback to improve the health program. The feedback is used to quickly tailor and refine the health program to optimize learning and potential positive impact in a particular setting. The feedback loop is completed in days or within a few weeks. Thus, data gathering, analysis, and sharing of results must be done very quickly. The focus is on the identification of health program problems, rough spots, or concerns so that they can be fixed quickly. This formative evaluation process can be repeated until the professional staff are satisfied that the health program is of high quality. Once the quality of the program is established, it is reasonable to move on to **summative evaluation** procedures. Summative evaluations are conducted to draw conclusions and make decisions about the impact, outcomes, and other benefits of a health program. Summative evaluations are often used to pass judgment on the worth of a health program.

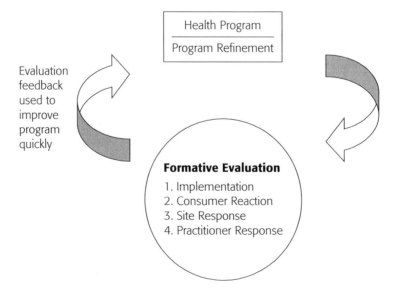

Figure 8.2 Formative evaluation: rapid feedback loop for program refinement.

When Is Formative Evaluation Needed?

When a new health education or health promotion program is being tested for the first time, a formative evaluation is indicated. Although a new program may be carefully developed based on needs assessment, health education principles, and sound theory, ultimately it must be accepted by professionals and the target audience. Formative evaluation is an essential first step to systematically looking at program acceptability.

A health education or health promotion program may have a track record of effectiveness and thus is being actively disseminated around the country. When an established program is adopted by a different community, a formative evaluation is recommended. With the new community come new professionals, new stakeholders, and new consumers. Each community can be viewed as possessing many features in common with other communities, but each community may also have unique features that may affect program relevance and effectiveness. The formative evaluation can help tailor the program to the specific needs and capabilities of the new setting.

Imagine that a hospital has developed a new diabetes education program that is computer-based. Newly diagnosed patients are offered the opportunity to participate in a self-guided, six-lesson program in diabetes self-care. Although the program is based on sound principles of health education practice, formative evaluation methods will be used to refine the program. Formative evaluation will monitor and provide feedback on program implementation, consumer response, health professional response, and site response.

Program Implementation

The degree to which programs are delivered as designed varies with different instructors, participants, and sites. A key question is how much the program can be modified and still be considered a quality program. For example, an instructor does not like a section of lesson 1 and so simply skips that section. Discussions with the instructor will be needed to determine why the section was not implemented. Perhaps the instructor lacked training, and thus did not see the relevance of the section. Another possibility is that the instructor knows from experience that the target audience is well versed in the content of the skipped section. Detailed analysis of the situation can reveal the best course of action for program refinement.

Not all deviations from the original program plan are bad. It may be discovered that health educators are modifying the program in response to consumers' interests and questions. Such discoveries can lead to program modifications to improve instructional effectiveness.

Consumer Response

Consumer response to the program can be assessed from a variety of perspectives. The first is consumer satisfaction: Did they judge the program to be useful, did they like the program, and was it worth the investment of time? Consumers' emotional response to the program is an important indicator of subsequent referrals and ultimately the reach of the program into the intended target audience. Consumer expectations and program acceptability are also critical. If a health program is not perceived as necessary and useful, a consumer is unlikely to participate fully. Consumer response can be assessed through satisfaction surveys, class observation, or focus groups.

Health Professionals' Response

Experienced professionals' input can be invaluable in making suggestions for program refinement. They are in a unique position to view the program from a delivery perspective and can also be astute observers of consumers' classroom behavior. They can identify sections of the program that are strong and useful, as well as sections that are not relevant or do not hold consumer interest. Importantly, direct involvement of professionals in the refinement of the program can increase their ownership and engagement in the health program and the evaluation. Health professionals' responses can be assessed in interviews, focus groups, and detailed questionnaires that carefully review each component of the health program.

Site Response

Health programs are implemented in communities with a wide range of competing concerns. How the new health program is viewed in the political environment of the responsible health agency and the community should be monitored. For example, are there competing programs that already exist in the community? Are professionals skeptical of the new program? Are there significant obstacles to program acceptance in the community? These concerns can often be constructively dealt with by open forums to explain the new program. In other cases, the program may need to be modified to be acceptable to community stakeholders. Meetings or interviews with stakeholders are an essential part of revealing site response to a health program.

Returning to the example of the computer-based diabetes education program, observations and records reveal that six patients volunteered to complete the course. Three patients completed two lessons and dropped out. The remaining three patients skipped over sections of the program and completed about 50% of the program. Interviews with dropouts revealed several reasons for not finishing the program. Traveling to the hospital to complete a 30-minute lesson was a concern. Dropouts also found the computer program confusing and often did not know how to complete the lesson. The patients who completed 50% of the program revealed other concerns. They found the waiting room of the hospital to be a distracting environment for taking a computer-based course. They also complained about not being able to ask personal questions about self-management. This information can be vital to professional staff in making specific modifications in hopes of improving the health program and the consumer educational experience. The formative evaluation process can be repeated over a period of months until the administration and staff are convinced that the program has been refined to the point of meeting professional standards for quality.

Contrast Between Formative Evaluation and Summative Evaluation

The purpose of formative evaluations is to provide rapid diagnostic feedback to improve or refine a health program. In contrast, summative evaluations are done to assign worth or pass judgment on a health program. Formative evaluations are completed in a very short time—typically in a matter of days or weeks the diagnostic feedback is presented and program refinements are actively considered. Summative evaluations typically take several months to possibly several years to assess the effects of the health program on consumer health behaviors and subsequent health status.

Formative evaluation will monitor and provide feedback on program implementation, consumer response, health professionals' response, and site response.

After a health program has been refined through the use of formative evaluation feedback, stakeholders will want to know how effective the program is in achieving stated goals and objectives. Summative evaluations systematically gather evidence to judge the effectiveness of a health program in achieving goals and objectives. Before investing resources and time in summative evaluation, it makes sense to use formative evaluation methods to optimize the health program for a particular community setting.

SKILL-BUILDING ACTIVITY

Imagine you been assigned to evaluate the Drug Abuse Resistance Education (DARE) program (http://www.dare.com). DARE is a police officer–administered substance abuse prevention program in grades K–12. What would be some targets of process evaluation? How will you ascertain implementation fidelity? Design an instrument to assess implementation fidelity of one session of the DARE program.

SUMMARY

The purpose of process evaluation is to document the quality of health interventions in the field. It seeks to describe what happens when the intervention is implemented in real-world conditions. Results from a process evaluation provide data about the interactions between intervention components and consumers. This data can be used as a quality control method and can ensure that standards are being met. This information is useful for program managers, funding agencies, and the general public. Process evaluation methods can also be used to document the actual level of implementation of the program in community settings. The results of a well-designed process evaluation can enhance stakeholders' ability to interpret impact and outcome evaluations of the same program.

Formative evaluation uses many of the same methods as process evaluation; the key difference is the purpose of the evaluation. Formative evaluation refers to the rapid, diagnostic feedback about the quality of implementation of health program methods, activities, and resources. The purpose of formative evaluation methods is to provide rapid, meaningful feedback to refine the health program implementation in a particular setting. The feedback is used to quickly revise and refine the health program to optimize learning and potential positive impact in a field setting. The feedback loop is completed in days or within a few weeks. Formative evaluation is a useful first step to systematically examining program acceptability. The formative evaluation can help tailor the program to the specific needs and capabilities of the new setting.

REVIEW QUESTIONS

1. Define process evaluation, formative evaluation, and quality control.
2. Identify the targets of process evaluation.
3. Define program accountability. List the different types of program accountability.
4. Describe the importance of implementation fidelity.
5. What is a Type III error? Discuss reasons why an intervention may not be implemented as planned.
6. Discuss methods to assess implementation fidelity.
7. Describe how process evaluation can be used as a quality control tool.
8. What is formative evaluation? Give indications for using formative evaluation.
9. Differentiate between formative and summative evaluation.

WEBSITES TO EXPLORE

Process Evaluations

http://www.emcdda.europa.eu/attachements.cfm/att_5866_EN_4_process_evaluations.pdf
This website provides a World Health Organization (WHO)–developed workbook on process evaluations. The what, why, and how of process evaluation are described. A highlight of this workbook is the case examples. *Read one case example and discuss its strengths and weaknesses.*

Process Evaluation as a Quality Assurance Tool

http://www.worldbridgeresearch.com/files/Process_Evaluation.pdf
This page of the Annie E. Casey Foundation website introduces the concept of process evaluation. Topics such as what is process evaluation, what are the main questions process evaluation can answer, when should process evaluation be conducted, methods of process evaluation, data sources for process evaluation, the importance of community involvement in process evaluation, and tools for process evaluation are covered. *Read this write-up and follow the recommendations for locating standard tools for process evaluation.*

Process Evaluation in Tobacco Use Prevention and Control

http://www.cdc.gov/tobacco/tobacco_control_programs/surveillance_evaluation/process_evaluation/pdfs/tobaccousemanual_updated04182008.pdf
This webpage of the Centers for Disease Control and Prevention (CDC) contains a 71-page document about using process evaluation in tobacco prevention and control programs. Discussed in this report are the purposes and benefits of process evaluation, key elements of process evaluation, and steps for managing process evaluation. *Review this document. What*

are the salient lessons you have been able to learn from the application of process evaluations in the tobacco prevention field?

Process Evaluation for Public Health Interventions

http://media.wiley.com/product_data/excerpt/66/07879597/0787959766.pdf

This website contains a chapter by Laura Linnan and Allan Steckler entitled, "Process Evaluation for Public Health Interventions and Research: An Overview." It provides a brief history and review of process evaluation, gaps in current knowledge, and advancing future public health-linked process evaluation efforts. *Read this chapter. Prepare a 250-word summary and critique.*

Workbook for Designing a Process Evaluation

http://health.state.ga.us/pdfs/ppe/Workbook%20for%20Designing%20a%20Process%20Evaluation.pdf

This website by the Georgia Department of Human Resources, Division of Public Health presents a 38-page workbook for designing and conducting process evaluation. Topics include what is process evaluation, why process evaluation is important, and the stages of process evaluation. *Use this workbook to design a process evaluation of a real health education program.*

REFERENCES

Basch, C. E., Sliepcevich, E. M., Gold, R. S., Duncan, D. F., & Kolbe, L. J. (1985). Avoiding type III errors in health education program evaluations: A case study. *Health Education Quarterly*, *12*, 315–331.

Hill, L. G., Maucicone, K., & Hood, B. K. (2007). A focused approach to assessing program fidelity. *Prevention Science*, *8*(1), 25–34.

Mark, M. M., & Pines, E. (1995). Implications of continuous quality improvement for program evaluation and evaluators. *Evaluation Practice*, *16*, 131–139.

Mihalic, S. F., Fagan, A. A., & Argamaso, S. (2008). Implementing the Lifeskills Training drug prevention program: Factors related to implementation fidelity. *Implementation Science*, *3*, 5.

Pearson, M. L., We, S., Schafer, J., Bonomi, A. E., Shortell, S. M., & Mendel, P. (2005). Assessing the implementation of the chronic care model in quality improvement collaboratives. *Health Services Research*, *40*, 978–996.

Rossi, P., Lipsey, M., & Freeman, H. (2004). *Evaluation: A systematic approach* (7th ed.). Thousand Oaks, CA: Sage.

Scheirer, M. A. (1994). Designing and using process evaluation. In J. S. Wholey, H. P. Hatry, & K. E. Newcomer (Eds.), *Handbook of practical program evaluation* (pp. 40–68). San Francisco: Jossey Bass.

Sobo, E. J., Seid, M., & Gelhard, L. R. (2006). Parent-identified barriers to pediatric health care: A process-oriented model. *Health Services Research*, *4*, 148–171.

Spilane, V., Byrne, M. C., Byrne, M., Leathem, C. S., O'Malley, M., & Cupples, M. E. (2007). Monitoring treatment fidelity in a randomized controlled trial of a complex intervention. *Journal of Advanced Nursing*, *60*, 343–352.

CHAPTER 9

Designs for Quantitative Evaluation

KEY CONCEPTS

- blinding
- double blinding
- evaluation design
- evaluation design notation
- external validity
- Hawthorne effect
- history
- instrumentation bias
- interactive effects
- internal validity
- maturation
- novelty effect

- participant attrition
- placebo effect
- Pygmalion effect
- random assignment
- selection bias
- social desirability
- statistical regression
- testable hypothesis
- testing
- triple blinding
- unobtrusive measures

CHAPTER OBJECTIVES

- Explain the importance of evaluation design
- Explain the relationship among internal validity, external validity, and evaluation design
- Identify real-world obstacles to evaluation design
- Describe the components of a testable hypothesis
- Identify threats to internal validity and propose methods to overcome the threats
- Identify threats to external validity and propose methods to overcome the threats
- Use evaluation design notation
- Identify common designs used in evaluation of health education and health promotion interventions
- Identify obstacles to randomization in health education and health promotion program settings

QUESTIONS IN EVALUATION

One of the bottom line questions for health education and health promotion evaluations is: "To what degree did the health program achieve its stated goals?" Specifically, did the health program help participants learn knowledge and skills enabling them to make informed decisions? Did the health program increase adherence to health behaviors that yielded improved health status for individuals and/or the community? Most important, has the evaluator produced clear, convincing evidence that the documented changes in learning, health behavior, or improved health status can be attributed to the health program? These are the fundamental questions that stakeholders and health promotion professionals want answered. Evaluation design is fundamental to creating a legitimate case for answering these questions. Adequate evaluation design requires careful planning, utilization of adequate evaluation resources, and a long-term commitment to rigorous evaluation methods. This chapter will review issues related to evaluation design for health education and health promotion interventions.

Stakeholders' bottom line question: To what extent did the health program achieve its stated goals and objectives?

Ultimately, stakeholders (funding agencies, administrators, tax-paying voters, program consumers) want to know how effective health education and health promotion programs are in promoting health. This is a decision that is best addressed by reliable knowledge produced by systematic evaluation efforts. Best, Brown, Cameron, Smith, and MacDonald (1989) argue that the first critical task for the evaluation team is to clearly identify the purpose of the health program. **Table 9.1** summarizes fundamental evaluation questions for health education and health promotion programs that can help identify the purpose of the program and the evaluation. These questions can be used to guide evaluation planning discussions to arrive at the set of questions that will be addressed. Rarely can a program evaluation address all of the questions listed in Table 9.1; priorities often must be established. What is critical is that program management, program staff, and evaluators all understand which questions will be addressed and which will not be addressed in the evaluation.

Gathering empirical evidence to support causal linkages is a challenging task. There are often a large number of alternative explanations to any observed change in health practices among any given target population (Biglan et al., 1996). The goals of evaluation design are

---

TABLE 9.1   Fundamental Evaluation Questions for Health Education and Health Promotion Programs

Did the health program produce meaningful learning among participants?

Did participants in the health program change their health practices as a function of learning?

Did participants in the health program maintain changes in their health practices for a period of time sufficient to produce changes in health status?

Did participants in the health program experience health status improvements as a result of changes in health practices?

Did the health program produce improvements in quality of life beyond health status?

to determine what the major threats are to a causal explanation, identify design strategies to control for these alternative explanations, garner resources to support evaluation design components, gather empirical evidence, and create a convincing case that indeed the health promotion intervention caused the favorable health changes in the target population.

EVALUATION DESIGN

Evaluation design specifies the conditions under which an evaluation will take place (Cook & Campbell, 1979). It describes how program participants will be selected and assigned to groups. It carefully plans who will implement which program procedures. Design also indicates when and how measurements will be administered. Evaluation design can be seen as a strategic set of actions evaluators take regarding sampling, intervention implementation, and measurement that are used to answer evaluation questions and create a ratio-

Evaluation design can be seen as a strategic set of actions evaluators take regarding sampling, intervention implementation, and measurement that are used to answer evaluation questions and create a rationale for causal reasoning.

nale for causal reasoning. The decisions made regarding evaluation design can increase or decrease the scientific rigor of the evaluation. In this direct manner, evaluation can enhance or detract from the confidence one places in the results of the evaluation. A carefully designed evaluation enables the evaluation team to estimate the level of change produced by the health promotion intervention.

Evaluation design can be used to increase the scientific rigor used in evaluations. It would make sense that the evaluation team would design a very rigorous evaluation. But in fact, there are many real-world conditions that present significant barriers to rigorous design. The evaluation team should map out the critical design decisions to be made. All feasible options for each decision should be listed. The resource costs of design options should be carefully considered. Then a critical analysis should be conducted to assure that the highest level of practical evaluation rigor is achieved. It is the rigor of the evaluation design and not the statistical analysis that allows one to make causal inferences.

The following list discusses real-world constraints that often prohibit the use of rigorous experimental designs. Each of these issues needs to be carefully considered when designing an evaluation.

- *Institutional/administrative constraints:* Policies at the program's setting (worksite, hospital, school, community organization) may constrain how subjects may be selected or assigned. These organizations may also have constraints on or conditions for how health education and health promotion interventions are delivered. An example of such a constraint is in the school setting, which has intact classrooms; the health educator may not be able to randomly assign the students into chosen categories because of the already existing classrooms.
- *Financial constraints:* Some elements of research design may take additional resources and thus cost more than other approaches. Often, but not always, more rigorous designs cost more. Sometimes the evaluation team can think of creative strategies to control costs and increase rigor.

- *Practical time constraints:* There are limits to how much time participants can devote to participation in health education and health promotion programs as well as the evaluation procedures for those programs. There also is a limit on how much time you can ask participants to devote to completing measurement tools for the purpose of the evaluation. Often the participants are not willing to devote more than a few minutes to completing the tools that the evaluator has designed. Sometimes incentives may have to be given for the participants to complete the measurement tools. Some evaluation designs require 6- or 12-month follow-up after the health program. Can the evaluator reach the health participants and are they willing to complete assessments 6 or 12 months after the health program?
- *Scientific constraints:* Progress in scientific methods is slow and gradual. Often measurement tools are not as sophisticated and refined as the evaluator would like. Are the measurement tools specifically designed to measure the variables targeted in the health program? The results of evaluation rely heavily on the quality of the measurement technologies used. Does the measurement technology being considered have established validity and reliability for the population you will be using it for?
- *Ethical constraints:* Evaluators should always be mindful of ethical treatment of human subjects. Health education and health promotion programs may target personal lifestyle practices among youth or disadvantaged members of the community. The evaluation team should be vigilant to maintain the highest ethical standards in studying human subjects.

These constraints to true experimental designs in health education and health promotion are summarized in **Table 9.2**.

COMPONENTS OF A TESTABLE HYPOTHESIS

Testable hypotheses drive decisions regarding evaluation design. A **testable hypothesis** is defined as the depiction of the relationship between independent and dependent variables in a given target population. It is an explanation of the relationship between independent and dependent variables that can be tested using empirical methods. A testable hypothesis requires a minimum of two variables. The evaluation hypothesis explicitly

TABLE 9.2   Constraints to True Experimental Designs in Health Education and Health Promotion

Constraints	Example
Institutional/administrative constraints	Intact classrooms in school settings that prevent random assignment of students to intervention and control groups
Financial constraints	Lack of money to cover cost of control group
	Lack of money preventing long-term follow-up data collections
Practical time constraints	Participants have limited time for completing evaluation instruments.
Scientific constraints	Lack of valid and reliable instruments to measure goals and objectives
Ethical constraints	Inability to observe certain health behaviors

states the expected relationships between the health education or promotion intervention (independent variable) and
the impact and outcome variables (dependent variables). The
hypothesis should indicate specifically who (target population)
will change what (dependent variable), by how much (magnitude of change), and by when (typically after the interven-

> *A testable hypothesis is one that depicts the relationship between independent and dependent variables in a given target population and can be tested empirically.*

tion). Therefore, a testable hypothesis must contain a phrase such as, "more than," "less
than," "increase," "decrease," "greater than," "less than," or the like. Another increasingly
important attribute is adherence: How long should changes produced by the intervention
continue into the future? All of these variables must be operationally defined by how they
will be measured. There must be an agreed-upon method of assessing key variables that
is acceptable to participants, is practical in the applied setting, and fits within the evaluation budget. **Figure 9.1** shows a logic diagram for enhancing understanding on testable
hypotheses.

INTERNAL VALIDITY

Internal validity is the degree of confidence one has that the results produced by the evaluation are causally linked directly to the intervention. It is the extent to which a measured
impact (learning, skill development, health behavior, or health status) can be attributed to
the health education or health promotion intervention. Is the health education or health
promotion intervention the only plausible explanation for the observed results, or could
the results be explained by other factors? To what degree could the results be explained
by other factors? What are the competing explanations for the observed results that have
been addressed by the evaluation design? The internal validity of the evaluation is reduced

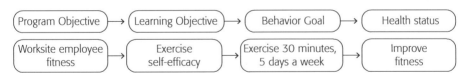

Examples of testable evaluation hypotheses at different levels:
Program impact on exercise self-efficacy
- Participants who complete the worksite fitness program will increase their scores on the exercise self-efficacy scale by five points.

Program impact on health behavior
- Participants who complete the worksite fitness program will increase their rates of 30-minute exercise bouts to 5 days a week as assessed by exercise logs.

Program impact on adherence to health behavior
- Participants who complete the worksite fitness program will maintain their rates of 30-minute exercise bouts 5 days a week at 6-month follow-up.

Program impact on health status
- Participants who complete the worksite fitness program will increase their estimated VO^2 by 10% (submax test) by the end of the program.

Figure 9.1 Logic model explaining testable evaluation hypotheses.

when the evaluator does not use evaluation design to control for or rule out competing explanations of the results. Cook and Campbell (1979) have summarized the most common factors associated with reductions in internal validity. These factors are commonly referred to as *threats* to internal validity.

Threats to Internal Validity

There are several potential threats to internal validity. These are as discussed in the following sections.

Testing

Testing is defined as the threat to internal validity caused by changes in observations as a result of the measurement. Pretest measurement procedures may alter participants' perceptions so that their responses to the posttest are no longer accurate. For example, responding to an interview question may encourage a person to overreport a health practice. Wearing a pedometer may cause a person to walk more. Tests of knowledge or skills on a pretest may produce "test learning," helping to artificially raise posttest scores. Measures of attitudes or health behavior may cue subjects to what the evaluator is seeking and thus may provoke overreporting of scores when subjects' attitudes or behavior have not changed. An equivalent control group may enable the evaluator to control for or estimate the extent of testing effects.

Selection Bias

Selection bias is a threat to internal validity caused by preexisting differences between groups under evaluation. When the comparison group and the intervention group are not equivalent on important variables it will have direct bearing on the interpretation of the evaluation results. Selection bias occurs when sampling procedures produce control/ comparison groups that are not equal to the experimental group on all relevant variables. Observed differences between the two groups might be due to differences that existed between groups before the intervention occurred. This form of bias can in part be verified and controlled for by comparison of pretest scores. An effective method to control for selection bias is randomization of subjects to treatment and control groups. If randomization is not feasible, it may be possible to match subjects in pairs on key variables and assign one to the treatment group and one to the control group.

Participant Attrition

Participant attrition is defined as the dropout of participants from the program or the lack of completion of the program in its entirety by the participants. Bias is introduced by systematic or excessive attrition in the control/comparison group or experimental group. There are many reasons why program participants drop out of health education and health promotion programs or control groups. Often dropouts from either group can result in differences between the groups at posttest.

Statistical Regression

Statistical regression is a threat to internal validity that is defined as the bias introduced by selection of subjects with unusually high or low levels of a variable. When measured later, the score will tend to move back (regress) towards the mean score. This threat is especially relevant to health education programs directed at high-risk groups in the community. High-risk groups tend to have high scores on risk behaviors and beliefs. As a group, there is a tendency for extreme scores to regress towards the population mean over time.

Instrumentation Bias

Instrumentation bias is the bias from changes in characteristics of measurement instruments between observations. This form of bias can be produced by changes in the instrument or changes in the conditions under which the instrument is taken between pretest and posttest. Instrumentation involves changes in the characteristics of the test or testers. Examples include changes in the wording of items (even if considered refinements) and changes in the motivation or skill level of the staff collecting measurements. A change in interviewers from pretest to posttest can create changes in data that are not caused by the intervention. One effective solution to control instrumentation bias is to have a true control group evaluation design and eliminate pretests. Another solution is to carefully choose valid and reliable instruments for measuring all variables and then carefully control the assessment protocol to eliminate any changes that might occur between pretest and posttest.

Maturation

Maturation refers to the growth occurring within the participants during the course of the evaluation as a result of time rather than the intervention. They are growing older and more experienced. It is the bias produced by changes in participants being measured over time (pretest and posttest). This threat is potentially increased when children or adolescents are the subjects in the evaluation. These stages of life are marked by rapid changes in social, biological, and cognitive maturation that could affect the evaluation results. Maturation can also be a threat if the evaluation takes place over one or more years. Maturation can also be a concern if the target population is experiencing a life transition, such as retirement, divorce, childbirth, transitioning from school to the workforce, unemployment, chronic disease diagnosis, or graduation.

History

History refers to the external events that happen at the same time as the intervention that could potentially affect the dependent variable. This is the bias produced by unplanned events or secular trends occurring before or during the health education program that could have affected the evaluation results. These effects are independent of the intervention and may produce learning or health behavior change among consumers.

One approach to controlling for secular trends is to establish a baseline of behavior prior to the beginning of any health education programming. Establish whether there are seasonal or historical trends in a health behavior; for example, physical activity rates are influenced by seasonal trends in many parts of the country. Historically, rates of seat belt utilization have slowly improved over the past 30 years. Many state health departments maintain a database of behavioral risk factors among the population. This data can be used to describe historical patterns in many health behaviors.

Extraneous events can also affect an evaluation sample. A successful television show on weight loss, or a community building a new fitness center, could have an effect on health practices separate from a health education program. The best way to estimate the effects of the extraneous event is to have a control or comparison group. This group will be exposed to the extraneous event but not the planned health education program. They will complete the data gathering instruments and thus provide an opportunity to estimate the impact of the extraneous event.

Interactive Effects

Interactive effects occur when a combination of the previously listed threats is present to produce bias. When multiple threats to internal validity are present, an interaction can occur. All these threats to internal validity are summarized in **Table 9.3**.

Counteracting Threats to Internal Validity

One of the most potent means of counteracting threats to internal validity is to have an evaluation design that has a control group. The control group participants should be similar to the participants in the intervention group; however, the control group does not receive the same health intervention as the experimental group. In this evaluation design, the only differentiating factor between the two groups is the health program being evaluated. Another approach to reducing threats to internal validity is using random assignment

TABLE 9.3 Threats to Internal Validity	
Threat	**Description**
Testing	The threat to internal validity due to changes in participants as a result of participants completing instruments or being measured
Selection bias	The threat to internal validity due to pre-existing differences between groups under evaluation
Participant attrition	The dropout of participants from the evaluation or lack of completion of the program in its entirety by the participants
Statistical regression	When subjects with unusually high or low levels of a variable of interest are selected for an evaluation, resulting in a tendency for scores to return to average independent of treatment effects
Instrumentation bias	The bias from changes in characteristics of measurement instruments between observations
Maturation	The growth occurring within the participants during the course of the evaluation as a result of time rather than the intervention
History	The events external to the intervention that have the potential to affect the dependent variable
Interactive effects	A combination of the above threats being present to produce bias

TABLE 9.4   Strategies to Counteract Threats to Internal Validity
Use an evaluation design with a control group.
Randomly assign participants between experimental and control groups.
Pretest differences on key variables between the treatment and control groups and make statistical adjustments.
Monitor and take actions to retain participants in both groups to reduce attrition.
Use valid and reliable instruments for measuring variables and carefully control measurement/assessment protocols.

of individuals between the two groups (intervention and control), so that the uncontrolled variables are equally distributed between the two groups. A third approach, when random assignment is not possible, is to use pretests to discern preexisting differences between the two groups. These preexisting differences can then be statistically controlled. Fourth, efforts should be made to carefully monitor and retain participants in the intervention and the control group, thereby reducing attrition to a bare minimum. Finally, the evaluator must carefully choose valid and reliable instruments for measuring all variables and then carefully control the assessment protocol to eliminate any changes that might occur between pretest and posttest. **Table 9.4** summarizes the strategies to counteract threats to internal validity.

> *One of the most potent means of counteracting threats to internal validity is to have an evaluation design that has a control group.*

EXTERNAL VALIDITY

External validity is the extent to which the positive results produced by the evaluation can be generalized to other settings with similar conditions. It is the extent to which a measured impact (learning, skill development, health behavior, or health status) can be generalized to similar populations or settings. For example, would a teen pregnancy prevention program designed for rural students living in Appalachia be equally effective for rural students who do not live in Appalachia? Further, would the pregnancy prevention program work for students living in urban areas? In the early stages of evaluation, evaluators might make reasoned arguments about generaliziblity based on the features of the evaluation design. Over time, the satisfactory way to resolve the proposed questions about external validity is through scientific testing. This would require replicating the program evaluation in a representative setting.

External validity or generalizability is reduced when the evaluation design produces reactive effects. The behavior of the evaluator or the requirements of the evaluation design cause subjects to react in different ways than if they had just received the health education program. This reactive effect is often produced when the evaluation design exerts too much control over subjects or creates a situation that is atypical of most health promotion interventions. In these cases, participants' behavior is influenced in ways that would not be representative of their typical behavior. External validity can also be reduced when the intervention is narrowly designed for a unique set of circumstances in a very specific target population.

Threats to External Validity

There are several threats to external validity. Some of these are described as follows:

- *Hawthorne effect:* The **Hawthorne effect** occurs when the observed effects on an intervention can be attributed to participants responding to the special attention being paid to them. If the evaluation procedures or intervention pay too much attention to the subjects, or make them feel too special or too unique, this may reduce the ability to generalize evaluation results to other settings. A key question would be: Are the intervention features that make subjects feel special or unique reliably reproducible? If these features can be replicated in other settings, external validity may be maintained.
- *Novelty effect:* The **novelty effect** occurs when participants react to the unique aspects of an innovative technology because it arouses interest and motivation due to its inherent newness. This reactive effect is likely to be reduced when the participants and the population in general become more familiar with the innovative technology.
- *Placebo effect:* The **placebo effect** occurs when people can improve their health based on faith in a treatment or provider. This effect is widely acknowledged. It is common in medical research to have a control group that receives a placebo treatment to control for this effect. Health promotion or evaluation staff might exert enough influence to change participants' beliefs or behavior independent of the intervention effects, thus causing a placebo effect.
- *Social desirability:* **Social desirability** occurs when participants want to please the evaluator, so they respond to evaluation measurements in ways they believe the evaluator wants. They seek to please the evaluation team rather than answer the measurement tools accurately.
- *Pygmalion effect:* The **Pygmalion effect** is the belief that if one expects another person to do something it is much more likely to happen. If the evaluation team holds a preconceived notion about participants it may subtly affect their interactions with the participants, making certain outcomes more likely. This effect is again independent of the health promotion intervention.

The threats to external validity are summarized in **Table 9.5**.

Counteracting Threats to External Validity

There are specific strategies an evaluation team can mobilize to reduce threats to external validity. Each of these strategies should be considered in the context of how important external validity is to the mission of a particular evaluation study. Generally, each of these strategies will add costs to the total budget of the evaluation, and thus should be considered carefully. These strategies are as follows:

- *Sampling:* Sampling is foundational to the external validity of evaluation studies. Critical to external validity is the careful definition of the target population followed by a sampling method that produces a representative sample of that population.

TABLE 9.5	Threats to External Validity
Threat	**Description**
Hawthorne effect	This occurs when the observed effects on an intervention can be attributed to participants responding to the special attention being paid to them.
Novelty effect	This occurs when participants react to the unique aspects of an innovative technology because it arouses interest and motivation due to its inherent newness.
Placebo effect	This occurs when participants improve their health based on faith in a program, treatment, or provider.
Social desirability	This occurs when participants want to please the evaluator; they respond to evaluation measurements in ways they believe the evaluator wants.
Pygmalion effect	This is the belief that if one expects a participant to do something it is much more likely to happen.

Conversely, an evaluation study using a sample of people who do not represent the intended target population will yield results of low external validity.

> *Critical to external validity is the careful definition of the target population followed by using a sampling method that produces a representative sample of that population.*

- *Unobtrusive measures:* Obtrusive measures mean that the subjects are aware of being measured. Completing instruments, wearing data collection devices, and maintaining logs can produce reactive effects in subjects. Completing a pretest might cue subjects to program expectations. Wearing a physical activity monitor might affect a subject's daily physical activity choices independent of the educational program. To an extent, a control or comparison group can help evaluators estimate and possibly control for the reactive effects of measures. But care should be given to reduce the reactive effects of data gathering methods. **Unobtrusive measures** imply that the participants do not know they are being measured. Examples of unobtrusive measures include abstracting data from existing records (medical, attendance, etc.) and observing participants in the community. The use of unobtrusive measures can reduce reactive effects and increase external validity.

- *Blinding:* **Blinding** means that the participants do not know whether they have been assigned to the experimental group or the control/comparison group. Over the past several decades, blinding participants to evaluation procedures has become more of a challenge. Current practices regarding informed consent procedures require that subjects know the purpose, risks, and involvement requirements of an evaluation study. But it is still possible to obtain informed consent for participation in an evaluation and randomly assign participants to experimental or control conditions. If the control condition provides some reasonable standard of health education intervention, it is possible to keep participants blinded as to their position in the design.

- *Double blinding:* When it is reasonable to assume that the participants and the professionals delivering the health education program may both be threats to external validity, double blinding may be useful. In **double blinding**, both the participants and the program delivery staff do not know whether they are part of the treatment or control conditions. If a program being tested has several methods or levels of

TABLE 9.6 Strategies to Counteract Threats to External Validity	
Strategy	**Description**
Sampling	Critical to external validity is the careful definition of the target population followed by using a sampling method that produces a representative sample of that population.
Unobtrusive measures	Assessments are taken in a manner in which the participants do not know they are being measured.
Blinding	This means that the participants do not know whether they have been assigned to the experimental group or the control/comparison group.
Double blinding	Both the participants and the program delivery staff do not know whether they are part of the treatment or control conditions.
Triple blinding	The participants, the program delivery staff, and the program evaluation staff do not know whether they are part of experimental or control conditions.

intervention, professional staff can be rotated through the different aspects of the program without knowing what the specific elements are that are being evaluated.

- *Triple blinding:* It is possible that evaluation staff or data collection staff could also influence the results of the evaluation. Generally they may exert subtle or even subconscious bias towards the experimental group. They might be more positive or motivational towards experimental subjects, and thereby influence the responsiveness of subjects. In these cases, it may be advisable for all parties to be blinded to experimental and control conditions. **Triple blinding** entails the participants, the program delivery staff, and the program evaluation staff not knowing who is part of the experimental or control conditions.

Table 9.6 summarizes the strategies to counteract threats to external validity.

EVALUATION DESIGN NOTATION

Over the years, scientists and evaluation specialists have developed a system of design notation to communicate design features precisely and efficiently. **Evaluation design notation** is the system of symbols and terminology used to depict evaluation designs. Listed in **Table 9.7** are the basics of evaluation design notation.

TYPES OF DESIGNS IN HEALTH PROMOTION AND EDUCATION

A variety of evaluation designs are commonly used in health promotion and education. The strengths of the designs reside in their respective abilities to control for threats to internal and external validity. The evaluation team should consider the strengths of each

TABLE 9.7	Evaluation Design Notation
Notation	**Definition**
E	Experimental/intervention group that is the planned intervention group and primary focus of the evaluation.
C	A control group established by random assignment only. The control group is essential to controlling for many threats to internal validity. A control group may receive no exposure to the intervention or limited exposure or a different intervention considered a standard in the field.
C̲	A comparison group established by a method other than randomization. Examples include a convenience sample or volunteers.
R	Random assignment of participants to either the experimental/intervention group or control group. Randomization is a key feature of true experimental designs.
X	Represents the intervention the evaluation team wishes to evaluate. X1, X2, ... represent different interventions or levels of intervention.
O	Observation or measurement to assess independent or dependent variables of interest to the evaluation team.

possible design in the context of the feasibility and costs of each design in the field. Some designs have requirements that may not be practical in a particular setting. Typical designs used in health promotion and education evaluations will be described in the following sections. Particular attention will be placed on practical considerations needed to use a design effectively in practice.

True Experimental Design with Posttests Only

R   E   X   O
R   C   O

Random assignment of participants to the experimental and control groups is essential for this design (Boruch, 1997). Neither group receives a pretest, thus minimizing testing bias. It is assumed that randomization makes both groups equivalent on variables of interest or reactivity. This distinction is critical; it eliminates biases that arise from groups not being equivalent, so any subsequent differences found on posttests can be attributed to the intervention (Mosteller & Boruch, 2002). For randomization to make the groups equivalent, a relatively large number of participants are required. The actual number of participants needed depends on several factors. It is advisable to consult with a statistician to ensure you have adequate numbers of participants in the experimental and control groups. The control group does not receive any health promotion intervention prior to posttest. This ensures that their posttest scores represent an unbiased meaningful comparison to the experimental posttest scores. This is a powerful design in which differences in posttest scores can be directly linked to the health promotion intervention.

True Experimental Design with Pretest and Posttest

R   E   O   X2   O
R   C   O   X1   O

Again, random assignment of participants to the experimental and control groups is essential for this design. This design enables evaluators to evaluate two different interventions. For example, X1 is a "standard intervention" and X2 is a "new intervention," which is presumed to be more powerful. Or, X1 could be an intervention delivered in the classroom and X2 is the same content delivered by computer to individuals. With sufficient numbers of participants randomized to the two groups, all independent and dependent variables of interest should not be significantly different (Glasgow, Nelson, Strycker, & King, 2006). A pretest is administered to both groups to establish baseline scores on all variables for meaningful comparison to posttest scores. In this way, changes in pretest and posttest scores can be contrasted by levels of intervention.

A variant of this design that is commonly used in health education and health promotion is the *group randomized control design*. In this design, the unit of randomization is not the individual but the group to which the individual belongs. For example, it may be the classroom in which the student is studying, the school in which the student is enrolled, or the community in which the person is residing that is randomized. Such designs are also called nested designs or partial hierarchical designs.

Quasi-experimental Design Nonequivalent Comparison Group

E   O   X   O
C̲   O   O

In this design, randomization of participants does not occur. The evaluation notation symbol $\underline{C}$ indicates a comparison group, not a control group. This is a critical distinction that can affect internal validity. This design is widely used in health promotion evaluations (Maticka-Tyndale, Wildish, & Gichuru, 2007). In many health program settings, randomization cannot be done. Public schools serve as one example. Students are assigned to intact classrooms for a variety of reasons related to school function. This situation generally prevents evaluators from random assignment of pupils. Lack of randomization introduces the possibility of threats to internal validity. Without the benefit of randomization, it is suggested that sampling procedures be used to minimize bias. Comparison of pretest scores can help identify any preexisting differences in relevant variables. Statistical procedures (analysis of covariance) can be used to statistically control for pretest differences (Heinsman & Shadish, 1996).

One Group, Time Series Design

E   O   O   O   X   O   O   O

This design can be useful when the entire population is the unit of analysis for the program evaluation (Shadish, Cook, & Campbell, 2002). For example, the purpose of an evaluation is to determine the impact of an intervention on an entire community, all of the employees at a worksite, or all of the students at a school. Conceptually, it is also important that the nature of the intervention be focused on the entire population as well. A health promotion intervention that utilizes policy, law, access to health services, a public media campaign, or altering the environment to influence health practices all serve as examples. Recent examples include bans on smoking in public areas, seatbelt laws, and media campaigns to increase exercise. This design is useful if data has been collected on the same group at several time points before the intervention and can be collected at several time points after the intervention. Because the unit of analysis is the entire population, there is no assumption that the same individuals need to be measured at each observation point. This design is easy to plan and has a relatively low cost if data surveillance systems are already in place. Many states gather behavioral risk factor data on an annual basis, and worksites often gather data about medical insurance utilization among their employees. When these types of surveillance are in place, incorporation into a time series design can be a low cost endeavor.

An important consideration is the number of observation points before and after the intervention. For statistical reasons, Tukey (1977) recommends five observations before and after the intervention. Less than three observations make it difficult to identify statistical trends before or after the intervention. Campbell and Russo (1999) note that this design is best used for evaluating interventions that are intended to have a dramatic impact on behavior in a short period of time. This is because the design does not control for several biases, particularly history. Population-based observations tend to be imprecise, and there are typically normal variations in observations from year to year.

Nonexperimental Design: One-Group Pretest-Posttest

E   O   X   O

The one-group pretest-posttest design is often used to evaluate health programs. This design does not allow the evaluator to estimate the degree of bias introduced by threats to internal validity (Stead, Hastings, & Eadie, 2002). It is difficult to create a sound rationale that observed changes were caused by the intervention. Although this design is very weak, it may be useful for pilot testing a new intervention. The evaluation team should take precautions to control for selection bias and make efforts to verify that participants are representative of the intended target audience. Using only instruments with established validity and reliability is also helpful. Administering pretests just before the intervention and posttests soon after the intervention (within 2–3 weeks) can partially control for history bias.

BARRIERS TO RANDOMIZATION

A review of the previous designs logically leads to an important question: If true experiments with randomization are so powerful in controlling for bias, why are these designs not used more often? There is no doubt that the science of health education and health promotion would be more rigorous if true experimental designs were used more often (Julnes & Rog, 2007). But there are many practical concerns and constraints that often prevent participant randomization from being used. A review of the barriers to randomization is offered in this section. It is hoped that evaluation teams will actively consider creative approaches to overcoming these barriers so that true experimental designs are used more often.

In many health program settings, ethical concerns may prevent the use of random assignment to receive or not receive a program (Resnicow et al., 2001). Evaluation teams and stakeholders should discuss the ethical issues in each case. In disadvantaged or vulnerable populations, randomization may not be acceptable to stakeholders. A community agency may resist withholding a health promotion program from all who are at high risk. Another barrier to randomization is the strong norm for voluntary participation in health promotion programs. If members of the target population volunteer to participate, staff often feel compelled to offer the health promotion program to all members of the target

---

FOCUS FEATURE 9.1   CONSIDERATIONS IN CHOOSING A DESIGN

An evaluator must consider several issues before choosing an evaluation design. The first consideration pertains to the type of evaluation question. If the purpose is to simply find out whether the intervention or program is effective, then designs that enhance internal validity can be chosen. If the purpose is to compare two or more programs for effectiveness, then the evaluator would benefit from looking at designs that increase internal validity. If the purpose is to generalize the results to other populations, then one must also pay attention to representativeness of the sample.

Evaluators also need to consider the budget available for evaluation when making the decision about the design. If the budget is limited, only simpler designs can be used. One would also need to look at the statistical capability one has when choosing the design. For example, group randomized control designs require greater understanding of procedures such as one-between, one-within repeated measures analysis of variance than would a one-group pretest-posttest design. Another consideration regards minimization of bias. If one wants to reduce bias to a large extent, then an experimental design would be more appropriate.

The following options provide guidance in choosing a design, starting from the most rigorous to the least rigorous options:

Option #1: True experimental design with pretest and posttest with random selection of the sample

Option #2: Option #1 without random selection of the sample

Option #3: Group randomized control design with pretest and posttest without random selection of the sample

Option #4: True experimental design with posttests only with random selection of the sample

Option #5: True experimental design with posttests only without random selection of the sample

Option #6: Quasi-experimental design

Option #7: Time series design

Option #8: One-group pretest-posttest design

population. The staff is concerned that volunteers will be disappointed or even angered by assignment to a control group. This is particularly true if the control group is seen as receiving "nothing" or an inferior intervention. If the evaluation design relies on voluntary participation, it is critical to note that all results should only be generalized back to volunteers within the target population.

The target population needs to be sufficiently large to produce adequate numbers of people to fulfill requirements for the experimental and control groups. In relatively small populations, it is often unrealistic to assume that a large proportion of the pool of potential participants will volunteer. The health promotion program itself should possess preliminary evidence that it can produce an impact of practical importance on the population. Generally speaking, a health promotion program should produce changes in behavior of sufficient magnitude to eventually yield improvements in health status. If this criterion is not met, it is hard to justify the expense of a true experimental design. It is vitally important that scientifically sound measures of the critical outcomes exist. This assessment method should be sensitive to the full, meaningful range of variability in the outcomes of interest.

Another barrier to experimental designs is that there must be an adequate budget to cover the costs of the large number of participants needed for randomization to be effective. When random assignment is used with inadequate numbers of participants, the treatment and control groups may not be theoretically equivalent, thus undermining the purpose of the design. If the program produces considerable changes in outcomes, and the assessment technologies can detect high levels of change, sample sizes for randomization go down. This increases the feasibility of using true experimental designs.

The evaluation team and stakeholders should consider the feasibility of using true experimental designs. The costs, scientific requirements, and ethical concerns should be openly discussed. Discussion combined with creative problem solving can often open doors to increased rigor in the evaluation design. At the least, such discussions identify potential concerns that need to be addressed regardless of the specific evaluation design chosen.

SKILL-BUILDING ACTIVITY

You have designed an intervention based on social cognitive theory to promote physical activity in upper elementary school children. You are interested in finding out whether this intervention is effective in meeting goals and objectives and whether it can be replicated in other schools. What will be your testable hypotheses? What design will you choose? What will be the threats to internal validity and external validity?

SUMMARY

Evaluation design specifies the conditions under which an evaluation will take place. It describes how program participants will be selected and assigned to groups. It would make sense that the evaluation team would design a very rigorous evaluation; however, there are many real-world constraints that present significant barriers to rigorous design. Considerations include institutional/administrative constraints, financial constraints, practical time constraints, scientific constraints, and ethical constraints.

The purpose of the evaluation is precisely expressed by a set of testable hypotheses. A testable hypothesis is defined as the depiction of the relationship between independent and dependent variables that can be tested empirically. A testable hypothesis requires a minimum of two variables.

There are two major considerations in evaluation design: internal and external validity. Internal validity is the degree of confidence one has that the results produced by the evaluation are causally linked directly to the intervention. External validity is the extent to which the observed results produced by the evaluation can be generalized to other settings with similar conditions. The threats to internal validity include testing, selection bias, participant attrition, statistical regression, instrumentation bias, maturation, history, and interactive effects. These threats can be counteracted by a variety of evaluation design elements. One option is using a control group and having random assignment between experimental and control groups. Pretesting the differences between intervention and control groups can enable the evaluator to make statistical adjustments. Taking actions to prevent participant attrition can reduce bias. Carefully choosing valid and reliable instruments also enhances internal validity. The threats to external validity include the Hawthorne effect, novelty effect, placebo effect, social desirability, and Pygmalion effect. These threats can be counteracted by representative sampling, unobtrusive measures, blinding, double blinding, and triple blinding.

Common designs in evaluating health programs are true experimental design with posttest only, true experimental design with pretest and posttest, group randomized control design, quasi-experimental design, time series design, and pretest-posttest design.

REVIEW QUESTIONS

1. What is an evaluation design? What are its benefits?
2. Identify constraints to true experimental designs in health education and health promotion.
3. Describe the components of a testable hypothesis. Give an example of a testable hypothesis.
4. Define internal validity. Identify threats to internal validity.
5. Discuss ways in which threats to internal validity can be counteracted.
6. Define external validity. Identify threats to external validity.
7. Discuss ways in which threats to external validity can be counteracted.
8. Define evaluation design notation. Depict and explain a design of your choice using notation.
9. Discuss the strengths and weaknesses of the true experimental design with pretest and posttest.
10. Discuss the strengths and weaknesses of the one-group pretest-posttest design.

WEBSITES TO EXPLORE

Evaluation Design Checklist

http://www.wmich.edu/evalctr/archive_checklists/evaldesign.pdf
This checklist was developed by Daniel Stufflebeam of the evaluation center at Western Michigan University. The checklist is designed as a general guide for decisions that are made when planning and conducting an evaluation. The checklist encompasses decisions needed for focusing an evaluation, collecting information, organizing information, analyzing information, reporting information, and administering the evaluation. *Review the checklist and apply it to developing an evaluation design for a real or imaginary problem.*

Evaluation Designs

http://go.worldbank.org/7M4NUSKE10
This website developed by World Bank discusses three types of evaluation designs: experimental design, quasi-experimental design, and nonexperimental design. Also discussed is selection bias. *With each design there is a link for key readings. Locate one or two key readings, read them, and summarize salient findings in a brief paper.*

Evaluation: Designs and Approaches

http://www.promoteprevent.org/publications/prevention-briefs/
evaluation-designs-and-approaches
This website was developed by the National Center for Mental Health Promotion and Youth Violence Prevention to discuss evaluation design and approaches. Four designs are discussed: one-group posttest-only design, one-group pretest and posttest design, pretest and posttest with comparison group design, and pretest and posttest with control group design. Also discussed are quantitative, qualitative, and mixed approaches to evaluation. *Read the discussion on the four types of design, review this chapter, and come up with a list of advantages and disadvantages for each of the four types of designs.*

Evaluation Design for Public Health Communication Programs

http://www.social-marketing.org/conference_readings/public_health_eval.pdf
This is a link to an epilogue by Robert Hornik of the University of Pennsylvania that discusses various facets of evaluation design. The issue of use of controls, time period of treatment, matching study populations and target audiences, units of analysis and treatments, and alternatives to ideal evaluation design are discussed. *Read this article and prepare a 250-word summary of salient findings.*

REFERENCES

Best, J. A., Brown, K. S., Cameron, R., Smith, E. A., & MacDonald, M. (1989). Conceptualizing outcomes for health promotion programs. In M. T. Braverman (Ed.), *Evaluating health promotion programs* (pp. 19–32). San Francisco: Jossey-Bass.

Biglan, A. D., Ary, H., Yudelson, T., Duncan, D., Hood, L., James., V., … Gaiser, E. (1996). Experimental evaluation of a modular approach to mobilizing antitobacco influences of peers and parents. *American Journal of Community Psychology, 24*(3), 311–339.

Boruch, R. F. (1997). *Randomized experiments for planning and evaluation: A practical guide.* Thousand Oaks, CA: Sage.

Campbell, D. T., & Russo, M. J. (Eds.). (1999). *Social experimentation.* Thousand Oaks, CA: Sage.

Cook, T. D., & Campbell, D. T. (Eds.). (1979). *Quasi-experimentation, design and analysis issues for field settings.* Chicago: Rand McNally.

Glasgow, R. E., Nelson, C. G., Strycker, L. A., & King, D. K. (2006). Using RE-AIM metrics to evaluate diabetes self-management support interventions. *American Journal of Preventive Medicine, 30*(4), 422–429.

Heinsman, D. T., & Shadish, W. R. (1996). Assignment methods in experimentation: When do nonrandomized experiments approximate the answers from randomized experiments? *Psychological Methods, 1,* 154–169.

Julnes, G., & Rog, D. J. (2007). Current federal policies and controversies over methodology in evaluation. *New Directions in Evaluation, 113,* 1–12.

Maticka-Tyndale, E., Wildish, J., & Gichuru, M. (2007). Quasi-experimental evaluation of a national primary school HIV intervention in Kenya. *Evaluation and Program Planning. 30,* 172–186.

Mosteller, F., & Boruch, R. (Eds.). (2002). *Evidence matters: Randomized trials in educational research.* Washington, DC: Brookings Institution.

Resnicow, K., Braithwaite, R., DiIorio, C., Vaughan, R., Cohen, M. I., & Uhl, G. (2001). Preventing substance abuse in high risk youth: Evaluation challenges and solutions. *Journal of Primary Prevention, 21,* 399–415.

Shadish, W. R., Cook, T. D., & Campbell D. T. (2002). *Experimental and quasi-experimental designs for generalized causal inference.* Boston: Houghton-Mifflin.

Stead, M., Hastings, G., & Eadie, D. (2002). The challenge of evaluating complex interventions: A framework for evaluating media advocacy. *Health Education Research, 17,* 351–364.

Tukey, J. W. (1977). *Exploratory data analysis.* Reading, MA: Addison-Wesley.

CHAPTER 10

Approaches to Qualitative Evaluation

INTRODUCTION TO QUALITATIVE EVALUATION AND RESEARCH

Discussing qualitative evaluation methodology is a topic for a complete textbook for two reasons. First, qualitative evaluation entails using verbose writing, and second, there are a plethora of techniques and differing traditions in this methodology that make it impossible to summarize this rich tapestry in a chapter format. This chapter will simply introduce qualitative methods; you are encouraged to read more about these methods from other sources. Bear in mind that the qualitative evaluation and research process is as rigorous, as disciplined, and as systematic as the quantitative research process. Qualitative evaluation often provides a viable complement to quantitative evaluation. You will see later in this chapter that qualitative and quantitative methods can be used together to enrich the evaluation.

Many terms have been used in the literature to denote qualitative evaluation and research, including cultural studies, constructivist paradigm, naturalistic inquiry, phenomenological inquiry, postmodernism, postpositivism approach, and poststructuralism (Schwandt, 2007). There are subtle differences among these terms, but exploration of those subtleties is beyond the scope of this chapter. **Qualitative evaluation** is defined as a method of assessing a program by using one of three approaches: (1) interviews or discussions consisting of open-ended questions, (2) observations based on field notes, or (3) review of written materials and other documents.

Qualitative evaluation and research owes its origin to the disciplines of anthropology and sociology. A growing number of applications of qualitative research are now being published in diverse fields such as criminal justice, education, health sciences, history, journalism, linguistics, management, marketing, mass communication, medicine, nursing, physical education, psychology, recreation, social work, and women's studies (Huberman & Miles, 2002; Paterson, Thorne, Canam, & Jillings, 2001; Patton, 2002; Wolcott, 2008). Denzin and Lincoln (2005) have classified the history of qualitative research into five distinct periods. The first period they call the *traditional period* (1900–1950). This period includes the work done by anthropologists such as Franz Boas, Ruth Benedict, and Margaret Mead that has influenced the qualitative methodology and paved the way for its future growth. One of the most famous initial works was by Margaret Mead, who in 1925 did her field work in Samoa observing adolescent girls growing up in that culture. The work was published as a book, *Coming of Age in Samoa* (Mead, 1928), which became a well-known international bestseller and has since been translated into several languages. She was among the first researchers who looked at human development from a cross-cultural perspective and provided qualitative research a respectable image.

The second period identified by Denzin and Lincoln (2005) is the *modernist* or *golden age* (1950–1970). The period consists of the post–World War II era and was marked by overall progress in all spheres. The quantitative mode of enquiry, which had become established as the mainstream method and was the dominant thinking at that time, began to be challenged by several arguments about its assumptions in the liberal environment that followed these postwar years. The period also witnessed growth in the feminist movement, the growing power of women, and the prolific growth of women scholars who added thrust to the qualitative mode of thinking.

The third period, according to Denzin and Lincoln (2005), is the *blurred genres* period (1970–1986). During this period, respect for qualitative research and qualitative researchers grew. Various traditions (such as phenomenology, feminism, cultural studies, and others) were established, several methods (such as case study and ethnography) were refined, and an authoritative body of knowledge emerged.

The fourth period as described by Denzin and Lincoln (2005) is the *crisis of representation* period (1986–1990). During this period, the assumptions of qualitative research were challenged. Discussion regarding validity, reliability, and generalization gained momentum, which led to the emergence of newer concepts in the next period.

The final period, as elaborated by Denzin and Lincoln (2005), is the *postmodern movement* (1990–present). During this period, unique terms specific to data interpretation of qualitative research are being established. For example, in the qualitative paradigm the term *dependability* has replaced the conventional concept of reliability used in the quantitative paradigm; *credibility* is being used for internal validity; and *transferability* for external validity. Furthermore, in this period, utilization of techniques for program evaluation is gaining importance and is, therefore, particularly relevant for health educators, who are often required to conduct program evaluations.

QUANTITATIVE VERSUS QUALITATIVE EVALUATION

The quantitative or positivist paradigm is based on what is called the **etic view**. In the etic view, the evaluator sets all the parameters or defines the reality. In contrast, an **emic view** is used in qualitative enquiry, where the meaning of any situation is perceived from the participant's viewpoint and the evaluator is a mere observer (Cresswell, 2006; Richards & Morse, 2006). For example, a quantitative evaluator, interested in measuring safer sex, makes *a priori* decisions about how to measure the number of times a person is using condoms, his or her number of partners, and so on. On the other hand, a qualitative evaluator when examining safer sex is more interested in what the meaning of safer sex is in the participant's life. He or she is also interested in why that activity (which the participant defines as safer sex) is being performed, feelings about safer sex, and many other details that are not included in any *a priori* plan but will become apparent during interaction with the participant(s). This difference can also be expressed epistemologically (or the relationship of the researcher with the research process) as the evaluator being independent from the subjects in the quantitative paradigm, versus the evaluator interacting and living with the participants in the qualitative paradigm.

The quantitative evaluation requires the evaluator to carefully conceptualize and then operationalize measurable definitions with specific variables that assume numbers. This method has often been criticized as **reductionism**, where reality is reduced to a number. Furthermore, the evaluator is encouraged to strip the context as much as possible to avoid contamination of the variable. In contrast, the qualitative evaluator is interested in the whole perspective or the **holistic perspective**, which includes underlying values and the

> *In qualitative enquiry an emic view is used, where the meaning of any situation is perceived from the participant's viewpoint and the evaluator is a mere observer.*

context as a part of the phenomenon (Morse, Swanson, & Kuzel, 2001). This is also called an *axiologic* difference or the variance due to the role of values in conducting research (Polit & Hungler, 1999). For example, a quantitative evaluator wanting to study physical activity behavior will reduce the reality to a number. He or she will be interested in observing or relying on self-reported data about how many minutes of moderate-intensity physical activity participants in his or her sample are engaging in and then comparing those against American College of Sports Medicine (ACSM) guidelines of a minimum of 30 minutes on most days of the week. The evaluator is not particularly interested in what physical activity, personal liking, with whom, where, when, how it was done, and other contextual details, which would be the main interest of a qualitative evaluator. If the quantitative evaluator does become interested in recording some of those aspects, he or she will also be reduced to numbers and the maximum number of objects under the study would be limited. In fact, in the quantitative paradigm parsimony is encouraged, whereas in the qualitative paradigm the richer the context, the better the research.

The quantitative paradigm is based on **logical positivism**, which assumes that a reality exists that can be objectively described (Polit & Hungler, 1999). The study of the cause–effect relationship between two variables is paramount in this approach. Qualitative enquiry, in contrast, is based on **postpositivism**, which states that only partially objective accounts of the world can be produced because all methods are flawed; hence reality is multiply constructed and multiply interpreted. For example, an evaluator in the quantitative paradigm, examining the relationship of an intervention on physical activity levels, finds the effect size (Cohen's d) to be 0.5 or medium effect size. Then the evaluator would be interested in looking at evidence from other similar evaluations (consistency), and examining the time sequence and the probable dose–response relationship. If these are positive, he or she would then conclude that the physical activity intervention is successful in changing physical activity behavior. On the other hand, the qualitative evaluator would look at all the facets of the intervention and at all the facets of physical activity. The evaluator would not be interested in establishing any causal relationships, but only in describing the observations. Therefore, sometimes the quantitative evaluation is also called hypothesis-confirming evaluation and qualitative evaluation is called hypothesis-generating evaluation.

> *Qualitative enquiry is based on postpositivism, which states that only partially objective accounts of the world can be produced because all methods are flawed; hence reality is multiply constructed and multiply interpreted.*

The quantitative research paradigm is based on **deductive reasoning**, in which logic proceeds from general to specific. For example, a health education intervention may be based on social cognitive theory, which has been found to be useful in changing behavior. So the general principles or constructs of this theory are used in designing a health education program for any given behavior. In the qualitative evaluation paradigm the logic is reversed or is **inductive reasoning**, in which logic proceeds from specific to general. For example, in a qualitative evaluation observations may be used to develop a theory.

The research design is fixed in the quantitative paradigm whereas it is dynamic or flexible in the qualitative paradigm. As an example, an evaluator writes her protocol, seeks institutional review board (IRB) approval for the instruments and procedures, and successfully obtains the permission. Now she begins to collect the data but wants to use another instrument or wants to switch to another method for collecting data, but cannot do so without having to go through the IRB approval process again. In contrast, if she were engaged in qualitative evaluation her design would allow her to make those adjustments depending on participant inputs with adequate and credible documentation of the process.

Finally, quantitative evaluation entails a high level of reliance on technology such as sophisticated measurement instruments and data analysis that always requires the use of statistics. These days, the statistical computations are not possible by hand; reliance on computer applications is not only the norm, but also mandatory. On the other hand, qualitative evaluation relies more on the participation of the participants under study. It does not necessitate use of technology to such an extent. Although computer and software producers continue to flood the market with sophisticated qualitative software programs, the crux of qualitative enquiry still lies in the process rather than any sophisticated analyses.

The differences between quantitative and qualitative paradigms are summarized in **Table 10.1**.

Several types of evaluations are based on the qualitative paradigm. We will discuss some of them, including empowerment evaluation, illuminative evaluation (also known as socio-anthropological evaluation, responsive evaluation, or transaction evaluation), participatory evaluation, the CIPP (Context, Input, Process, Product) model of evaluation, utilization-focused evaluation, and goal-free evaluation.

TABLE 10.1	Comparison of Qualitative Paradigm and Quantitative Paradigm	
Attribute	**Qualitative Paradigm**	**Quantitative Paradigm**
View	Emic view (reality is defined by the participants).	Etic view (evaluator defines the reality).
Perspective	Holistic perspective (context and values preserved).	Reductionism (concepts reduced to context-free numbers).
Role of the evaluator	Evaluator is an interactive observer.	Evaluator is independent.
Richness of context	Studying the rich context is encouraged.	Parsimony is encouraged (ability of a few variables to predict or explain).
Reality	Postpositivist (reality is multiply constructed and multiply interpreted).	Positivist (reality can be objectively measured).
Purpose	Hypothesis generation.	Hypothesis confirmation.
Reasoning	Inductive (specific to general).	Deductive (general to specific).
Design	Dynamic (no set protocol, flexible).	Fixed (protocol once set is etched in stone).
Technology	People centered.	Highly technocentric.
Statistics	Not required.	Required.

EMPOWERMENT EVALUATION

Empowerment evaluation is the "use of evaluation concepts, techniques, and findings to foster improvement and self determination" (Fetterman, 1996, p. 4). Even though we are discussing empowerment evaluation as a predominantly qualitative evaluation, it also uses techniques from quantitative evaluation. The distinctive feature of empowerment evaluation is that it builds on collaboration of community members and is not done by a single individual. Empowerment evaluation aims at building the skills of community members so that they can become independent problem solvers and decision makers. In contrast to traditional evaluation, it places the responsibility for evaluation on program participants (Fetterman, 2001). Besides the health field, it has been used in higher education, government, public education, crime prevention, agriculture and rural development, and evaluations in the not-for-profit sector. Empowerment evaluation is a relatively inexpensive alternative to traditional evaluations in low-income communities and developing country settings.

> "*E*mpowerment evaluation is the use of evaluation concepts, techniques, and findings to foster improvement and self determination."
>
> —Fetterman, 1996, p. 4

The principles of empowerment evaluation are derived from community psychology and action anthropology (Fetterman, 1996). Community psychology deals with groups, associations, and communities who want to gain control over their affairs, and action anthropology deals with how anthropologists can help groups achieve their goals and objectives. Self-determination, or the ability to plan one's own path in life, is the foundation of empowerment evaluation.

There are five facets of empowerment evaluation—training, facilitation, advocacy, illumination, and liberation. These facets are summarized in **Table 10.2**.

The following 10 principles of empowerment evaluation have been identified (Fetterman, 2005):

1. *Improvement:* It seeks continual enhancement.
2. *Community ownership:* It starts with involvement of community members.
3. *Inclusion:* It includes all stakeholders.
4. *Democratic participation:* It is based on rules of democracy.
5. *Social justice:* It aims at ensuring equity and justice for all.
6. *Community knowledge:* It builds on the collective knowledge of all community members.
7. *Evidence-based strategies:* It suggests focusing on time-tested approaches.
8. *Capacity building:* It promotes self-collection and self-analysis of data by the community.
9. *Organizational learning:* It focuses on collective learning by all involved.
10. *Accountability:* It promotes holding one another accountable.

There are several steps in conducting empowerment evaluation: (1) defining a mission, (2) taking stock, (3) setting goals, (4) developing strategies, (5) documenting progress, and (6) creating a program theory. These steps are summarized in **Table 10.3** (Fetterman, 1996, 2001).

TABLE 10.2 Facets of Empowerment Evaluation

Facet	Description
Training	Empowerment evaluator teaches the participants or community members to conduct self-evaluation and become self-sufficient. The evaluator helps in desensitizing and demystifying evaluation and enables people to self-reflect and self-assess.
Facilitation	Empowerment evaluator serves as a coach or catalyst in enabling people to conduct their own evaluation. The process entails identifying goals and people selecting their own performance indicators.
Advocacy	Empowerment evaluator acts as a direct advocate to help groups become empowered through evaluation. The process entails writing in public forums to change public opinion, influencing lobbyists, and providing information to assist in policy making.
Illumination	This is an experience that provides a new insight. Empowerment evaluation aims at having these insights at various levels of the project. This involves a dynamic involvement of learners or community members as they engage in self-analysis.
Liberation	This is the process of freeing oneself from preexisting roles and limitations. It entails new understanding of what one's roles are and the roles of others.

TABLE 10.3 Steps in Conducting an Empowerment Evaluation

Step	Description
1. Defining a mission	Empowerment evaluator facilitates an open session with program staff and participants to generate key phrases that symbolize the mission of their project. These are recorded and shared with the group. Collectively, a mission statement and values are developed.
2. Taking stock	This step has two parts. In the first part, a list of activities being done by the project are generated and prioritized for evaluation. In the second part, the program staff and participants are asked to rate each activity on a scale of 1 (lowest) to 10 (highest) and share their rating with the group. The average of the group can be used to compare change over time and initiate a dialogue. It also sensitizes the participants about their own ratings—whether they are overrating or underrating.
3. Setting goals	In this step, participants and program staff are asked how they would like to improve what they do well and what they do less well. Participants set specific and realistic goals in conjunction with program staff that are related to the program's activities, talents, resources, and scope of capability.
4. Developing strategies	In this step, participants and program staff select and develop strategies to accomplish program goals. The processes of brainstorming, critical review, and arrival of consensus are followed.
5. Documenting progress	In this step, participants and program staff decide on the type of documentation and evidence for monitoring progress in accomplishing the goals. The documentation chosen must be credible and rigorous and not self-serving.
6. Creating a program theory	In this step, a logic model is created using the previous steps and a theory is developed grounded in participants' own experiences, which will guide the program.

Empowerment evaluation and related evaluation has been used by several health education and health promotion projects. Some of these are as follows:

- Evaluation of safe community, drug/HIV prevention, and elderly quality of life programs in Rapla, Estonia (Kasmel & Andersen, 2011)
- Evaluation of a cardiovascular health promotion program offered to low-income women in Korea (Ok Ham & Jeong Kim, 2011)
- Evaluation of a health-promoting community-oriented radio station in a rural village in Bali, Indonesia (Waters, James, & Darby, 2011)
- Formative evaluation of Strengths, Prevention, Empowerment, and Community Change (SPEC) Learning and Changing by Doing, a 3-year action research and organizational change project designed to promote social justice and well-being in a community in Florida (Evans et al., 2011)
- Evaluation of 24 community-based organizations' efforts for HIV/AIDS education and prevention in the southern United States (Mayberry et al., 2009)
- Evaluation of Expect Respect, a teen dating violence prevention program in Texas (Ball, Kerig, & Rosenbluth, 2009)
- Empowerment evaluation for violence prevention public health programs (Goodman & Noonan, 2009)
- Empowerment evaluation with programs designed to prevent first-time male perpetration of sexual violence (Noonan & Gibbs, 2009)
- Empowerment evaluation in Toronto Public Health's nutrition programming redesign (Dwyer et al., 2006)

Empowerment evaluation is not without its limitations. Scriven (2005) criticizes empowerment evaluation as being inherently biased because it is a self-evaluation and is not conducted by an objective expert who is authoritative in drawing evaluation conclusions. Second, empowerment evaluation claims to use both qualitative and quantitative methods and conducts training to program participants and program staff on these approaches. A short training session cannot produce sufficient learning in the intricacies of these paradigms in a relatively small period of time. Most traditional evaluators spend several years in postgraduate education learning these essentials, and a short training program cannot make lay people experts. Hence, the evaluation remains a mere token in many cases. Third, it takes a lot of lead time to implement this sort of evaluation. The time and resources for evaluation are limited, and time often is not readily available to invest in training and planning. Finally, Fetterman (1996, p. 21) notes that "empowerment evaluation is designed to address a specific evaluative need. It is not a substitute for other forms of evaluative inquiry or appraisal." It is evident that empowerment evaluation cannot completely replace traditional evaluation, and is only one form of evaluation that offers potential benefits in some situations.

ILLUMINATIVE EVALUATION

Illuminative evaluation, also known as **socio-anthropological evaluation**, **responsive evaluation**, or **transaction evaluation**, is a type of qualitative evaluation that seeks to illuminate or clarify answers to questions pertaining to a program that are lying latent or dormant; it uses methods from social anthropology rather than psychology. It reflects a phenomenological (a perspective as experienced from the first-person point of view), ethnomethodological (codes and conventions that underlie everyday social interactions and activities), or holistic (complete picture) approach to evaluation (Gordon, 1991). It is based on an anthropological line of enquiry in which the field worker

Illuminative evaluation takes into consideration wider contexts than quantitative evaluation and is primarily interested in description and interpretation as opposed to measurement and prediction.

immerses him- or herself in the field to comprehend the culture being studied. Likewise, in this type of evaluation the evaluator immerses him- or herself in the program. This evaluation is also based on the grounded theory approach described by Barney Glaser and Anselm Strauss (Glaser & Strauss, 1967) and leads to development of a theory. It is also based on the social reconstruction of reality as described by Berger and Luckmann (1967).

Illuminative evaluation takes into consideration wider contexts than quantitative evaluation and is primarily interested in description and interpretation as opposed to measurement and prediction. In illuminative evaluation, the evaluator is interested in finding out how the program works, how it is influenced by internal and external forces, what its advantages and disadvantages are as experienced by those associated with the program, and how clients, patients, or participants are affected by the program. The basic idea in illuminative evaluation is for the evaluator to hang out with the participants to identify how they think and feel about the situation, and what the important underlying issues are. The context in illuminative evaluation is viewed as a transactional field in which the participants are inseparable from their setting.

The scope of an illuminative evaluation is very broad. This approach also emphasizes flexibility in response to ongoing change. A three-stage process is suggested in carrying out illuminative evaluation: (1) observation, (2) further enquiry, and (3) explanation (Parlett, 1972). The primary aim of this type of evaluation is description and interpretation that leads to understanding and improvement; therefore, a large amount of descriptive data is gathered and recorded. Observation and interviewing (unstructured or semi-structured) are the predominant methods of data collection. Triangulation (the use of multiple methods, multiple data, or multiple analysts) or use of theory to aid in data interpretation is commonly done in illuminative evaluation. Some examples of illuminative evaluation include the following:

- Evaluation of a breastfeeding education package for general practitioners in the United Kingdom (Burt, Whitmore, Vearncombe, & Dykes, 2006)
- Evaluation of skills rehearsal in a mentorship course (Clemow, 2007)
- Primary healthcare team development in the United Kingdom (Macfarlane, Greenhalgh, Schofield, & Desombre, 2004)
- General practice evaluation in the United Kingdom (Galvin, Sharples, & Jackson, 2000)

There are some limitations to this approach. First, it is not an inexpensive approach; it is rather costly in terms of resources to be invested. It entails producing copious amounts of descriptive data, which requires time and money. Editing and triangulation of data are also very costly. Second, it requires a high level of skills on the part of the evaluator, which is difficult to find. It requires a high level of interpersonal skills, diplomatic skills, and the ability to avoid own biases. Finally, an illuminative evaluation does not provide the strict controls and strength of inference offered by experimental evaluations.

PARTICIPATORY EVALUATION

Participation of the target audience in the research process is an integral and unique characteristic of the qualitative paradigm. **Participatory evaluation** has emerged and become popular in health education based on rural development work done around the world, especially in India (Tandon & Brown, 1981) and the adult literacy work from Latin America based on Freire's model (1970). Participatory evaluation has its roots in the principles of liberation theology (Alinsky, 1972), social activism (Rappaport, 1987), community psychology, and rural development (Chambers, 1983). Fernandes and Tandon (1981) have described participatory evaluation as a mode of inquiry designed and conducted by people themselves to trace the influence of knowledge as a means of power and for

> *The hallmark of participatory methodology is the fundamental technique of problematizing or problem posing.*

the purpose of generating some action. The hallmark of participatory methodology is the fundamental technique of *problematizing* or problem posing (Freire, 1970). The emphasis lies in raising questions without any predetermined answers. Paulo Freire (1976) in his book, *Education: The Practice of Freedom*, has explicated the framework of his methodology, which in essence is a simple three-phase process. First is the *naming* phase, where one asks the question, *What is the problem?* or *What is the question under discussion?* Second is the *reflection* phase, where one poses the question, *Why is this the case?* or *How do we explain this situation?* The third phase is the *action* phase, characterized by the question, *What can be done to change this situation?* or *What options do we have?* So this approach is *process centered* as opposed to *outcome centered* or *product centered*. It does not prescribe any acceptable end product in the beginning, but only specifies the approach to be adhered to.

The salient principles of participatory methods are summarized in **Table 10.4**.

TABLE 10.4   Principles of Participatory Evaluation
Involvement of the participants in learning logic and skills for goal setting, establishing priorities, focusing questions, interpreting data, decision making, and connecting processes to outcomes.
Participants in this evaluation *own* the research.
Participation is real and *not* token.
Participants focus on a purpose they consider important and to which they are committed.
Participants work together as a group. The facilitator supports group cohesion and collective enquiry.
All aspects of the problem-solving process are clear, understandable, and meaningful to the participants.
Internal self-accountability is highly valued—accountability to themselves first before external accountability.
The facilitator is a collaborator and a learning resource. The participants are the decision makers.
The facilitator recognizes and values the participants' perspectives and expertise and works for participants to recognize and value their own and each other's expertise.
The status difference between facilitator and participants is minimized.

There are several variants in implementing participatory evaluation. A practical step-by-step application of this model using a Freirian approach that helps in remembering all the facilitation steps has been described by Wallerstein and Bernstein (1988). They applied Freire's ideas to the evaluation of alcohol and substance abuse prevention programs in youth and coined the acronym SHOWED. The SHOWED model, as adapted to participatory evaluation, is depicted in **Table 10.5**.

In this approach the evaluator is a facilitator. He or she first brings the participants together and poses the question by narrating a story, saying a word, or showing a picture about the program. The first question posed is, "What do we see here?" The discussion alludes to problems or issues facing the program. Then the facilitator asks: "What is really happening? This question explores the deeper causes of the problems. The next question posed is, "How does this issue relate to our lives?" Through this question, the relation of the program and its various aspects to the lives of the participants is explored. The next question posed is, "Why did the program acquire the problem?" Through this question, the political and structural root causes are explored. The next question posed is, "How is it possible for this program to become empowered?" This discussion brings forth ways to strengthen the program. The final question posed is, "What can we do about it?" This question leads to specific things each participant can do to strengthen the program.

The chief advantage of participatory methods is the community empowering process or the essential skill acquisition by the participants. Participatory techniques are quite helpful in the community development process, and their primary purpose is action. For example, Cheadle and colleagues (2002) used this approach to provide assistance to community-based organizations (CBOs) in Seattle, Washington. Participatory approaches are useful in understanding social determinants of health problems. For example, Schulz and colleagues (2002) used this model to assess social determinants of health in the East Side Village Health Worker Partnership Project. Sanchez and colleagues (2011) implemented participatory evaluation with the New Mexico Health Department and its 32 county-based health councils.

One of the disadvantages of participatory evaluation lies in the long lead time required to build community capacity. Another disadvantage is that often the process remains merely at the problem-posing phase or token solution level with no true solutions emerging.

TABLE 10.5   SHOWED Model: A Practical Way to Apply Participatory Evaluation
What do we **s**ee here?
What is really **h**appening?
How does the issue relate to **o**ur lives?
Why did the program acquire the problem?
How is it possible for this program to become **e**mpowered?
What can we **d**o about it?

FOCUS FEATURE 10.1   CASE STUDY OF PARTICIPATORY EVALUATION IN VIETNAM

This section describes an account of participatory evaluation conducted in Vietnam in 1999 by one of the authors of this book. A detailed account of this evaluation can be found in: Sharma, M., & Deepak, S. (2001). A participatory evaluation of community-based rehabilitation program in North Central Vietnam. *Disability and Rehabilitation, 23,* 352–358.

Introduction

Vietnam is among the poorest nations of the world, with a per capita annual gross domestic product of $3,100 (Central Intelligence Agency, 2010). Vietnam is also a densely populated country with a current population of 90.5 million and a growth rate of 1.1% (Central Intelligence Agency, 2010). The country stretches over 1,600 kilometers along the eastern coast of the Indochinese peninsula, with a land area of 310,070 square kilometers. The health indicators of Vietnam are very similar to those of many developing countries. Twenty-five percent of the population is below 14 years of age and 70% of the population is rural (Central Intelligence Agency, 2010). The life expectancy at birth is 72.18 years, and the infant mortality rate is 20.9 deaths per 1,000 live births. The total fertility rate is 1.91 per woman. Infectious diseases are very common.

In 1976, the World Health Organization (WHO) estimated that 90% of persons with disabilities (PWDs) were totally neglected in developing countries; therefore it developed the community-based rehabilitation (CBR) strategy (WHO, 1976). Because the populations in developing countries were (and are) largely rural and without access to institutional rehabilitation facilities, WHO developed a CBR approach designed to integrate with the primary healthcare (PHC) approach. The goals of CBR are that a PWD should be able to look after him- or herself, move around the house and village, attend school, do a job and carry out household activities, enjoy family life, and take part in community activities (Helander, Mendis, Nelson, & Goerdt, 1989). The five basic principles of CBR strategy are:

- Utilization of available resources in the community

- Transfer of knowledge about disabilities and skills in rehabilitation to people with disabilities, families, and communities

- Community involvement in planning, decision making, and evaluation

- Utilization and strengthening of referral services at district, provincial, and national levels that are able to perform skilled assessments with increasing sophistication, make rehabilitation plans, and participate in training and supervision

- Utilization of a coordinated, multisectoral approach

In essence, the primary tenet of CBR is to provide primary care and rehabilitative assistance to persons with disabilities by using human and other resources already available in their communities. In the CBR approach, rehabilitation work can be carried out safely and effectively by laypersons, such as family members, significant community members, or persons with disabilities themselves.

CBR methodology (*Phuc Hoi Chuc Nang Dua Vao Cong Dong* in Vietnamese) was introduced in Vietnam in 1987. In 1992, a new nongovernmental organization, VIetNAm REHabilitation Association (VINAREHA) was formed to deliver CBR. The acronym in *Kinh* (the local language) means "victory for the persons with disability." This arrangement was made to reduce bureaucratic difficulties and explore the feasibility of an association to serve as "the long arm of the government." Because the needs were highest in the area of

FOCUS FEATURE 10.1   CASE STUDY OF PARTICIPATORY EVALUATION IN VIETNAM (Continued)

self-care and mobility, a 3-year pilot project based on the WHO model was designed for implementation through VINAREHA, focusing exclusively on medical aspects in the province of Thai Binh. In June 1996, a full-scale 3-year project co-funded by the European Union became functional in five north-central provinces: Ha Nam, Nam Dinh (in the initial part of the project these two districts were administratively under the name of Nam Ha), Thai Binh, Hoa Binh, and Ninh Binh. In 1999, a participatory evaluation was commissioned by Associazione Italiana Amici Di Raoul Follereau (AIFO) and the European Union (EU) to facilitate collective understanding and documentation of the lessons learned during the past 3 years, and jointly examine ways to strengthen the program while enhancing the participatory skills used for self-evaluation at all levels of the program. The approach utilized in this evaluation was based on a postmodernist paradigm that discards the notion of objective reality and emphasizes the value of meaning and interpretation (Lysack, 1997).

Methods

For this evaluation, a collective framework of Strengths, Weaknesses, Opportunities, and Threats (SWOT) analysis was chosen (Sharma & Bhatia, 1996). SWOT analysis is a management tool that is widely used in business and market planning (Hansler, 1998; NcNutt, 1991). Because the purpose of this evaluation was to reflect on past accomplishments and plan for the future, it was collectively decided that this framework would be well suited. For understanding the strengths, the primary question posed for reflection was, "What are some of the strong aspects of the program that you think the program has been able to accomplish in the past 3 years?" For understanding the weaknesses, the primary question posed for reflection was, "What are some of the difficulties that you think the program has encountered in the past 3 years?" For understanding the opportunities, the primary question posed was, "What are some of the areas that you think the program can consolidate and augment over the next 3 years?" Finally, for understanding the threats, the primary question posed was, "What are some of the areas that you think the program will face difficulties in over the next 3 years?" Discussion was conducted around these questions, probing was done where needed, and participant-initiated directions were diligently pursued. In addition, periodic reports prepared for monitoring at all levels that were provided by the program were also reviewed.

Participatory data collection was done at the village level, commune level, district level, provincial level, and central level. Due to the constraints imposed by time, travel, and resources for making this plan feasible, the village and commune levels were combined and semi-structured interviews were conducted at this level in three provinces. The program personnel selected the communes. The district and province levels were combined, and focus group discussions were facilitated involving participants from all 10 districts and all 5 provinces of the program. At the central level, both semi-structured interviews and focus group discussions were conducted.

At the central level, communication in English posed almost no difficulty. However, at all levels below the provincial level, because the primary language of communication is *Kinh*, the method of translation-retranslation was utilized. The facilitator posed questions that were translated into *Kinh* and the responses were translated into English. At the end of the session, the transcript was then relayed back to the participants to ensure accuracy, sometimes with the help of another translator and sometimes with the help of the same translator. Data from the village and commune level was collected through a total of 20 semi-structured interviews. The following people participated:

- A CBR supervisor at Dong Phong commune (Tien Hai district, Thai Binh)

- A CBR worker at Dong Phong commune (Tien Hai district, Thai Binh)

(continues)

FOCUS FEATURE 10.1   CASE STUDY OF PARTICIPATORY EVALUATION IN VIETNAM *(Continued)*

- A 72-year-old man with moving difficulty at Dong Phong village (Tien Hai district, Thai Binh)
- A 13-year-old child with disability due to fits and his mother at Dong Phong village (Tien Hai district, Thai Binh)
- A CBR supervisor at Yen Xa commune (Y Yen district, Nam Dinh)
- Two CBR workers at Yen Xa commune (Y Yen district, Nam Dinh)
- A 32-year-old woman with moving disability at Yen Xa commune (Y Yen district, Nam Dinh)
- A 35-year-old man with disability due to strange behavior at Yen Xa commune (Y Yen district, Nam Dinh)
- A CBR supervisor at Yen Dung commune (Y Yen district, Nam Dinh)
- Two CBR workers at Yen Dung commune (Y Yen district, Nam Dinh)
- A 65-year-old man with moving disability at Yen Dung commune (Nam Dinh)
- A 2-year-old child with cerebral palsy and his mother at Yen Dung (Nam Dinh)
- Two CBR supervisors from Hoa Lu district (Ninh Binh)
- Two CBR supervisors from Tam Diep district (Ninh Binh)
- A 34-year-old person with moving difficulty due to limestone burns (Ninh Binh)
- A 9-year-old child with cerebral palsy and his mother (Ninh Binh)

Data about provincial- and district-level functioning was collected through six focus group discussions. One focus group discussion was done exclusively with province-level personnel, one exclusively with district-level personnel, and four with combined participants from the district and provincial levels. Following was the composition of each of the six focus groups:

1. Two members of the Thai Binh provincial steering committee and two members of the Tien Hai district steering committee (total 4)
2. Three members of the Nam Dinh provincial steering committee (total 3)
3. Five members of the Y Yen district steering committee of Nam Dinh province (total 5)
4. Two members from the CBR steering committee of Ninh Binh province, two members of the steering committee from Hoa Lu district, and two members from the Tam Diep district (total 6)
5. Two members from the Ha Nam province steering committee, two members from the Kim Bang district, and two members from the Binh Luc district (total 6)
6. Two members from the Hoa Binh province steering committee, two members from the Lac Son district, and two members from the Kim Boi district (total 6)

Data from the central level was collected individually and collectively from six key informants. They were:

1. President of VINAREHA (who is also head of the Rehabilitation department at Bach Mai Hospital, Hanoi)
2. Vice President of VINAREHA (who is also the director of CBR at the Ministry of Health)

FOCUS FEATURE 10.1   CASE STUDY OF PARTICIPATORY EVALUATION IN VIETNAM *(Continued)*

3. Secretary General of VINAREHA (who is also the deputy director of international cooperation in the Ministry of Health and head of the Rehabilitation department at NIP in Hanoi)
4. Vice Secretary General of VINAREHA (who is also deputy chair of the Rehabilitation department at Bach Mai Hospital in Hanoi)
5. Vice Secretary General of VINAREHA (who is also a faculty member at Hanoi Medical University and a specialist in the Rehabilitation department at Bach Mai Hospital in Hanoi)
6. Country representative, Associazione Italiana Amici di Raoul Follereau (AIFO) in Vietnam

Results

The *strengths* identified from data collected across all the levels were as follows:

- PWDs were identified through house-to-house surveys. The mean disability rate from this data was found to be 8.6% (with a range from 5.6% in Kim Bang to 12.3% in Binh Luc). The data about PWDs were collected and are available in the eight categories of disabilities at the village, commune, district, and provincial levels.

- People's attitudes changed towards PWD and attitudes of PWD. Some of the comments in this regard from CBR personnel included: "There is less stigma," "They feel equal to other people." One of the PWD said, "I feel confident in my new business of stitching clothes."

- Community mapping at each commune (rough community map depicting location of houses of persons with disabilities in the commune) is maintained. Each CBR worker who was visited was able to show the community map.

- The CBR program has assisted several PWDs in making progress towards their rehabilitation goals. In gauging the progress of PWDs, the program followed 23 criteria including performance of activities of daily living (ADLs), self-care, playing, schooling, taking part in family activities, taking part in social activities, and taking part in income generation activities. The program has been able to demonstrate progress in 25% of those needing rehabilitation and to integrate another 19% of those needing rehabilitation. The integration of children with moving difficulty into schools was mentioned as a strength.

- A good ratio of CBR workers and PWDs was found. A CBR worker was found to be dealing with two to four PWDs.

- Emotional support was provided to PWDs. In Yen Xa village, a 35-year-old amputee lost her 2-year-old son to encephalitis during her rehabilitation period. She mentioned that "[the CBR worker] visited me every day just to talk."

- Simple prosthetic, orthotic, and orthopedic devices were produced.

- The medical referral system utilized by the CBR program was mentioned as a strength at all levels.

- The system of cross-assessment between one commune and another commune and one district and another district utilizing pre-established criteria was mentioned as a strength.

- The WHO manual was translated into *Kinh* and 10,000 copies were printed.

(continues)

FOCUS FEATURE 10.1   CASE STUDY OF PARTICIPATORY EVALUATION IN VIETNAM *(Continued)*

- Planned seminars were conducted for province and district leaders, CBR supervisor training, and CBR worker training at district and commune levels. Up to 2,235 CBR workers were trained. Further, the program created a nucleus of trainers well versed in CBR methodology at the provincial level who in turn can train commune-level supervisors and workers.

The *weaknesses* identified from data collected across all the levels were as follows:

- Supplementation and reinforcements in CBR worker training were needed. The medical budget remains low; for example, Ninh Binh had a budget of 20,000 dongs per person per year (about US$2) and Ha Nam 5,000 dongs per person per year (about US$0.50). Mobilization of local funding remains a challenge. Further, training was pointed out as being of a theoretical nature.

- Income generation by PWDs was mentioned as a weakness, because the component has been in effect only since 1998. One woman interviewed in Yen Xa village who had started a small kiosk mentioned earning "50,000 dongs a month" (about US$3) and said, "(it) is not enough."

- A multiplicity of tasks need to be done by CBR workers from several vertical programs, such as a family planning program, immunization program, infectious diseases control programs, iodine deficiency disorders programs, and others.

- Centralized planning—there was limited cooperation from people other than the Ministry of Health. The active members of steering committees are mainly people involved in the medical system.

- There was irregularity in steering committee meetings and modest documentation.

The *opportunities* identified from data collected across all the levels were as follows:

- The best CBR workers are family members of PWDs. Efforts need to be made in future programming to recruit such people.

- Skill-building activities need to be included in CBR workers' and CBR supervisors' training. Some CBR workers felt that there should be a periodic newsletter sent to them after training to increase their knowledge, provide them with new ideas, and keep their interests in rehabilitation-related issues alive.

- The program should be expanded to all communes in the district, not just a few.

- There is a need to enhance the number of PWDs in the composition of steering committees. At present the number of PWDs varies from one to two people (10–20%) in most of the committees.

- A need was expressed to enhance the participation of all members at the commune, district, and provincial levels in the steering committees. CBR leaders' training needs to include more specific information about involving political leaders, ways of ensuring participation in steering committee meetings, and ways to mobilize local funding.

- There is a need to enhance firm commitment from People's Committee chairpersons and vice chairpersons to provide support for local funding.

FOCUS FEATURE 10.1   CASE STUDY OF PARTICIPATORY EVALUATION IN VIETNAM *(Continued)*

The *threats* identified from data collected across all the levels were as follows:

- In most interviews, CBR workers were mentioned performing several duties in different areas such as family planning, immunization, teaching, and so on.

- CBR supervisors and workers felt that there are numerous difficulties in extending rehabilitation beyond medical work, particularly due to lack of training. Some of the members of the team were humble enough to admit that they had limited knowledge and expertise with regard to aspects other than medical.

- The approach as laid out in the WHO manual is very theoretical.

- Issues pertaining to funding, availability of trainers, and availability of participants without incentives were pointed out as potential threats to training.

- Cooperation with other programs and other sectors was mentioned as a major challenge in the coming years.

- Motivation of the CBR worker through incentives or monetary reimbursement was an issue brought up at almost all focus group discussions.

- Self-sufficiency of the program still remains elusive.

Discussion

The purpose of this participatory evaluation was to facilitate collective understanding and documentation of the lessons learned during the past 3 years and jointly find ways to strengthen the program. In this section, an attempt is being made to:

- Establish a summarization across different levels while examining the findings against the WHO principles of CBR and developing implications for future CBR programming

- Discuss the limitations of this evaluation

With regard to *utilization of available resources*, findings from across the levels seem to suggest that for the CBR program in North Central Vietnam, this is indeed a strong component. Resources in the community include both human and material resources. The CBR workers were selected and trained locally. The rehabilitation materials used at the village level were locally available. Examples of such materials included crutches and exercise aids made of bamboo. Furthermore, after training, a cadre of local trainers was created who have the potential to continue training and retraining in the future. Also, efforts have been initiated to mobilize some local funding. In the future, perhaps it would be more beneficial if firm and regular local funding could be harnessed.

Transfer of knowledge about disabilities again seems to be an area of strength. Across all levels, identification of PWDs using a house-to-house survey was acclaimed as being a strong component of this program. Collection and reporting of data in this regard also supports this notion. This collected data can serve a useful purpose for persons with disability because the data provides the capacity to discuss with local authorities the need to allocate regular funding. Such strategies have been used by several groups in other countries. For example, in the slums in Bombay (Mumbai, India), Society for the Promotion

(continues)

FOCUS FEATURE 10.1   CASE STUDY OF PARTICIPATORY EVALUATION IN VIETNAM *(Continued)*

of Area Resource Centres (SPARC) facilitated a cluster profiling during a census that besides providing useful data, enabled women to become aware of their community, initiated a process of reflection (because this was designed with women requiring consultation with each other), and provided the basis for asking for more funds from local authorities. Mapping the community at the village level and using it for tracking PWDs is again an excellent example of an effective tool. Further, in some focus groups, especially at the village level, it was mentioned how important it is that the program has been able to change attitudes about PWDs in the community as well as the attitudes of people with disability. However, there is a need to obtain more information about which attitudes have been influenced and which attitudes have been resistant to change, so that those can be targeted using focused strategies.

With regard to *transfer of knowledge about skills in rehabilitation*, it seems that skills pertaining to activities of daily living (ADLs), self-care, and mobility-related exercises have been done well, especially at the village level. Another very significant progress that has been made is the development of a cadre of trainers at the province and district levels. This core group of trainers will be very useful in future expansion of the program. In the future, however, there is a need to improve CBR workers' skills further with regard to learning disability, hearing disability, speech disability, seeing disability, strange behavior, and multiple disabilities. Besides addressing the "content" needs in training, "process" needs in training will also have to be addressed. Experimentation with techniques that develop skill transfer and not merely knowledge transfer will be mandatory for future programs. Such measures will also ensure retention of skills for longer periods of time. Allowing for more practice sessions, breaking down the skills into small steps, facilitating observational learning, incorporating simulations, presentation of actual problems, and group exploration of ways to deal with those would be helpful techniques in developing actual skills. Some form of refresher training of trainers in training methodology would be a useful investment for improving skill-developing training in the future. Such training may include aspects of adult learning principles, roles and responsibilities of trainers, facilitating small group discussion, conducting structured experiences, and introduction to self-efficacy–building techniques. Also, the suggestion in some focus groups with regard to conducting CBR worker training in a phased manner (twice a year) with appropriate timing linked to after the harvest will go a long way in strengthening this aspect.

Community involvement in planning and decision making has clearly been one of the challenges in this program in North Central Vietnam, as has been pointed out in focus groups at all levels. There are several factors inherent in the cultural milieu and system-wide constraints that impede maximization of participation. Sometimes while working in the field, one experiences the acme of what Freire (1970) talked about as the "culture of silence." However, being a nongovernmental organization (NGO) offers a unique advantage to VINAREHA that can be judiciously invoked to enunciate the voice of PWDs. It may be worthwhile for VINAREHA to look into management practices of some of the NGOs in other countries. Of particular relevance would be sharing of experiences from an NGO in India, Social Work and Research Centre (SWRC), Tilonia (Rajasthan), because that organization also operates as the "long arm of the government" (Tandon, 1993) and has experimented with several ways to improve community participation. However, even if drastic changes are not possible, even simple changes such as including more PWDs in steering committees at all levels, having effective intra- and inter-steering committee communications, improving the regularity of steering committee meetings, inculcating a sense of ownership of the program in all steering committee members, and increasing the willingness to incorporate the wishes of PWDs would be useful steps in that direction. At present, the process of refining the WHO manual is done by "experts" at the central level and some at the provincial level. Involvement of CBR workers and PWDs in this exercise will benefit the refinement a great deal.

FOCUS FEATURE 10.1   CASE STUDY OF PARTICIPATORY EVALUATION IN VIETNAM *(Continued)*

With regard to *community involvement in evaluation*, reporting of monitoring data is a regular practice and needs to continue. The idea of cross-assessments has a great deal of merit; however, it can benefit from greater rigor. What can be added is to critically and continually reflect on problems, discard irrelevant issues, focus on pertinent concerns, identify several ways of dealing with those, discuss the pros and cons of different methods, and then experiment with innovative solutions. Incorporating this practice as a routine in all steering committee meetings would also help in rejuvenating these important structures. It may also be worthwhile to translate and share this report at all levels and critically examine all the issues raised.

Utilization and strengthening of referral services are again identified as strong components of the CBR program at all levels. Vietnam has a good primary healthcare system and an effective referral chain. The AIFO-VINAREHA partnership has made useful strides in utilizing this chain and deserves unequivocal kudos.

Utilization of a coordinated multisectoral approach has again been a challenge for this program. With this issue there are no easy answers. Centralized administration, bureaucracy, diverse mandates, and reporting regulations make establishing collaboration between agencies a very slow and challenging process. The quote of one AIFO country representative, "[a] small step is a big success" is quite pertinent in this regard. The participatory focus group discussions introduced the need for collaboration; however, with regard to the issue of how, no clear answers emerged. Some of the needs that focus groups seemed to suggest were in the areas of income generation, credit schemes, and inclusive education. Many of these approaches appear promising on paper, but in my opinion, before AIFO-VINAREHA gets on the bandwagon of some of these approaches, it may be worthwhile to wait and watch how they shape up. Over the past 6 years, the AIFO-VINAREHA partnership has developed substantial experience utilizing primarily medical rehabilitation, importantly in disability identification, and assisting with self-care and mobility needs. It would be only logical to consolidate these aspects and make the coverage universal in these five provinces before embarking upon some of the newer challenges. However, in the areas where needs with regard to self-care and mobility have been met, it may be possible to gradually introduce some of these aspects (as has been done over the past year) and guardedly track the outcome. Such a slow and cautious approach would be helpful for the program.

Let us also discuss some of the limitations of this evaluation. For a reader, coming from a purely quantitative, modernist paradigm expecting an immaculate, objective, scientific evaluation, this evaluation would pose some difficulty in comprehension. For qualitative, postmodernist evaluators, many of the aspects also may be unpalatable. It is evident in this evaluation that an attempt was made to utilize participatory methods. The participatory approach is a process on a continuum. The circumstances in the CBR program posed several challenges that prevented maximization of participation. Language was a major constraint that was addressed partially by using translators and applying a translation-retranslation method. However, this method poses several inherent weaknesses such as the quality of translation, loss of accurate meaning, and misinterpretation. It is my hope that in the future, perhaps using the same method with some local person(s) would facilitate a better process. The other limitation was the method of recording that was done by note taking. Ideally, it would have been desirable to record conversations and then transcribe the transcripts using the translation-retranslation method. However, limitations of resources and other factors precluded such an approach. Also, the translators chosen for this evaluation were members of the central team. Again this poses a threat in terms of honest and free expression of thoughts. On the other hand, it offers an advantage in terms of introducing a person

(continues)

FOCUS FEATURE 10.1   CASE STUDY OF PARTICIPATORY EVALUATION IN VIETNAM *(Continued)*

that the people already know and feel more comfortable with. It also reduces the time entailed in establishing rapport. Another limitation was that the communes and evaluation processes were selected by the program personnel. Random selection of which communes needed to be visited was not done. Clearly, random selection would have added objectivity to the data collection. However, the purpose of this evaluation was to collectively understand the processes and not to maximize objectivity; therefore, selection by the program staff provided definitive advantages. Further, no specific training was given to translators. Again this was in consonance with the participatory philosophy of having "faith" in the inherent potential of people. Further, it was possible to conduct only 20 semi-structured interviews at the village and commune level, 6 focus groups with the province- and district-level people, and 1 focus group with six individual discussions at the central level. Clearly, if more time was available more data could have been collected. However, there was substantial repetition of themes that would indicate that not much more would have been gained by carrying on with the process any further. It can be safely assumed that the data gathered and presented here has been fairly representative of the entire program area.

Another limitation was in terms of a lack of prior familiarity of the facilitator with the country, people, or program. Besides posing problems, this also offered some advantage by providing the ability to look at the situation as a blank slate. The political, cultural, and historical location of the program was also not very conducive to classical participatory "dialogue" and can be considered in the limitations. A limited amount of time availability was another major constraint. This was addressed by tapping and relying extensively on the potential of the people involved in the program who provided all the insights.

Finally, an important limitation was that no specific concrete time-bound action plans emerged. Ideally, the participatory approach should enable generation of action plans. It is my ardent hope that this report will be used as a tool for further reflection and articulation of concrete action plans at all levels.

CIPP MODEL OF EVALUATION

One of the models that evolved in the field of education as an alternative to the dominant, objectives-based approach to evaluation is the CIPP (Context, Input, Process, Product) model (Stufflebeam, 1983, 2003). The **CIPP model of evaluation** consists of *context*, which is the needs assessment; *input*, which is the design; *process*, which is the implementation; and *product*, which includes the outcomes. The shortcomings of the objectives-based evaluation are that it assumes the program staff and participants can determine the behavioral objectives and it also assumes that these objectives are constant from the beginning through the end of the program. The CIPP model does not start with predetermined objectives, and perceives evaluation as a tool to help improve programs for the people they are intended to serve. The CIPP model is decision-oriented and aims to promote the growth of programs, ensure optimal utilization of resources, and improve programs.

In determining the context, the following aspects are assessed: relationship of the program with other programs, adequacy of time for the program, external factors associated with the program, whether it is an integrated or a separate program, links with other programs, and the need for the program. Some of the considerations in determining input are the ability of the participants; motivation of the participants; living conditions of the participants; knowledge, skills, attitudes, and behaviors of the participants; suitability of the objectives; and abilities of the health educators. The process identifies the following: problems related to program implementation, problems confronting the participants, and problems confronting the health educators. The product focuses on quality of assessment, lessons learned, and how participants use what they have learned. Some of the methods the CIPP model uses are discussions, informal conversation, observation, individual participant interviews, organizational documents, self-assessment, and videotapes.

Some of the applications of the CIPP model for evaluation in health have been the following:

- Evaluation of the Suicide Prevention Program in Kaohsiung City, Taiwan (Ho et al., 2010)
- Evaluation of the Community Medical Care Unit (CMU) in Mahasarakham Hospital, Thailand (Asavatanabodee, 2010)
- Evaluation of a patient safety initiative in the United States (Farley & Battles, 2009)

One of the limitations of this approach is that it may be driven by outsiders or experts and thus may not have the involvement of all the stakeholders.

UTILIZATION-FOCUSED EVALUATION

Utilization-focused evaluation as an approach was suggested by Michael Patton (2008). This evaluation is conducted for specific and intentional uses along with and for primary users of the program. The underpinning of this type of evaluation is that the evaluation must be user-driven. This evaluation begins with identification of key decision makers and users who are likely to use the information resulting from the evaluation. The focus of utilization-focused evaluation is therefore on "intended use by intended users" (Patton, 2002, 2008).

> *In utilization-focused evaluation the evaluator poses the questions: What difference will this evaluation make? and What would you do with the answers that the evaluation will provide?*

The intended users may include program staff, program participants, funders, administrators, and board members. Stakeholder identification is crucial to utilization-focused evaluation (Bryson, Patton, & Bowman, 2011). The evaluation facilitator works with these people to decide what kind of evaluation they want. These people are tapped to develop the evaluation questions. Based on these evaluation questions, the research methods and data analysis techniques evolve. This type of evaluation does not recommend any set content, model, theory, or approach. It is all guided by the situation. But the underlying theme in evaluation is the "use." The evaluator poses the questions: What difference will this evaluation make? and What would you do with the answers that the evaluation will provide? It usually uses qualitative approaches, although quantitative approaches may also be used (Patton, 2002).

Utilization-focused evaluation has been used in the health field in the evaluation of several programs, including medical education in Oklahoma (Vassar, Wheeler, Davison,

& Franklin, 2010), a conservation education program in Montana (Flowers, 2010), and a Compassionate Care Benefit program in Canada (Williams, 2010).

GOAL-FREE EVALUATION

Goal-free evaluation is different from a traditional evaluation. In goal-free evaluation, the goals of the program are not known. This type of evaluation aims at eliminating (or reducing) evaluator bias. In conducting this type of evaluation, the program's preset objectives are not revealed to the evaluator. As a result, a program's intended and unintended effects are both studied. This type of evaluation was first proposed by Michael Scriven (1972). In goal-free evaluation, emphasis is placed on fieldwork that gathers data on potential outcomes and compares it with the needs of the people. So the data is collected at two levels, needs assessment and potential outcomes.

Patton (2002) identifies four distinct reasons for doing goal-free evaluation: (1) to study unintended outcomes, (2) to eliminate negative undertones such as the label of "side effect" associated with unintended effects, (3) to reduce evaluator bias, and (4) to preserve the evaluator's independence. The goal-free evaluator asks, What does the program actually do?, rather than, What does the program intend to do? This type of evaluation uses predominantly qualitative approaches because it requires capturing the actual experiences of the program participants. However, it can use both qualitative and quantitative approaches. Goal-free evaluation has been used in the health field, for example, in the evaluation of a respite program for persons with Alzheimer's disease (Perry & Bontinen, 2001). One of the disadvantages of this type of evaluation is its lack of objectives and clear methodology.

QUALITATIVE DATA ANALYSIS AND INTERPRETATION

For qualitative research, *interviews* or *discussions*, and *observation* remain the key means for collecting data. Qualitative interviewing or discussions usually require use of open-ended questions. The delivery of questions could be as follows (Patton, 2002):

- *Informal conversational interviews:* The evaluator does not make any *a priori* preparations and is solely guided by his or her probing self. This permits rich exploration of the subject. However, it makes summarization of results across participants difficult.
- *Semi-structured interviews:* A script, an interview guide, or a schedule is organized for this type of interview, but the interviewer is free to probe, skip questions, and add questions. This provides some flexibility. It also makes it easier to summarize data and productively use limited time.
- *Standardized, open-ended interviews:* These interviews contain a set of questions that have been pretested, and the interviewer sticks to these questions. These are most useful when multiple sites have to be covered and time is of the essence.

With interviews, most qualitative evaluators normally suggest the use of audio recording. These recordings are then transcribed and used in data analysis. This process is helpful in accurate data collection. Some evaluators also use videotaping, which captures the gestures and other forms of nonverbal communication. However, some evaluators recommend against the use of audio- and videotaping due to their intrusive nature, potential technical failures, and the lack of viability in remote locations.

Observation is the other method of data collection used by qualitative evaluators. This often requires more resources, especially time, than interviews and necessitates the evaluator becoming the "true instrument" for evaluation to a greater extent. Depending on the evaluation topic, opportunity, feasibility, and IRB approval, the evaluator may choose to be:

- *A concealed observer:* The observer is hidden from the participants and the participants do not know they are being observed. People may behave quite differently when they know they are being observed. Therefore, these types of covert observations are more likely to be close to what is actually happening. However, it is usually difficult to get permission from an IRB for these types of observations.
- *A passive, unobtrusive observer:* In this observation, the observer passively observes (does not interact with) the participants, but is visible to the participants.
- *A limited interaction observer:* The observer has limited interaction with the participants in the form of, for example, asking a few questions.
- *A completely participatory observer:* The observer acts like a participant and participates in all activities and interacts freely with the participants.

The main benefit of observation over interview is its ability to capture the context. The main drawback of observation is the requirement of a higher degree of acumen on the part of the observer, who must be adept at noticing verbal content and nonverbal cues, must have command of the local language and dialect, and must be versatile with field-based note taking.

In its initial stages, the data analysis in qualitative evaluation is an ongoing activity in which the evaluator processes data and analyzes his or her strategy on a daily or weekly basis during data collection. In qualitative evaluation, data collected is usually quite plentiful. This preliminary data analysis helps the evaluator determine when to stop further data collection. This ongoing data analysis also provides insight for identifying concepts for open coding.

There are three steps in qualitative data analysis. These are:

1. *Open coding:* **Open coding** or substantive coding is where the evaluator decides on tentative conceptual categories into which the data will be coded. For this purpose, the evaluator may choose words, items, phrases, events, timings, and so on. This coding is often done in the margin of the field notes.
2. *Audit trail:* In an **audit trail**, the evaluator links the data identified in open coding with the source and context. This can be done simply in a table format in a notebook. Sometimes one can use a word processor, or some qualitative software such as N-Vivo. In this step, salient quotes from the sources are also very important to keep in the records.
3. *Axial coding:* In **axial coding**, the evaluator begins to put together the complete picture, in which events pertaining to the evaluation topic, related topics, implications

from evaluation, and a description of a proposed conceptual model are weaved together and presented.

In completing these steps of data analysis, the evaluator polishes the script and addresses concerns of data interpretation, namely trustworthiness, triangulation, credibility, coherence, dependability, transferability, and confirmability.

- *Trustworthiness:* **Trustworthiness** is about how much the evaluator has adhered to the procedures specific to the chosen method, exercised rigor in inquiry, and is open about describing the procedures.
- *Triangulation:* **Triangulation** is the use of multiple methods, multiple data, or multiple analysts, or the use of theory to aid in data interpretation.
- *Credibility:* **Credibility** is the extent to which the evaluation is considered to be believable from the perspective of the participants. It is similar to the concept of internal validity in quantitative research. The qualitative evaluation assumes multiple realities that are multiply interpreted, and credibility is a reflection of this richness. The participants are the only ones who can legitimately judge this attribute.
- *Coherence:* **Coherence** is the extent to which the final evaluation write-up makes sense, the extent to which conclusions are supported by data, and the extent to which multiple data sources were used in the evaluation.
- *Dependability:* **Dependability** refers to whether we would obtain the same results if we could observe the same thing twice. It is a function of detailed description of the method by one evaluator in one study, and another evaluator closely following the same steps in another study. Dependability is a concept similar to reliability in the quantitative paradigm.
- *Transferability:* **Transferability** is the degree to which the results of qualitative evaluation can be transferred to other contexts or settings. The issue of transferability is similar to the concept of external validity in the quantitative paradigm.
- *Confirmability:* **Confirmability** is the degree to which the results can be confirmed or corroborated by others. To establish confirmability, the evaluator can document the procedures for checking and rechecking the data throughout the study.

Several computer programs are available to aid the qualitative evaluator. Although a discussion on their merits, demerits, or usage guidelines is beyond the scope of this book, a brief description of some commonly used software is presented as follows:

- *ATLAS ti:* This software is designed for visual analysis of text, audio, graphical, or video data. It helps in selecting, coding, annotating, and comparing marked segments.
- *Ethnograph:* This software is used for analysis of textual data. It assists in locating open-coded data.
- *HyperRESEARCH:* This software is available for both PC and Macintosh computers, and assists in working with textual and multimedia data.
- *QSR NVivo:* This software assists in code-based theorizing and has the ability to search for a word, sound, or image.

- *MAXQDA:* This is versatile software that can analyze text-based data from focus groups, unstructured interviews, case histories, field notes, observation protocols, document letters, and other written materials.

SKILL-BUILDING ACTIVITY

Take a real or fictitious health education program and develop a protocol for conducting a focus group among participants for process or impact evaluation. Focus group discussions are a common method of data collection in qualitative evaluations. The focus group method entails developing a detailed protocol. In developing the protocol, the evaluator must decide on the topic. The protocol must include the method of recruiting participants (8–12 persons with a minimum of 4–5 groups for each topic). The length of time for conducting a focus group is usually between 1 and 2 hours. The protocol must include directions for conducting the discussion. It should elaborate the introductory comments from the moderator. The protocol must also include the set of questions to be asked, which can be derived from a theory or previous studies. The questions must be open ended and not amenable to a yes/no response. The protocol must also specify the roles and responsibilities of the moderator. Finally, the protocol must provide guidance for data analysis and interpretation.

SUMMARY

Qualitative evaluation is defined as a method of assessing a program using one of three approaches: (1) interviews or discussions consisting of open-ended questions, (2) observations based on field notes, or (3) review of written materials and other documents. An emic view is used in qualitative enquiry, where the meaning of any situation is perceived from the participant's viewpoint and the evaluator is a mere observer. The qualitative evaluator is interested in the whole perspective or the holistic perspective, which includes underlying values and the context as a part of the phenomenon. The qualitative enquiry is based on postpositivism, which states that only partially objective accounts of the world can be produced because all methods are flawed; hence, the reality is multiply constructed and multiply interpreted. In the qualitative evaluation paradigm, the logic is inductive reasoning in which logic proceeds from specific to general. The research design is dynamic or flexible.

Several types of evaluation are based on the qualitative paradigm, such as empowerment evaluation, illuminative evaluation (also known as socio-anthropological evaluation, responsive evaluation, or transaction evaluation), participatory evaluation, the CIPP (Context, Input, Process, Product) model of evaluation, utilization-focused evaluation, and goal-free evaluation. Empowerment evaluation is the use of evaluation concepts, techniques, and findings to foster improvement and self-determination. Illuminative evaluation is a qualitative evaluation that seeks to illuminate or clarify answers to questions pertaining to a program that are lying latent or dormant, using methods from social anthropology rather than psychology. Participatory evaluation is a mode of inquiry designed and conducted by people themselves to trace the influence of knowledge as a means of power and for the purpose of generating some action. The CIPP model of evaluation is composed of *context*, which is the needs assessment; *input*, which is the design; *process*, which is the implementation; and *product*, which includes the outcomes. Utilization-focused evaluation is conducted for specific and intentional uses along with and for primary users of the program. Goal-free evaluation aims at eliminating (or reducing) evaluator bias. In conducting this type of evaluation, a program's preset objectives are not revealed to the evaluator.

REVIEW QUESTIONS

1. Delineate the historical genesis of qualitative research.
2. Differentiate between qualitative and quantitative paradigms.
3. Explain the facets and principles of empowerment evaluation.
4. Describe the steps for undertaking empowerment evaluation.
5. What is illuminative evaluation?
6. List the principles of participatory evaluation.
7. Describe the CIPP model of evaluation
8. Differentiate between utilization-focused evaluation and goal-free evaluation.

WEBSITES TO EXPLORE

Empowerment Evaluation Blog

http://eevaluation.blogspot.com
This blog on empowerment evaluation comes mostly from the originator of this form of evaluation, Dr. David Fetterman. This is the place for dialogue on theory and practice pertaining to empowerment evaluation. You can also read the profile and bio sketch of Dr. Fetterman on this website. *Read one or more of the blog postings and provide your comment in the section where it asks for comments.*

What Is Evaluation?

http://www.enquirylearning.net/ELU/Issues/Research/Res1Ch6.html
This website presents a chapter on evaluation and discusses traditional evaluation, illuminative evaluation, bureaucratic evaluation, autocratic evaluation, and democratic evaluation. *Read this account and prepare a table that differentiates these five kinds of evaluations.*

Participatory Evaluation

http://meera.snre.umich.edu/plan-an-evaluation/related-topics/participatory-evaluation
This is the website of a group called MEERA (My Environmental Education Evaluation Resource Assistant). The website describes what participatory evaluation is and how it is conducted. It also describes why and how to involve youth. It has links to case studies in participatory evaluation. *Choose any one case study, read it, and discuss the strengths and weaknesses of participatory evaluation.*

Society for Participatory Research in Asia (PRIA)

http://www.pria.org

This is the website of an organization in India that was formed in 1982 and has been involved with systematic participatory evaluations. The website has links related to the organization, projects, strategic partners, media, resources, working with the organization, and contact information. *Browse through these links and pay attention to the projects that have been undertaken by this organization. Read at least one of the case studies presented and discuss the strengths and weaknesses of participatory approaches.*

Utilization-Focused Evaluation Checklist

http://www.idrc.ca/uploads/user-S/10905198311Utilization_Focused_Evaluation.pdf

This website presents a checklist for conducting utilization-focused evaluation developed by Michael Patton, the originator of this model. *Review the checklist. Then, adapt this checklist for conducting a real or fictitious evaluation of a program of your choice.*

REFERENCES

Alinsky, S. (1972). *Rules for the radicals* (pp. 37–52). New York: Random House.

Asavatanabodee, P. (2010). The evaluation of primary care unit of Mahasarakham Hospital. *Journal of Medical Association of Thailand, 93*(2), 239–244.

Ball, B., Kerig, P. K., & Rosenbluth, B. (2009). "Like a family but better because you can actually trust each other": The Expect Respect dating violence prevention program for at-risk youth. *Health Promotion Practice, 10*(1 Suppl.), 45S–58S.

Berger, P. L., & Luckmann, T. (1967). *The social construction of reality.* Garden City, NY: Anchor.

Bryson, J. M., Patton, M. Q., & Bowman, R. A. (2011). Working with evaluation stakeholders: A rationale, step-wise approach and toolkit. *Evaluation and Program Planning, 34*(1), 1–12.

Burt, S., Whitmore, M., Vearncombe, D., & Dykes, F. (2006). The development and delivery of a practice-based breastfeeding education package for general practitioners in the UK. *Maternal and Child Nutrition, 2*(2), 91–102.

Central Intelligence Agency. (2010). The world fact book. Retrieved from https://www.cia.gov/library/publications/the-world-factbook/geos/vm.html

Chambers, R. (1983). *Rural development: Putting the "last first"* (pp. 28–72). Harlow, England: Longman.

Cheadle, A., Sullivan, M., Krieger, J., Ciske, S., Shaw, M., Schier, J. K., & Eisinger, A. (2002). Using a participatory approach to provide assistance to community-based organizations: The Seattle Partners Community Research Center. *Health Education and Behavior, 29*, 383–394.

Clemow, R. (2007). An illuminative evaluation of skills rehearsal in a mentorship course. *Nurse Education Today, 27*(1), 80–87.

Creswell, J. W. (2006). *Qualitative inquiry and research design. Choosing among five traditions* (2nd ed.). Thousand Oaks, CA: Sage.

Denzin, N. K., & Lincoln, Y. S. (Eds.). (2005). *Handbook of qualitative research* (3rd ed.). Thousand Oaks, CA: Sage.

Dwyer, J. J., Vavaroutsos, D., Lutterman, A., Hier, M., Hughes, M., & Makarchuk, M. J. (2006). Empowerment evaluation in redesigning a public health unit nutrition program. *Canadian Journal of Dietetic Practice and Research, 67*(1), 36–40.

Evans, S. D., Prilleltensky, O., McKenzie, A., Prilleltensky, I., Nogueras, D., Huggins, C., & Mescia N. (2011). Promoting strengths, prevention, empowerment, and community change through organizational development: Lessons for research, theory, and practice. *Journal of Prevention and Intervention in the Community, 39*(1), 50–64.

Farley, D. O., & Battles, J. B. (2009). Evaluation of the AHRQ patient safety initiative: Framework and approach. *Health Services Research, 44*(2 Pt 2), 628–645.

Fernandes, W., & Tandon, R. (1981). *Participatory research and evaluation: Experiments in research as a process of liberation.* New Delhi: Indian Social Institute.

Fetterman, D. M. (1996). Empowerment evaluation: An introduction to theory and practice. In D. M. Fetterman, S. J. Kaftarian, & A. Wandersman (Eds.), *Empowerment evaluation. Knowledge and tools for self-assessment and accountability* (pp. 3–48). Thousand Oaks, CA: Sage.

Fetterman, D. M. (2001). Empowerment evaluation and self determination: A practical approach toward program improvement and capacity building. In N. Schneiderman, M. A. Speers, J. M. Silva, H. Tomes, & J. H. Gentry (Eds.), *Integrating behavioral and social sciences with public health* (pp. 321–351). Washington, DC: American Psychological Association.

Fetterman, D. M. (2005). A window into the heart and soul of empowerment evaluation: Looking through the lens of empowerment evaluation principles. In D. M Fetterman & A. Wandersman (Eds.), *Empowerment evaluation principles in practice* (pp. 1–26). New York: Guilford Press.

Flowers, A. B. (2010). Blazing an evaluation pathway: Lessons learned from applying utilization-focused evaluation to a conservation education program. *Evaluation and Program Planning, 33*(2), 165–171.

Freire, P. (1970). *Pedagogy of the oppressed.* New York: Continuum.

Freire, P. (1976). *Education: The practice of freedom.* London: Writers and Readers Cooperative.

Galvin, K., Sharples, A., & Jackson, D. (2000). Citizens Advice Bureaus in general practice: An illuminative evaluation. *Health and Social Care in the Community, 8*(4), 277–282.

Glaser, B. G., & Strauss, A. L. (1967). *The discovery of grounded theory: Strategies for qualitative research.* Chicago: Aldine.

Goodman, R. M., & Noonan, R. K. (2009). Empowerment evaluation for violence prevention public health programs. *Health Promotion Practice, 10*(1 Suppl.), 11S–18S.

Gordon, V. H. (1991). Improving practice through illuminative evaluation. *Social Service Review, 65*(3), 365–378.

Hansler, D. F. (1988). Market planning—SWOT analysis. *Fund Raising Management, 19*, 78.

Helander, E., Mendis, P., Nelson, G., & Goerdt, A. (1989). *Training in the community for people with disabilities.* Geneva: World Health Organization.

Ho, W. W., Chen, W. J., Ho, C. K., Lee, M. B., Chen, C. C., & Chou, F. H. (2010). Evaluation of the suicide prevention program in Kaohsiung City, Taiwan, using the CIPP Evaluation Model. *Community Mental Health Journal* [Epub ahead of print] PMID: 21132460.

Huberman, A. M., & Miles, M. B. (Eds.). (2002). *The qualitative researcher's companion. Classic and contemporary readings.* Thousand Oaks, CA: Sage.

Kasmel, A., & Andersen, P. T. (2011). Measurement of community empowerment in three community programs in Rapla (Estonia). *International Journal of Environmental Research and Public Health, 8*(3), 799–817.

Lysack, C. (1997). Modernity, postmodernity and disability in developing countries. *International Journal of Rehabilitation Research, 20*, 121–128.

Macfarlane, F., Greenhalgh, T., Schofield, T., & Desombre T. (2004). RCGP Quality Team Development programme: An illuminative evaluation. *Quality and Safety in Health Care, 13*(5), 356–362.

Mayberry, R. M., Daniels, P., Yancey, E. M., Akintobi, T. H., Berry, J., Clark, N., & Dawaghreh, A. (2009). Enhancing community-based organizations' capacity for HIV/AIDS education and prevention. *Evaluation and Program Planning, 32*(3), 213–220.

McNutt, K. (1991). SWOT before you start. *Nutrition Today, 26,* 48–51.

Mead, M. (1928). *Coming of age in Samoa: A psychological study of primitive youth for Western civilization.* New York: Morrow.

Morse, J. M., Swanson, J., & Kuzel, A. J. (2001). *The nature of qualitative evidence.* Thousand Oaks, CA: Sage.

Noonan, R. K., & Gibbs, D. (2009). Empowerment evaluation with programs designed to prevent first-time male perpetration of sexual violence. *Health Promotion Practice, 10*(1 Suppl.), 5S–10S.

Ok Ham, K., & Jeong Kim, B. (2011). Evaluation of a cardiovascular health promotion programme offered to low-income women in Korea. *Journal of Clinical Nursing, 20*(9–10), 1245–1254. doi: 10.1111/j.1365-2702.2010.03580.x.

Parlett, M. (1972). Evaluating innovations in teaching, In H. J. Butcher & E. Rudd (Eds.), *Contemporary problems in higher education* (pp. 144–154). London: McGraw-Hill.

Paterson, B. L., Thorne, S. E., Canam, C., & Jillings, C. (2001). *Meta-study of qualitative health research. A practical guide to meta-analysis and meta-synthesis.* Thousand Oaks, CA: Sage.

Patton, M. Q. (2002). *Qualitative research and evaluation methods* (3rd ed.). Thousand Oaks, CA: Sage.

Patton, M. Q. (2008). *Utilization-focused evaluation* (4th ed.). Thousand Oaks, CA: Sage.

Perry, J., & Bontinen, K. (2001). Evaluation of a weekend respite program for persons with Alzheimer disease. *Canadian Journal of Nursing Research, 33*(1), 81–95.

Polit, D. F., & Hungler, B. P. (1999). *Nursing research. Principles and methods* (6th ed.). Philadelphia: Lippincott.

Rappaport, J. (1987). Terms of empowerment/exemplars of prevention: Toward a theory of community psychology. *American Journal of Community Psychology, 15,* 121–148.

Richards, L., & Morse, J. M. (2006). *Read me first for a user's guide to qualitative methods* (2nd ed.). Thousand Oaks, CA: Sage.

Sanchez, V., Carrillo, C., & Wallerstein, N. (2011). From the ground up: Building a participatory evaluation model. *Progress in Community Health Partnerships: Research, Education and Action, 5*(1), 45–52.

Schulz, A. J., Parker, E. A., Israel, B. A., Allen, A., Decarlo, M., & Lockett, M. (2002). Addressing social determinants of health through community-based participatory research: The East Side Village Health Worker Partnership. *Health Education and Behavior, 29,* 326–341.

Schwandt, T. A. (2007). *Dictionary of qualitative inquiry* (3rd ed.). Thousand Oaks, CA: Sage.

Scriven, M. (1972). Pros and cons about goal free evaluation. *Evaluation Comment, 3,* 1–7.

Scriven, M. (2005). Book review: Empowerment evaluation principles in practice. *American Journal of Evaluation, 26*(3), 415–417.

Sharma, M., & Bhatia, G. (1996). The voluntary community health movement in India: A strengths, weaknesses, opportunities, and threats (SWOT) analysis. *Journal of Community Health, 21,* 453–464.

Stufflebeam, D. L. (1983). The CIPP model for program evaluation. In G. F. Madaus, M. Scriven, & D. L. Stufflebeam (Eds.), *Evaluation models: Viewpoints on educational and human services evaluation* (pp. 279–318). Boston: Kluwer Nijhof.

Stufflebeam, D. L. (2003). The CIPP model for evaluation. In T. Kelleghan & D. L. Stufflebeam (Eds.), *International handbook of education evaluation* (pp. 31–62). London: Kluwer Academic Press.

Tandon, R. (1993). Trends in voluntary action. *Health for the Millions, 19,* 20–22.

Tandon, R., & Brown, L. D. (1981). Organization building for rural development: An experiment in India. *Journal of Applied Behavioural Science, 17,* 172–189.

Vassar, M., Wheeler, D. L., Davison, M., & Franklin, J. (2010). Program evaluation in medical education: An overview of the utilization-focused approach. *Journal of Educational Evaluation for Health Professions, 7,* 1.

Wallerstein, N., & Bernstein, E. (1988). Empowerment education: Freire's ideas adapted to health education. *Health Education Quarterly, 15,* 379–394.

Waters, D., James, R., & Darby, J. (2011). Health promoting community radio in rural Bali: An impact evaluation. *Rural and Remote Health, 11*(1), 1555.

Williams, A. M. (2010). Evaluating Canada's Compassionate Care Benefit using a utilization-focused evaluation framework: Successful strategies and prerequisite conditions. *Evaluation and Program Planning, 33*(2), 91–97.

Wolcott, H. F. (2008). *Writing up qualitative research* (3rd ed.). Thousand Oaks, CA: Sage.

World Health Organization (WHO). (1976). *Resolution on disability, prevention and rehabilitation (A29.68).* Geneva: Author.

CHAPTER 11

Sampling

CHAPTER OBJECTIVES

- Identify sampling as a fundamental evaluation design issue
- Describe how sampling should match the purposes of both the health program and the program evaluation
- Explain how a representative sample can increase the value of the results of health evaluations by increasing generalizability
- Distinguish between types of probability sampling and nonprobability sampling
- Identify barriers to using probability samples in health promotion and education evaluations
- Describe the relationship between sampling and the internal and external validity of evaluation results
- Identify factors that affect participant response rates in evaluation projects
- Identify factors that influence sample size estimation
- Describe how sample size can be estimated based on statistical considerations
- Distinguish between descriptive generalization and explanatory generalization
- Explain how adequate sample size is foundational to making statistical decisions

WHAT IS A SAMPLE?

From a statistical perspective, a **sample** is a subset of a population used in an evaluation to represent the target population. A measurement taken on the sample is called a *statistic*. The population value for that measurement is called a *parameter*. For example, a mean knowledge test score computed on a sample is a statistic. If the entire population of interest takes the knowledge test, the mean score would be considered a parameter. The goal of sampling is for the knowledge test statistic to be as close as possible to the population knowledge test parameter. Thus the goal of the sample is to represent the larger population. Stated another way, the goal of sampling is to minimize bias by selecting participants who represent the important attributes of the population.

Health promotion and education interventions are designed to address the health behaviors of a **target population** (Alfonso et al., 2008). The target population is composed of all people (or other units: schools, communities, etc.) in a defined group of interest. In some cases, the target population is very small and specific—for example, 86 seventh graders at a local high school. In other cases the target population can be diverse and large, such as all residents of a county. In many instances, target populations are defined by age (e.g., adults in the workforce), gender (e.g., women of child-bearing age), health status (e.g., recent diagnosis of diabetes), or risk behavior (e.g., sedentary). When designing an evaluation, it is critical to know the specific parameters of the target population (Faugier & Sargeant, 1997). More specifically, a well-defined target population is essential for designing a method of generating a representative sample.

A **sampling frame** is an essential link between the target population and the sample to be used in an evaluation. The sampling frame is a list of all units (people, communities, worksites, etc.) in the target population that are available for selection into a sample. Contact information is essential to inviting members of a target population to participate in an evaluation. For example, you wish to conduct an evaluation of a smoking cessation program at a worksite. Currently you do not have information that identifies the employees who are smokers. A survey, health screening, or drug test could be used to identify smokers. This list of smokers, along with their contact information, becomes the sampling frame for that worksite. If certain smokers went undetected, they are not part of the sampling frame.

One important goal of sampling methods is to minimize sampling error. **Sampling error** is inaccuracy introduced into an evaluation by measuring a sample rather than the entire target population. Error is observed when comparing the sample statistic (e.g., mean knowledge score) to the target population parameter (e.g., mean knowledge score). Sampling error is estimated by subtracting the value of a population parameter from the corresponding sample statistic. The goal is to keep sampling error to a minimum. This is accomplished by using probability sampling methods to increase the representativeness of the sample. The evaluator needs to take steps to actively prevent participant attrition. Participant attrition can introduce bias, reducing the representativeness of the sample.

Sampling procedures are carefully defined to ensure that the evaluation is conducted on participants who represent the target population of a program.

Evaluations are conducted to understand how well health education programs work. Sampling procedures are carefully designed to ensure that the evaluation is conducted on participants who represent the target population of a program. Sophisticated tools are available for generating **probability samples** that represent the target population. These samples enable the evaluator to claim that the data-producing sample in the evaluation is representative of the target population. To the extent that the sample is representative, one can generalize evaluation findings to the target population. This effort can substantially increase the quality and usefulness of the evaluation results. The effectiveness of a health education/promotion program should be considered in the context of the sample it was tested on. It is generally assumed that the results of the evaluation will be generalized back to a target population.

PROBABILITY SAMPLING

Using probability sampling, each member of the target population has a known chance of being chosen for the evaluation sample. Probability samples enable the evaluator to generalize the results from the sample to the population with a specified level of confidence. Thus, probability sampling provides a clear rationale for generalizing the observed results in a sample to the target population. It allows the evaluator to present the sample as representative of the intended target population. The following list describes the different types of probability samples used for evaluations of health programs. Table 11.1 summarizes the major types of probability samples.

> *Probability samples enable the evaluator to generalize the results from the sample to the population with a specified level of confidence.*

- *Simple random sample:* With a **simple random sample**, all members of the target population have an equal chance of selection into the sample. The evaluator starts with a sampling frame, a complete list of all accessible people in the target population. Then a table of random numbers or a computer program to generate random numbers is used to select the random sample.
- *Stratified random sample:* Health educators are often interested in specific subsets within the total community. Many health behavior change programs have different rates of effectiveness depending on variables like gender, age, educational status, socioeconomic status, and other potential modifying factors. A **stratified random sample** is generated when the target population is sorted into distinct categories (race, gender, age groups) and placed into independent subpopulations (strata). Participants are then randomly selected from each of the subpopulations. It is critical to define each stratum, so that each element (person) in the population appears in only one stratum. Using this method can ensure that the critical elements of the population are represented in the sample. For example, you may wish to evaluate the impact of a health behavior program on different age groups in the community. By stratifying the sample frame by age (20–29, 30–39, 40–49), the evaluation team can ensure that all age strata are represented in the sample. Evaluation questions related to effectiveness of the health behavior program by age can be examined.
- *Systematic sample:* For a **systematic sample**, all members of the target population are ordered by a variable (e.g., alphabetical order of last name, address, etc.). The

first unit (person) is chosen randomly from the sampling frame. Then, using a constant (e.g., every eighth person on the list), the remainder of the sample is chosen. If the units on the original list were randomly ordered, the systematic approach will yield the same result as the simple random sample. However, if the list of units is not randomly ordered this approach could produce selection bias. If the sampling frame list was rank ordered by income, achievement, health status, risk behavior, or the like, the systematic sampling approach could oversample some attribute and not represent the target population. If the evaluator has any suspicion that the sampling frame is ordered in any way that will bias the sample, it is advisable to use simple random sampling procedures.

- *Cluster sample:* **Cluster sampling** is a probability sampling method in which the unit of randomization is groups rather than individuals. The target population is divided into naturally occurring groupings (clusters). For example, the evaluator may select existing census tracts, schools, classrooms, churches, worksites, hospitals, or neighborhoods at random. Using random selection, a preset number of clusters is chosen for the sample. All or some of the elements (people) in a cluster may be part of the final sample.
- *Multistage sample:* A **multistage sample** is a probability sampling technique in which clusters are selected first, and then the sample is drawn by simple random sampling in each cluster. This technique is efficient when an exhaustive list is impossible or impractical. A possible disadvantage of this method is that bias in cluster selection may become a factor.

Table 11.1 summarizes the types of probability samples.

BARRIERS TO PROBABILITY SAMPLES IN HEALTH PROMOTION AND EDUCATION EVALUATIONS

There are clear statistical and scientific advantages to probability samples. Black (1999) suggests that probability sampling should always be considered a desirable first option when conducting evaluations. Yet it is clear that many health program evaluations are conducted without the benefit of probability samples. There are important reasons why probability

TABLE 11.1	Types of Probability Samples
Type	**Description**
Simple random	All members of the target population have an equal chance of selection.
Stratified random	Members of each stratum have an equal chance of selection.
Systematic	Members are selected by a constant interval from a list after the first member is selected randomly.
Cluster	Preexisting groups rather than individuals are selected randomly.
Multistage	Clusters are selected first, and then a sample is drawn by simple random sampling in each cluster.

samples are often not used in health promotion evaluations, such as when the purpose of an evaluation is to describe a sample and not to generalize from that sample to a target population. The sample of program participants is considered the only group of interest. In this case, stakeholders are only interested in the response of specific participants to the health program. No reference to statistical significance hypothesis testing is made and no effort to generalize evaluation results to a larger population is claimed.

Budgets for evaluations of health promotion programs are often modest. Money, staff, time, and access to program participants may be limited. Administrators may find themselves in a situation where each dollar spent on evaluation is a dollar taken from health programming efforts. Many times the resources needed to generate and recruit a probability sample simply may not be available (Chemimsky, 2007). In such cases, it is generally better to conduct an evaluation on a nonprobability sample than to conduct no evaluation at all. Having some form of evaluation is essential for making evidence-based decisions about health programs. All parties need to be cognizant of the limitations of the evaluation and make decisions accordingly. Data-based decision making is generally preferred over decisions not based on data. But it is critical that the limitations of the data be fully appreciated.

There any many challenges to maintaining the quality of a random sample in practice. In many health behavior change programs, participation is voluntary. Recruitment of subjects based on random sampling may generate a large number of people who decline participation and a large number of people who drop out of the program. Participant attrition may be substantial, making it hard to maintain the integrity of the randomly generated sample. This is particularly a concern in health behavior change programs that require considerable investment of time and effort on the participants' part. Other threats to a probability sample include staff errors in drawing and assigning random numbers, or staff replacing subjects incorrectly. Without the resources needed for quality control of sampling procedures, it may be advisable to use nonprobability sampling.

NONPROBABILITY SAMPLES

Nonprobability samples recruit participants who are readily accessible to the evaluator. More importantly, not all members of the target population have an equal chance of being selected for the sample. Technically, nonprobability samples are produced when methods of selecting participants result in some members of the population having no chance of being selected. The chance of each member of the target population being chosen for the evaluation sample is not known. Thus the evaluator cannot claim that the sample is representative of the target population. Nonprobability samples are often easier and less expensive to recruit than probability samples; however, this convenience results in a reduced ability to generalize the results of the evaluation.

The following are some common types of nonprobability samples:

- *Convenience samples:* **Convenience samples** are a type of nonprobability sample in which participants are drawn from the portion of the target population that is easily accessible. Samples of convenience use preexisting groups as a basis for recruitment. Examples include employees participating in a fitness program, seventh-grade students in a required health class, or newly diagnosed cancer patients attending a patient education class. The people in these examples are already participating in an existing group. They are a captive audience who can be asked to participate in an evaluation. This form of convenience sampling is widely used in evaluations of health programs. Muhib, Lin, and Stueve (2001) assert that in some cases, venue-based sampling is an effective approach for hard-to-reach populations. A variant of convenience sampling is snowball sampling or network sampling. In this type of sampling, participants are recruited and then asked to provide the names of friends and acquaintances who might meet the criteria. This leads to a snowball effect. Convenience samples do not enable the evaluator to make claims that this existing group represents any particular population. Generalizing to a population should not be attempted.

- *Volunteer sample:* This is a nonprobability sample in which participants take an active role in seeking out membership in the sample. The participants in a **volunteer sample** possess an interest or a motive that prompts them to actively seek inclusion into the sample. A common example is a health promotion program at the workplace. A smoking cessation program is being offered to employees for no charge. At any given time, only a percentage of smokers at a worksite will actively volunteer to participate in the cessation program. The motives of the volunteers are not known, but it is clear that they have actively sought out the opportunity. An evaluation of this cessation program can take advantage of their voluntary participation and solicit the participants' consent to participate in an evaluation of the program.

- *Quota sample:* In a **quota sample**, first the target population is segmented into exclusive subgroups using relevant variables (e.g., gender, race, educational status, age, health status). Next, specific numbers of participants are selected from each subgroup. This is a nonprobability sample because the units selected for each subsample are not selected randomly. Often the evaluator will seek to determine the rates or percentages of critical variables in the target population. Quotas are set to match the rates of these critical variables in the target population. For example, in a given community, the percentage of women with a college degree may be 28%, and the percentage of men with a college degree may be 23%. These numbers could be used as quotas for recruitment. Some health studies in the past underrepresented women and certain racial groups. It is not possible to generalize the findings of these health studies to these underrepresented groups. To correct for this, many federally funded studies require these groups be adequately represented.

SAMPLE SIZE: HOW MANY PARTICIPANTS ARE NEEDED FOR THE EVALUATION?

The results of evaluations will be viewed from different perspectives by program stakeholders. The evaluator should make a specific effort to increase the confidence stakeholders have in the evaluation results by employing methods that meet scientific standards for rigor. One key area of evaluation rigor is including an adequate number of participants in the evaluation. Sample size estimation identifies how many participants are needed to answer evaluation questions with sufficient practical and statistical rigor. There are statistical methods for estimating the sample size needed, but practical considerations also impact on **sample size estimation**.

The evaluator should make a specific effort to increase the confidence stakeholders have in the evaluation results by employing methods that meet scientific standards for rigor.

There are several factors to consider when establishing the sample size needed to support the overall purposes of the evaluation being conducted (Kraemer & Thiemann, 1987). Having an adequate sample can increase both the statistical power and external validity of the evaluation. Increasing the sample size also can substantially increase the amount of time and money that will be needed to complete the evaluation. Dynarski (1997) makes the case that there are tradeoffs to be made in striking a balance between adequate sample size to answer the evaluation questions and the amount of resources needed. Generally speaking, these considerations can be divided into two categories: statistical and practical.

Practical Considerations Affecting Sample Size

There are a host of practical considerations when establishing the sample size for an evaluation. Some of these considerations are time, budget, accessibility to subjects, and "after the program" evaluations (Huby & Hughes, 2001). Each evaluation must be completed in a specific time frame. Administrators and other stakeholders will expect the results at a time useful for making decisions. This often coincides with funding cycles and fiscal year planning. As a consequence, evaluators must work with program staff to determine how often a program can be offered and how many participants can be expected to complete the program in a defined time frame. Related to time considerations and sample size are budget concerns. More participants in the sample often require a greater budget. More programs need to be offered and more professional staff hours are needed to deliver those programs. Realistic estimates of the capacity of an organization to serve the participants need to be determined.

Accessibility to participants is critical. Many contextual factors can affect accessibility. How large is the defined target population for the health program? How many of the defined target population are willing, able, or incentivized to participate in the program? For example, you are evaluating a worksite-based smoking cessation program. There are 1,000 employees working at this company, but only 230 of the employees smoke cigarettes. If the employer requires all smokers to participate in the smoking cessation program in the next year, you can reasonably expect 230 participants. In contrast, the employer may make participation voluntary. In this instance, you might expect 30 to 50 participants rather than 230 in a given year. As a third option, the employer might incentivize employees to participate in smoking cessation classes. Depending on the magnitude of the incentive, somewhere between 100 and 200 may participate. In each of these cases, the evaluator should take care to describe the contextual factors (i.e., mandatory, incentivized, voluntary) that produced the participating sample.

A final consideration is "after the program" evaluations. The program evaluation is initiated after the health program has concluded. The evaluator is brought into the project after the program is completed and asked to "make sense" of the data. The evaluator did not design an evaluation or gather data. The evaluator must work with the conditions and decisions that were made earlier. In this scenario, it is obvious that the sample size is fixed and may or may not be adequate for making sound decisions. If demographic data was not gathered on the participants, it may be impossible to adequately describe the sample.

In contrast, we recommend a participatory approach to evaluation. In this approach, the evaluator is involved in the program planning phase, well before the program implementation phase. This enables the evaluator to carefully construct an evaluation that meets the interests of different stakeholders. It also enables the skilled evaluator to design an evaluation of sufficient rigor to support data-based decision making. Finally, it enables the evaluator to monitor all aspects of the evaluation implementation to maintain standards of rigor. The authors strongly encourage evaluators to avoid the pitfalls of "after the program" evaluations when possible.

Practical considerations may affect sampling type (probability versus nonprobability) and sample size. Practical considerations should not be an excuse to compromise evaluation design quality. Creative problem solving should be used to address practical constraints while maintaining evaluation rigor. The evaluator should promote the use of appropriate samples to address the purposes of the evaluation. The evaluator may need to educate professional staff and administrators about the important advantages to rigorous sampling methods. Specifically, the evaluator should describe statistical considerations in establishing sample size. In any case, the evaluator has the responsibility to precisely describe the data generating the sample. Evaluation results should be described in the context of the sample, with particular attention given to limitations. Readers of the evaluation report should be cautioned about threats to internal or external validity caused by sampling methods used.

> *Practical considerations should not be an excuse to compromise evaluation design quality. Creative problem solving should be used to address practical constraints while maintaining evaluation rigor.*

Statistical Considerations Affecting Sample Size

Power analysis is the statistical method of analyzing the relationships between the type of statistical test, the number of variables, the expected effect size, and the sample size recommended (Cohen, 1988). **Table 11.2** lists a set of statistical considerations that allows an evaluator to estimate the sample size needed for adequate statistical power. (These are then discussed in the following sections.) Statistical power is the ability of a statistical analysis to reveal true effects between variables. Power is an issue of balance. Too much power can produce a statistically significant test of little practical importance. Too little statistical power will fail to detect differences of practical importance. In general, it is recommended that most evaluations attempt to achieve a balanced power of 0.80.

In a carefully planned evaluation, power analysis can consider all of the relevant factors and precisely estimate the number of subjects needed for an adequately powered statistical test. But in many evaluations of health programs, the number of participants may be determined by other factors, such as the program already having been implemented and the number of participants being set. Another factor may be that time or funding is

TABLE 11.2 Statistical Considerations That Affect Sample Size
Precision: level of accuracy required (10% vs. 5% sampling error)
Variability in important target variables
Sample representativeness
Reliability of measurement tools
Effectiveness of the health program (effect size)
Subclass analysis

limited, and an adequate number of subjects cannot be recruited and exposed to the program. In these circumstances, power considerations work in reverse. Statistical analysis is conducted and the power of the test is determined. If the power is adequate (typically 0.80), stakeholders can place more confidence in the results. If power is low, stakeholders need to be very cautious about interpreting the data. If power is inadequate, failure to identify statistical significance may be due to a lack of statistical power. In such cases, interpretation of the evaluation results is speculative and open to different interpretations. Essentially, this becomes an evaluation failure in which conclusions are not clear.

Precision

Precision is the degree to which measured values accurately reflect true values. Evidence of precision is the degree to which repeated measures produce the same value. Another way of saying this is the degree to which variables (statistics) produced by the sample accurately represent those same variable values (parameters) in the target population. Precision, then, is an estimate of reliability. Probability samples enable evaluators to establish the degree of precision needed before any data is collected. The evaluation team decides how wide the confidence interval can be (e.g., plus or minus 10 points) at a predetermined level of confidence (e.g., 90% or 95%). This estimate then needs to be considered in the context of the other factors that influence sample size. Many resources exist to calculate sample sizes for probability samples (Cohen, 1988).

Data Variability

Data variability is the degree to which measured values are spread out or dispersed. The range or standard deviation is commonly reported to describe the degree of data variability. The evaluation team needs to identify the key variables for a particular evaluation. The variability produced by measures of these key variables will, in part, affect the sample size needed. In general, the more heterogeneous the population, the more variability will be reported on key variables. Under these circumstances, a larger sample will be needed in order to represent the population accurately. It is helpful to have experience with the measurement of the key variables in the target population. First, a track record of assessment of key variables allows evaluators to estimate variance based on experience. Second, a refined, valid instrument can reduce variability by eliminating error variance. The formula for estimating sample size considers both the variance of the key variable and target confidence intervals.

Sampling Method

The **sampling method** is a precisely described approach for selecting a sample of participants from a defined target population. If the sampling method employs probability methods, an evaluator can accurately estimate how many subjects will be needed to represent the population. Nonprobability sampling will not allow the evaluator to estimate the needed sample size. Each type of probability sampling has advantages. When working with a diverse, heterogeneous population, simple random samples may not be the most cost-effective choice. Stratified random sampling can offer distinct advantages in lower sample size and cost if homogeneous strata can be identified that reduce variability in key variables. When working with large populations, sampling randomly selected clusters is less expensive than a simple random sample from the entire population.

Effectiveness of the Health Education/Promotion Intervention

As a general principle, the larger the impact of the health intervention on the target variables (knowledge, skill, motivation, health behavior), the smaller the sample needed to yield statistical significance. For example, a health intervention increases scores on a skill measure by 5 points. With program refinement, the health intervention can now increase scores on the same skill measure by 20 points. This increase in effect size will now require a smaller sample size to produce a statistically significant result. A series of formative evaluations conducted in the field could provide evidence of the impact on variables. With program refinement, the impact should be increased to a level of practical importance. Refined health promotion interventions with a track record of solid effect sizes on key variables can be adequately tested with smaller samples.

Subclass Analysis

Subclass analysis refers to analysis of different subgroups within a sample. Evaluators often expect different subgroups within the sample to respond differently to the intervention. Age, gender, and socioeconomic status are examples of variables that may explain different responses (e.g., attendance, learning, behavior change) to the program. For example, male and female participants may respond differently to the same health program. Gender may be associated with different levels of skill development, motivation, or actual health behavior change. Dividing the sample by gender variables and analyzing the data may provide valuable insights. Anticipating these analyses, the evaluation team should ensure that estimates for sample size include consideration of subclass analysis. In addition, recruitment efforts should ensure adequate representation of members of each subclass. Dividing a sample by gender for subclass analysis could double the sample needed for adequate power. Thus subclass analysis should be selected with care and a consideration for cost.

RESPONSE RATES

The evaluation **response rate** is the number of participants who complete the evaluation protocol divided by the number of participants in the complete sample. It is the percentage of participants who complete the evaluation protocol. It is assumed that after careful sampling and recruitment procedures, a total sample has been drawn. However, there are many reasons why a participant may not complete all of the required phases of the evaluation. Prospective participants may not accept the conditions of informed consent and thus do not volunteer to be part of the evaluation. Participants may lose interest in the health program and drop out. Outside obligations (work, family, illness, etc.) may prevent subjects from completing the health program. Participants may not complete measurement tools correctly or adequately. For a wide range of reasons, only a percentage of the sample will complete all of the steps in the evaluation protocol. Procedures should be put in place to anticipate and mitigate the factors that contribute to participants dropping out. The goal is to retain as high a percentage of the sample as possible. It may be helpful for the evaluators to attempt to follow up with dropouts to see if they can be brought back into the project. High dropout rates suggest that the health intervention is not addressing the participants' needs adequately. Evaluators should investigate this possibility to make recommendations on how to reduce dropout rates. In all cases, the evaluator should report response rates and discuss how the dropout rate (high or low) affects the interpretation of the evaluation results.

Nonresponse is also due to participant **attrition**. Sample size and quality are reduced when participants drop out of an evaluation before all data is gathered. Attrition can threaten both the internal and external validity of an evaluation design. Attrition can occur for a variety of reasons. Participants may not meet criteria for program or evaluation participation, they may move away or experience illness, or family circumstances may change. Attrition is an expected part of all health program evaluations. Sample size should take expected attrition into account. Attrition of 10% to 40% can be expected, depending of the demands of the intervention or evaluation protocol. Some evaluators use oversampling to deal with expected attrition. With oversampling, one may lose participants but still maintain adequate numbers in the sample. Although oversampling may ensure that adequate statistical power is maintained, it is important to note that attrition may bias the sample. The evaluator should check to determine whether the participant attrition was systematic; for example, did a disproportionate number of participants drop out of the evaluation based on gender, race, age, socioeconomic status, or some other reason. This attrition should be noted, and its potential influence on the interpretation of the results should be described as a limitation.

FOCUS FEATURE 11.1   CALCULATING SAMPLE SIZE USING G*POWER

G*Power is a free power analysis software. It is available in two equivalent versions, one for the Macintosh operating system and the other for Windows. At the time of writing this text, the latest version of this software was Version 3. You can download G*Power from: http://www.psycho.uni-duesseldorf.de/abteilungen/aap/gpower3/download-and-register

(continues)

FOCUS FEATURE 11.1   CALCULATING SAMPLE SIZE USING G*POWER *(Continued)*

Its developers include Dr. Franz Faul of Christian-Albrechts University, Dr. Edgar Erdfelder of Mannheim University, Dr. Albert-Georg Lang of Heinrich-Heine University, and Dr. Axel Buchner of Heinrich-Heine University.

Several articles have been published in English and other languages on its utility and applications. Some resources on G*Power in English are:

Erdfelder, E., Faul, F., & Buchner, A. (1996). GPOWER: A general power analysis program. *Behavior Research Methods, Instruments and Computers, 28*, 1–11. This article describes G*Power's capabilities and program handling.

Erdfelder, E., Faul, F., & Buchner, A. (2005). Power analysis for categorical methods. In B. S. Everitt & D. C. Howell (Eds.), *Encyclopedia of statistics in behavioral science* (pp. 1565–1570). Chichester, UK: John Wiley & Sons. This chapter describes how to compute power and sample size for categorical data.

Kornbrot, D. E. (1997). Review of statistical shareware G*Power. *British Journal of Mathematical and Statistical Psychology, 50*, 369–370. This is a review of the G*Power program.

Thomas, L., & Krebs, C. J. (1997). A review of statistical power analysis software. *Bulletin of the Ecological Society of America, 73*, 126–139. This includes a review of the G*Power program.

In conducting a sample size estimation, one must first make a choice regarding the family of statistical tests one wants to use. G*Power provides a choice of exact tests, F-tests, t-tests, chi square tests, and z tests. The most common tests used in evaluation are either a paired t-test or a repeated measures ANOVA. The first would be found in the family of t-tests and the second in the F-tests. For paired t-test, G*Power lists it as "Means: Difference between two dependent means (matched pairs)." Next, choose the type of power analysis, which would be "A priori: Compute required sample size—given alpha, power and effect size." Then you can choose the input parameters and a one-tailed or two-tailed test, depending on your hypothesis. The most common alpha chosen is 0.05, and the power is usually 0.80. For the effect size, you would have to review previous studies and find out what effect sizes previous studies have yielded and then make an estimate. If no effect size studies are available, then one can assume a medium effect size, which is usual in health education evaluations (Lipsey & Wilson, 1993). After inputting these parameters, G*Power will calculate the sample size as well as a graphic plot.

GENERALIZING EVALUATION RESULTS

There are cases when stakeholders have no interest in **generalizing evaluation results**. The evaluation is viewed as a case study. The sample used in the evaluation is considered the complete target population of interest. The results of the evaluation will only be used to describe the effects of the health program on the sample participants involved. In such a case, it is important for the evaluator to make sure all important stakeholders agree with this position before the evaluation begins. If agreement can be reached, then nonprobability samples may be an acceptable approach to conducting the evaluation. However, all stakeholders should understand that the results of the evaluation cannot be generalized to any other population of interest.

In many cases, stakeholders and evaluators are interested in generalizing the results of an evaluation. Generalizing evaluation results involves making inferences from the observed sample to the intended target population. There are two types of generalization, descriptive and explanatory. Descriptive inferences occur when sample characteristics are generalized to the target population; for example, an evaluation reveals that at pretest newly diagnosed patients with diabetes have very low knowledge of self-care behaviors to prevent complications. A descriptive inference is dependent upon valid, reliable measurement; a probability sample; and an adequate response rate. If these conditions are met, it is scientifically reasonable to generalize to the target population of all newly diagnosed patients with diabetes.

In contrast, explanatory research attempts to test theories to identify the reasons why observed events occur. Rigorous design methods are used to enhance the internal validity of an evaluation design. Specific attention is placed on the assessment of theory-based variables. For example, a randomized control trial could be implemented to determine if a theory-based health intervention can increase recently diagnosed diabetes patients' self-efficacy for exercise. The design would allow evaluators to determine whether increases in self-efficacy for exercise were linked to increases in patient exercise behavior. The results would test theoretical links between self-efficacy and behavior, and thus would contribute to our understanding of the mechanisms of behavior change. The confidence placed on the explanatory inference is dependent on the validity and reliability of the measures and the internal validity of the evaluation design.

DESCRIBING THE EVALUATION SAMPLE AND POPULATION

Regardless of the sampling method used, it is critical for the evaluation team to provide a detailed description of the target population, the participating sample, and the final data-producing sample. These descriptions provide a context for the subsequent interpretation of evaluation findings. First describe the target population. Describe the setting or community where the population resides and the historical circumstances that produced the need for the health intervention. Perhaps there are public health data, including morbidity, mortality, or medical care costs, that help explain the need for the health program. Detail the demographic variables, including socioeconomic status, that may be associated with evaluation results. Next, provide a detailed description of the sampling procedures. Provide enough detail in the description so that other health professionals could reproduce the sampling procedures used. Some professional readers may want to replicate your evaluation methods. Many readers will want to interpret the results of the evaluation in the context of the methods used. Describe how recruitment procedures were mobilized to attract the drawn sample. This includes methods of contacting and attracting members of the target population to participate in the evaluation. Detail any participation requirements, screening procedures, and informed consent methods used. Report an accounting of members of the population who refused to participate, as well as program dropouts. Detail the minimum requirements for a consenting subject to be considered part of the data-generating sample (consent, completion of measurements, attendance, etc.). This description should be detailed, so that others can judge the relevance of the evaluation findings to other settings, communities, or populations.

SKILL-BUILDING ACTIVITY

This activity will help you learn how to use a software program to establish sample size for an evaluation. The program is called G*Power, and it can be downloaded for free at http://www.psycho.uni-duesseldorf.de/abteilungen/aap/gpower3/download-and-register. Download and install the program on your computer. The website provides Windows- and Mac-based versions of the program.

Exercise 1: The first exercise will help you establish the needed sample size for a health program evaluation in which an X^2 test will be used to analyze the data. You are evaluating a smoking cessation program. The design is a treatment group and control group. The treatment group received an innovative, classroom-based program to use self-regulation strategies to quit smoking over a period of 8 weeks. The control group received a self-guided booklet on quitting smoking developed by the American Cancer Society. At 6 months post–program completion, both groups will be measured as either smoke free or relapse. Using G*Power, estimate the *a priori* sample size needed for the following parameters:

> X^2 goodness of fit test
> Effect size $w = 0.5$
> Error probability = 0.05
> Power = 0.80
> Degrees of freedom (df) = 3

> 1. How many subjects did G*Power calculate were needed?
> 2. If you reduce the effect size from 0.5 (large effect size) to 0.3 (medium effect size), how does it affect the estimated sample size needed?
> 3. If you adjust the error probability from 0.05 to 0.01, how does it affect the estimated sample size needed?

Exercise 2: Refer back to the same smoking cessation program evaluation described in Exercise 1. This time you will use a scale of 6 months to measure the number of cigarettes smoked in the past 2 days. You will use a different statistical test to analyze the smoking quit data. Select the following choices:

> t-test difference between two independent means (two groups)
> Tail(s) = one
> Effect size = 0.80
> Alpha = 0.05
> Power = 0.80
> Allocation ratio N2/N1 = 1

1. How many subjects did G*Power indicate are needed for the treatment and control groups?
2. If you reduce the effect size from 0.8 (large) to 0.5 (medium), how does it affect the estimated sample size for the treatment and control groups?
3. If you change from a one-tailed to a two-tailed test, how does it affect sample estimation?
4. If you change the power from 0.80 to 0.95, how does it affect sample estimation?

SUMMARY

From a statistical perspective, a sample is a subset of a population used in an evaluation to represent the target population. A measurement taken on the sample is called a statistic. The population value for that measurement is called a parameter. The target population is composed of all people (or other units: schools, communities, etc.) in a defined group of interest. The sampling frame is a list of all units (people, communities, worksites, etc.) in the target population that are available for selection into a sample. One important goal of sampling methods is to minimize sampling error. Sampling error is the inaccuracy introduced into an evaluation by measuring a sample rather than the entire target population. Sampling error is reduced by using probability sampling methods to increase the representativeness of the sample.

There are five types of probability samples: (1) simple random samples, in which all members of the target population have an equal chance of selection; (2) stratified random samples, in which members of each stratum have an equal change of selection; (3) systematic samples, in which members are selected by a constant interval from a list after the first member is selected randomly; (4) cluster samples, in which preexisting groups rather than individuals are selected randomly; and (5) multistage samples, in which clusters are selected first and then the sample is drawn by simple random sampling in each cluster. Sometimes it is not possible to have probability samples; in these cases, nonprobability samples are used. Examples of nonprobability samples are convenience sample, volunteer sample, and quota sample.

There are practical and statistical considerations in determining sample size. Practical considerations include time, budget, accessibility to subjects, and "after the program" evaluations. Statistical considerations include precision, variability, sample representativeness, reliability of measurement tools, effect size, and subclass analysis.

REVIEW QUESTIONS

1. Explain how a representative sample can increase the value of the results of health evaluations by increasing generalizability.
2. Describe the key attributes that distinguish probability sampling from nonprobability sampling.
3. Create a realistic health promotion setting in which the barriers to using probability samples justify the use of nonprobability sampling.
4. Describe the relationship between sampling the internal and external validity of evaluation results.

5. Identify five factors that contribute to participant attrition. Identify strategies to reduce the effects of these attrition factors.

6. Identify five statistical factors that influence sample size estimation.

WEBSITES TO EXPLORE

G*Power

http://www.psycho.uni-duesseldorf.de/abteilungen/aap/gpower3/

G*Power is a Web-based program that will estimate sample sizes needed. At the time of writing, G*Power 3 was available. *Review the information about G*Power. How can you use it in your work?*

Java Applets for Power and Sample Size Estimation

http://www.stat.uiowa.edu/~rlenth/Power/index.html

This website provides several Java applets for power and sample size estimations. The software on this website is intended for planning evaluation studies. It is not intended for data that has already been collected. *Use an applet for an evaluation study that you are planning to do. Compare the results with those from G*Power. Did you find the same results, or were there differences?*

Power Analysis

http://www.statsoft.com/textbook/power-analysis/

This site provides a detailed discussion of statistical power and sample size. Also included are links on sampling theory, hypothesis testing logic, calculating power, calculating required sample size, and graphical approaches to sample size. *Review this discussion to enhance your knowledge about sample size estimation. What are some factors you need to consider when determining sample size?*

Sample Size Calculator for Multiple Regression

http://danielsoper.com/statcalc3/calc.aspx?id=1

This site provides an *a priori* sample size calculator for multiple regression. Links to formulas, references, and other related calculators are also provided. Some of the related calculators are for sample size calculation in student t-test, sample size estimation in hierarchical multiple regression, and effect size calculation in multiple regression. *Review these calculators and compare the results with those from G*Power. Did you find the same results, or were there differences?*

Sampling

http://www.csulb.edu/~msaintg/ppa696/696sampl.htm

This is a module on sampling developed at California State University, Long Beach. Topics discussed include why to sample, types of samples, how big a sample is needed, sample size formula, sample size table, and sample size quality. *Review the information provided on this website, and then complete the exercises provided.*

REFERENCES

Alfonso, M. L., Nickelson, J., Hogeboom, D. L., French, J., Bryant, C. A., & McDermott, R. J. (2008). Assessing local capacity for health intervention. *Evaluation and Program Planning, 31*(2), 145–159.

Black, T. R. (1999). *Doing quantitative research in the social sciences: An integrated approach in research design, measurement and statistics.* London: Sage.

Chemimsky, E. (2007). Factors influencing the choice of methods in federal evaluation practice. *New Directions for Evaluation, 113,* 13–33.

Cohen, J. (1988). *Statistical power analysis for the behavioral sciences* (2nd ed.). Hillsdale, NJ: Lawrence Erlbaum.

Dynarski, M. (1997). Trade-offs in designing a social program experiment. *Children and Youth Services Review, 18*(7), 525–540.

Faugier, J., & Sargeant, M. (1997). Sampling hard-to-reach populations. *Journal of Advanced Nursing, 26*(4), 790–797.

Huby, M., & Hughes, R. (2001). The effects on using material resources in social research. *Social Work and Social Sciences Review, 9,* 5–16.

Kraemer, H. C., & Thiemann, S. (1987). *How many subjects? Statistical power analysis in research.* Newbury Park, CA: Sage.

Lipsey, M. W., & Wilson, D. B. (1993). The efficacy of psychological, educational, and behavioral treatment: Confirmation from meta-analysis. *American Psychologist, 48*(12), 1181–1209.

Muhib, F. B., Lin, L. S., & Stueve, A. (2001). A venue-based method for sampling hard to reach populations. *Public Health Reports, 116*(1 Suppl.), 216–222.

CHAPTER 12

Quantitative Data Analysis

INTRODUCTION

Stakeholders and evaluators want to know whether a health education or health promotion intervention is effective. Evaluations are designed to answer this question in a scientifically rigorous manner. Specifically, can the evaluator provide evidence that the health education or health promotion intervention was able to achieve the stated goals and objectives in a target population? Attention to evaluation designs, sampling, and measurement create a foundation upon which confidence in the statistical analysis is based (Abelson, 1995). **Statistics** is a set of scientific methods that focuses on collection, analysis, and interpretation of data. Evaluators use statistics to describe a set of data, to make inferences, and to identify relationships among variables (Glass & Hopkins, 2008). This chapter will describe how quantitative data analysis can be used to describe the sample of participants, make decisions about program effectiveness, and consider the possibility of making inferences from the sample to a target population (Newcomer, 1994). Although evaluations rely on statistics to present data and make decisions, statistics is a scientific discipline in its own right. The field of statistics is large and complex.

*E*valuators use statistics to describe a set of data, to make inferences, and to identify relationships among variables.

This chapter can serve as a brief introduction to how statistics may be used in evaluations. The goal of this chapter is to emphasize the usefulness of statistics to evaluation and to introduce some statistical tools. We encourage those who wish to engage in evaluation to seek out additional training in statistics. In practice, evaluators often consult with statisticians to complete a project.

Some stakeholders have had bad experiences with evaluation. These experiences produce beliefs that suggest evaluations generate large amounts of boring data of questionable value. Stakeholders may feel overwhelmed and confused by complex data sets and complicated statistical analysis (Alkin, 1980). The connection between the data and conclusions is not always clear. Evaluations can then be seen as restating the obvious while being cautious regarding practical conclusions. These perceptions leave stakeholders frustrated and skeptical about the value of evaluation. This text emphasizes performing evaluations that engage stakeholders in the program planning and evaluation process. Stakeholder engagement works in several ways. First, stakeholders can articulate what they value as relevant to the evaluation of the program. This can help the evaluator keep the data analysis closely aligned with the purposes of the evaluation. Second, engagement allows stakeholders to learn how evaluation data can be used in making decisions. A large part of this process is explaining how the evaluation will gather relevant data, analyze the data, and draw conclusions that are evidence based. Third, engagement can be educational; stakeholders can learn about evaluation methods and thus feel more confident in understanding evaluation conclusions. Finally, engagement can produce a sense of investment in the process and a sense ownership in the evaluation results. A key to effective evaluation is linking health program objectives, evaluation questions, valid measures, relevant analysis, and evidence-based conclusions into a meaningful evaluation report (Rossi & Freeman, 1993).

DATA MANAGEMENT

You have been charged with the evaluation of a health promotion program. Pretests and posttests were administered to the intervention and control groups. Before you can conduct statistical analysis, the data needs to be entered into a computerized database. A key decision to make is which statistical software will be used for the project. There are many powerful commercial products on the market, including IBM-SPSS and SAS. Another option is free software such as EpiInfo, which is available from the Centers for Disease Control and Prevention (CDC). Most statistical software programs have a data entry system, but many programs will also accept data that has been entered into spreadsheets such as Microsoft Excel. Once a statistical package and data management software have been chosen, a data entry system needs to be developed.

Data management formalizes a step-by-step plan for transferring data from completed instruments to databases or statistical software. The plan for data management must be very precise, so that all data management personnel are consistent in how they transfer data. Often several people are responsible for data entry, so it is critical that all staff enter the data in a consistent and correct way (Black, 1999). First, all data-gathering instruments are collated, accurately labeled (pretest–posttest, intervention group–control group), and securely stored. Trained staff carefully transfer the data from instruments to a computerized database. Typically, when entering data into a spreadsheet each row represents a participant in the evaluation, and each column represents one variable. For example, in **Table 12.1**, column one represents Participant ID, column two represents Treatment Group (1 = intervention group, 0 = control group), column three represents Age, column 4 represents Gender (1 = male, 2 = female), columns 5–8 represent responses to a multiple choice knowledge pretest (a = 1, b = 2, c = 3), and columns 9–12 represent responses to a multiple choice knowledge posttest (a = 1, b = 2, c = 3). It is not uncommon for each participant to have over 100 columns of variables associated with all of the scales administered during the evaluation.

It is critical that all data entry be consistent among data entry personnel. It is also advisable to have a formal system for checking the accuracy of data transfer from the instrument to the database. The paper records should not be discarded until the evaluation project is complete and evaluation reports have been accepted. Even then, it is a good practice to keep the records available in case there is a need to check the accuracy of data entry. During analysis, spurious data may be discovered in the data set; occasionally, going back to the original source instrument can provide accurate values to correct the data set.

TABLE 12.1	Sample Data Entry Table										
Participant ID	Treatment Group	Age	Gender	Item 1	Item 2	Item 3	Item 4	Pitem 1	Pitem 2	Pitem 3	Pitem 4
001	1	35	1	2	1	3	3	2	1	2	1
002	1	42	2	3	1	3	2	2	1	3	1
003	0	41	2	1	2	3	2	2	1	3	2
004	0	33	1	2	1	2	2	1	1	2	3

Statistical packages have input statements in which you indicate where each variable appears in the spreadsheet. Further, you provide instructions for how to "grade" or transform data. In Table 12.1, Items 1–4 need to be graded for correct responses, and then these item scores need to be added together for a total knowledge test score. The capability of the statistics program to grade scales and create total scores for each scale is a time saver when dealing with large data sets.

DATA CLEANING

After the data is transferred from instruments to a data spreadsheet, and before data analysis can begin, data cleaning is an important step (Tabachnick & Fidell, 2007). **Data cleaning** involves checking for data entry errors. Data entry is a tedious task, and errors do occur. If data entry personnel skip a column or lose their place in the spreadsheet, all data entry after that point is out of place and inaccurate. Such errors can render any statistical analysis meaningless. The first step in data cleaning is to have the statistical software produce frequency distributions for all relevant variables.

Outliers

Table 12.2 presents an example frequency table with data that should be examined for outliers. **Outliers** are data values for variables that are plausible but extremely high or low; they are values at extreme ends of the frequency distribution. In Table 12.2, the evaluator notices one score of 20 that is clearly an outlier. The evaluator knows the possible range of scores on this scale is 0 to 20; so 20 is a possible score, but the distribution of scores suggests that all of the other scores were 12 or lower. The evaluator might check to see whether the score of 20 was accurately coded or computed. If possible, the evaluator might try to determine whether the participant who received this score was unique in some way. Perhaps

TABLE 12.2 Sample Frequency Distribution with Outliers and Missing Values			
Test Score	**Frequency**	**Cumulative Frequency**	**Cumulative Percentage**
87	1	60	100
20	1	59	98.33
12	2	58	96.6
10	5	56	93.394
9	14	51	85.84
8	12	37	61.656
6	9	25	41.6
5	7	16	26.6
.	9	9	14

the participant was highly educated or had work experience that produced this very high score. Other examples of outliers would include a participant who reports a body weight of 645 pounds, a participant who reports 17 planned bouts of exercise in one week, or a participant who reports consuming 200 calories daily. In each case, the evaluator should check the outliers for measurement error or data entry error.

If the outlier value is not an error, the evaluator still must make a decision about retention of the outlier data in the final analysis. Outliers can influence statistical results by shifting the mean and increasing variance in the sample. This distortion effect is especially true in relatively small samples (less than 30 participants in the intervention group). The evaluator needs to decide whether the outlier data will distort the final analysis. Decisions regarding outlier values (retention or deletion) should be carefully explained in the evaluation report.

Implausible Values

Carefully examine the distribution looking for variable values that are not plausible. **Implausible values** are data entered into the data set that are beyond the range of the instrument or coding values. In Table 12.2, the test score of 87 is problematic. The possible range of values on the test score variable is 0 to 20. Clearly, the test score of 87 is not an outlier, but an erroneous entry. The score should be traced to the original participant document. This is usually done by assigning participants an ID number that is entered into the database and written on the source document. Review of the source document should enable the evaluator to replace 87 with the correct value for that participant.

Missing Values

The frequency distribution should also be checked for missing values. **Missing values** generally are represented in a database as a "." or a blank space, and are not equivalent to zero. Missing values occur when no value appears in the data set for a particular variable. There are two primary sources of missing values (Little & Schenker, 1995). Participants who fail to respond to items on a scale can generate missing values in the database. Missing values also can be generated by a data entry staff member who fails to report a value from the scale to the database. In Table 12.2, missing values are represented by a ".". A review of this table indicates that there were 9 occurrences of missing values for this variable. If a variable has many missing values, the evaluator should first determine the cause—participant failure or data entry failure. The evaluator may consider dropping those variables from the analysis.

It is also wise to try to determine why there is a pattern of low response rate. Sometimes the problem can be solved by redesign of the instrument or instructions (Bradburn & Sudman, 1982). If a specific participant has a pattern of missing values, it will be necessary to make a decision about dropping that participant from the analysis (Kalton & Kasprzyk, 1986). Generally, evaluators set exclusion criteria; if a participant has missing values above a set limit, they are dropped from the analysis. Similarly, if a participant has not met the criteria for adequate participation in an intervention (attendance, completion of assignments, and completion of assessments), a decision needs to be made regarding retaining or dropping that participant from the final analysis. The evaluator should explicitly describe all exclusion criteria and describe the sample of participants who were not included in the final sample. Sometimes techniques such as imputation of the mean for missing values is done.

DESCRIBING THE SAMPLE

After the data has been fully entered, errors corrected, and data cleaned, data analysis can begin. The analysis should begin with a detailed description of the data-producing sample. The **data-producing sample** is all of the evaluation participants (including both control and intervention groups) that meet all criteria for retention in the evaluation sample. **Inclusion criteria** are all of the evaluation protocol steps that must be completed by participants to remain in the evaluation sample. **Table 12.3** lists examples of typical inclusion criteria for health education evaluations. The purpose of these inclusion criteria is to maintain a level of quality control over the integrity of the sample and the data.

The detailed description of the sample begins with a detailed summary of the demographic characteristics of the intervention and control groups. Typically, frequency distributions and measures of central tendency are used to summarize variables including age, gender, race, and educational status of the data-producing sample. There are several reasons for describing the sample. First, the sample make-up provides a context for interpreting the results of the evaluation. Second, the evaluator would like to describe the sample as representing the intended target population. Careful examination of the demographic profile can help the evaluator decide whether the sample is representative of the target population. Finally, the evaluator would like to make a case that the intervention group and the control group are equivalent. In this case, review of the demographics information, as well as descriptive statistics on critical variables, can help determine whether the intervention group and control group are equivalent. The evaluator will generally find it useful to also describe the samples on key variables from the pretest. This description will create an image of where the sample values lie before the intervention.

TABLE 12.3   Examples of Inclusion Criteria for the Data-Producing Sample
Participants sign required consent forms to participate in the evaluation.
Participants complete pretests meeting criteria for missing values or errors.
Intervention group participants meet expectations for attendance and completion of health promotion activities.
Intervention group participants complete course assignments.
Control group participants complete evaluation protocol expectations. Some control groups do not receive an intervention, but in some cases the control group may receive a standard level of intervention that must be completed.
All participants complete posttests meeting criteria for missing values or errors.
All participants complete follow-up data collections (if part of protocol).

DATA ANALYSIS: DESCRIPTIVE METHODS

The data has been entered; checked for errors, outliers, and missing values; and cleaned. Now statistical analysis can begin. The first step is to provide a full description of all of the variables for the intervention group and the control group (if a control group is included in the design). **Descriptive statistics** provide simple numerical summaries of the measures taken on a sample. Examples of descriptive statistics include frequency distributions, measures of central tendency, and measures of variability. Providing a detailed description of the data set is important. It provides the evaluator and the stakeholders with a "mental picture" of the sample. A complete description of the variable values generated by the sample provides a context for interpreting the evaluation results. Each of the questions listed in **Table 12.4** will be discussed in the following section in the context of preparing an interpretation of evaluation data.

Were the Demographic Characteristics Similar Between the Intervention and Control Groups?

A control or comparison group is useful only if it can be considered equivalent to the intervention group on relevant variables. Evaluators assign participants in a manner intended to produce this equivalence. Descriptive data analysis can help verify that the assignment was successful in producing equal groups. Demographic variables such as age, gender, educational status, and race are used to describe the control and intervention samples. The evaluator should look for over- or underrepresentation of a demographic variable in either sample that would suggest systematic bias. Ideally, this bias would be minimized by future sampling.

> *A complete description of the variable values generated by the sample provides a context for interpreting the evaluation results.*

Are the Demographic Characteristics Representative of the Intended Target Group?

As an extension of point one, the distribution of demographic variables for both the treatment and control groups can also be used to determine whether the two groups are representative of the intended target population. Most health education/promotion programs

TABLE 12.4   Questions to Consider When Reviewing Descriptive Statistics
Were the demographic characteristics similar between the intervention and control groups?
Are the demographic characteristics representative of the intended target group?
How were the scores distributed on important variables at pretest?
Were the pretest scores equivalent for the intervention and control groups?
Did scores on important variables change in the expected direction at posttest?
Did participants score relatively low or high on important variables at posttest?
Were changes in scores at posttest distributed across many participants or a few?

seek to promote the health of defined target populations. Illustrative examples might include smokers at a worksite, women at risk for breast cancer between the ages of 24 and 55, adolescents at risk for obesity, and postretirement adults who are sedentary. Evaluators should make sure they gather the appropriate descriptive data, so they can verify that the sampling methods employed yielded participants who represent the intended target population.

How Were the Scores Distributed on Important Variables at Pretest?

Once pretests have been gathered, coded, and cleaned, frequency distributions for each variable should be examined for several attributes. An often-overlooked, but fundamental assumption of variables is that they must produce a variety of scores in the sample. Imagine for a moment an intended variable that does not vary. For the sake of illustration, consider a 10-item scale that is supposed to assess knowledge of self-care behaviors to prevent complications due to diabetes. All of the participants in the intervention and control groups get a perfect score of 10 correct on the pretest. The distribution of scores at pretest should leave room for improvement on the scale. The first concern is that the scale did not produce variability or differences between participants. Serious questions must be asked about the validity, reliability, and scientific soundness of an instrument that produces no variability. It may be necessary to secure a better instrument. The ceiling effect is a major concern in this case. The **ceiling effect** occurs when pretest scores are high and participants have little to no room to improve scores on a measure. In this example, it is obvious that posttests would not detect improvement in participants' scores, even if the participants benefited from the instructional intervention.

There are other important attributes of the scoring distribution to examine. Examining the frequency distribution is important to determine whether the values are widely distributed or narrowly distributed, or possibly have a bimodal distribution. Although variability is essential, if the distribution is widely variable more participants may be needed to sufficiently power statistical tests (see the discussion on sampling earlier). A bimodal distribution may suggest that there are two distinct groups that make up the evaluation sample. Subgroup analysis may reveal important differences and trends within the groups.

Were the Pretest Scores Equivalent for the Intervention and Control Groups?

The evaluator should compare pretest scores on all relevant variables expected to change as a result of the intervention. Example variables might include knowledge scores, skill measures, motivation levels, self-efficacy, and behavioral capability. The frequency distribution of these variables should be checked for several attributes. First, does the distribution of scores reveal good variability? Are ceiling effects avoided (does each scale have room for improvement at posttest)? Are the measures of central tendency and measures of variability similar for the intervention and control groups? This is a check on whether participant assignment to treatment and control groups was unbiased. To the extent the evaluator can demonstrate the two groups were equivalent at pretest, a case can be made that the evaluation design was sound and a fair and rigorous test of intervention impact can be conducted.

Did Scores on Important Variables Change in the Expected Direction at Posttest?

Evaluators examine the descriptive data from the posttest to determine which of the important targeted variables improved as a result of the health intervention. The participants in the intervention group should produce scores that are substantially higher on posttests. Evaluators should have a clear estimate of how much a score should improve to be of **practical importance**. If the control group also experiences improvement in posttest scores, it suggests that factors other than the intervention may have played a role in score improvement. (See the earlier discussion on threats to internal validity.)

Did Participants Score Relatively Low or High on Important Variables at Posttest?

Evaluators generally report whether changes in scores are statistically significant. A follow-up question of equal importance is: What is the professional interpretation or practical meaning of the scores? This question addresses the meaning of the scores on different instruments used in the evaluation. For example, how much of an increase in a knowledge score would be considered of practical importance? The knowledge test is 10 items and the possible range of scores is 0 to 50 points. Is a 5-point increase on this knowledge test important? Is a 10-point increase important? The answers to these questions can be based on professional judgment and expert opinion. Another method for answering these questions is empirical. How much change in knowledge test scores is associated with favorable changes in motivation or health behavior change?

Haertel (1985) encourages the use of criterion-referenced testing for evaluations. In contrast, many instruments used in evaluations are norm-referenced. A **norm-referenced test** produces an estimate of the position of one individual's score relative to a predefined population. The primary interpretation of the scores is that the test taker did better than others with lower scores and worse than people with higher scores. In contrast, a **criterion-referenced test** is designed to translate test scores into a statement about the capability of the test taker. The criterion is the domain of knowledge or skill set that the test is designed to assess. Generally speaking, if a cut score on a criterion-referenced test is achieved by participants, the evaluator can assume those participants have met an established standard of competence or behavioral capability. For example, there are tests of behavior capability for skill in providing cardiopulmonary resuscitation. If a participant passes the test, you can assume they have the knowledge and skills necessary to provide cardiopulmonary resuscitation. The development and use of criterion-referenced tests in health education evaluations would enable evaluators to make clear statements about the instructional benefits of a health intervention.

Were Changes in Scores at Posttest Distributed Across Many Participants or a Few?

Assuming there were score increases in targeted variables, the question is how these increments are distributed. First, were increases in scores evenly distributed among the full range of pretest scores? In effect, did all participants increase approximately the same amount of points from pre- to posttest? Often, some participants benefit disproportionately from the intervention. Sometimes the participants with the highest scores at pretest experience the biggest gains at posttest. In contrast, it may be the participants with the low pretest scores who increase scores at posttest, whereas the remaining participants do not improve scores at all. If score increases are not evenly distributed among participants, subclass analysis methods can be used to explain who benefited and how the benefits of health intervention are most plausibly explained.

FREQUENCY DISTRIBUTIONS

A first step in organizing data for review and interpretation is to create frequency distributions for each variable of interest. **Frequency distributions** arrange variable scores by size, specifying how many times each score occurs in the sample. This can be followed by columns to indicate cumulative frequency and cumulative percentage. **Table 12.5** lists a frequency distribution for the following set of scores: (5,5,5,5,5,5,5,6,6,6,6,6,6,6,6,6,6,8,8,8,8, 8,8,8,8,8,8,8,8,9,9,9,9,9,9,9,9,9,9,9,9,9,9,10,10,10,10,10,12,12,12). The frequency distribution

The frequency distribution organizes the scores so the reader can quickly grasp the overall arrangement of values for each variable.

organizes the scores so that the reader can quickly grasp the overall arrangement of values for each variable. As mentioned earlier in the chapter, frequency distributions can help the evaluator spot data errors and outliers. Table 12.5 has already had missing values and outliers removed from the data set.

MEASURES OF CENTRAL TENDENCY

Measures of central tendency are statistics that describe the typical, average value for a variable. These measures can provide an impression of where the bulk of scores in a distribution lie. Measures of central tendency are the most widely used descriptions of data. One advantage of reporting measures of central tendency is that they are widely understood. For the sake of illustration, consider the following data set: (5,5,5,5,5,5,5,6,6,6,6,6,6, 6,6,6,8,8,8,8,8,8,8,8,8,8,8,9,9,9,9,9,9,9,9,9,9,9,9,9,9,10,10,10,10,10,12,12,12).

TABLE 12.5   Sample Frequency Distribution of Knowledge Test Scores

Test Score	Frequency	Cumulative Frequency	Cumulative Percentage
12	3	50	100
10	5	47	94
9	14	42	84
8	12	28	56
6	10	16	32
5	7	7	14

Mode: The **mode** is the score that occurs most frequently in a distribution. In the set of scores listed, the mode is 9. The value 9 appears 14 times, which is more than any other value. The mode is not affected by extreme values. However, some score distributions may have more than one value that occurs at the same high frequency.

Median: The **median** is the 50th percentile of a score distribution; it is the point below which half of the scores fall. Scores on a variable are rank ordered, and the 50% rank is easily located (see Table 12.5, the frequency distribution table, for the scores). In the set of scores listed, the median is 8; 16 of 50 scores occur below the value 8 and 22 scores are above 8. This is unique, and not drastically affected by extreme values.

Mean: The **mean** is the arithmetic average of all the scores in a distribution. It is calculated by adding all of the scores and dividing the resulting sum by the number of scores in the sample. In the data set listed in Table 12.5, the sum of all values is 403 divided by the number of scores (50), producing a mean score of 8.06. Take note that the value 7 does not occur in the distribution of scores listed. The mean of 7 is unique, but its calculation is affected by all of the actual scores in the distribution.

As illustrated in the examples, the mode, median, and mean are often different for the same set of numbers. Therefore, it is important that the measures of central tendency reported are labeled and explained. It is up to the evaluator to decide which set of measures of central tendency to report to provide the most accurate description of the data set. It is acceptable to list all three measures of central tendency in the evaluation report.

MEASURES OF VARIABILITY

Measures of central tendency provide an impression of where the bulk of scores in a distribution lie, but they do not provide insight into the shape of the distribution. **Measures of variability** describe how widely scores are dispersed from each other in the sample. It can help us understand how spread out the scores are along a possible range of values. How the scores are distributed can provide many insights to the careful evaluator. Are the majority of the scores clustered around the mean, suggesting a homogeneous sample? A bimodal distribution occurs when scores are widely dispersed, with some scores clustering low in the range of scores and some scores clustering high in the range of scores. In a bimodal distribution, the mean or other measures of central tendency may not be a representative statistic. Are pretest scores clustered together close to the maximum score on a scale? This may suggest that the sample is well versed or experienced in whatever the scale measures.

Range

A **range** is the difference between the highest and lowest scores in the sample. For example, if the highest score on a knowledge test was 80 and the lowest was 30, the range would be 50. Although the meaning of the range is clear, it does not take into account the dispersion of all the scores. One very high or low score (outlier) can increase the range and distort the meaning of the range.

Standard Deviation

The **standard deviation** is a measure of variability that is sensitive to all scores in the sample distribution. Conceptually the standard deviation is a measure of how far each value in a distribution falls from the mean for that variable. Based on the normal curve, 68% of the score distribution falls between 1 standard deviation above and 1 standard deviation below the mean score. Two standard deviations above and below the mean score capture 95% of the variation in scores. Because the standard deviation is based on all of the scores, it is less affected by outlier scores when compared to the range. The formula for calculating the standard deviation is:

$$\text{Standard deviation} = \sqrt{\frac{\text{Sum (Each score} - \text{Sample mean)}^2}{\text{Number in sample} - 1}}$$

GRAPHING DATA

For many, reviewing large sets of numbers is a tedious task that does not lead to an understanding of the data. Do not underestimate the appeal and value of using graphs to present data. **Graphing data** provides a visual representation of data, often illustrating important features regarding the distribution of scores. Often graphs can provide visual interest and ease of interpretation for stakeholders (Tufte & Cheshire, 2001). For example, **Figure 12.1** presents a bar graph of the frequency distribution on pretest knowledge scores for the intervention group that was first presented in Table 12.5. Figure 12.1 adds the knowledge test score distribution for the comparison group as well. This graph allows the reader to make a quick visual comparison of the two groups on this variable. Using graphs is an important method of communicating evaluation results. Graphing of data can help stakeholders develop a clear understanding of the data.

> *Graphing data provides a visual representation of data, often illustrating relationships between variables.*

Scores distributed normally produce a symmetrical, bell-shaped curve. It is important to determine whether the score distribution for variables in an evaluation are distributed normally. Figure 12.1 shows the data distribution is somewhat symmetrical, but does skew a bit to the left. Skewness is the degree to which scores fall more on one side of the curve than the other. Software programs can test for the degree of skewness. This is important, because parametric statistical tests assume that the data is normally distributed. If the data is not normally distributed, then a nonparametric test (e.g., chi square test) may be used. A review of the distribution in Figure 12.1 would raise questions about representing a normal distribution. It would be advisable to test the degree of skewness before making a final decision about which statistical test to use.

Figure 12.2 presents a line graph summarizing a main result of an evaluation. The figure compares mean knowledge test scores at pretest, posttest, and follow-up for the intervention and control groups. Notice that the line graph presents parallel changes between the groups over time. The following is clear from the line graphs:

- Both groups' pretest knowledge scores were equal, verifying that the control group was equivalent to the intervention group on this variable.

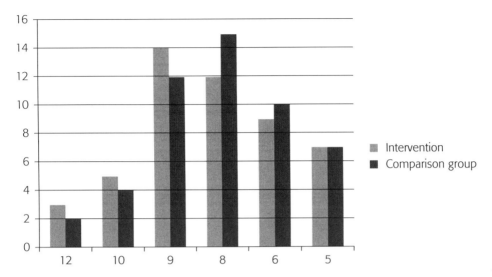

Figure 12.1 Comparison of pretest knowledge score distributions between intervention and comparison groups.

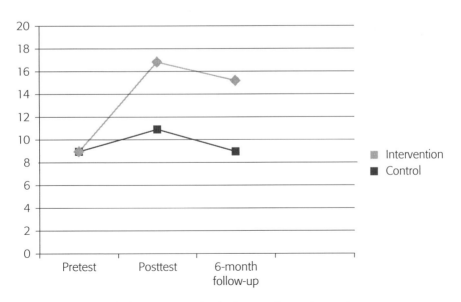

Figure 12.2 Mean knowledge test scores for the intervention and control groups.

- Whereas the control group's scores increased by 1 point at posttest, the intervention group's scores increased by 8 points. This supports the hypothesis that the health intervention was effective in increasing knowledge test scores.
- The intervention group score increase was substantial, with a mean score of 18 that approaches the maximum score on the test of 20.
- At 6-month follow-up, both groups experienced a small decline in test scores. The intervention group maintained six of the eight points gained in test scores.

Stem and Leaf Plots

Stem and leaf plots are an easy method of showing the frequency with which values occur in a data set. As an example, let's assume you have the following test scores: 12, 22, 25, 29, 31, 43, 56, 49, 28, 44, 66, 21, 57, 62, 33, 45, 51, 63, 48. Now we can enter these scores in a stem and leaf plot. The stem is the left column, which represents the tens units. The leaves are the lists in the right column plotting the ones values for all of the tens, twenties, thirties, forties, fifties, and sixties. See **Figure 12.3**.

The stem and leaf plot provides a visual representation of the distribution of scores. A unique feature of the stem and leaf plot is that it retains the original test scores in the plot. For example, the reader can clearly see that there were the following scores in the twenties: 22, 25, 28, 29. Also note the key at the bottom of the chart to assist the reader in interpretation of plot.

Stem	Leaf				
1	2				
2	2	5	8	9	
3	1	3			
4	3	4	5	8	9
5	1	6	7		
6	2	3	6		

Key: 2 | 2 = 22   stem unit: 10.0   leaf unit: 1.0

Figure 12.3   Stem and leaf plot showing distribution of scores.

Pie Charts

Figure 12.4 presents another option for the visual presentation of data. In this case, the racial breakdown of a sample is presented as a pie chart. A pie chart is circular and divided into proportional sectors. The pie chart can be effective in representing the proportional size of each slice of the whole. It can provide the reader with a visual map of proportions.

Box Plot

When presenting descriptive statistics, a box plot is an effective method of graphically depicting data with a five-number summary. The five-number summary consists of the smallest value, lower quartile, median, upper quartile, and largest value. In **Figure 12.5**, the box plot for the treatment group indicates that the smallest exam score was 22, the lower quartile exam score was 30, the median score was 58, the upper quartile exam score was 77, and the largest exam value was 91. The box plots allow for visual comparison of the dispersion of exam scores for the treatment and control groups. Box plots illustrate differences between populations without imposing assumptions regarding underlying statistical distributions, and thus are nonparametric.

Graphs can be an effective method of studying data visually. Evaluators can use graphs as a detective tool to study patterns in the data and make visual comparisons between groups. Graphs can effectively communicate observations. Evaluators can use graphs to help stakeholders visualize the evaluation data. The thoughtful use of graphs can draw attention to selected aspects of the evaluation data. Thus, graphs can help emphasize important points in the evaluation report.

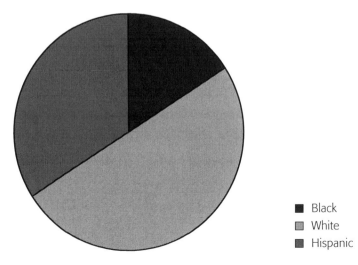

■ Black
▨ White
▩ Hispanic

Figure 12.4 Pie chart illustrating race distribution in a sample.

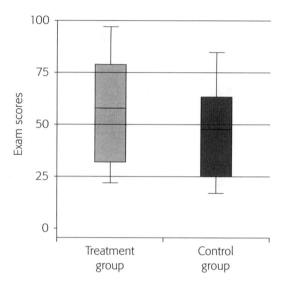

Figure 12.5   Box plot illustrating distributions on an exam score.

STATISTICAL INFERENCE

The main use of **statistical inference** is as a method of drawing conclusions from data that is subject to random variation. It is a mathematically based approach to obtaining knowledge about a target population from a relatively small number representing that population, also known as a sample. Inferential statistics use inductive reasoning—from the observed sample to the unobserved population. Inferential reasoning addresses questions like: Will the increase in seat belt use (from 45% to 65%) produced in the health intervention evaluation sample be as effective in the target population? The ability to draw inferences from the sample to the target population is influenced by the sampling method employed. Probability samples are foundational to making statistical inferences (see the previous discussion on sampling). Evaluators often use nonprobability samples when conducting evaluations. In these cases, interpretations of evaluation data should consistently caution against making inferences to the target population. When using a nonprobability sample, there is no statistical basis for inference.

HYPOTHESIS TESTING

Evaluations are designed to detect changes brought about by health promotion and education activities (Veany & Kaluzny, 1998). An evaluation **hypothesis** is a statement about anticipated changes produced by health promotion and education interventions that is testable. There are several considerations when crafting a useful, testable hypothesis for a health intervention evaluation. First, a hypothesis should be composed with a clear intent of serving the decisional purposes of the evaluation. During the initial stages of an evaluation

TABLE 12.6   Questions to Refine the Purpose of the Evaluation

What decisions will be made based on the evaluation results?

What types of evaluation evidence are needed to support the decisions that need to be made?

What changes in health program participants (e.g., knowledge, skills, health behavior, health status) should be measured?

What changes beyond the health program participants (e.g., program implementation, professional staff performance, environmental issues, policy) should be measured?

How many components are used in the health intervention (e.g., instruction, social media, screenings, policy, incentives, environmental supports) to produce targeted changes?

What is a reasonable amount of time needed for implementation of health intervention components and subsequent changes in target outcomes?

How important is the maintenance of targeted outcomes to decision making regarding the health intervention?

project, key stakeholders (funding agencies, administrators, program staff, and evaluation staff) should openly discuss the intended purpose of the evaluation. This is to ensure that the goals and methods of the subsequent evaluation directly address the purpose of the evaluation. Key issues to discuss are summarized in **Table 12.6**.

Answers to these questions are critical to clarifying the purposes of the evaluation. Discussions around these questions can help set priorities and allocate appropriate levels of resources to evaluation activities. Discussions between evaluators and stakeholders promote the setting of realistic expectations for the goals and objectives of the health intervention. They also provide an opportunity to detail the types of information the evaluation can realistically produce and to link this to the decisional purposes of the evaluation.

For evaluations employing quantitative methods, evaluation results are based on hypothesis testing. A hypothesis is a statement of the expected relationships between the independent variables (health intervention) and the dependent variable (knowledge, skills, motivation, health behavior, health status). These variables are operationally defined by the measurement used in the evaluation. There are many methods of measuring health behaviors or health status. **Table 12.7** presents some of the measurement methods reported

TABLE 12.7   Examples of Measurement: Physical Activity Behavior and Health Status Measures

Physical Activity Behavior	Health Status Associated with Physical Activity
Self-report of exercise	VO^2 exercise stress test
Pedometers (step counts)	Field-based fitness measure
Accelerometers	Blood pressure/resting heart rate
Caloric expenditure recorders	Body composition
Daily logs	Body weight loss/maintenance
Exercise class attendance	Medical care utilization
GPS recorders	Morbidity (absenteeism, sick days)
Doubly labeled water	Mortality

For evaluations employing quantitative methods, evaluation results are based on hypothesis testing.

in the literature for evaluation of health programs promoting physical activity. There are many factors to consider in the choice of measurement methods, but it is critical that the measure of behavior be directly linked to plausible changes in the chosen health status within the time frame of the evaluation. Reviewing the measurement methods listed in Table 12.7, it is plausible that changes in daily activity levels could produce changes in fitness in a matter of two or more months. But changes in mortality or morbidity produced by changes in physical activity levels would take many years.

Hypotheses are statements that specify the nature of relationships between variables. A hypothesis can be tested using scientific methods. A scientific hypothesis is constructed to be falsifiable. Falsifiability is the logical possibility that a hypothesis can be contradicted by a scientific experiment. For evaluations, the hypothesis should state the expected relationships between the health intervention (independent variable) and the impact on participants' learning, behavior, or health (dependent variable). Evaluators generally start with the goals and objectives of a health program and refine these objectives into a hypothesis for the evaluation. The hypothesis needs to be stated in a form that is scientifically testable. In most cases, that means stating the hypothesis in its null form. The null hypothesis typically states that there is no relationship between two variables or that an intervention has no effect. An alternative hypothesis is proposed in the case that statistical analysis determines that the null hypothesis is rejected. The alternative hypothesis indicates that a relationship between variables does exist. For example, when evaluating a smoking cessation intervention, the null and alternative hypotheses might be:

Null hypothesis: The number of ex-smokers in the intervention group will be equal to the number of ex-smokers in the control group.
Alternative hypothesis: The number of ex-smokers in the intervention group will be higher than the number of ex-smokers in the control group.

During statistical analysis, it will be determined whether the quit rate is significantly higher in the intervention group. **Statistical significance** would indicate whether the observed difference in number of quitters between the intervention and control groups is unlikely to be due to chance. Evaluators generally use probability levels of 0.01 (the observed differences would be due to chance 1 time in 100) or 0.05 (the observed differences would be due to chance 5 times in 100). If the statistical analysis yields a probability level of 0.01 or 0.05, then the null hypothesis is rejected in favor of the alternative hypothesis. Statistical significance allows the evaluator to assert that observed differences are not likely to be due to chance. When statistical significance is reported the evaluator should also comment on whether observed differences are also of practical importance. This judgment is based on professional criteria and reasoning.

STATISTICAL TESTS USED IN HEALTH EVALUATIONS

There are a large number of statistical tests. The appropriate statistical test for a particular evaluation is based on several considerations. Generally speaking, health promotion evaluators should consult with a statistician to arrive at well-informed choices regarding the best statistical test for a particular application. For the sake of illustration, we will examine the use of chi-square tests and t-tests in conducting analysis.

Chi-Square Test Used in Evaluation

In some health programs the outcome variable is dichotomous, which means there are two categories of outcome. For example, in smoking cessation programs, one outcome variable typically is: 12 months postintervention, how many of the participants remained ex-smokers (abstain from smoking)? The outcome variable can take on two values: ex-smoker or smoker. For the purpose of illustration, we offer the following example: Four hundred smokers are identified at a worksite. These 400 smokers are randomized to treatment and control conditions. The treatment group receives a program that offers a wide range of self-regulation techniques. The class meets once a week for 8 weeks. The control group members do not receive the cessation program, but are encouraged to quit on their own. At 12 months postintervention, all subjects take a test to determine their smoking status. **Table 12.8** presents the results of a contingency table. Each participant is placed in one of four sections of the table based on their smoking status and their membership in the control or treatment condition. The null hypothesis for this study is the number of successful ex-smokers in the treatment group will equal the number of successful ex-smokers in the control group. Using statistical software (e.g., IBM-SPSS, SAS, etc.), the probability of null hypothesis is rejected based on a statistical significance ($p < 0.05$). This means that the higher success rate in the intervention group would be observed by chance less than 5 times out of 100. The null hypothesis is rejected in favor of the alternative: The smoking cessation class produced more ex-smokers than did the control condition.

Note that statistical significance only refers to the likelihood of this data occurring by chance. Effect size should be estimated to describe the results. The effect size will estimate the strength of the relationship between the smoking cessation class and abstinence from smoking. We can compute a **relative risk**, which in this case is the likelihood of remaining smoke-free based on membership in the treatment or control group. For this contingency table, relative risk (RR) would be computed as follows:

$$4 = \frac{20 / 200 \text{ (treatment group)}}{5 / 200 \text{ (control group)}}$$

Membership in the smoking cessation class increased the likelihood of remaining smoke-free by a factor of 4. Stated another way, you were 4 times more likely to quit smoking if you were in the smoking cessation class as compared to the control condition.

TABLE 12.8 Results of a Smoking Cessation Program: Chi-Square Analysis		
	12 months smoke-free	**Resumed smoking**
Smoking cessation class	20	180
Control (self-help)	5	195

Chi square: probability < 0.05

There are some advantages to reporting relative risk. First, it helps stakeholders understand and estimate the effectiveness of the intervention. This is easier to apply than a probability statement like statistical significance. Second, relative risk estimates are not affected by sample size. As long as results are consistent from one evaluation to the next, relative risk will provide a meaningful comparison regardless of sample size.

t-Test for Two Independent Samples

The t-test for two independent samples fits well with a commonly used evaluation design, the randomized treatment control group posttest design. An applied example will illustrate the use of the t-test for the evaluation of a health intervention. A new Web-based program has been developed to enhance participants' exercise self-efficacy. Self-efficacy is the perceived ability to overcome barriers to exercise. An evaluation is being conducted to determine whether the program is more effective than classroom-based instruction for the same purpose. Thirty participants have volunteered for the evaluation. Fifteen participants are randomly assigned to the treatment group, and 15 participants are assigned to the control group. The treatment group received five Web-based lessons designed to enhance exercise self-efficacy. The control group received five classroom-based lectures on exercise self-efficacy.

Note that sometimes in t-tests, the control group receives no treatment. In other cases, the control group may receive a treatment considered to be a standard of care in the field. Although different types of control groups are useful, it is important that the evaluator clearly state which type of control group is being employed. In this example, the two samples (treatment and control groups) are considered independent of each other. They are separate samples containing different sets of participants.

After exposure to treatment and control conditions, all participants complete a posttest that measures exercise self-efficacy. The scores on this scale are listed in **Table 12.9**. The null hypothesis: the Web-based group mean score on self-efficacy will equal the mean score on self-efficacy for the control group. The mean score for the treatment group was 23.13 and the control group mean score was 20.87. Is this difference statistically significant?

TABLE 12.9   A t-Test for Independent Samples

Treatment Group: Web-Based Exercise Self-Efficacy Scores	Control Group: Classroom Exercise Self-Efficacy Scores
26, 21, 22, 26, 19,	18, 23, 21, 20, 20,
22, 26, 25, 24, 21,	29, 20, 16,20, 26,
23, 23,18, 29, 22	21,25, 17,18, 19
Mean = 23.13	Mean = 20.87

degrees of freedom = 28, standard deviation = 1.19, t value = 1.9, probability < 0.05

Using statistical software, the t-test procedure on this data produces a t value of 1.9, which is significant at the 0.05 level. The likelihood that the observed difference in this evaluation could have been produced by random variability is less than 5 times out of 100. Thus, we can assert with about 95% confidence that the observed difference can be attributed to the treatment differences. The alternative hypothesis is accepted: The Web-based group mean score for exercise self-efficacy is significantly larger than the control group's score.

Now that you know the difference between the two groups is statistically significant, it would be helpful to estimate the effect size to help explain the magnitude of the difference. The effect size, "take[s] into account the size of the difference between the means" (Fraenkel & Wallen, 1990). The formula for one method to estimate effect size is as follows:

$$\text{Effect size} = \frac{(\text{Mean of the experimental group}) - (\text{Mean of the control group})}{\text{Standard deviation of the control group}}$$

Applying this formula to the example illustrated in Table 12.8 shows the following:

$$\text{Effect size} = \frac{23.13 - 20.81}{1.19} = 1.95$$

One interpretation of this effect size calculation is that the difference in mean scores between the two group is 1.95 standard deviations. Fraenkel and Wallen (1990) recommend that an effect size of 0.5 or larger should be considered an important result.

Change Scores

Evaluators expect health interventions to produce changes in participants' scores, so evaluators need to conceptualize the types of changes meaningful to a particular project (Rossi & Freeman, 1993). The first way to assess change is to subtract pretest values before the intervention from posttest scores after the intervention. This type of change score is used when the evaluation design is pretest-posttest one group (no control group) design. For each participant, the change score is calculated and then averaged across all participants. This type of change score is computed using the following formula:

$$\text{Change score} = \frac{\text{Sum (Each posttest score} - \text{Each pretest score})}{\text{Number of paired scores}}$$

A different form of change score involves subtracting the mean score of the intervention group from the mean score of the control group. This type of change score is based on a treatment/control group posttest-only design:

Change score = (Mean posttest score intervention group) − (Mean posttest score control)

Evaluation design with pre- and posttests and treatment and control groups is a superior design allowing better estimation of program effect. The control group change is subtracted from the intervention group change. This strengthens the position that changes other than those produced by the health program have been removed from the change score.

Change score = (Mean intervention posttest score – Mean intervention group pretest score) – (Mean control group posttest score – Mean control group pretest score)

Some Other Common Inferential Tests

Several inferential tests are used in the evaluation of health education and promotion programs. Some commonly used ones are summarized in **Table 12.10**. Although a detailed discussion of these is beyond the scope of this text, IBM-SPSS instructions for using two commonly used ones—paired t-test and repeated measures ANOVA—are presented in **Focus Feature 12.1** and **Focus Feature 12.2**, for the interested reader.

TABLE 12.10   Commonly Used Inferential Tests in Evaluation of Health Education and Health Promotion Programs

Inferential Test	Description
Paired t-test	To investigate the difference between two samples obtained in pairs such as pretest-posttest data
Analysis of variance (ANOVA)	Technique by which the total variation present in a data set can be partitioned into two or more components, and it is possible to ascertain the magnitude of contributions of each of these sources to total variation; usually used when there are three or more groups
Repeated measures ANOVA	Usually used when there are three or more observations on each subject in the evaluation
Regression	To predict, explain, or estimate a dependent variable from *fixed* independent variables
Correlation	To establish strength of association between *random* independent and dependent variables
Logistic regression	To predict, explain, or estimate a dichotomous dependent variable
Log linear models	To establish associations among categorical variables
Wilcoxon signed-rank test	Nonparametric counterpart of paired t-test when one of the assumptions is violated for single sample or paired data
Wilcoxon rank-sum (Mann-Whitney) test	Nonparametric test for two independent samples
Kruskal-Wallis test	Nonparametric counterpart of one-way ANOVA
Freidman test	Nonparametric counterpart of two-way ANOVA
Spearman rank correlation coefficient (r_s)	Nonparametric counterpart of correlation

FOCUS FEATURE 12.1   USING IBM-SPSS FOR A PAIRED T-TEST

Enter data such that the first-time measurement and second-time measurement are in the same row for each subject.

1. From the data editor screen, click *Analyze*. Then click *Compare Means*, and then *Paired Samples T Test*.
2. From the left display column, select the first measurement and move it to *Pair 1, Variable 1*.
3. From the left display column, select the second measurement and move it to *Pair 1, Variable 2*.
4. Repeat the same process for all variables on which you want to do a paired t-test.
5. Click OK.

Table 1 shows sample results.

Table 1

Sample Output Table: Paired Samples Test

	Paired Differences							
	Mean	**Std. Dev.**	**Std. Error Mean**	**95% CI of the Difference**		**t**	**df**	**Sig. (two-tailed)**
				Lower	**Upper**			
Pair 1 Variable 1– Variable 2								

Interpretation: Interpret the significance level.

FOCUS FEATURE 12.2   USING IBM-SPSS FOR REPEATED MEASURES ANOVA

Enter data such that the first-time measurement, second-time measurement, and all subsequent measurements are in the same row for each subject.

1. From the data editor screen, click *Analyze*. Then click *General Linear Model*, and then *Repeated Measures*.
2. Give *Within-Subject Factor Name* a name. The default is factor1.
3. Specify the number of *Levels* (how many measurements).
4. Click *Add*, and then click *Define*.
5. From the left display column, select the first measurement and move it to the *Within-Subject Variables* panel labeled (1).
6. From the left display column, select the second measurement and move it to the *Within-Subject Variables* panel labeled (2). Repeat for all measurements.
7. Define the *Model*. The default is factorial.
8. Define the *Contrasts*. The default is polynomial.
9. Define the *Plots*. (You can leave it as it is.)
10. Choose the *Post hoc*. (We recommend using *Bonferroni* for most applications.)

(continues)

FOCUS FEATURE 12.2   USING IBM-SPSS FOR REPEATED MEASURES ANOVA *(Continued)*

11. Choose the *Save* option to obtain predicted values, diagnostics (such as Cook's distance), residuals, and coefficient statistics (You can leave it as it is.)
12. Choose the *Options* to get descriptive statistics, estimates of effect size, and several other things. (We would suggest clicking descriptive statistics and effect size.)
13. From the left display column, select the *Between-Subjects Factor(s)* and any *Covariates* and move to the appropriate panels.
14. Click OK.

Table 2 shows sample results.

Table 2

Sample Output Table: Repeated Measures Test Mauchly's Test of Sphericity

Within-Subjects Effect	Mauchly's W	Approx. Chi-Square	df	Sig.	Epsilon		
					Greenhouse Geiser	Huynh-Feldt	Lower Bound

Interpretation: This table tests the assumption for repeated measures. If the significance of Mauchly's test is greater than 0.05, then the assumption of sphericity is met. If it is less than 0.05 then the assumption is violated. If the assumption is violated, one may use Greenhouse-Geiser estimates.

Table 3

Test of Within-Subjects Effects

Source	Type III Sums of Squares	df	Mean Square	F	Sig.	Partial Eta Squared
Factor 1						
Sphericity Assumed						
Greenhouse-Geiser						
Huynh-Feldt						
Lower Bound						

Interpretation: This shows the main result of ANOVA. A two-way ANOVA will have three effects: a main effect of each variable and interaction between the two. If the sphericity assumption is met, then look at the *Sphericity Assumed* row. If the sphericity assumption is not met, then look at the *Greenhouse-Geiser* row. In the column labeled *Sig.*, if the value is < 0.05 then the means of the groups are significantly different.

USING EFFECT SIZES TO COMMUNICATE EVALUATION RESULTS _____

Effect sizes enable evaluators to communicate the practical importance of evaluation results. **Effect sizes** are the magnitude of association between two variables (Cohen, 1988). Effect sizes allow the evaluator to judge how meaningful results are. Program effects can be stated as the difference between the

> *Effect sizes are the magnitude of association between two variables. Effect sizes allow the evaluator to judge how meaningful results are.*

treatment group mean and the control group mean on a variable. For example, a program is designed to increase knowledge of factors that contribute to hypertension. The treatment group's posttest knowledge test score mean was 35 and the control group's mean was 25. The evaluator can describe a mean 10-point gain in hypertension knowledge as an effect size. This information is helpful, but it is specific to the particular knowledge test used in the evaluation. Only persons with an in-depth familiarity with the instrument are likely to fully understand this effect size.

To provide a more general description of effect size, it is often more meaningful to state it in a way that is not closely linked to a particular instrument. One alternative is to state effect size in terms of a percentage increase. The hypertension knowledge test difference could be stated at 40% higher; that is, the treatment group mean of 35 was 40% higher that the control group mean of 25 (10 mean difference / 25 control group mean). However, one could criticize using percentages if the variable does not have a true zero. In this case, is there a true zero in knowledge? So although effect sizes stated in percentages might be useful for cigarettes smoked or days of exercise, it is less appropriate for measures of knowledge, attitudes, skills, and other factors that support adoption of a health behavior. Measures of these variables tend to be scaled in arbitrary units. Because many measures used in health program evaluations are scaled in arbitrary units and lack a true zero, it is recommended that evaluators consider using an effect size statistic. An effect size statistic describes the magnitude of program effect in standardized form. This standardization makes effect sizes comparable across different scales.

A common effect size statistic is the standardized mean difference, which is computed by subtracting the control group mean score from the intervention group mean score divided by the standard deviation for that variable. In effect, this describes the size of a program effect in standard deviation units. Referring back to the hypertension knowledge test example, the 10-point difference between the intervention and control groups would be divided by the standard deviation, which in this case was 5. The standardized mean difference is 2, that is to say two standard deviations difference. This value can then be compared to other standardized mean difference scores.

$$\text{Standardized mean difference} = \frac{35 \text{ (Intervention group mean)} - 25 \text{ (Control group mean)}}{5 \text{ (Standard deviation pooled for both groups)}}$$

Some outcomes of health program evaluations are binary, meaning the participants are assessed as having changed or not changed. Examples include becoming pregnant, receiving a diagnosis for a disease, or quitting smoking. With binary outcomes, a relative risk ratio effect size can be used to describe magnitude of effect. A relative risk ratio of 1.0 indicates that the intervention group and the control group were equal. A relative risk ratio

TABLE 12.11 Evaluation of an Innovative Smoking Cessation Program		
	Quit Smoking	**Did Not Quit Smoking**
Innovative Treatment Group	21	79
No Treatment Control Group	7	93

above 1.0 signifies that the intervention group experienced more change. The relative risk is defined as the risk of success in the treatment group relative to the success in the control group, For example, an innovative smoking cessation program produces a 6-month success rate of 21%. The no-treatment, control group yielded a 7% cessation rate at 6 months. The results are presented in **Table 12.11**. The relative risk of 3 indicates that the participants in the treatment group were three times more likely to quit smoking than participants in the control group.

$$\text{Relative risk} = \frac{\text{Treatment group } (21 / 100)}{\text{Control group } (7 / 100)} = \frac{0.21}{0.7} = 3$$

SKILL-BUILDING ACTIVITY

A study to promote physical activity at the worksite has been conducted. The study randomly assigned 30 employees to an experimental group and 30 employees to a control group. The treatment group received a theory-based program to increase self-regulation of physical activity. The control group received an incentive-based program. Pre- and post-test data are presented in the table below. The table below lists the data for the following variables:

    Treatment E = experimental group   C = control group
    Knowledge = pre-test scores
    Self-efficacy = pre-test scores
    Self-regulation = pre-test scores
    Activity = pre-test minutes of activity
    pKnowledge = post-test scores
    pSelf-efficacy = post-test scores
    pSelf-regulation = post-test scores
    pActivity = post-test minutes of activity

Data for Worksite Physical Activity Promotion Evaluation

Treatment	Knowledge	Self-efficacy	Self-regulation	Activity	pKnowledge	pSelf-efficacy	pSelf-regulation	pActivity
E	12	12	4	40	14	14	7	44
E	11	13	5	24	12	15	6	34
E	5	14	8	33	11	15	8	36
E	8	15	7	42	12	16	7	42

Data for Worksite Physical Activity Promotion Evaluation *(Continued)*

Treatment	Knowledge	Self-efficacy	Self-regulation	Activity	pKnowledge	pSelf-efficacy	pSelf-regulation	pActivity
E	9	11	4	22	13	14	5	44
E	9	5	2	44	14	8	7	77
E	12	13	9	77	15	15	9	88
E	14	11	7	12	16	13	8	22
E	12	3	4	0	12	6	5	22
E	11	18	2	0	17	17	8	66
E	13	14	8	2	16	15	8	22
E	15	13	7	3	18	18	9	33
E	11	12	4	77	14	14	8	87
E	12	17	6	44	18	17	7	54
E	12	15	3	54	13	18	8	54
E	12	13	9	23	15	14	9	33
E	11	13	8	23	13	14	8	23
E	11	12	2	78	14	12	7	70
E	10	12	4	98	11	14	8	94
E	10	11	6	23	16	15	9	33
E	9	10	1	12	11	15	5	22
E	9	10	3	43	9	16	6	44
E	9	12	8	78	10	13	8	78
E	9	11	7	22	10	14	7	33
E	9	10	8	23	11	11	8	44
E	9	19	9	23	15	18	9	33
E	4	12	7	7	8	14	7	22
E	3	12	3	55	9	15	6	55
E	8	11	6	45	9	14	8	45
E	2	9	8	33	6	10	9	33
C	11	8	7	22	12	8	7	22
C	12	7	3	2	14	8	3	6
C	11	3	5	40	13	4	4	30
C	2	6	1	22	4	7	2	21
C	6	8	3	32	7	8	3	22

(continues)

Data for Worksite Physical Activity Promotion Evaluation *(Continued)*

Treatment	Knowledge	Self-efficacy	Self-regulation	Activity	pKnowledge	pSelf-efficacy	pSelf-regulation	pActivity
C	6	11	6	42	8	11	7	33
C	8	11	8	22	9	11	8	22
C	9	11	9	32	11	11	9	32
C	7	12	8	71	9	12	8	66
C	10	12	5	32	13	12	5	22
C	11	15	3	3	14	16	4	22
C	12	14	2	4	14	14	3	12
C	12	14	7	5	13	13	7	12
C	11	13	8	3	13	13	8	23
C	15	13	2	70	16	12	4	60
C	15	13	3	41	16	13	3	41
C	10	13	8	44	11	13	8	44
C	12	13	7	23	13	11	7	23
C	9	17	3	23	9	17	3	33
C	8	16	5	78	9	15	5	70
C	7	16	3	98	8	16	4	66
C	4	11	4	23	6	13	4	22
C	11	11	3	12	13	11	3	11
C	13	10	2	43	15	10	4	43
C	12	9	8	78	14	9	8	66
C	11	8	7	22	11	9	7	32
C	11	4	2	23	11	5	3	23
C	9	3	4	23	10	5	4	23
C	8	8	5	7	8	9	5	11
C	10	7	4	55	10	7	4	44

Use statistical software to analyze the data presented in the data table above. Use descriptive statistics to best represent patterns in the data. Use a statistical test to determine if there were significant increases in the variables from pre- to post-test. Were there significant differences between the treatment and control group?

SUMMARY

Stakeholders and evaluators want to know whether a health education or health promotion intervention is effective. Attention to evaluation designs, sampling, and measurement create a foundation upon which confidence in the statistical analysis is based. Evaluators use statistics to describe the sample of participants, to make decisions about program effectiveness, and to consider the possibility of making inferences from the sample to a target population. The first step in statistical analysis is to develop systematic procedures for standardizing data entry. Then the data set needs to be carefully reviewed and corrective actions taken for implausible values, outliers, and missing values.

Descriptive statistics are used to provide simple numerical summaries of the variables measured during the evaluation. Examples of descriptive statistics include: frequency distributions, measures of central tendency (mean, mode, median), and measures of variability (range and standard deviation). Providing a detailed description of the data set is important for creating a mental picture of the sample used in the evaluation. A complete description of the variable values generated by the sample provides a context for interpreting the evaluation results. The use of graphs to present descriptive data provides a visual representation often illustrating relationships between variables. Often graphs can provide visual interest and ease of interpretation for stakeholders.

Evaluations are designed to detect changes brought about by health promotion and education activities. An evaluation hypothesis is a statement about anticipated changes produced by health promotion and education interventions that is testable. For evaluations employing quantitative methods, conclusions are based on hypothesis testing. Statistical tests such as the chi-square and t-test can be used to determine whether the null hypothesis is retained or rejected. This statistical test is a probability statement (e.g., probability = 0.05) indicating how likely the observed results can be explained by chance. Effects sizes should also be reported to enhance the stakeholders' understanding of the magnitude of observed intervention impact on target variables.

REVIEW QUESTIONS

1. Define statistics. What is its use in evaluation?
2. What is data management? Identify the importance and methods of data cleaning.
3. What is a data-producing sample? What are some examples of inclusion criteria in a data-producing sample?
4. What are some questions to consider when reviewing descriptive statistics?
5. Describe the measures of central tendency.
6. Describe the measures of variability.
7. Differentiate between norm-referenced and criterion-referenced tests.
8. What is statistical inference? How is it done?
9. Differentiate between statistical significance and practical importance of evaluation results.

WEBSITES TO EXPLORE

Statistical Decision Tree

http://www.microsiris.com/Statistical%20Decision%20Tree/
This website provides an online decision tree to help make decisions about which statistical test to use in different evaluation situations. The material used on this website is based on the book, *A Guide for Selecting Statistical Techniques for Analyzing Social Science Data*,

2nd edition, produced at the Institute for Social Research, at The University of Michigan, under the authorship of Frank M. Andrews, Laura Klem, Terrence N. Davidson, Patrick O'Malley, and Willard L. Rodgers in 1981. *Use this tree for an actual or imaginary problem that you want to evaluate.*

Statistical Education Through Problem Solving (STEPS)

http://www.stats.gla.ac.uk/steps/

This site contains free software to download designed to provide education through applied problem solving. The software includes problem-based modules to support the teaching of statistics in biology, business, geography, and psychology. It can be used to enhance understanding about statistics and evaluation. *Download the software and complete at least one module.*

Statistics Site

http://www.statsoft.com/textbook/

This is the website for the Statsoft electronic statistics textbook. The site provides definitions, explanations, and computational formulas for a wide variety of statistical analysis. *Browse through the "Basic Statistics" link and write down five things that you learned.*

Topics in Statistical Data Analysis

http://home.ubalt.edu/ntsbarsh/stat-data/topics.htm#rrtopic

This website was developed by Professor Hossein Arsham of the University of Baltimore. It discusses several topics pertaining to statistics. *Choose the topics, "ANOVA," "What is the Effect Size?," "Different Schools of Thought in Statistics," and "Test for Normality." Read these topics and summarize each in 250 words, describing what you understood.*

REFERENCES

Abelson, R. (1995). *Statistics as principled argument.* Hillsdale, NJ: Lawrence Erlbaum.

Alkin, M. C. (1980). *A user focused approach in conducting evaluations: Three perspectives.* New York: Foundation Center.

Black, T. R. (1999). *Doing quantitative research in the social sciences: An integrated approach to research design, measurement and statistics.* London: Sage.

Bradburn, N., & Sudman, S. (1982). *Asking questions: A practical guide to questionnaire construction.* San Francisco: Jossey-Bass.

Cohen, J. (1988). *Statistical power analysis for the behavioral sciences* (2nd ed.). Hillsdale, NJ: Lawrence Erlbaum.

Fraenkel, J. R., & Wallen N. D. (1990). *How to design and evaluate research in education.* New York: McGraw-Hill.

Glass, V. G., & Hopkins, K. D. (2008). *Statistical methods in education and psychology* (3rd ed.). Boston: Allyn & Bacon.

Haertel, E. (1985). Construct validity and criterion-referenced testing. *Review of Educational Research, 55*(1), 23–46.

Kalton, G., & Kasprzyk, D. (1986). The treatment of missing survey data. *Survey Methodology, 12,* 1–16.

Little, R., & Schenker, N. (1995). Missing data. In G. Arminger, C. Clogg, & M. Sobel (Eds.), *Handbook of statistical modeling for the social and behavioral sciences* (pp. 39–69.). New York: Plenum.

Newcomer, K. E. (1994). Using statistics appropriately. In J. Wholey, H. Hatry, & K. Newcomer (Eds.), *Handbook of practical program evaluation* (pp. 389–416). San Francisco: Jossey-Bass.

Rossi, P. H., & Freeman, H. E. (1993). *Evaluation: A systematic approach.* Beverly Hills, CA: Sage.

Tabachnick, B. G., & Fidell, L. S. (2007). Cleaning up your act. Screening data prior to analysis. In B. G. Tabachnick & L. S. Fidell (Eds.), *Using multivariate statistics* (5th ed., pp. 60–116). Boston: Pearson/Allyn and Bacon.

Tufte, E. R., & Cheshire, C. T. (2001). *The visual display of quantitative information.* Cheshire, CT: Graphics Press.

Veany, J. E., & Kaluzny, A. D. (1998). *Evaluation and decision making for health services* (3rd ed.). Chicago: Health Administration Press.

CHAPTER 13

Data Interpretation and Report Writing

INTRODUCTION

This chapter will review a variety of themes related to the interpretation of the evaluation results. Statistical analyses are useful methods of describing data and testing hypothesis. This approach is an important method of enhancing the reliability and scientific rigor of decision making in evaluation. But statistical analysis is only one type of tool that evaluators use. Evaluators also employ a set of conceptual tools to interpret and explain the evaluation results. This chapter begins with a review of some conceptual tools evaluators use.

This chapter also proposes a comprehensive table of contents for an evaluation report. Each section of the report is described and explained. Evaluation results are of little value if they are not effectively communicated to decision makers and stakeholders. It is the decision makers, professional staff, and stakeholders who are in a position to refine health programs and allocate resources. Ergo, it is essential that these folks understand and appreciate the meaning of evaluation results (Black, 1999). The evaluation report is also a historical record of methods, results, and conclusions. It can be used as a reference point for future evaluations and, if effective, can inform current health program practices.

INTERPRETATION OF EVALUATION RESULTS: CONCEPTUAL TOOLS

Green and Lewis (1986) compare the interpretation of evaluation results to detective work. Detectives need to dig deeply into the evidence, trying to develop a full understanding of the health program being evaluated. Evaluation detectives are sensitive to context, realizing certain variables have been measured, others variables controlled for by evaluation design, and many variables left unexamined. Practically speaking, many factors impact consumer health actions. Many of these factors are beyond the direct influence of health education and health promotion programs, such as access to resources, discretionary time, community norms, occupation responsibilities, and family responsibilities. In a similar fashion, health program evaluations do not measure all possible factors that can impact participants' health practices. It is important for evaluators to keep this perspective in mind. Doing so can assist evaluators in placing evaluation results in the context of the everyday circumstances in which participants live. Health promotion detectives are skilled in the use of evaluation design, but also have a toolbox of conceptual analysis methods. These conceptual tools are used to discover important findings, explain evaluation results, and communicate the results of evaluations. This chapter discusses several conceptual tools that may be useful in critically reviewing and explaining the results of an evaluation. The reasoned use of these tools can provide context for the statistical results of an evaluation, enabling more sophisticated explanations. This process can provide a more detailed understanding of the results, leading to effective refinements of program efforts in the future.

Evaluation reports should avoid overwhelming stakeholders with statistics. More is not necessarily better when it comes to statistics. Tukey (1977) cautions against reporting data analysis that lacks focus and creates the impression of random analysis in search of significant results. The evaluation report should clearly convey a sense of focus, using statistics to describe the data and test hypotheses linked directly to the purpose of the evaluation. After these carefully targeted analyses have been completed, the detective work begins. Using the conceptual tools of the evaluation detective, the results are carefully scrutinized for critical review, practical meaning, and program application. Stakeholders are more likely to find evaluation reports using this method useful in making decisions.

STATISTICAL SIGNIFICANCE AND PRACTICAL IMPORTANCE

Statistical tests are used to test hypotheses in health program evaluation. Evaluators should take special care in describing evaluation results that are statistically significant. Unfortunately, the everyday, nontechnical use of the word *significance* implies importance. This can lead stakeholders to misunderstand the meaning of statistical significance as it would appear in an evaluation report. The evaluator is using the phrase *statistical significance* as a technical term. **Statistical significance** is a statement regarding the likelihood that observed variable values occurred by chance. Statistical significance is affected by several design features including sample size. In some health evaluations there may be 100 or more participants. As sample sizes get larger, statistical power increases and very small differences in values can be statistically significant. In the case of large sample sizes, it is generally a sound practice to check statistical power. As power goes over 0.8, an evaluator should consider replacing the p-value of 0.05 with the more rigorous standard of a p-value of 0.01.

> *The p-value (usually 0.05 or 0.01) is not the same as an effect size. An effect size has direct, substantive meaning.*

The p-value (usually 0.05 or 0.01) is not the same as an effect size, which has direct, substantive meaning. Statistical significance is a useful decision-making tool for rejecting a null hypothesis when the appropriate statistical analysis is used with adequate, but not too much, statistical power. An experienced researcher will carefully adjust statistical power so that statistical significance coincides with a result of practical importance. An appropriate test of a hypothesis requires power that is neither too low nor too high. In most cases, 80% power is considered a balanced, recommended level of statistical power. A responsible evaluator follows a report of statistical significance with a detailed discussion of effect size and the practical importance of a finding. This is especially important for evaluations with large sample sizes and highly powered statistical tests. The evaluation report should emphasize that statistical significance does not mean practical significance. A significant finding simply is a result unlikely to be explained by chance. Thus, statistical significance is a necessary first step requirement for practical importance, but by itself is not sufficient.

Practical importance is an interpretation of evaluation results that considers the relevance of effect sizes in the context of the professional practice of health promotion and education. Practical importance speaks to how likely the intervention is to benefit participants or stakeholders. It is critical that the evaluator interpret results to show practical implications for stakeholders (Datta, 1980). This interpretive step is often critical to the success of the evaluation project. If evaluation results can be understood in practical terms, they are more likely to be translated into practice. From a stakeholder's point of view, a large statistical effect may be of little practical importance. Conversely, a small statistical effect may be very important. For example, a large score change

> *Practical importance is an interpretation of evaluation results that considers the relevance of effect sizes in the context of the professional practice of health promotion and education.*

in consumer satisfaction has considerably fewer financial consequences than a relatively small effect size that reduces absenteeism for a worksite health promotion program. The health program participant context is critical for determining the practical implications of an evaluation result.

Determinations of practical importance can be based on several methods. Statistically significant results can often be translated back in terms of the original outcome measurement scale. This is effective if the scale has a relevant interpretation. For example, a scale measure could be participants' days of physical activity per week. The results can be translated into increased days per week attributed to the intervention. This interpretation can be compared to recognized recommendations for physical activity as well as pretest scores. Stakeholders will have an intuitive understanding of the increase that allows them to interpret the importance of the finding. Many measures used in health program evaluations, including reduced absenteeism, reduced healthcare expenditures, and improvements in fitness and health measures, can be stated in term of practical importance. Projected cost savings can also be associated with many of these outcomes. The advantage of this approach is that the outcomes are directly linked to program objectives and possess a meaning that stakeholders are likely to understand and value. Stating evaluation outcomes in practical terms can contribute to public understanding regarding the contribution health behavior change programs can make to public health.

Some outcome measures may not possess inherently meaningful interpretations. Theory-based variables, which by nature are abstract concepts, fall into this category. Examples of theory-based variables include perceived threat, personal susceptibility, self-efficacy, behavioral capability, and perceived barriers. How much change in these variables is needed to be considered important? For example, among evaluation studies, how much change in "perceived threat" is reported in the literature? How much change in perceived threat is associated with positive changes in health behavior? Professional judgment is often used. Professional judgment is based on knowledge of the professional literature. A review of the program evaluation literature may reveal effect sizes for targeted theoretical variables. These effect sizes can be an important standard of comparison. It often takes repeated evaluation trials to determine how to effectively promote change in theoretical variables. It takes more trials to determine how much change in theoretical variables produces changes in health practices. The cumulative professional literature can provide an empirical basis for establishing meaningful standards of change in theory-based variables.

Another commonly used approach to describing practical significance is to use conventional guidelines. Cohen (1988) suggests general effect size standards for "small," "medium," and "large" effect sizes in educational and behavioral research. Cohen developed these standards as an aid to doing power analysis. Over time, these standards have been adopted as general rules of thumb for judging intervention effects. Using standardized mean difference effect sizes, Cohen claims that 0.20 is a small effect, 0.50 is a medium effect, and 0.80 is a large effect. If an evaluator is going to use these standards, it is important to describe how they were computed and how they can be interpreted.

Another commonly used method is historical analysis. If an evaluation has been run for several years, current results can be judged against results from previous years. Using this historical method, it may be possible to link positive changes produced by health programs with socially valued outcomes. For example, it may be observed that participants in worksite wellness programs who reach certain thresholds of enrollment in health incentive programs become consistent consumers of prevention programming, which leads to reductions in medical care expenditures. In this case, the evaluator can suggest that the threshold of incentive participation is an indicator of practical importance. Over time, refinements in the health program can lead to steady improvement. With a consistent record of achievement in the literature, professional organizations may adopt and promote professional standards that can be used for comparison.

An extension of the historical approach for gauging practical importance is grounded in logic model testing, or what is sometimes referred to as theory testing. **Figure 13.1** illustrates a typical logic model for a health program. Outputs is the health program, which is designed to create learning experiences that will enhance participants' knowledge, motivation, and self-regulation skills and provide incentives to support a health behavior.

To test the logic of this model, the evaluator carefully identifies changes produced by the health program. Examples include increases in participant knowledge, motivation, skills, or other factors that contribute to behavioral capability. The evaluator then strategically uses evaluation design and statistical analysis to identify the combination of logic model variables that produces meaningful changes in targeted health behavior.

For example, an evaluator may notice that 20% of program participants possess the following profile:

- Score of 80% or better on a knowledge test of health benefits of exercise
- Report four or more motivations for adhering to their exercise goals
- Report the consistent use of five or more self-regulation strategies
- Enroll in the sponsored incentive program for exercise

When participants have this profile, they are three times more likely to report successful adherence to 6-month exercise goals. Essentially, the evaluator is attempting to identify how much change is needed in predisposing and enabling factors to support health behavior change. Using this method requires consistent use of rigorous evaluation methods over a period of several years. This method empowers the health promotion and education

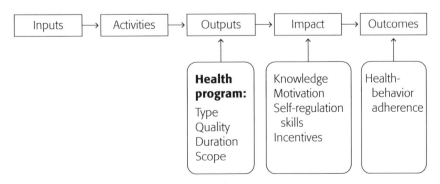

Figure 13.1   Health program logic model.

field to assert there is a threshold level of health programming needed to attain a critical level of learning and environmental support that are linked to health behavior change.

There is no single best method to explain the practical importance of evaluation results. It is clear that statements of statistical significance are necessary, but are not sufficient methods of communicating the importance of findings. The evaluator should consult with stakeholders to identify the best way to communicate the practical importance of evaluation results. The evaluator needs to be prepared to provide several translations for the statistical results. The importance of describing effect size in practical terms cannot be overstated.

POTENTIAL FAILURES IN INTERPRETATION

There are several ways in which failure can occur in the interpretation of evaluations of health education and health promotion programs. These are discussed in the following sections and summarized in **Table 13.1**.

Statistical Power Failure

Statistical power is the ability of a statistical analysis to reveal true effects between variables. **Statistical power failure** can occur with too little or too much power. Too much power can produce a statistically significant test of little practical importance. Too little statistical power will fail to detect differences of practical importance. An appropriate level of power is a balance. It is recommended that most evaluations attempt to achieve a power of 0.80. Too much power and too little power both create problems of interpretation. It is always recommended that an evaluator review factors that can affect statistical

TABLE 13.1   Different Types of Failures That Can Occur in Interpretation of Evaluations of Health Education and Health Promotion Programs

Type of Failure	Description
Statistical power failure	Too much power can produce a statistically significant test of little practical importance. Too little statistical power will fail to detect differences of practical importance.
Participant retention failure	Participant attrition affects statistical power or generializiblity of results.
Recruitment failure	When evaluation sampling procedures do not produce a sample representative of the target population, then the results cannot be generalized.
Measurement failure	An assessment tool used in an evaluation does not accurately assess a variable.
Implementation failure	A health program is not delivered to participants as it was designed.
Behavior theory failure	The health program evaluation reveals that the targeted theoretical constructs were successfully changed but the health behavior change predicted by the theory did not follow as predicted.
Behavioral adherence failure	Changes in health behavior do not produce the anticipated changes in health status.
Ecological fallacy	An incorrect assumption that a group characteristic applies to all individuals in the same group.

power prior to the evaluation and draw an appropriate size sample to ensure recommended levels of power.

As the evaluation plan is implemented, some of these factors affecting statistical power (e.g., participant attrition) may change in unanticipated ways, resulting in statistical tests that are over- or underpowered. Many statistical packages have the capability of calculating the precise power for a statistical test being run. Evaluators should check the power of all important statistical tests. If the power is very high (e.g., > 0.95), very small and sometimes trivial differences in observed variables may test as statistically significant. The usefulness of significance testing is reduced. In this case, the evaluator should focus on presentation of effect sizes and discuss the practical significance of the results. If the power is too low (e.g., < 0.70), important differences in observed variables may not be statistically significant. Again, the evaluator should discuss the practical significance of the observed differences and indicate that the finding was not statistically significant. A caution about the low statistical power should be provided as a possible explanation for the lack of significance.

When statistical power is too high or too low, the evaluator should pay close attention to the practical importance of effect sizes. The goal is to carefully establish the correct sample size to achieve the recommended level of statistical power (0.80) and take steps to prevent participant attrition. By following these steps, the difficulties involved in the interpretation of over- and underpowered statistical tests is avoided.

Participant Retention Failure

Participant retention failure occurs when participant attrition affects statistical power or the generalizability of results. Despite our best efforts, participants in evaluations drop out before the evaluation is completed. Dropouts can be caused by health program factors such as program time requirements, lack of participant satisfaction, lack of convenience, and the like; however, dropouts also can be caused by factors unrelated to the health program, such as family or work responsibilities, injury, or illness. In either case, participant dropouts can produce serious consequences for the interpretation of evaluation results. First, attrition from either the intervention or the control group can reduce statistical power. The more subjects drop out, the larger the reduction in statistical power. Reduced power reduces the usefulness of significance testing (see the previous section on statistical power failure).

Participant satisfaction may be low or the time demands of the program may be too high for many. When program factors are contributing to attrition, it is likely to exert a systematic influence on dropouts. In these cases, sampling bias can occur. Several concerns arise. Is the final data-producing sample still representative of the intended target population? Generalization of results is influenced by this consideration. Did participant attrition bias the final results in an important way? For example, was there a discernable pattern in the type of participants dropping out? The evaluator can examine demographic information (age, gender, race, etc.) to help determine whether systematic attrition occurred. The evaluator also can review pretest data to determine whether the knowledge, motivation, health practices, or other variables assessed were different between the final data-generating sample and the dropouts. The key issue is whether detected differences between dropouts and the final sample affected the final results. If so, the evaluator should provide an explanation for how he or she believes the results have been affected.

Recruitment Failure

Recruitment failure occurs when evaluation sampling procedures do not produce a sample representative of the target population, and the results cannot be generalized. Health education and health promotion programs, and subsequently health program evaluations, are typically designed for specific target populations within the community. For example, many physical activity promotion programs are designed for sedentary and low-active populations. A key concern is whether the sampling procedures produced a sample that adequately represents the intended target audience. Evaluators should describe the data-producing sample in detail. If the data-producing sample does not represent the intended target population, some corrective steps should be considered. First, if discovered early, steps may be taken to refine sampling and recruitment methods to ensure a representative sample. If it is too late for corrective sampling, the evaluator should carefully describe the sample, identify specific features of the sample, and discuss how these features could affect the results of the evaluation. The evaluator should also discuss how the final data-producing sample will affect the ability to generalize the results to the intended population. Referring back to the example, it has been observed that a physical activity promotion program may attract individuals who are already physically active. If a substantial amount of the sample is active, it can contribute to a ceiling effect. This occurs when subjects enter the program with preexisting high levels of targeted health practices. There is no room for improvement among these participants, and thus they suppress the potential health behavior gains produced by the health program.

Measurement Failure

Measurement failure occurs when an assessment tool used in an evaluation does not accurately assess a variable. Experience suggests that measurement is often a weak link in the evaluation design methods used in health education and health promotion. There are several reasons for this. First, the development of valid and reliable instruments takes considerable time and resources. Often evaluators do not have the resources needed to develop instruments specifically tailored to a health program. Evaluators are left to review the literature to see whether an instrument that approximates current needs is available. A second approach is to quickly develop an instrument that appears to match program evaluation needs. But again, resources are not available to actually test and refine the instrument for reliability and validity. In either case, the link between health program objectives and the items on the instrument are often low. For example, there are many instruments reported in the literature to measure social support. Several social support instruments focus on health-related practices (e.g., diet, exercise, etc.). The items that comprise these measures of social support should correspond directly to the way in which social support is operationalized in the health program being evaluated. If the health program promotes the development of skills for providing emotional and instrumental social support for regular exercise, the instrument should precisely target these types of social support. Too often, evaluators rely on instruments that do not correspond to the specific objectives of a program. The sensitivity and precision of measurement for a particular health program deteriorates as a consequence. Weak, imprecise measurement increases error and decreases the overall rigor of the evaluation. Ideally, evaluators have access to valid and reliable instruments that precisely correspond to the way in which important constructs are taught in the health program.

Implementation Failure

Implementation failure occurs when a health program is not delivered to participants as it was designed. If a program was not delivered to participants as it was designed, the evaluator runs the risk of a Type III error (Basch, Sliepcevich, Gold, Duncan, & Kolbe, 1985). A Type III error occurs when an evaluator assumes that a health program has been implemented fully and correctly when it has not been. The remainder of the evaluation project is profoundly affected by this incorrect assumption. The evaluation results are not based on implementation of the health program. In applied health education settings, implementation is generally judged by a matter of degree. Many health staff members actively adjust elements of the program design to suit their preferences or the presumed needs of program participants. Unforeseen events in class (e.g., low attendance, off-task discussions, class interruptions) can also substantially reduce implementation fidelity. Based on these and other circumstances, it is safe to presume that implementation will be less than perfect. It is important that evaluators use implementation fidelity measures to document the extent of implementation. This enables the evaluator to describe subsequent evaluation results in the context of degree of implementation. If the evaluator has several program sites, it may be possible to compare different levels of implementation fidelity to determine how they impact evaluation results. In this circumstance, it may be possible to establish an association between degree of implementation and subsequent health program impact. It may also be important for the evaluator to study the factors that reduce implementation fidelity in the field. This line of inquiry could prove beneficial in promoting program quality.

Behavior Theory Failure

Behavior theory failure occurs when the program evaluation reveals that the targeted theoretical constructs were successfully changed, but theoretically predicted health behavior change did not occur. Behavior theory is sometimes integrated into the logic model or program model in the professional practice. Many health programs are based on a variety of health behavior theories. These programs will focus on constructs of the theory in an effort to increase health behavior change in participants. Many health behavior theories have not been consistently tested and are not empirically confirmed. It is entirely possible that health behavior theories could be an explanation for lower than predicted levels of behavior change.

Some evaluations will measure changes in health behavior theory constructs. In these cases, the evaluator has the opportunity to evaluate theory on two levels. First, did participation in the health program produce favorable changes in targeted theoretical constructs? Several critical things can be learned. What types of educational experiences produce gains in theoretical constructs? How much programmatic effort, what types of conditions, or what resources are required to produce meaningful gains in theoretical constructs? What constructs seem particularly resistant to change via health promotion activities? All of these questions help the evaluator describe health program effectiveness in changing theoretical constructs that are hypothesized to support change in health behavior. Second, are documented changes in theory-based constructs associated with changes in health behavior? It is at this point that theory failure is a potential explanation. If the health program successfully produced changes in constructs among participants, and this does not produce predicted changes in health behavior, theory failure is a consideration. Evaluators should clearly discuss the evidence and elaborate on the possibility that health behavior theory is a contributing factor to less than expected levels of health behavior change.

Behavioral Adherence Failure

Behavioral adherence failure occurs when changes in health behavior do not produce anticipated changes in health status. Many health programs produce learning, skill development, and health behavior changes among a meaningful proportion of participants. Evaluators are sometimes puzzled when important changes in health behavior do not produce anticipated changes in health status. Examples include when a reduction in caloric intake does not produce anticipated changes in weight loss, when increases in physical activity do not lead to changes in fitness, and when increases in smoking cessation do not lead to decreases in healthcare costs. There are several possible explanations for these observations. An important perspective to consider is the many factors that contribute to any particular health status. The target health behavior is important, but it may not be sufficient by itself to support health status change. It is also entirely possible that other factors or practices negate the health effects of a newly adopted health practice. For example, increases in physical activity will not produce reductions in body weight if caloric consumption increases with activity level.

In addition to these concerns is the possibility that health behavior changes are not maintained long enough to produce health status change. The key issue is whether the participants in the program maintain health practices long enough to produce detectable changes in health status. Health behavior adherence is a key and fundamental question for many health programs. If an evaluation wants to address this issue empirically, several adjustments are required in overall evaluation design. First, does the evaluation design allow for follow-up assessments over time to track health behavior adherence? This requires developing methods of maintaining communication with participants weeks, months, or even years after participation in the health program. A practical and valid measure of the targeted health behavior is needed to gather data during the follow-up period to verify health behavior adherence levels. A reasonable estimate of the duration of health behavior adherence to promote health status change is needed to inform data gathering. Gathering data on long-term adherence can be expensive, but it is an important step to empirically testing the ability of health programs to promote sustainable changes in health practices. Equally important, it tests the presumption that health behavior adherence produces meaningful changes in health status.

Ecological Fallacy

Ecological fallacy is the incorrect assumption that a group characteristic applies to all individuals in that same group (Milcarek & Link, 1981). For example, an evaluation reports that the average education level of participants was a high school degree (12 years). The ecological fallacy is to assume that any or all participants had 12 years of education. It is possible that the participants may include a substantial portion of people with a college education and another group with less than 12 years of education. This distribution could produce an average of 12 years of education when many of the participants had more or less education. The frequency distributions of all important variables should be reviewed with this fallacy in mind. If the review of the distribution is bimodal or suggests that there are important clusters within the sample, this should be reported. Analysis that examines differences among subgroups may be indicated. For example, participants with different educational levels may respond very differently to the health program. It is possible that the health program was effective for one group and not another. Overlooking this possibility and not doing a subclass analysis based on education could potentially miss an important result.

In summary, the chapter began with the suggestion that evaluators should take on the role of detective to dig deeper into the evaluation results. This chapter has presented a set of conceptual tools that may be useful in helping better understand the results of an evaluation. These tools can be used to discover "hidden" findings, that is, insights that might be overlooked. These tools can be helpful in providing context for understanding factors that may have influenced the evaluation results. Some of these factors may turn out to be **limitations of evaluation**. Limitations are shortcomings in the evaluation methods that should be considered when interpreting the results. The reasoned use of these tools can enhance understanding and provide context for the statistical results of an evaluation. This process can provide a more complete understanding of the results, leading to effective refinements of program efforts in the future.

EVALUATION STANDARDS: HOW MUCH IS ENOUGH?

Evaluations are designed to encourage evidence-based decision making. Statistical data does not speak for itself. The interpretation of data is not self-evident or obvious. This is particularly true for professionals whose training and experience with statistics is limited. Standards inevitably are involved in making comparisons and judgments about evaluation results. In health promotion evaluation, several types of standards are commonly used.

Historical Standards

Historical standards are benchmarks to compare results from the current evaluation effort to results from prior years. Health programs may have a track record of evaluation results accumulated over a period of years. One method of demonstrating progress is to compare results from the current evaluation effort to results from prior years. With accumulated experience and program refinements based on previous evaluations, results should improve over time. For example, a smoking cessation program demonstrates the 6-month cigarette smoking quit rates have improved from a success rate of 10% of participants to the current rate of 18%.

Normative Standards

Normative standards compare results from one group to results from another group. If an evaluation design employs a control group, it may serve as the norm for comparison. Referring back to the smoking cessation example, we might find that a no-treatment control group produced a 6-month cigarette smoking quit rate of 4% whereas participants in the treatment group who received the smoking cessation program produced an 18% quit rate.

Empirical Standards

Empirical standards are derived from an in-depth knowledge of the professional literature. Over time, the published literature in the field eventually arrives at a typical standard of performance for similar programs. For example, smoking cessation programs often produce 6-month quit rates that range between 15% and 20%.

Absolute Standards

Absolute standards focus on 100% success rates. A smoke-free America is an example of an absolute standard. Often laypeople with little experience in prevention or health behavior change want to "stamp out" a behavior with zero tolerance approaches. Using absolute standards usually sets health education and health promotion programs up for failure. With experience, absolute standards should evolve into more realistic and useful standards. Evaluators should resist efforts to employ absolute standards for decision making. Referring back to the smoking cessation example, an absolute standard of 100% expected success rate will be of little value for interpreting or reporting evaluation results.

Diagnostic Threshold Standards

Diagnostic threshold standards are an empirically validated critical level of changes needed to yield improvements in health. For example, professional organizations and government agencies have developed threshold standards for recommended levels of physical activity, dietary standards, and body mass index. When a threshold is accepted, it can be used to explain evaluation results. For example, the proportion of intervention group participants who meet the threshold can be compared to the proportion of control group participants who meet the threshold. For example, at posttest, 35% of intervention group participants met the American College of Sports Medicine standard of 300 minutes or more of moderate-intensity aerobic physical activity a week. In contrast, 20% of the control group met this standard.

Statistical Convention Standards

Statistical convention standards are benchmarks developed over time by statisticians for labeling the magnitude of standardized effects. Statisticians put considerable thought into methods of standardizing effect sizes. Cohen (1988) provides guidelines for identifying effects sizes for the educational and social sciences. For standardized mean difference effect size, he suggests that 0.20 is a small effect, 0.50 is a medium effect, and 0.80 is a large effect. Some evaluations in the literature report these standards to compare to results.

Consensus Standards

Consensus standards are a combination of the different standards that stakeholders agree to use for an evaluation project. With thoughtful deliberation, stakeholders can arrive at a set of standards that are meaningful and realistic. Consensus standards informed by historical and empirical standards can be a particularly useful tool in utilization-based evaluations. The use of multiple standards is a common and recommended evaluation practice.

> *Consensus standards informed by historical and empirical standards can be a useful tool in utilization-based evaluations.*

EFFECTIVELY COMMUNICATING STATISTICAL RESULTS

Evaluations report statistical results. Statistics is a language that many professionals do not understand well. As a consequence, statistics can be a barrier to communication. This is particularly true of decision makers who do not have training in the use of statistics. Stakeholders are often reluctant to read through page after page of statistics. Evaluators should work to present statistical results in a manner that is easily understood and directly linked to the purposes of the evaluation. Communication is the key to the effective use of statistics. Abelson (1995) has identified five concepts to help effectively communicate statistical results: magnitude of effect, articulateness, generalizability, interest level, and credibility. These concepts can help make statistical results both understandable and persuasive.

> *Five concepts to effectively communicate statistical results are magnitude of effect, articulateness, generalizability, interest level, and credibility.*

Magnitude of the effect is the amount of change in key variables that was produced by the health program (Sechrest & Yeaton, 1982). The larger the magnitude of effect, the more persuasive the data will be. The magnitude of the effect size should be stated in terms that are clearly understood. For example, a community program to promote physical activity increased minutes of weekly exercise by 30% among program participants. It may be more effective to report: "Among program participants, weekly exercise increased from two bouts of exercise per week to three bouts, thus meeting program objectives."

Articulateness refers to the clarity and detail of the evaluation report. Decision makers should perceive the report results as direct, clear, and easy to understand. Statistical jargon should be replaced with language that describes the meaning of the results. The use of charts or graphs may be helpful in visualizing or communicating statistical results.

Getting feedback on initial drafts of the report from stakeholders can help the evaluator decide how best to explain the results.

Generalizability of results will also have an impact on how persuasive the report will be. Imagine an evaluation report in which the methods were so flawed that the results do not generalize to any other population. The report only applies to the sample participating in the evaluation, and only applies to the sample during the immediate past implementation of the health program. In this case, the evaluation report would be reduced to a curiosity with no relevance to the future. Decision makers often complain that evaluation reports say a great deal about very little. By parsing statements, qualifying each conclusion, and being overly cautious about generalizing results, evaluation reports can disappoint decision makers. Taken to the extreme, the report may indicate that the results only apply to the program, setting, and sample described in the evaluation. Such a report is of no use to decision makers. Evaluators need to carefully describe the evaluation methods employed (sampling, evaluation design, etc.), and actively describe reasonable approaches to generalizing the evaluation.

Evaluation reports can be written in a mechanical way with heavy reliance on the use of technical and statistical jargon. The goal of a well-written report is to present the results of the evaluation in a manner that increases the reader's comprehension and **interest level**. There are several methods for increasing interest level. First, the evaluation reporting should be clear and concise. Speak directly to the intended audience using language they will understand. Next, present statistical results in a manner that directly addresses the decisions that need to be made. When findings lead to important claims or are surprising, they will attract attention. Results also can be compared to previous trials or program evaluations reported in the literature, if it helps underscore the importance of the findings. Finally, the relevance of the results should be emphasized. Do the results clearly explain the relevance of the results so that the question, "So what?" is answered?

The findings of the report will be more persuasive if the credibility of the evaluation is communicated. **Credibility** is the extent to which decision makers place confidence in the results of the evaluation. Attention to reporting on the strengths of the evaluation methods can substantially increase the credibility of the findings. The report should emphasize how those methods will enhance the rigor and quality of the evaluation data. If evaluation methods are compromised or flawed, that should be reported as well. Above all, the evaluation report should be perceived as objective and fair. The strengths and weaknesses of the evaluation should be discussed, particularly how the strengths and weaknesses affect the interpretation of the data.

Taken together, magnitude of effect, articulateness, generalizability, interest level, and credibility can serve as a guide for composing and reviewing the evaluation report. Attention to these concepts can increase the persuasiveness and the utilization of the report.

EVALUATION REPORT WRITING

Conducting an evaluation involves a complex series of decisions regarding purposes, measurement, design, sampling, data gathering, analysis, and interpretation. All of these decisions are described in the evaluation report. Some of the decisions will be influenced by practical, fiscal, or ethical factors. These factors should be explained in the report as well. The purpose of the report is to communicate the results of the evaluation in a thorough manner that helps stakeholders make decisions about the health program that is being evaluated. Because the evaluation report should help stakeholders make decisions, it must be clear, concise, and logically linked to the decisions to be made. Different sections of the evaluation report and specific conclusions should be labeled as relevant to particular decisions. Detailed explanations should describe how results and conclusions can be applied to the decisional purposes of the evaluation. Working closely with stakeholders from the beginning to the end of the project will help ensure the report is on target with their needs and is understood. Evaluation reports are only useful if they are read, understood, and used by decision makers.

The evaluation report needs to describe the evaluation methods in a clear and consice manner, so that readers could replicate the evaluation. They also must be described in sufficient detail to be reproducible. A critical principle of science is **replication**. If the evaluation methods are employed with a similar sample in the future, those evaluators should expect similar results. The report enables replication by describing all evaluation methods. The description of evaluation methods also helps the reader to make informed judgments about the rigor and quality of the evaluation. The reader can then consider the results and conclusions in the context of the rigor of the evaluation methods. Results of evaluations are affected by evaluation methods. Often in the field, evaluators must make decisions that to some extent affect the rigor of the evaluation design. For example, a common weakness in some evaluations is measurement. The use of instruments that do not have established reliability and validity can call into question the quality of measurement and ultimately the results. It is also possible that an instrument with established validity and reliability does not match the precise measurement needs of an evaluation. Many health programs address social support as an important construct to support health behavior change. There are many different types of social support. The limited number of published social support instruments available may not match the precise way in which social support is used in a particular program. Often evaluators find that random selection or random assignment procedures cannot be used due to time or resource constraints. In each of these cases, the evaluator is making pragmatic decisions regarding evaluation methods. Each of these design adaptations contributes to the limitations of the evaluation. These limitations create a context in which the results of the evaluation must be described. The evaluator should carefully describe the evaluation methods, specifically how these methods affect the interpretation of the results. Professional evaluators should also be provided with enough information about evaluation methods so that they can make an informed, independent decision regarding the interpretation of the results.

The evaluation report describes a health concern, a health program to address the health concern, and an evaluation of how well the health program addressed the health concern. Evidence is presented to document the implementation of the health program in the field. It also describes who participated in the program and what benefits participation in the program yielded. The goal of the report to is help stakeholders make data-based decisions about the health program. **Figure 13.2** is an outline of an evaluation report for a comprehensive evaluation. In the outline process, impact and outcome evaluations are

Title page

Title of evaluation project

Time period covered by evaluation

Author of evaluation report

Members of the evaluation team

Agency evaluation was conducted for

Date report was submitted

Executive Summary

Purpose of the evaluation

Health program decisions to be made based on evaluation results

Purpose of the health program being evaluated

Main results, conclusions, and recommendations

Table of Contents

Chapter titles

List of tables

List of figures

Appendices

Health Program Evaluated

Program history

Health concern: Purpose of the program

Program setting/target population

Program theory/logic model

Health program goals and objectives

Program content/process/staff

Process Evaluation

Purpose of process evaluation

Health program objectives

Evaluation methods: sampling, recruitment, instruments

Timeline for assessments/observations

Data coding/data analysis

Results: descriptive statistics, hypothesis testing, effect sizes

Process evaluation: conclusions

Implications/application of process evaluation conclusions

Impact Evaluation

Purpose of the impact evaluation

Health program objectives

Evaluation methods: sampling, recruitment, instruments

Timeline for assessments/observations

Data coding/data analysis

Results: descriptive statistics, hypothesis testing, effect sizes

Impact evaluation: conclusions

Implications/application of impact evaluation conclusions

Outcome Evaluation

Purpose of outcome evaluation

Health program objectives

Evaluation methods: sampling, recruitment, instruments

Timeline for assessments/observations

Data coding/data analysis

Results: descriptive statistics, hypothesis testing, effect sizes

Outcome evaluation: conclusions

Implications/application of outcome evaluation conclusions

Conclusions and Recommendations

Summary of conclusions: process, impact, and outcome evaluations

Synthesis of conclusions from the process, impact, and outcome evaluations

Summary of recommendations for health program improvement

Limitations of evaluation methods

Recommendations for future evaluations of the health program

Figure 13.2   Health education/health promotion program evaluation report outline.

included. Many evaluations do not include all three levels of evaluation, and thus the outline would be adjusted accordingly.

Who Will Read the Evaluation Report?

Before report writing begins, carefully consider the intended audience. Identify the stakeholders that will be reading the report. What is their professional background and training? Be mindful of their technical expertise. Present the report in a direct and understandable manner. What is their level of statistical training? Make sure data is presented in a manner that can be understood. This may require presenting the report in several versions. What decisions do they need to make based on the evaluation results? Write the report directly to the intended decision makers. Your goal is to encourage and support evidence-based decision making. The report may be disseminated to a large number of stakeholders with a wide range of backgrounds and technical expertise. If so, the evaluators may find themselves writing to several audiences. Several versions of the report may need to be tailored to different audience needs.

SECTIONS OF THE EVALUATION REPORT

The following sections provide a detailed description of the sections that make up an evaluation report.

Title Page

An example title page appears in **Figure 13.3**. The title page should contain critical information describing the evaluation project. The title of the evaluation should be descriptive and avoid jargon or technical language. The time period covered by the evaluation should identify the date range from the start of evaluation planning to the date of report completion. The author(s) of the evaluation report should be listed. This is followed by a listing of the members of the evaluation team, if they are different from the authors of the evaluation report. This text advocates for a team approach to evaluation planning. The hope is that the evaluation team will involve a range of stakeholders in the process of designing

---

An Evaluation of the "Walk for Health" Program at Acme Whistle Company

Camillus, New York

Evaluation Report submitted by: A. Lingyak and V. Mature

Evaluation Team: A. Lingyak, B. Joiana, V. Damone, M. Ray

Evaluation time frame: May 2013–April 2014

Submitted to: Human Resources Department, Acme Whistle Company

June 2014

Figure 13.3 Example title page for an evaluation report.

a relevant, utilization-based evaluation. The agency that the evaluation is being submitted to also should be listed. Finally the date the report is submitted should appear on the title page.

Executive Summary

The first section of the report is typically the last section composed. The executive summary is a concise (one- to two-page) summary of the main evaluation findings. Included in this section are the purpose of the evaluation, program objectives, evaluation methods, main results, and main conclusions. However, the approach is not to be exhaustive, but brief. The summary should be clear, direct, and seek to engage decision makers. To generate interest, avoid jargon, speak directly to the purposes of the evaluation, and state the results in a manner the stakeholders can appreciate. If this section is successful, decision makers will want to read the rest of the report. The evaluator will need to have composed the results sections of the process, impact, and outcome evaluations before a concise synthesis is possible; thus, the executive summary is typically written last.

Table of Contents

Evaluation reports are comprehensive by nature. As a consequence, most readers refer to specific sections of the document. The table of contents is a time management tool for many professionals. The evaluation report is often examined in sections. Decision makers jump from section to section as they seek specific information to make different decisions. Make sure to include a list of tables and a list of figures, as well. Descriptive titles for each table and figure help decision makers find what they seek quickly. Evaluation reports can be many pages long, with considerable amounts of technical information. Without a table of contents, decision makers may not find the information they need.

Description of the Health Program Evaluated

The report should include a complete description of the program being evaluated. This provides a context for understanding the design of the evaluation and the evaluation results. Explain the history of the program, including when the program was developed, how often it has been implemented, and any previous evaluations conducted. Explain the health concern the program addresses, the purpose of the program, the setting in which it operates, and the intended target population. Describe the community setting and the nature of the target population. It is critical to present the program logic model, goals, and objectives. This information is key to the design of the evaluation.

Process, Impact, and Outcome Evaluations

Comprehensive evaluation projects conduct all three levels of evaluation (process, impact, and outcome). **Figure 13.4** presents a logic model for evaluation.

The logic model illustrates the functional relationships among the process, impact, and outcome evaluations. Many of the evaluation methods are similar among them. When composing the report, an evaluator may be tempted to combine any or all levels of evaluation

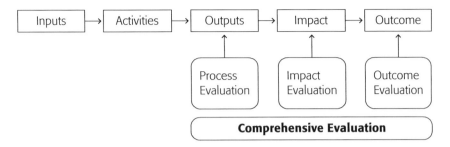

Figure 13.4   A logic model for a comprehensive evaluation.

into one section. The recommended table of contents in Figure 13.2 clearly recommends separate treatment of the process, impact, and outcome evaluations. There are several reasons for this perspective. First, each level of evaluation has different purposes and results, and significant variations in methods. It is helpful for decision makers to keep these different types of evaluations distinct. They should be able to apply the appropriate evaluation to the appropriate programmatic decision. In the report, each level of evaluation should be linked to a specific purpose. This purpose should be associated with the decisions that will be made based on results. Another reason to report the levels of evaluation separately is practical. Evaluation reports can be many pages long. Often the evaluation report is used as a reference document. Decision makers will often use the table of contents to locate, and then refer directly to the section of the document they need to make a decision. Thus, it is important that each level of evaluation be fully reported separately. Doing so is end user friendly and can increase conceptual understanding of the different levels of evaluation.

Process Evaluation

The outputs section of the logic model is the direct services that participants receive as delivered by the health program. These program activities are designed to promote participant behavioral capability and provide environmental supports to encourage health practices and enhance health status. This includes health education programs, as well as environmental supports including health policy, incentives, and access to facilities. Process evaluation can determine whether the program participants are members of the intended target audience. Further, the evaluation can assess program reach—what percentage of the intended target audience was reached by the program. Process evaluation can also assess the quality and degree of health program delivery. Process evaluation is needed to verify that the program was delivered as designed. This step is essential to preventing Type III error. As mentioned earlier, Type III error is basing results of the impact and outcome evaluations on the assumption that the program was delivered as designed when it was not. In practice, programs are rarely delivered exactly as designed. It is more accurate to conceptualize implementation of programs as a matter of degree. As a consequence, it is important for the evaluator to look for relationships between the degree of implementation and subsequent impact of the health program.

The process evaluation section of the evaluation report should begin with a purpose statement. Most process evaluations focus on a small number of the potential targets described earlier. The health program educational objectives and programmatic objectives should be listed and linked to the purposes of the evaluation. Process evaluation methods and protocols should be precisely described. This enables professionals to replicate the process evaluation methods in the future. It also enables stakeholders to consider the results of the process evaluation in the context of the evaluation methods. Results are systematically presented. First, descriptive statistics are used to describe program participants. This is followed by descriptive information on data-gathering instruments. The descriptive data allows the reader to examine distributions and patterns in the data. This is followed by hypothesis testing and presentation of effect sizes to help stakeholders understand the magnitude of change produced in targeted variables.

Evaluators have the responsibility to conservatively formulate conclusions that are evidence based. The conclusions should be presented in the context of the strengths and limitations of the evaluation methods employed. Special care should be taken to ensure that the conclusions are unbiased and objective. Generally speaking, implications should not be prescriptive. Do not tell decision makers what they should do. Rather, the implications should suggest a range of options for program refinement that are linked to the evaluation evidence.

Impact Evaluation

The impact section of the logic model represents the changes in health program participants' knowledge, skills, motivation, and health behavior. The impact section also includes environmental supports participants are exposed to. Examples of environmental supports include incentives, public recognition, access to facilities, and policies that support health practices. Short-term impact is measurable from the final session of the health program to 6 months after program exposure. The evaluator should focus on several critical questions to support the logic model approach to evaluation. A fundamental question is to determine whether health program participants acquired the intended knowledge, skills, and motivation targeted in program objectives. A related issue is whether the increases in knowledge, skills, and motivation were sufficient to promote and sustain health behavior change in participants. Did the participants receive targeted environmental supports? What effects did the environmental supports have on the participants? Were the targeted health behaviors practiced with sufficient quality to produce changes in health status targeted in the outcome evaluation? A final key question is to determine whether the health behaviors are sustained over time to maintain changes in health status. It is important to keep in mind that the potential impact evaluation questions listed here are not exhaustive; still, it is unlikely that any particular evaluation will address all of these potential questions. To do so would in many cases be very costly and go beyond the evaluation needs of decision makers in a particular setting.

The impact evaluation section of the evaluation report should begin with a purpose statement. The statement clearly identifies and delimits the purpose of the impact evaluation. The health behavior objectives should be listed and linked to the purposes of the evaluation. Impact evaluation methods and protocols should be precisely described. This enables professionals to replicate the impact evaluation methods in the future. It also enables stakeholders to consider the results of the impact evaluation in the context of the methods. Results are systematically presented. Descriptive statistics are used to describe participants. Descriptive data on instruments used to gather information on participant impact is presented. The descriptive data enables the reader to examine distributions and patterns in the data. This is followed by hypothesis testing and presentation of effect sizes to help stakeholders understand the magnitude of change produced in targeted educational, environmental, and behavioral variables. Evaluators have the responsibility to conservatively formulate conclusions that are evidence based. The conclusions should be presented in the context of the strengths and limitations of the impact evaluation methods employed. Care should be taken to ensure that the conclusions are unbiased and objective. Implications should not be prescriptive, telling decision makers what they should do. Rather, the implications should suggest a range of options for program refinement that are linked to the evaluation evidence.

Outcome Evaluation

Outcomes in the logic model are the changes in community participants. Outcomes generally focus on issues related to health status or quality of life produced by the health education/promotion program activities. The time frame for outcome-level changes depends on the temporal relationship between health behavior change and detectable changes in health status. Typically, evaluators look for changes in health status starting about 6 months after the health program concludes. Changes in some programs may be more evident 1 to 2 years after the health program. For example, a physical activity program can produce changes in physical fitness in as quickly as 8 to 12 weeks. But changes in body mass or blood lipid profiles may take several months to be detectable. Changes in healthcare costs or morbidity may take several years to detect. Another critical issue is whether the changes in health status are short lived or maintained over time. The maintenance of health status gains would be dependent on several factors, including continuation of health program delivery, a population that can be tracked over time, and no major outside factors influencing health status. Again, long-term monitoring would be required to address maintenance of health outcomes.

The outcome evaluation section of the evaluation report should begin with a purpose statement. The statement clearly identifies and delimits the purpose of the outcome evaluation. The health status goals should be listed and linked to the purposes of the evaluation. Outcome evaluation methods and protocols should be precisely described. This enables professionals to replicate the outcome evaluation methods in the future. It also enables stakeholders to consider the results of the outcome evaluation in the context of the methods. Results are systematically presented. Descriptive statistics are used to describe participants. This is followed by descriptive data on instruments used to gather information on participant outcomes. The descriptive data enables the reader to examine distributions and patterns in the data. This is followed by hypothesis testing and presentation of effect sizes to help stakeholders understand the magnitude of change produced in health status or quality of life variables. Evaluators have the responsibility to conservatively formulate conclusions that are evidence based. The conclusions should be presented in the context of the strengths and limitations of the outcome evaluation methods employed. Care should be taken to ensure that the conclusions are unbiased and objective. Implications should not be prescriptive, telling decision makers what they should do. Rather, the implications should suggest a range of options for health program refinement that are linked to the evaluation evidence.

Conclusions and Recommendations

Summary of Conclusions: Process, Impact, and Outcome Evaluations

The final section of the evaluation report should be composed with **sensitivity** to the purposes of the evaluation and the political context in which the health program exists (Mohr, 1992). It would be naïve for an evaluator to assume that an evaluation does not exist in a political climate. Programs and professionals are being judged and worth is being estimated. Stakeholders may have widely different views on the interpretation of evidence or even the validity of evidence. For example, a rigorous evaluation of a teen pregnancy prevention program has been conducted. Regardless of the results of the evaluation, interpretations of the data may vary widely. Supporters and opponents of the program are likely to have sharply different conclusions. Opponents may question the need for the program regardless of the evaluation results. An evaluator should expect decision makers (program funders, program managers, program professionals) to carefully scrutinize the evaluation results in the context of a whole range of political concerns. Evaluators should attempt to identify the stakeholders of a health program. By identifying the motives of stakeholders, the evaluator can attempt to respond to the wide range of concerns that will ultimately determine the usefulness of an evaluation. Evaluation reports have the potential to be used by stakeholders to forward personal agendas. Their personal agendas can be supportive of the health program, but also can be contrary to the program. The goal of the evaluator is to be objective and balanced. All conclusions should be grounded in evaluation evidence. Evaluators should be particularly careful to ensure that their personal values and beliefs do not influence the interpretation of the results.

Evaluation conclusions should focus specifically on the needs of consumers and practitioners. This view is essential to designing an evaluation that is relevant to stakeholders (Cronbach, 1982). The goal is to provide useful information that is sensitive to political realities and program constraints. Patton (1997) argues that the primary concern is utilization of evaluation results. As a consequence, the evaluation should be designed around the information needs of program managers, program staff, and consumers (Mercier, 1997). This text strongly advocates for the formation of evaluation teams and the utilization-focused evaluation approach. To conduct a utilization-focused evaluation requires the evaluator to actively engage decision makers (e.g., funders, program managers, professional staff) in the evaluation planning process. And the evaluation needs to provide a utility in the real world (Dibella, 1990). The evaluator needs to discuss the principles of utilization-focused evaluation with decision makers. These principles include active engagement of decision makers, clearly identifying program decisions to be made, specifying the evidence needed to make a decision, and developing a plan for implementing decisions. The evaluator should outline the potentials and the limitations of the evaluation data in hopes of setting realistic expectations. A critical step is carefully defining the evidence needed to make program decisions. Generally speaking, the rigor of the evaluation (measurement, design, etc.) should match the importance and consequences of the decision to be made. For example, if an evaluation is being conducted to determine whether a health program should be eliminated or expanded, considerable rigor and evaluation resources should focus on program effectiveness. Finally, a method for implementation of decisions should be outlined (Florio, Behrmann, & Goltz, 1995). This step clarifies the specifics of how the evaluation data will be interpreted and how the evaluation conclusions will be used by the organization to improve or refine the health program. The goal of utilization-based evaluation is fairness and transparency. The evaluation is designed to answer questions that have been publicly discussed and agreed upon. Further, an agreed-upon method of generating credible evidence is established. These steps can build trust and cooperation directed towards the constructive and continuous refinement of health programs.

Conclusions should be stated in clear and concise language. Technical and statistical jargon should be avoided. Descriptive statistics and hypothesis tests were reported earlier in the report. Conclusions should focus on the practical significance of the evidence. Specific efforts should be made to describe effect sizes in practical terms. Take time to explain meaningful changes in impact and outcome measures produced by participation in the health program. Answer fundamental questions related to health program effectiveness. Was the program delivered as designed? How much did participants learn? Was learning linked to health behavior changes? Is there evidence that health behavior changes were maintained? Were changes in health behavior linked to improvements in health status? Practical and precise answers to these questions go a long way towards helping stakeholders appreciate the utility of the evaluation report.

Synthesis of Conclusions from the Process, Impact, and Outcome

The synthesis of conclusions from the process, impact, and outcome evaluations is an important part of the evaluation report (Hendricks & Papagiannis, 1990). This text supports the use of the logic model for health program and evaluation planning. The logic model maps the intended linkages between the health program and outputs, impact, and outcomes. The synthesis section of the evaluation report attempts to directly comment on the intended linkages between health programs, participant learning, and health status. Clearly, there are strong conceptual linkages illustrated in the logic model. Many of the functional relationships are examined by careful synthesis of results across the three levels of health program evaluation. The results of the process, impact, and outcome evaluations should be considered parts of a meaningful whole. Taken together, the synthesis of results from the three levels of evaluation can yield information about the effectiveness of health programs that separate analyses of process, impact, and outcome evaluations cannot

TABLE 13.2 Potential Functional Relationships Among Process, Impact, and Outcome Evaluations		
Process Evaluation	**Impact Evaluation**	**Outcome Evaluation**
Program recruitment	Participant learning	Health status change
Program reach	Health behavior change	Health status maintenance
Program quality	Link between learning and behavior	Quality of life
Program implementation	Behavior mediators	Medical care costs
Environmental supports	Health behavior maintenance	Productivity
Participant satisfaction	Social support	

produce. **Table 13.2** depicts the functional relationship among factors targeted in process, impact, and outcome evaluations.

Most evaluations will not address all of these potential factors, but most evaluations will address many of them. This section of the evaluation report should explicitly address the linkages that were tested in the evaluation. For example, if the evaluation can link health program implementation fidelity to health behavior maintenance, which in turn can be associated with improvements in health status, this is powerful evidence that the program is indeed effective.

Conclusions and Recommendations

This section begins with a summary of the conclusions from the process, impact, and outcome evaluations. But this section is not just a compilation of previously stated conclusions; rather, it is a reasoned analysis of the inter-relationships among the process, impact, and outcome evaluations. Based on the logic model, recruitment strategies will reach the intended target audience. The health program will be implemented as designed. Participation in the health program is designed to produce changes (knowledge, skill, motivation, etc.) in participants that cause changes in health behaviors. Adherence to health behaviors are thought to be linked to changes in health status. By careful synthesis of the process, impact, and outcome evaluations, the logic model can be tested to determine which relationships are supported and which are not. Conversely, this synthesis can also identify weak links in the causal chain mapped by the logic model. This synthesis can lead to important insights for program improvement.

For example, a process evaluation might reveal considerable variability in the fidelity of implementation across different settings for the same program. An important question is whether implementation fidelity is linked to participant learning. If implementation is linked to learning, evidence exists for program effectiveness. If implementation is not linked to learning, it suggests that the program should be revised. Taking this example one step further, are higher levels of participant learning linked to higher levels of behavior change? If so, then the assumptions of the program logic model are supported. If not, the evaluator may try to determine whether there are alternative explanations for health behavior change. But clearly, the program logic model was not supported. The same type of analysis can be applied to the assumed linkages between health practices and anticipated changes in health status. These logic model questions are answered by synthesizing the results of the three levels of evaluation.

Limitations of Evaluation Methods

It is common for the evaluator to gain valuable experience in the field while implementing the evaluation. Evaluation in applied settings often requires that methods be adapted and sometimes compromised. Real-world constraints on resources (e.g., time, money) and unanticipated factors require adaptations to the original evaluation plan. For example, many health promotion settings do not allow random assignment of participants to treatment and control conditions. As a consequence, there are often limitations in evaluation methods, which the evaluator should list. This section should explicitly describe the limitations of the evaluation methods. An effort should then be made to describe how the limitation did affect or could have affected the results and conclusions of the evaluation. Referring back to the inability to use random assignment, it is clear that many threats to internal validity cannot be strictly controlled. The evaluator should always explicitly describe limitations that could affect the interpretation of results.

Recommendations for Future Evaluations of the Health Program

After implementation of the evaluation plan in real-world conditions and after composing the evaluation report, the evaluator has had time to reflect on the entire project. It is an opportune time to make recommendations for future evaluations. What questions should be asked? Should different evaluation methods be employed? Should different measurement methods be considered? In retrospect, the evaluator can think of creative solutions to enhance the scientific rigor and utility of future evaluations. The evaluator is offering a set of constructive suggestions about how to improve the evaluation in the future.

FOCUS FEATURE 13.1   EXAMPLE OF AN EVALUATION REPORT IN HEALTH EDUCATION

Purpose of the project: To recruit and train promotora (lay person promoters, educators) to educate about the healthy management of diabetes among Spanish-speaking members of the community.

Purpose of the evaluation: An impact evaluation to determine the effects of promotora training on participant comfort level to present diabetes information, confidence to answer questions about diabetes, and attitudes towards diabetes.

(continues)

FOCUS FEATURE 13.1   EXAMPLE OF AN EVALUATION REPORT IN HEALTH EDUCATION *(Continued)*

First-Year Evaluation Report of Training of Promotoras on Diabetes Mellitus

Evaluation report submitted by:

Manoj Sharma, MBBS, PhD

Evaluation time frame: June 2012–May 2013

Submitted to: Knox County Health Department

May 2013

Executive Summary

This report summarizes the results from first-year evaluation of the project X funded through Foundation XX to Agency Y in City YY. For this evaluation, a pretest–posttest single group design was chosen. A Diabetes Knowledge Test (DKT) and Diabetes Attitude Scale (DAS-3), developed and validated by Michigan Diabetes Research and Training Center (MDRTC), were used for this evaluation. The results of the evaluation will be used to improve the training program.

A total of 21 participants completed the training between September 2006 and May 2007. This number fell short of the target planned by the project. The majority of participants were women (93.8%). The age of the participants ranged from 30 years to 63 years, with a mean of 43.13 years. More than half (53.3%) of the participants were unemployed. The majority (87.5%) of the participants were Hispanic Americans. The majority of the participants were from Mexico (41.17%).

The purpose of this evaluation of training of promotoras focused on three aspects. The first aspect was the self-perception in comfort level to present information to clients, confidence to answer questions about diabetes, and perception about having all the information about diabetes. With regard to this first aspect, the training program was a success. The training increased the number of participants who agreed or strongly agreed that they had the comfort level to present information to clients, they had the confidence to answer questions about diabetes, and they had all the information about diabetes.

The second aspect was knowledge gain as measured on the Michigan Diabetes Knowledge Test (DKT); in this regard the training has not been able to demonstrate any change. This could be due to lack of consonance between the program and the tests, not enough emphasis on retention of salient aspects, and not enough time to apply the knowledge acquired. Future training programs should make efforts to improve knowledge acquisition.

The third aspect pertained to the five types of attitudes as measured on the Michigan Diabetes Attitude Scale (DAS-3). These five categories of attitudes were (1) need for special training, (2) seriousness of non-insulin-dependent diabetes mellitus (NIDDM), (3) value of tight control, (4) psychosocial impact of diabetes mellitus (DM), and (5) patient autonomy. The training was able to demonstrate change in two aspects: seriousness of NIDDM and psychosocial impact of DM. These represent a success of the program. With regard to the attitude of needing special training, there was no need to emphasize this aspect because it was found to be already quite high in the participants. But there is a need to underscore the attitudes of value of tight control and patient autonomy in the future training programs.

FOCUS FEATURE 13.1   EXAMPLE OF AN EVALUATION REPORT IN HEALTH EDUCATION *(Continued)*

Table of Contents

List of Tables

(continues)

FOCUS FEATURE 13.1   EXAMPLE OF AN EVALUATION REPORT IN HEALTH EDUCATION *(Continued)*

List of Figures

Promotora Training Program

This report summarizes the results from first-year evaluation of project X, funded through Foundation XX to Agency Y in City YY. In the first year, the project planned on training a cadre of Latino *promotores de salud* in the area of diabetes mellitus. A three-session training program was developed. Each session consisted of 4 hours of training (total of 12 hours of training). The first session included a 1-hour pretest and 3 hours of general information on diabetes mellitus. The second session consisted of more information on diabetes mellitus and information on nutritional aspects pertaining to diabetes management. The third session was geared toward exercise and also had hands-on practice sessions on blood pressure testing, use of glucometers, and the like. The session concluded with the administration of the posttest. All sessions were conducted in Spanish.

Evaluation Design and Instrumentation

For this evaluation, a pretest–posttest single group design was chosen. The instruments chosen for this evaluation were the instruments developed and validated by Michigan Diabetes Research and Training Center (MDRTC). The first instrument was the Diabetes Knowledge Test (DKT), which is a multiple choice test consisting of 23 knowledge test items. These 23 items represent a test of general knowledge of diabetes. The first 14 items are general and the next 9 items are the insulin use subscale. Both subscales are valid and reliable (Fitzgerald et al., 1998). The scale has also been validated in Spanish (Campo, Vargas, Martinez-Terrer, & Cia, 1992). The 23-item test takes approximately 15 minutes to complete.

The second instrument chosen was the Diabetes Attitude Scale (DAS-3). This is the third version of the scale, and is congruent with current scientific knowledge about diabetes, has improved internal reliability scores, and is shorter with 33 items (Anderson, Fitzgerald, Funnell, & Gruppen, 1998). It has five discrete subscales. The subscales measure attitudes pertaining to:

FOCUS FEATURE 13.1   EXAMPLE OF AN EVALUATION REPORT IN HEALTH EDUCATION *(Continued)*

- Need for special training to provide diabetes care

- Seriousness of type 2 diabetes mellitus or NIDDM

- Value of tight glucose control

- Psychosocial impact of diabetes

- Attitude toward patient autonomy

It is a valid and reliable scale that is used for comparison across different groups of healthcare professionals and/or patients. The scale's developers also recommend this scale for program evaluations (Anderson, Fitzgerald, Funnell, & Gruppen, 1998).

In addition, seven demographic questions pertaining to group of training, sex, age, education, employment, national origin, and race were also included on the pretest. Further, three training process questions each were asked on the pretest and posttest. These questions pertained to comfort level in presenting information to clients, confidence to answer questions correctly about diabetes, and information needed to share with clients about diabetes.

The pretests were collected at the first session and the posttests were collected at the last session. All data were analyzed using SPSS, Version 14.0.

Evaluation Results

A total of 21 participants completed the training between September 2006 and May 2007. The training was held in four groups. The first group was trained by the educator from University YYY and the training was conducted in Spanish. The remaining three training programs were conducted in Spanish by the staff and Agency X. The second group received training on three Saturdays between 9 am and 1 pm. The third group received training on three weekday mornings between 9 am and 1 pm, and the fourth group received training on three weekday afternoons between 2 pm and 6 pm. **Table 1** and **Figure 1** summarize the distribution of participants in each of the four groups of training.

Table 1

Distribution of Participants by Group of Training

		Frequency	Percentage	Valid Percentage	Cumulative Percentage
Valid	Group 1	5	23.8	23.8	23.8
	Group 2	3	14.3	14.3	38.1
	Group 3	8	38.1	38.1	76.2
	Group 4	5	23.8	23.8	100.0
	Total	21	100.0	100.0	

(continues)

FOCUS FEATURE 13.1   EXAMPLE OF AN EVALUATION REPORT IN HEALTH EDUCATION *(Continued)*

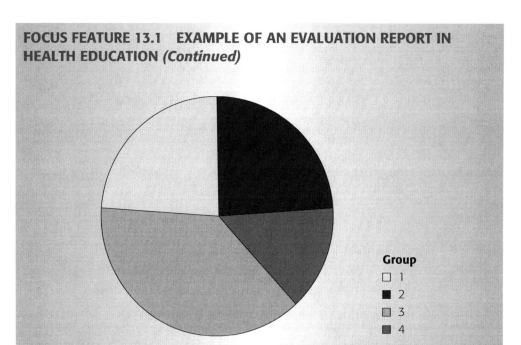

Group
☐ 1
■ 2
▨ 3
■ 4

Figure 1   Distribution of participants by training group (*n* = 21).

Table 2 summarizes the sex of participants. It is worth noting that the majority of participants were women (93.8%). The age of the participants ranged from 30 years to 63 years, with a mean of 43.13 years (standard deviation 12.13).

Table 2

Distribution of the Sex of Participants

		Frequency	Percentage	Valid Percentage	Cumulative Percentage
Valid	Female	15	71.4	93.8	93.8
	Male	1	4.8	6.3	100.0
	Total	16	76.2	100.0	
Missing	System	5	23.8		
	Total	21	100.0		

FOCUS FEATURE 13.1   EXAMPLE OF AN EVALUATION REPORT IN HEALTH EDUCATION *(Continued)*

Table 3 summarizes the employment status of the participants. More than half (53.3%) of the participants were unemployed.

Table 3

Distribution of Employment Status of Participants

		Frequency	Percentage	Valid Percentage	Cumulative Percentage
Valid	Unemployed	8	38.1	53.3	53.3
	Part time	0	0.0	0.0	53.3
	Full time	7	33.3	46.7	100.0
	Total	15	71.4	100.0	
Missing	System	6	28.6		
Total		21	100.0		

Table 4 summarizes the distribution of racial status of the participants. The majority (87.5%) of the participants were Hispanic Americans. **Table 5** summarizes the national origin of the participants. The majority of the participants were from Mexico (41.17%). One participant was from the United States.

Table 4

Distribution of Racial Status of Participants

		Frequency	Percentage	Valid Percentage	Cumulative Percentage
Valid	Caucasian American	1	4.8	6.3	6.3
	Hispanic American	14	66.7	87.5	93.8
	Asian American	1	4.8	6.3	100.0
	Total	16	76.2	100.0	
Missing	System	5	23.8		
Total		21	100.0		

(continues)

FOCUS FEATURE 13.1   EXAMPLE OF AN EVALUATION REPORT IN HEALTH EDUCATION *(Continued)*

Table 5

Distribution of the Country of Origin of Participants

Country	Frequency	Percentage
Mexico	7	41.17
Peru	3	17.64
Panama	3	17.64
Honduras	2	11.76
Guatemala	1	5.88
United States	1	5.88
Total	17	100.00

Table 6 summarizes the responses to the question about how comfortable the participants were about presenting diabetes information to clients at pretest. The majority (78.6%) felt comfortable. **Table 7** presents the response to the same question at posttest. It is worth noting that all 100% either agreed or strongly agreed with this aspect. It would be fair to say that the training program made all the participants comfortable about presenting diabetes information.

Table 6

Distribution of Responses About Being Comfortable Presenting Diabetes Information at Pretest

		Frequency	Percentage	Valid Percentage	Cumulative Percentage
Valid	Disagree	3	14.3	21.4	21.4
	Agree	5	23.8	35.7	57.1
	Strongly agree	6	28.6	42.9	100.0
	Total	14	66.7	100.0	
Missing	System	7	33.3		
Total		21	100.0		

FOCUS FEATURE 13.1   EXAMPLE OF AN EVALUATION REPORT IN HEALTH EDUCATION (Continued)

Table 7

Distribution of Responses About Being Comfortable Presenting Diabetes Information at Posttest After Training

		Frequency	Percentage	Valid Percentage	Cumulative Percentage
Valid	Agree	6	28.6	40.0	40.0
	Strongly agree	9	42.9	60.0	100.0
	Total	15	71.4	100.0	
Missing	System	6	28.6		
Total		21	100.0		

Table 8 summarizes the information about how confident participants were about answering questions about diabetes correctly at pretest. A majority of the participants (57.1%) were not confident. **Table 9** summarizes the information about how confident participants were about answering questions about diabetes correctly at posttest. All 100% of the participants either agreed or strongly agreed with this aspect at posttest. The self-perception of the participants about answering questions related to diabetes increased as a result of the training.

Table 8

Distribution of Responses About Being Confident to Answer Questions About Diabetes Correctly at Pretest

		Frequency	Percentage	Valid Percentage	Cumulative Percentage
Valid	Strongly disagree	2	9.5	14.3	14.3
	Disagree	6	28.6	42.9	57.1
	Agree	3	14.3	21.4	78.6
	Strongly agree	3	14.3	21.4	100.0
	Total	14	66.7	100.0	
Missing	System	7	33.3		
Total		21	100.0		

(continues)

FOCUS FEATURE 13.1   EXAMPLE OF AN EVALUATION REPORT IN HEALTH EDUCATION *(Continued)*

Table 9

Distribution of Responses About Being Confident to Answer Questions About Diabetes Correctly at Posttest After Training

		Frequency	Percentage	Valid Percentage	Cumulative Percentage
Valid	Agree	7	33.3	46.7	46.7
	Strongly agree	8	38.1	53.3	100.0
	Total	15	71.4	100.0	
Missing	System	6	28.6		
Total		21	100.0		

Table 10 summarizes the distribution of responses about having all the information about diabetes at pretest. A majority of the respondents (76.9%) thought they did not have adequate information about diabetes at pretest. **Table 11** summarizes the distribution of responses about having all the information about diabetes at posttest. All 100% of the participants either agreed or strongly agreed with this aspect at posttest. The self-perception of the participants about the training having provided all the information they needed to share with the clients improved as a result of the training.

Table 10

Distribution of Responses About Having All the Information About Diabetes at Pretest

		Frequency	Percentage	Valid Percentage	Cumulative Percentage
Valid	Strongly disagree	3	14.3	23.1	23.1
	Disagree	7	33.3	53.8	76.9
	Agree	3	14.3	23.1	100.0
	Total	13	61.9	100.0	
Missing	System	8	38.1		
Total		21	100.0		

FOCUS FEATURE 13.1   EXAMPLE OF AN EVALUATION REPORT IN HEALTH EDUCATION *(Continued)*

Table 11

Distribution of Responses About Having All the Information About Diabetes at Posttest After Training

		Frequency	Percentage	Valid Percentage	Cumulative Percentage
Valid	Agree	6	28.6	40.0	40.0
	Strongly agree	9	42.9	60.0	100.0
	Total	15	71.4	100.0	
Missing	System	6	28.6		
Total		21	100.0		

Table 12 summarizes the distribution of knowledge scores by group at pretest and posttest on the Michigan Diabetes Knowledge Test (DKT). The maximum possible score of 23 was not achieved by any of the participants at either the pretest or the posttest. The minimum score at pretest was 0 and at posttest 5. The maximum score at pretest was 15 and at posttest 18. The mean score at pretest was 11.20 and at posttest it was 12.05. As shown in **Table 13** there was no significant difference between mean pretest and posttest scores on knowledge both overall and for individual groups.

Table 12

Distribution of Knowledge Scores by Group at Pretest and Posttest

Group (*n*)	Pretest Mean	Pretest Standard Deviation	Posttest Mean	Posttest Standard Deviation
1 (5)	12.40	1.95	13.20	3.63
2 (3)	12.67	1.15	10.33	3.05
3 (8)	11.62	1.19	13.00	2.67
4 (4)	7.75	5.19	10.00	4.69
Total (20)	11.20	3.00	12.05	3.46

(continues)

FOCUS FEATURE 13.1   EXAMPLE OF AN EVALUATION REPORT IN HEALTH EDUCATION *(Continued)*

Table 13

Repeated Measures Analysis of Variance on Pretest and Posttest Knowledge Scores by Group

Source	factor1	Type III Sum of Squares	df	Mean Square	F	Sig.
factor1	Linear	2.408	1	2.408	0.621	0.442
factor1 * Group	Linear	20.229	3	6.743	1.739	0.199
Error (factor1)	Linear	62.046	16	3.878		

Table 14 summarizes the mean scores by group on pretest and posttest on the need for special training subscale of the Michigan Diabetes Attitude Scale (DAS-3). There are five items on this subscale. At both pretest and posttest, the attitude mean was quite high. Most participants believed that there is a need for special training on diabetes for promotoras and healthcare professionals. Because the attitude mean was already quite high, there was no statistically significant increase between pretest and posttest, as shown in **Table 15**.

Table 14

Distribution of Scores on Attitudes Pertaining to Need for Special Training

Group (*n*)	Pretest Mean	Pretest Standard Deviation	Posttest Mean	Posttest Standard Deviation
1 (5)	4.60	0.42	4.56	0.22
2 (3)	4.73	0.23	4.87	0.23
3 (7)	4.46	0.56	4.60	0.35
4 (4)	4.45	0.44	4.70	0.48
Total (19)	4.54	0.44	4.65	0.32

FOCUS FEATURE 13.1   EXAMPLE OF AN EVALUATION REPORT IN HEALTH EDUCATION *(Continued)*

Table 15

Repeated Measures Analysis of Variance on Pretest and Posttest Scores on Attitudes Pertaining to Need for Special Training by Group

Source	factor1	Type III Sum of Squares	df	Mean Square	F	Sig.
factor1	Linear	0.128	1	0.128	1.022	0.328
factor1 * Group	Linear	0.100	3	0.033	0.266	0.849
Error (factor1)	Linear	1.873	15	0.125		

Table 16 summarizes the mean scores by group on pretest and posttest on the seriousness of NIDDM subscale of the Michigan Diabetes Attitude Scale (DAS-3). This is an average score on seven items. **Table 17** shows the results from repeated measures analysis of variance and signifies that there is statistically significant improvement in the scores from pretest to posttest. The training has been successful in improving the attitude pertaining to seriousness of NIDDM among the promotoras.

Table 16

Distribution of Scores on Attitudes Pertaining to Seriousness of NIDDM

Group (*n*)	Pretest Mean	Pretest Standard Deviation	Posttest Mean	Posttest Standard Deviation
1 (5)	4.20	0.35	4.31	0.25
2 (3)	3.29	0.52	3.71	1.27
3 (8)	3.64	0.52	3.59	0.74
4 (4)	3.61	0.80	4.39	0.24
Total (20)	3.72	0.59	4.05	0.73

(continues)

FOCUS FEATURE 13.1   EXAMPLE OF AN EVALUATION REPORT IN HEALTH EDUCATION *(Continued)*

Table 17

Repeated Measures Analysis of Variance on Pretest and Posttest Scores on Attitudes Pertaining to Seriousness of NIDDM by Group

Source	factor1	Type III Sum of Squares	df	Mean Square	F	Sig.
factor1	Linear	0.895	1	0.895	4.981	0.040
factor1 * Group	Linear	1.032	3	0.344	1.915	0.168
Error (factor1)	Linear	2.874	16	0.180		

Table 18 summarizes the mean scores by group on pretest and posttest on the value of tight control subscale of the Michigan Diabetes Attitude Scale (DAS-3). This is an average score on seven items. **Table 19** shows the results from repeated measures analysis of variance and signifies that there is no significant change between pretest and posttest scores. This is an aspect that needs greater attention during future training.

Table 18

Distribution of Scores on Attitudes Pertaining to Value of Tight Control

Group (n)	Pretest Mean	Pretest Standard Deviation	Posttest Mean	Posttest Standard Deviation
1 (5)	4.11	0.29	4.14	0.67
2 (3)	3.33	0.46	3.52	0.82
3 (8)	3.62	0.64	3.80	0.71
4 (4)	3.29	0.16	3.61	0.24
Total (20)	3.63	0.54	3.81	0.64

FOCUS FEATURE 13.1   EXAMPLE OF AN EVALUATION REPORT IN HEALTH EDUCATION *(Continued)*

Table 19

Repeated Measures Analysis of Variance on Pretest and Posttest Scores on Attitudes Pertaining to Value of Tight Control by Group

Source	factor1	Type III Sum of Squares	df	Mean Square	F	Sig.
factor1	Linear	0.285	1	0.285	2.599	0.126
factor1 * Group	Linear	0.097	3	0.032	0.295	0.829
Error (factor1)	Linear	1.752	16	0.110		

Table 20 summarizes the mean scores by group on pretest and posttest on the psychosocial impact of DM subscale of the Michigan Diabetes Attitude Scale (DAS-3). This is an average score on six items. **Table 21** shows the results from repeated measures analysis of variance and signifies that there is statistically significant improvement in the scores from pretest to posttest. The training has been successful in helping the promotoras appreciate the psychosocial impact of diabetes mellitus.

Table 20

Distribution of Scores on Attitudes Pertaining to Psychosocial Impact of DM

Group (*n*)	Pretest Mean	Pretest Standard Deviation	Posttest Mean	Posttest Standard Deviation
1 (5)	3.87	0.30	4.17	0.62
2 (3)	3.94	0.58	4.39	0.42
3 (8)	3.65	0.65	3.52	0.69
4 (4)	4.08	0.17	4.46	0.60
Total (20)	3.83	0.50	4.00	0.71

(continues)

FOCUS FEATURE 13.1   EXAMPLE OF AN EVALUATION REPORT IN HEALTH EDUCATION *(Continued)*

Table 21

Repeated Measures Analysis of Variance on Pretest and Posttest Scores on Attitudes Pertaining to Psychosocial Impact of DM by Group

Source	factor1	Type III Sum of Squares	df	Mean Square	F	Sig.
factor1	Linear	0.544	1	0.544	5.716	0.029
factor1 * Group	Linear	0.587	3	0.196	2.055	0.147
Error (factor1)	Linear	1.524	16	0.095		

Table 22 summarizes the mean scores by group on pretest and posttest on the patient autonomy subscale of the Michigan Diabetes Attitude Scale (DAS-3). This is an average score on eight items. **Table 23** shows the results from repeated measures analysis of variance and signifies that there is no significant change between pretest and posttest scores. This is an aspect that needs greater attention during future training.

Table 22

Distribution of Scores on Attitudes Pertaining to Patient Autonomy

Group (*n*)	Pretest Mean	Pretest Standard Deviation	Posttest Mean	Posttest Standard Deviation
1 (5)	4.02	0.37	4.02	0.48
2 (3)	4.08	0.26	3.96	0.71
3 (8)	3.62	0.59	4.02	0.67
4 (4)	4.25	0.46	4.47	0.61
Total (20)	3.92	0.51	4.10	0.60

FOCUS FEATURE 13.1 EXAMPLE OF AN EVALUATION REPORT IN HEALTH EDUCATION *(Continued)*

Table 23

Repeated Measures Analysis of Variance on Pretest and Posttest Scores on Attitudes Pertaining to Patient Autonomy by Group

Source	factor1	Type III Sum of Squares	df	Mean Square	F	Sig.
factor1	Linear	0.129	1	0.129	0.783	0.389
factor1 * Group	Linear	0.401	3	0.134	0.811	0.506
Error (factor1)	Linear	2.638	16	0.165		

Discussion

In the first year of the program, 21 participants have been trained thus far. This number has fallen short of the target that was planned by the project. It is difficult to recruit promotoras, but clearly more effort needs to be undertaken to identify and train more promotoras.

This evaluation of training of promotoras focused primarily on three aspects. The first aspect was the self-perception in comfort level to present information to clients, confidence to answer questions about diabetes, and perception about having all the information about diabetes. The second aspect was knowledge gain as measured on the Michigan Diabetes Knowledge Test (DKT). The third aspect pertained to changes in the five types of attitudes as measured on the Michigan Diabetes Attitude Scale (DAS-3). These five categories of attitudes were (1) need for special training, (2) seriousness of NIDDM, (3) value of tight control, (4) psychosocial impact of diabetes mellitus, and (5) patient autonomy.

With regard to the first aspect (improving the self-perception of the participants), the training program was a success. The training increased the number of participants who agreed or strongly agreed that they had the comfort level to present information to clients, they had the confidence to answer questions about diabetes, and they had all the information about diabetes. Improving this confidence level of the participants is an important part of being able to function as a promotora for diabetes education. Future training efforts should continue to build on this aspect.

With regard to the second aspect (knowledge gain), the training has not been able to demonstrate any change. Several things need to be done for future training programs. First, there must be a direct link between the program content and what is being tested on the knowledge test. Second, there must be an emphasis to help participants retain important information. A fact sheet or something of that nature can be designed to improve retention. Third, there could be a follow-up test after the participants have had a chance to work in the field and apply some of the knowledge they have learned. This could also show some improvement in their knowledge.

With regard to the third aspect (the five categories of attitudes), the training was able to demonstrate change in two aspects: seriousness of NIDDM and psychosocial impact of DM. This is a success of the program. With regard to the attitude of needing special training, there is no need to emphasize this because it is already quite high in the participants. However, there is a need to underscore the attitudes of value of tight control and patient autonomy in future training programs.

(continues)

FOCUS FEATURE 13.1   EXAMPLE OF AN EVALUATION REPORT IN HEALTH EDUCATION *(Continued)*

References

Anderson, R. M., Fitzgerald, J. T., Funnell, M. M., & Gruppen, L. D. (1998). The third version of diabetes attitude scale. *Diabetes Care, 21*(9), 1403–1407.

Campo, J. M., Vargas, M. E., Martinez-Terrer, T., & Cia, P. (1992). [Adaptation and validation of a test on knowledge about diabetes mellitus][Spanish]. *Aten Primaria, 9*(2), 100–105.

Fitzgerald, J. T., Funnell, M. M., Hess, G. E., Barr, P. A., Anderson, R. M., Hiss, R. G., & Davis, W. K. (1998). The reliability and validity of a brief diabetes knowledge test. *Diabetes Care, 21*(5), 706–710.

SKILL-BUILDING ACTIVITY

A study to promote physical activity at the worksite has been conducted. The study randomly assigned 30 employees to an experimental group and 30 employees to a control group. The treatment group received a theory-based program to increase self-regulation of physical activity. The control group received an incentive-based program. Pre- and post-test data are presented in the table below. The table below lists the data for the following variables:

    Treatment E = experimental group   C = control group
    Knowledge = pre-test scores
    Self-efficacy = pre-test scores
    Self-regulation = pre-test scores
    Activity = pre-test minutes of activity
    pKnowledge = post-test scores
    pSelf-efficacy = post-test scores
    pSelf-Regulation = post-test self regulation scores
    pActivity = post-test minutes of activity

Data for Worksite Physical Activity Promotion Evaluation

Treatment	Knowledge	Self-efficacy	Self-regulation	Activity min	pKnowledge	pSelf-efficacy	pSelf-regulation	pActivity min
E	12	12	4	40	14	14	7	44
E	11	13	5	24	12	15	6	34
E	5	14	8	33	11	15	8	36
E	8	15	7	42	12	16	7	42
E	9	11	4	22	13	14	5	44
E	9	5	2	44	14	8	7	77
E	12	13	9	77	15	15	9	88

Data for Worksite Physical Activity Promotion Evaluation *(Continued)*

Treatment	Knowledge	Self-efficacy	Self-regulation	Activity min	pKnowledge	pSelf-efficacy	pSelf-regulation	pActivity min
E	14	11	7	12	16	13	8	22
E	12	3	4	0	12	6	5	22
E	11	18	2	0	17	17	8	66
E	13	14	8	2	16	15	8	22
E	15	13	7	3	18	18	9	33
E	11	12	4	77	14	14	8	87
E	12	17	6	44	18	17	7	54
E	12	15	3	54	13	18	8	54
E	12	13	9	23	15	14	9	33
E	11	13	8	23	13	14	8	23
E	11	12	2	78	14	12	7	70
E	10	12	4	98	11	14	8	94
E	10	11	6	23	16	15	9	33
E	9	10	1	12	11	15	5	22
E	9	10	3	43	9	16	6	44
E	9	12	8	78	10	13	8	78
E	9	11	7	22	10	14	7	33
E	9	10	8	23	11	11	8	44
E	9	19	9	23	15	18	9	33
E	4	12	7	7	8	14	7	22
E	3	12	3	55	9	15	6	55
E	8	11	6	45	9	14	8	45
E	2	9	8	33	6	10	9	33
C	11	8	7	22	12	8	7	22
C	12	7	3	2	14	8	3	6
C	11	3	5	40	13	4	4	30
C	2	6	1	22	4	7	2	21
C	6	8	3	32	7	8	3	22
C	6	11	6	42	8	11	7	33
C	8	11	8	22	9	11	8	22
C	9	11	9	32	11	11	9	32

(continues)

Data for Worksite Physical Activity Promotion Evaluation *(Continued)*

Treatment	Knowledge	Self-efficacy	Self-regulation	Activity min	pKnowledge	pSelf-efficacy	pSelf-regulation	pActivity min
C	7	12	8	71	9	12	8	66
C	10	12	5	32	13	12	5	22
C	11	15	3	3	14	16	4	22
C	12	14	2	4	14	14	3	12
C	12	14	7	5	13	13	7	12
C	11	13	8	3	13	13	8	23
C	15	13	2	70	16	12	4	60
C	15	13	3	41	16	13	3	41
C	10	13	8	44	11	13	8	44
C	12	13	7	23	13	11	7	23
C	9	17	3	23	9	17	3	33
C	8	16	5	78	9	15	5	70
C	7	16	3	98	8	16	4	66
C	4	11	4	23	6	13	4	22
C	11	11	3	12	13	11	3	11
C	13	10	2	43	15	10	4	43
C	12	9	8	78	14	9	8	66
C	11	8	7	22	11	9	7	32
C	11	4	2	23	11	5	3	23
C	9	3	4	23	10	5	4	23
C	8	8	5	7	8	9	5	11
C	10	7	4	55	10	7	4	44

Use statistical software to analyze the data. Use descriptive statistics to accurately represent patterns in the data. Use statistical tests to determine if the experimental treatment had a positive effect on learning and a positive effect on physical activity. Use statistics to determine if the experimental treatment was more effective than the control group method. Write a report that presents the data and provides a set of evidence-based conclusions regarding the effectiveness of the experimental and control group programs. Compare your conclusions to other students in your class.

SUMMARY _____

Statistical analyses are essential methods of describing data and testing hypotheses. Statistics is an important tool for enhancing the rigor of decision making in evaluation. But statistical analysis is only one of many tools that evaluators use. This chapter recommends evaluators assume the role of detective to "dig deeper," using detective work that goes beyond the numbers to help reveal a full description of the results. The chapter presented a set of conceptual tools that evaluators should review before drawing a final conclusion on an evaluation. These tools may reveal hidden findings or new insights that can enhance the interpretation of the evaluation results.

Second, the chapter proposed a comprehensive table of contents for an evaluation report. Each section of the report was described and explained. Rarely do stakeholders read the report cover to cover in a single sitting. It is recommended that each section of the report be complete so that readers of individual sections do not develop misconceptions. Clear use of headings and a table of contents direct the readers to the section(s) of the report they need.

All evaluation methods should be reported in sufficient detail to allow future replication of the study. This level of reporting also enables readers to critically examine the methods for strengths and weaknesses. Evaluation results are of little value if they are not effectively communicated to stakeholders. Evaluators should make a specific effort to describe results in effect sizes that can be stated in terms of practical significance. It is the decision makers and stakeholders who are in a position to refine health programs and allocate resources. Ergo, it is essential that stakeholders understand and fully appreciate the meaning of evaluation results. The evaluation report is a historical record of evaluation purpose, methods, results, and conclusions.

REVIEW QUESTIONS

1. Differentiate between statistical significance and practical significance.
2. Define the following terms: statistical power failure, participant retention failure, recruitment failure, measurement failure, implementation failure, behavior theory failure, behavioral adherence failure, and ecological fallacy.
3. Describe the common standards used in evaluation of health education and health promotion programs.
4. Differentiate between absolute and consensus standards. Which of these two is more useful in evaluation of health education and health promotion programs?
5. Describe the five criteria for effectively communicating statistical results.
6. Discuss salient aspects of writing an evaluation report.
7. Discuss the potential functional relationships among process, impact, and outcome evaluations.

WEBSITES TO EXPLORE

About Monitoring and Evaluation

http://www.ces-vol.org.uk/index.cfm?pg=40

This website by Charities Evaluation Services in the United Kingdom is devoted to all aspects of reporting evaluations. Links have been provided on the topics of what is monitoring, what is evaluation, monitoring and evaluation resource guide, theory of change, and more. *Browse through this website. Pay special attention to the theory of change. How can this be applied for health education and health promotion programs?*

Two Research Fallacies

http://www.socialresearchmethods.net/kb/fallacy.php
This website was developed by William Trochim, Professor in the Department of Policy
Analysis and Management at Cornell University. The webpage presents descriptions of
two research fallacies or errors in reasoning. We have discussed ecological fallacy in this
text. The other fallacy that this webpage discusses is exception fallacy. *Review this webpage
and discuss the implications of these two fallacies in the evaluation of health education and health
promotion programs.*

UNICEF Evaluation Report Standards

http://www.unicef.org/evaldatabase/files/UNICEF_Eval_Report_Standards.pdf
This document was produced by UNICEF as a transparent tool for quality assessment of
evaluation reports. It outlines the standards used by UNICEF and their rationale. *Review
this 35-page document. Compare the standards described in this document with those in this text.
What similarities and differences did you notice?*

USAID: Constructing an Evaluation Report

http://pdf.usaid.gov/pdf_docs/PNADI500.pdf
This website provides access to a publication produced by the United States Agency for
International Development (USAID) on constructing evaluation reports. The document
starts with an introduction about style and format. The components of an evaluation report
are then presented. *Review this 17-page report. Compare it with the guidelines provided in this
text. What similarities and differences did you notice?*

REFERENCES

Abelson, R. (1995). *Statistics as principled argument*, Hillsdale, NJ: Lawrence Erlbaum.

Basch, C. E., Sliepcevich, E. M., Gold, R. S., Duncan, D. F., & Kolbe, L. J. (1985). Avoiding type
III errors in health education program evaluations: A case study. *Health Education Quarterly,
12*, 315–331.

Black, T. R. (1999). *Doing quantitative research in the social sciences: An integrated approach to research
design, measurement and statistics.* London: Sage.

Cohen, J. (1988). *Statistical power analysis for the behavioral sciences* (2nd ed.). Hillsdale, NJ: Lawrence
Erlbaum.

Cronbach, L. (1982). *Designing evaluations of educational and social programs.* San Francisco: Jossey-Bass.

Datta, L. (1980). Interpreting data: A case study from the career intern program evaluation. *Evaluation Review, 4*, 481–506.

Dibella, A. (1990). The research manager's role in encouraging evaluation use. *Evaluation Practice,
11*(2), 115–119.

Florio, D. H., Behrmann, M., & Goltz, D. L. (1995). What do policy makers think of evaluational
research and evaluation? Or do they? *Educational Evaluation and Policy Analysis, 1*, 61–87.

Green, L. W., & Lewis. F. M. (1986). *Measurement and evaluation in health education and health promotion.* Palo Alto, CA: Mayfield.

Hendricks, M., & Papagiannis, M. (1990). Do's and don'ts for offering effective recommendations.
Evaluation Practice, 11(2), 121–125.

Mercier, C. (1997). Participation in stakeholder-based evaluation: A case study. *Evaluation and Program Planning, 20*(4), 467–475.

Milcarek, B. I., & Link, B. G. (1981). Handling problems of ecological fallacy in program planning and evaluation. *Evaluation and Program Planning, 4*(1), 23–28.

Mohr, L. B. (1992). *Impact analysis for program evaluation.* Newbury Park, CA: Sage.

Patton, M. Q. (1997). *Utilization focused evaluation: The new century text* (3rd ed.). Thousand Oaks, CA: Sage.

Sechrest, L., & Yeaton, W. H. (1982). Magnitudes of experimental effects in social science research. *Evaluation Review, 6*(5), 579–600.

Tukey, J. W. (1977). *Exploratory data analysis.* Reading, MA: Addison-Wesley.

Glossary

A

absolute standards: Standards that focus on 100% success rates.

acquiescence bias: Occurs when people responding to an instrument agree with all statements, irrespective of their content. *See also* yeasayers bias.

activities: In the logic model, this refers to all of the educational processes, tools, and events that make up the health education/promotion program designed to achieve program objectives.

alternative-forms reliability: The estimation of correlation between parallel tests. Another name for this is equivalence.

articulateness: The clarity and detail of an evaluation report.

attitudes: Relatively constant feelings, predispositions, or sets of beliefs directed toward an idea, object, person, or situation; they also can be considered as beliefs with an evaluative component.

attrition: Participants dropping out before completing the program. Sample size and quality are reduced when participants drop out of an evaluation before all data is gathered. Attrition can threaten both the internal and external validity of an evaluation design.

audit trail: This is the second step in qualitative data analysis, in which the evaluator links the data identified in open coding with the source and context. *See also* axial coding *and* open coding.

axial coding: This is the third step in qualitative data analysis, in which the evaluator begins to put together the complete picture with events pertaining to the evaluation topic, related topics, implications from evaluation, and description of a proposed conceptual model weaved together and presented. *See also* audit trail *and* open coding.

B

behavior theory failure: This occurs when the health program evaluation reveals that the targeted theoretical constructs were successfully changed but the health behavior change predicted by the theory did not follow as predicted.

behavioral adherence failure: This occurs when changes in health behavior do not produce anticipated changes in health status.

beliefs: Convictions that a phenomenon is true or real; also, statements of perceived fact or impressions about the world.

bias: Type of error in measurement that occurs due to a systematic mechanism of either increasing or decreasing the true score. *See also* systematic error.

blinding: The participants do not know whether they have been assigned to the experimental group or the control/comparison group.

C

categorical variables: Type of variables that categorize or classify individuals, objects, issues, or events into different groups (e.g., sex, race, marital status, etc.). Also known as nominal variables, grouping variables, or qualitative variables.

ceiling effect: This occurs when pretest scores are high and participants have little to no room to improve scores on a measure.

central tendency bias: Caused by some individuals only endorsing the middle range of possible responses. *See also* end aversion bias, extreme responses bias, *and* middle range bias.

Certified Health Education Specialist (CHES): A person who has met the standards of competence in health education established by the National Commission for Health Education Credentialing (NCHEC) and has successfully passed the CHES examination.

Certified in Public Health (CPH): A person who has met the standards of competence in public health established by the National Board of Public Health Examiners (NBPHE) and has successfully passed the CPH examination.

CIPP model of evaluation: Composed of the *context*, which is the needs assessment; *input*, which is the design; *process*, which is the implementation; and *product*, which includes the outcomes.

classical test theory: A set of propositions that was developed to explain the concept of reliability.

cluster sample: A probability sampling method in which the unit of randomization is groups rather than individuals. For example, an evaluator may select schools, classrooms, churches, worksites, hospitals, or neighborhoods. An attempt is then made to gather data on all of the individuals in the selected clusters.

Cohen's kappa: When there are two observers and interrater reliability is desired between qualitative (categorical) items, then Cohen's kappa is calculated. The formula for Cohen's kappa is:

$$\kappa = Pr(a) - Pr(e) / 1 - Pr(e)$$

where,

Pr(a) = Observed percentage of agreement
Pr(e) = Expected percentage of agreement

coherence: The extent to which the final evaluation write-up makes sense and conclusions are supported by data, and multiple data sources have been used in the evaluation.

communality: In factor analysis, the proportion of variance on a variable accounted for by the set of factors.

comprehensive evaluation: An evaluation that includes process, impact, and outcome evaluation methods.

concept: An abstract idea that cannot be directly measured or observed.

concurrent validity: Measures the degree of correlation between two instruments at the same point in time.

confirmability: The degree to which the results of a study can be confirmed or corroborated by others. In order to establish confirmability, the evaluator can document the procedures for checking and rechecking the data throughout the study.

confirmatory factor analysis: Seeks to determine whether the number of factors and the loadings of measured variables or indicator variables on them conform with what is expected on the basis of theory.

consensus standards: A combination of the different standards that stakeholders agree to use for an evaluation project.

construct: A concept adopted for use in theory.

construct validity: The degree to which an instrument measures the same variable it purports to measure.

constructed response items instruments: These measure knowledge in which the test taker develops his or her own answers in response to the questions.

consumer response: Reaction of the clients to a given health education or health promotion program in terms of how satisfied they are with the program and to what extent their expectations have been met.

consumer satisfaction: The extent to which a health program meets or exceeds the expectations of participants.

content validity: Measures whether the items on the instrument adequately assess each construct within the universe of content as operationally defined.

continuous health program improvement: A cyclical model that starts with the skilled application of the health education knowledge base that informs needs assessment, leading to high quality program planning and implementation. This is followed by program evaluation, which contributes back to the health education knowledge base.

convenience sample: A type of nonprobability sample in which participants are drawn from the portion of the target population that is easily accessible.

convergent validity: The degree to which constructs (consisting of items measuring alternative but related substrata or dimensions) relate to each other.

cost-benefit evaluation: A type of evaluation in which analysis is carried out using only financial costs and financial benefits. A financial (dollar) value is placed on every cost and every benefit, and then a comparison is made.

cost-effectiveness evaluation: A type of evaluation that analyzes the impact of a program as a ratio of program costs to some naturally occurring outcome, such as cost per case of breast cancer prevented.

coverage accountability: The extent to which the intended target audience receives the health program.

credibility: The extent to which decision makers and participants can have confidence in the results of the evaluation.

criterion-referenced test: This is designed to translate test scores into a statement about the capability of the test taker. Generally speaking, if a cut score on a criterion-referenced test is achieved by participants, the evaluator can assume those participants have met an established standard of competence or behavioral capability.

criterion validity: The extent of correlation of an instrument with another instrument of the same phenomenon.

Cronbach's alpha: A summary measure of internal consistency and reliability based on calculating the amount of intercorrelation or relationship among all items of an instrument designed to measure one construct.

cumulative scale: A scale for measuring attitudes that is composed of a set of items arranged by their degree of positivity or favorableness toward the variable under study. *See also* Guttman scale.

D

data cleaning: Checking for data entry errors.

data management: The process of formalizing a step-by-step plan for transferring data from completed instruments to databases or statistical software.

data-producing sample: All of the evaluation participants (including both control and intervention groups) that meet all criteria for retention in the evaluation sample.

data variability: The degree to which measured values are spread out or dispersed. The range or standard deviation is commonly reported to describe the degree of data variability.

deductive reasoning: The basis of the quantitative evaluation paradigm; it is based on logic that proceeds from general to specific. *See also* inductive reasoning.

dependability: Whether a researcher would obtain the same results if he or she could observe the same thing twice. It is a function of a detailed description of the method being provided by an evaluator in one study and another evaluator closely following that description.

descriptive statistics: These provide simple numerical summaries of the measures taken on a sample. Examples include frequency distributions, measures of central tendency, and measures of variability.

deviation bias: Caused by the tendency of some respondents to respond to test items with deviant responses, such as extreme responses.

diagnostic threshold standards: An empirically validated critical level of change needed to yield improvements in health.

dichotomous variable: A categorical variable or nominal-level variable that has only two categories (e.g., gender).

discriminant validity: The degree to which constructs (dimensions) are not correlated with the constructs (dimensions) with which they are not expected to correlate.

double blinding: Both the participants and the program delivery staff do not know whether they are part of the treatment or control condition.

Dunning-Kruger effect: In reality, a person may score low on performance of any given task even though that person tends to overestimate his or her test performance and competence.

E

ecological fallacy: The incorrect assumption that a group characteristic applies to all individuals in that same group.

effect size: The magnitude of association between two variables.

effectiveness: The extent to which an existing or tested approach produces an impact (cognitive or behavioral changes) and/or outcome (changes in health indicators such as mortality, morbidity, etc.) as tested under real-world or practice conditions.

efficacy: The extent to which a new or untested approach produces an impact (cognitive or behavioral changes) and/or outcome (changes in health indicators such as mortality, morbidity, etc.) as tested under *optimal* conditions.

efficiency: Health program resources are used without waste or redundancy.

Eigenvalue: The amount of variance in the original variable set that is explained by each component in factor analysis. *See also* Kaiser criterion *and* scree test.

emic view: The basis of qualitative enquiry, in which the meaning of any situation is perceived from the participant's viewpoint, and the evaluator is a mere observer. *See also* etic view.

empirical standards: Criteria derived from an in-depth knowledge of the professional literature, which over time arrives at a typical standard of performance for similar programs.

empowerment evaluation: The use of evaluation concepts, techniques, and findings to foster improvement and self-determination.

end aversion bias: Caused when some individuals only endorse middle range choices. *See also* central tendency bias, extreme responses bias, *and* middle range bias.

equal-appearing interval scale: Consists of items measuring attitude, with each item having a scale value indicative of the strength of attitude toward the item. *See also* Thurstone scale.

equivalence: The estimation of correlation between parallel tests. Another name for this is alternative-forms reliability.

etic view: The basis of quantitative enquiry, in which the evaluator sets all the parameters or defines the reality. *See also* emic view.

evaluation: To judge the strong points and weak points of programs/interventions, policies/procedures, personnel/staff, products/materials, and organizations/institutions to enhance their effectiveness.

evaluation design: The blueprint that specifies the conditions under which an evaluation will take place. Evaluation design includes sampling, intervention implementation, and measurement decisions that are used to answer evaluation questions and create a rationale for causal reasoning. The decisions made regarding evaluation design can increase or decrease the confidence one places on the evaluation results.

evaluation design notation: The system of symbols and terminology used to depict evaluation designs.

evaluation rigor: The use of scientific methods, including measurement, sampling, and control groups, to ensure high levels of internal and external validity.

expectation bias: This type of bias occurs in instruments requiring observation when the observer may tend to observe things in favor of the treatment group.

exploratory factor analysis: Used for data reduction to a smaller number of factors, to ascertain the minimum number of unobservable common factors that can account for observed correlations among variables, or for exploring the underlying dimensions in a data set.

external validity: The extent to which the results produced by an evaluation can be generalized to other settings with similar conditions.

extreme responses bias: Occurs when individuals have a tendency to express their attitudes in extreme terms (such as strongly agree or strongly disagree).

F

face validity: Measures whether each item measures the intended construct as operationally defined and whether the instrument looks like an instrument.

factor analysis: A statistical method in which correlations between items are measured, and as a result factor scores are developed.

factor loadings: Pearson product moment correlation coefficients between items and factors.

faking bad bias: When the opposite of social desirability bias occurs, and the respondent portrays him- or herself as bad. *See also* social desirability bias.

fiscal accountability: Resources are used in accordance with an approved budget.

Flesch-Kincaid Grade Level score: Rates text on a U.S. school grade level. For example, a score of 5.0 means that a fifth grader can understand the document. The formula for the Flesch-Kincaid Grade Level score is:

$$(0.39 \times ASL) + (11.8 \times ASW) - 15.59$$

where,

ASL = Average sentence length (the number of words divided by the number of sentences)

ASW = Average number of syllables per word (the number of syllables divided by the number of words)

Flesch Reading Ease score: Rates text on a 100-point scale; the higher the score, the easier it is to understand the document. The formula for the Flesch Reading Ease score is:

$$206.835 - (1.015 \times ASL) - (84.6 \times ASW)$$

where,

ASL = Average sentence length (the number of words divided by the number of sentences)

ASW = Average number of syllables per word (the number of syllables divided by the number of words)

forced choice (paired comparisons) scale: Measures attitudes by having a respondent select one choice from two choices.

formative evaluation: Rapid, diagnostic feedback about the quality of implementation of health program methods, activities, and resources for the purpose of program refinement. It is done during development and/or implementation of a health education or health promotion intervention. It is usually done on a smaller scale as a pilot study or a field study, and entails monitoring of activities.

frequency distribution: Arranging variable scores by size and specifying how many times each score occurs in the sample.

G

generalizability: The extent to which evaluation results can be considered representative of the target population. Projecting results from a sample to the population.

generalizing evaluation results: Making inferences from the observed sample with regards to the intended target population.

goal-free evaluation: This type of evaluation aims at eliminating (or reducing) evaluator bias. In conducting this type of evaluation, a program's preset objectives are not revealed to the evaluator.

goal-oriented evaluation: This type of evaluation is based on predetermined objectives. It usually uses quantitative experimental designs that are typically grounded in theory.

graphing data: Provides a visual representation of data, often illustrating relationships between variables.

grouping variables: Another name for nominal-level variables or categorical variables.

Guttman scale: A type of scale composed of a set of items arranged by their degree of positivity or favorableness toward the variable under study. *See also* cumulative scale.

H

halo effect: When the ratings made on individual aspects of a person's performance or behavior are influenced by the respondent's overall impression of the person.

hatchet evaluation: The purpose of this evaluation is to demonstrate the weaknesses and failures of a program or an organization. The motive for such an evaluation is to discredit the program so that funding or political support is diminished or completely removed.

Hawthorne effect: Occurs when the observed effects of an intervention can be attributed to participants responding to the special attention being paid to them.

Health and Psychosocial Instruments (HaPI): A specialized database that lists only instruments in health-related disciplines, behavioral and social sciences, and organizational behavior such as checklists, coding schemes/manuals, index measures, interview schedules, projective techniques, questionnaires, rating scales, vignettes/scenarios, and tests.

health education: Systematic application of a set of techniques to voluntarily and positively influence health by changing the antecedents of behavior (awareness, information, knowledge, skills, beliefs, attitudes, and values) in individuals, groups, or communities.

health promotion: The process of empowering people to improve their health by providing educational, political, legislative, organizational, social, and community supports.

historical standards: Benchmarks to compare results from the current evaluation effort to results from prior years.

history: The external events that occur at the same time as the intervention and have the potential to affect the dependent variable.

holistic perspective: This perspective is used in qualitative enquiry and includes the underlying values and the context as a part of the phenomena.

hypothesis: A statement of the expected relationships between the independent variables (health intervention) and the dependent variable (knowledge, skills, motivation, health behavior, health status).

I

illuminative evaluation: A qualitative evaluation that seeks to illuminate or clarify answers to questions pertaining to a program that are lying latent or dormant using methods from social anthropology rather than psychology. Also known as socioanthropological evaluation, responsive evaluation, or transaction evaluation.

impact: In the logic model, this refers to the changes in participants' knowledge, skills, motivation, and health behavior.

impact accountability: How program participants benefit from the health program.

impact evaluation: A type of evaluation concerned with assessing changes in health-related cognitive and behavioral domains. The usual time frame for this evaluation is 6 months to 2–3 years. This type of evaluation usually uses experimental or quasi-experimental designs.

implausible values: Data entered into the data set that is beyond the range of the instrument or coding values.

implementation failure: Occurs when a health program is not delivered to participants as it was designed.

implementation fidelity: The degree to which a health program was delivered as planned.

inclusion criteria: All of the evaluation protocol steps that must be completed by participants to remain in the evaluation sample.

indicator: A construct with specific properties.

inductive reasoning: The basis of the qualitative evaluation paradigm; it is based on logic that proceeds from specific to general. *See also* deductive reasoning.

ingratiating evaluation: The primary purpose of this type of evaluation is to show the success and strengths of the program.

inputs: In the logic model, this refers to the human, financial, and community resources that are available to support the health education/promotion program.

insensitive measure bias: Occurs when the instrument used is not sensitive enough to detect what might be important differences in the variable of interest.

instrument: A tool that helps measure concepts and constructs by reducing them to variables. See also *questionnaire*.

instrumentation bias: Bias from changes in characteristics of measurement instruments between observations.

interactive effects: Occur when a combination of the internal validity threats are present to produce bias.

interest level: The extent to which a report is able to capture the attention and curiosity of a reader.

internal consistency: The indication about how much each item in a scale relates to other items in the scale or how much the items gel together.

internal consistency reliability: Measures the extent to which each item in an instrument is related to other items in the instrument.

internal validity: The degree of confidence one has that the results produced by the evaluation are causally linked directly to the intervention.

interobserver reliability: Calculated when different observers are using the same instrument to measure the same phenomena at the same time. Also known as rater–interrater reliability.

interval scale: Used to classify individuals, objects, issues, or events into categories that have a meaningful order, implying higher levels have more of the attribute. This scale also has equal intervals, so it is possible to tell how much difference there is between different categories.

intervention: A more sophisticated term for a program. It refers to the health education or health promotion program.

intraobserver reproducibility: The extent to which a single rater agrees upon the characteristics of an observation repeatedly over time. Also known as intrarater reliability.

intrarater reliability: The extent to which a single rater agrees upon the characteristics of an observation repeatedly over time. Also known as intraobserver reproducibility.

K

Kaiser criterion: Used in factor analysis, which specifies one can retain those components that have an Eigenvalue greater than 1. *See also* Eigenvalue *and* scree test.

knowledge: Learning of facts and gaining of insights.

Kuder-Richardson Formula-20 (KR-20): A method of internal consistency reliability testing. It is employed when a scale consists of dichotomous items.

Kuder-Richardson Formula-21 (KR-21): A statistic related to KR-20. It represents a lower limit for the computed value of KR-20 and is also used for determining internal consistency reliability of dichotomous scales.

L

legal accountability: Determining that legal and ethical standards are maintained.

Likert scale: Lists several statements about an object and then asks respondents whether they strongly agree, agree, disagree, or strongly disagree with each statement.

limitations of evaluation: Restrictions and conditions placed on the interpretation of evaluation results when elements of evaluation design reduce scientific rigor.

logic model: A systematic graphic representation of how an intervention is designed to produce its results by showing its relationship to resources and activities.

logical positivism: The basis of the quantitative paradigm. It assumes that a reality exists that can be described objectively.

M

magnitude of the effect: The amount of change in key variables that was produced by the health program.

Master Certified Health Education Specialist (MCHES): A person who has met the standards of competence in health education established by the National Commission for Health Education Credentialing (NCHEC), including 5 years of work experience, and has successfully passed the MCHES examination.

maturation: The growth or development occurring within the participants during the course of the evaluation as a result of time rather than the intervention.

mean: The arithmetic average of all the scores in a distribution.

measurement: The systematic application of a set of procedures and processes so that concepts can be objectively reduced to numbers for the purpose of comparison.

measurement error: The degree of deviation from a high level of validity and reliability.

measurement failure: This occurs when an assessment tool used in an evaluation does not accurately assess a variable. This failure can produce spurious evaluation results.

measures of central tendency: Statistics that describe the typical, average value for a variable.

measures of variability: These describe how widely scores are dispersed from each other in the sample.

median: The 50th percentile of a score distribution; it is the point below which half of the scores fall.

metric scale: Both interval and ratio scales are often referred to as metric scales or quantitative variables.

middle range bias: Caused by individuals who only endorse the middle range of responses. *See also* end-aversion bias, central tendency bias, *and* extreme response bias.

missing values: These occur when no value appears in the data set for a particular variable. This can be caused by a participant failing to respond to an item or it may be due to a data entry error.

mode: The score that occurs most frequently in a distribution.

multistage sample: A probability sampling technique in which clusters are first selected, and then the sample is drawn by simple random sampling in each cluster.

N

nay sayers bias: The opposite of acquiescence bias; occurs when the respondent disagrees with each item irrespective of the content. *See also* acquiescence bias *and* yeasayers bias.

negative predictive value: The conditional probability of absence of disease given that the test is negative. The formula for negative predictive value is as follows:

P (No Disease | Test –) = TN / TN + FN

where,

P = Probability
TN = True negatives
FN = False negatives
See also predictive value sensitivity *and* specificity.

nominal scale: Used to categorize or classify individuals, objects, issues, or events into different groups (e.g., sex, race, marital status, etc.). Also known as categorical variable, grouping variable, or qualitative variable.

nonprobability sample: Any method of selecting participants in which some members of the population have no chance of being selected. The chance of each member of the target population being chosen for the evaluation sample is not known. Thus, the evaluator cannot claim that the sample is representative of the target population.

normative standards: These compare results from one group with results from another group.

norm-referenced test: Produces an estimate of the position of one individual's score relative to a predefined population. The primary interpretation of the scores is that the test taker did better than others with lower scores and worse than people with higher scores.

novelty effect: Occurs when participants react to the unique aspects of an innovative technology because it arouses interest and motivation due to its inherent "newness."

O

observation of behavior: A method of measuring behavior that requires two or more observers to directly see the behavior.

observer reactivity: In situations where an observer is observing a phenomenon (usually behavior), the behavior of participants is altered.

open coding: The first step of qualitative data analysis, in which the evaluator decides on tentative conceptual categories into which the data will be coded. *See also* audit trail *and* axial coding.

optimizing approach: The respondent tries to do his or her best with the most optimal mental attitude, such as when taking an exam on which he or she will be graded. *See also* satisficing approach.

ordinal scale: Used to classify individuals, objects, issues, or events into categories that have a meaningful order.

outcome: In the logic model, this refers to the changes in participants' or communities' health status or quality of life produced by the health education/promotion program activities.

outcome evaluation: A type of evaluation concerned with assessing changes in health indicators such as mortality and morbidity in the target population. The time frame for this evaluation is usually long, often entailing 5–10 years.

outliers: Data values for variables that are plausible but extremely high or low. Outliers are values at extreme ends of the frequency distribution.

outputs: In the logic model, these refer to the direct services to be delivered by the program. These services are what the program participants receive.

P

parallel tests: Tests that have the same mean, variance, and correlations as other tests, such as Form A and Form B on the GRE.

participant attrition: The dropout of the participants from the program or lack of completion of the program in its entirety by the participants.

participant retention failure: Evaluation participant attrition that affects the statistical power or generalizability of the results.

participatory evaluation: An evaluation involving partnership among all stakeholders—program developers, program implementers, target population, and funders—to develop a joint evaluation framework and implement it together.

placebo effect: Occurs when people can improve their health based on faith in a treatment or provider.

political climate: An environment consisting of stakeholders representing a wide range of concerns and motivations, to which evaluators must be sensitive.

postpositivism: States that only partially objective accounts of the world can be produced because all methods are flawed; hence, the reality is multiply constructed and multiply interpreted. Qualitative enquiry is based on postpositivism.

practical importance: An interpretation of evaluation results that considers the relevance of effect sizes in the context of the professional practice of health promotion and education. Practical importance speaks to how likely the intervention is to have a benefit of value to participants or stakeholders.

precision: The degree to which measured values accurately reflect true values. Evidence of precision is the degree to which repeated measures produce the same value.

predictive validity: Measures the degree of correlation between one instrument and a future measure of the same observable fact.

predictive value: The conditional probability of a disease being present given that the test is positive. The formula for predictive value is as follows:

P (Disease | Test +) = TP / TP + FP

where,

P = Probability
TP = True positives
FP = False positives
See also negative predictive value sensitivity *and* specificity.

probability sample: Each member of the target population has a known chance of being chosen for the evaluation sample. Probability samples enable the evaluator to generalize the results from the sample to the population with a specified level of confidence.

process evaluation: An evaluation concerned with finding out to what extent the program adhered to the written plan. It is also interested in finding out the satisfaction of the recipients, implementers, sites, and other personnel associated with the program. Assurance of quality is another purpose of process evaluation.

program accountability: Documentation that health education or health promotion programs were delivered.

program management: The program's compliance with the requirements of professional standards, legal standards, funding agencies, and agency administration.

program reach: The degree to which the health education or health promotion program was able to recruit and retain members of the intended target audience.

program stakeholder: A person or organization having a keen interest in the development, implementation, or evaluation of a health education/promotion program.

p-value: Probability of obtaining, when the null is true, a value of the test statistic as extreme or more extreme (in the appropriate direction) than the one actually computed.

Pygmalion effect: The belief that if one expects another person to do something, it is much more likely to happen.

Q

qualitative evaluation: A method of assessing a program by using one of three approaches: (1) interviews or discussions consisting of open-ended questions, (2) observations based on field notes, or (3) review of written materials and other documents.

qualitative variables: Variables that yield nominal-level data; they classify into qualitative categories and not quantitative categories. *See also* nominal scale, categorical variable, *and* grouping variable.

quality: Level of appropriateness of a set of defined professional procedures for a health education or promotion program.

quality control: A set of procedures designed to ensure that a program or intervention adheres to a defined set of characteristic criteria or meets the requirements of the participants or consumers.

quality standards: A minimum acceptable level of performance established by expert opinion.

quantitative variables: Both interval and ratio scales are often referred to as metric scales or quantitative variables.

questionnaire: A tool used to measure concepts and constructs by reducing them into variables. *See also* instrument.

quota sample: First, the target population is segmented into exclusive subgroups using relevant variables (e.g., gender, race, educational status, age, health status). Next, specific numbers of participants are selected from each subgroup. This is a nonprobability sample because the quotas for each subsample are not selected randomly.

R

random assignment: Placement of participants into experimental and control groups using methods that insure that each subject has an equal chance of being assigned to each group. This method ensures that any differences between the groups are due to chance and not systematic bias.

random error: The type of error in measurement that occurs due to chance.

range: The difference between the highest and lowest scores on a particular variable in a sample.

rater–interrater reliability: Calculated when different observers are using the same instrument to measure the same phenomena at the same time.

ratio scale: Has all the characteristics of an interval scale, and in addition has a true zero point. *See also* interval scale.

recall or memory bias: In instruments requiring recall of a behavior or another attribute, a potential measurement bias of erroneous recall.

recruitment failure: When evaluation sampling procedures do not produce a sample representative of the target population, then the results cannot be generalized.

reductionism: Evaluation and research method where the reality is reduced to a number.

relative risk: The ratio of incidence of a condition in those exposed to a risk factor (e.g., smokers) to the incidence in those not exposed (e.g., nonsmokers). A relative risk of 1.0 indicates no greater risk in those exposed than in the nonexposed, a relative risk higher than 1.0 signifies greater risk, and a relative risk less than 1.0 signifies a protective effect.

relevance: The instrument is appropriate and important to the measure being examined.

reliability: The ability of the instrument to measure repeatedly the same results and be internally consistent.

replication: The process by which the evaluation processes and procedures can be repeated at a different site or with a different sample.

response rate: The number of participants who complete the evaluation protocol divided by the number of participants in the complete sample.

response sampling error: When errors result from selection of items that have been chosen from the pool of potential items.

response set biases: Systematic measurement errors that occur when people provide responses that are not related to the content of the item but instead provide responses based on some other criteria.

responsibility: Health professionals ensuring that a program and services are delivered according to quality standards.

responsive evaluation: A qualitative evaluation that seeks to illuminate or clarify answers to questions pertaining to a program that are lying latent or dormant using methods from social anthropology rather than psychology. Also known as illuminative evaluation, socioanthropological evaluation, or transaction evaluation.

S

sample: A subset of the population used in an evaluation to represent the target population.

sample size estimation: Estimating how many participants are needed to answer evaluation questions with sufficient practical and statistical rigor.

sampling error: The inaccuracy introduced into an evaluation by measuring a sample rather than the entire target population. Sampling error is estimated by subtracting the value of a population parameter from the corresponding sample statistic.

sampling frame: A list of all units (people, communities, worksites, etc.) in the target population that are available for selection into a sample.

sampling method: A precisely described approach for selecting a sample of participants from a defined target population.

satisficing approach: When a respondent puts in just enough effort, such as when completing a questionnaire for a researcher in which there is no tangible benefit to him or her. *See also* optimizing approach.

scree test: In this method, the Eigenvalues are plotted on the vertical axis and their ordinal rank on the horizontal axis. The magnitude of the successive Eigenvalues drops off sharply and then levels off. The Kaiser criterion recommends retention of all factors in the sharp descent of the curve before the first Eigenvalue on the line where the Eigenvalues begin to level off or where the "elbow" is getting formed. *See also* Eigenvalue, Kaiser criterion.

selected response items instruments: Measure knowledge; the test takers choose the answers from a set of possible answers.

selection bias: The threat to internal validity due to preexisting differences between groups under evaluation.

self-report of behavior: A method of measuring behavior that requires the respondents to provide guidance about their actions on their own.

semantic differential rating scale: Measures attitudes by using bipolar adjectives.

sensitivity: The conditional probability that a test is positive given that there is disease. The formula for determining sensitivity is as follows:

$$P \text{ (Test + } | \text{ Disease)} = TP \text{ / } TP + FN$$

where,

P = Probability
TP = True positives
FN = False negatives
See also negative predictive value, predictive value, *and* specificity.

service accountability: Determining that the intervention is provided as planned.

simple random sample: Sampling method in which all members of the target population have an equal chance of selection into the sample.

situational validity: The phenomenon that an instrument measuring one characteristic is valid for only one group of people—it may or may not be valid for another group of people.

skills: Acts involving physical movement, coordination, and use of motor function.

social desirability: Occurs when participants want to please the evaluator, so they respond to evaluation measurements in ways they believe the evaluator wants.

social desirability bias: When respondents mark responses such that they want to portray a favorable image of themselves. *See also* faking bad bias.

socio-anthropological evaluation: A qualitative evaluation that seeks to illuminate or clarify answers to questions pertaining to a program that are lying latent or dormant using methods from social anthropology rather than psychology. Also known as illuminative evaluation, responsive evaluation, or transaction evaluation.

Spearman-Brown split-half reliability method: A technique by which an instrument is divided into two equal parts and the correlation between these two halves is considered as an estimate of the instrument's internal consistency reliability. It is also called the split-half method.

specificity: The conditional probability that a test is negative given that there is no disease. The formula for specificity is as follows:

P (Test − | No Disease) = TN / TN + FP

where,

P = Probability
TN = True negatives
FP = False positives
See also negative predictive value, predictive value, *and* sensitivity.

split-half method: The technique by which an instrument is divided into two equal parts and the correlation between these two halves is considered as an estimate of the instrument's internal consistency reliability. It is also called the Spearman-Brown split-half reliability method.

stability: The degree of association between two or more measurements of the same instrument taken over time. Also known as test–retest reliability.

standard deviation: A measure of variability that is sensitive to all scores in the sample distribution. Conceptually, the standard deviation is a measure of how far each value in a distribution falls from the mean for that variable.

statistical convention standards: Over time, statisticians have developed general rules of labeling the magnitude of standardized effects. For standardized mean difference effect size, it is generally suggested that 0.20 is a small effect, 0.50 is a medium effect and 0.80 is a large effect.

statistical inference: A method of drawing conclusions from data that is subject to random variation. It is a mathematically based approach to obtain knowledge about a target population from a relatively small number representing that population, known as a sample.

statistical power failure: Too much power can produce a statistically significant test of little practical importance. Too little statistical power will fail to detect differences of practical importance. It is recommended that most evaluations attempt to achieve a power of 0.80.

statistical regression: The threat to internal validity that is defined as the bias introduced by selection of subjects with unusually high or low levels of a variable.

statistical significance: A statement regarding the likelihood that observed variable values occurred by chance.

statistics: A set of scientific methods that focuses on collection, analysis, and interpretation of data.

stratified random sample: Sampling method in which the target population is sorted into distinct categories (e.g., race, gender, age groups) and placed into independent subpopulations (strata). Participants are randomly selected from each of the subpopulations.

subclass analysis: Analysis of different subgroups within a sample.

summated rating Likert scale: Scale composed of items that are approximately equal in their attitudinal value. Respondents respond to these items in terms of the extent of agreement or disagreement.

summative evaluation: Conducted to draw conclusions and make decisions about the impact, outcomes, and other benefits of a health program. It is usually done on a large scale and uses quantitative designs.

systematic error: A type of error in measurement that occurs due to a systematic mechanism of either increasing or decreasing the true score. *See also* bias.

systematic sample: When all members of the target population are ordered by a variable (e.g., alphabetical order of last name, address, etc.). The first unit (person) is chosen randomly from the sampling frame. Then, using a constant (e.g., every eighth person on the list), the reminder of the sample is chosen.

T

target population: All people (or other units: schools, communities, etc.) in a defined group of interest.

team approach to program planning and evaluation: A joint collaboration between those responsible for planning the health education or health promotion program and those responsible for evaluating it.

testable hypothesis: The depiction of the relationship between independent and dependent variables in a given target population that can be tested empirically.

testing: A threat to internal validity due to changes in observations as a result of the pretest.

test–retest reliability: The extent of association between two or more measurements of the same instrument taken over time. Also known as stability.

Thurstone scale: A type of equal-appearing interval scale that consists of items measuring attitude. Each item has a scale value that is indicative of the strength of attitude toward the item. See also *equal-appearing interval scale*.

transaction evaluation: A qualitative evaluation that seeks to illuminate or clarify answers to questions pertaining to a program that are lying latent or dormant using methods from social anthropology rather than psychology. Also known as illuminative evaluation, socio-anthropological evaluation, responsive evaluation.

transferability: The degree to which the results of a qualitative evaluation can be transferred to other contexts or settings.

triangulation: The use of multiple methods, multiple data, or multiple analysts or the use of theory to aid in data interpretation.

triple blinding: The participants, the program delivery staff, and the program evaluation staff do not know whether they are part of the experimental or control conditions.

trustworthiness: How much the evaluator has adhered to the procedures specific to the chosen method, exercised rigor in inquiry, and is open about describing the procedures.

Type III error: Assuming a health program has been implemented fully and correctly when it has not been.

U

unobtrusive measures: The participants do not know they are being measured.

utilization-focused evaluation: An evaluation in which the evaluator actively engages decision makers (e.g., funders, program managers, professional staff) in the design of the evaluation for the purpose of increasing the use of evaluation results in future intervention efforts.

V

validity: The degree to which an instrument is actually measuring what it is purporting to measure.

values: Enduring beliefs or systems of beliefs regarding whether a specific mode of conduct or end state of behavior is personally or socially preferable.

variable: A quantitative score that varies from one individual to another. A variable can be measured and observed. It takes on different values in the form of numbers.

variance: The variation or dispersion in a set of scores or a measure of how far a set of numbers are spread out from each other.

visual analog scale (VAS): A type of graphic rating scale that measures attitudes.

volunteer sample: A nonprobability sample in which participants take an active role in seeking out membership in the sample. The participants possess an interest or a motive that prompts them to actively seek inclusion into the sample.

Y

yeasayers bias: In responding to an instrument, some people tend to agree with all statements irrespective of their content. *See also* acquiescence bias.

Index